The
Guinness
Book of
CURIOUS
PHRASES

Leslie Dunkling

GW00722589

GUINNESS PUBLISHING

Editor: Beatrice Frei
Design and Layout: Mandy Sedge

The Work Copyright © Leslie Dunkling, 1993

The right of Leslie Dunkling to be identified as the Author of this
Work has been asserted in accordance with the Copyright, Design
and Patents Act 1988.

This Publication Copyright © Guinness Publishing Ltd., 1993
33 London Road, Enfield, Middlesex.

'GUINNESS' is a registered trade mark of Guinness Publishing
Ltd.

All rights reserved. No part of this publication may be reproduced,
stored in a retrieval system, or transmitted in any form or by any
means, electronic, mechanical, photocopying, recording or
otherwise, without prior permission in writing of the publisher.

Typeset in Times New Roman by Ace Filmsetting Ltd., Frome,
Somerset.
Printed and bound in Great Britain by The Bath Press, Bath

A catalogue record for this book is available from the British
Library.

ISBN 0–85112–593–X

The
Guinness
Book of

CURIOUS
PHRASES

CONTENTS

WORD AND PHRASE

PREFACE

Why do we say some of the strange things we do say? Why, for example, do we announce that we are **full of beans**, say that we want to **get down to brass tacks**, comment that two people are **in cahoots with** each other? Hundreds of such phrases, used in everyday conversations, are decidedly curious when examined closely. *The Guinness Book of Curious Phrases* sets out to tell their stories.

The book consists of some two hundred or so separate articles, each of which is based on a key word. Since many expressions could have been dealt with equally well under more than one word, the Index should be consulted for a particular phrase.

I have made liberal use of quotations throughout the book for several reasons. They demonstrate that the phrases are widely used, and that literary artists often comment on them. C.S. Lewis also said in his *Studies in Words*: 'One understands a word much better if one has met it alive, in its native habitat. So far as is possible our knowledge should be checked and supplemented, not derived, from the dictionary.' That is obviously true not only of words but of phrases.

I have avoided jargon as much as possible when discussing the phrases.

Occasionally terms more complex than simile, metaphor, alliteration, euphemism and the like are used, but they are usually glossed in context. Readers with a special interest in rhetorical technicalities are recommended to consult a work such as *A Dictionary of Stylistics*, by Katie Wales.

Throughout the book 'he' is used to mean 'he or she'. This is simply a long-established grammatical convention, made necessary by the lack in English of a singular pronoun of common gender. I have no intention of reinforcing sexual stereotypes. It is, as it happens, common practice to use one term of a pair to cover the range of meaning between them, as when we say that a baby is three days old rather than three days young, but the he/she issue is, of course, far more sensitive.

Finally, on a personal note, I would like to dedicate this book to those who love the English language and whom it has been my pleasure to meet or communicate with in many parts of the world. I hope I shall hear from them again, about matters discussed in these pages or other topics of interest.

Leslie Dunkling

INTRODUCTION

The word 'phrase' as used in this book refers to a group of words generally recognized to be a self-contained unit. A simple diagnostic test for such a phrase is to omit a key word and see whether native-speakers consistently use it to fill the gap. To reveal a secret, for example, is to 'let the . . . out of the bag'. There is little doubt that most informants would immediately say that 'cat' is the missing word.

English-speakers, as they speak or write, are able to draw on a large stock of such phrases, much as they draw on a stock of individual words. Each phrase is like a pre-fabricated component. It is used to do a specific job – convey a particular meaning – within the complex assembly that we call a conversation or a connected piece of spoken or written English.

'You must excuse me, my English is not so very good; I do not follow this about bees, was it? Bees in the bonnet?'

Mary Stewart *This Rough Magic*

Many phrases, when we look at them closely, are indeed 'curious'. They frequently say things, as with **let the cat out of the bag**, which the speaker does not literally mean. It can be a salutary experience to use such an expression to a child or foreigner who is not familiar with it. We may be asked in a puzzled way about what cat in which bag. This book partly sets out to give the kind of explanation that becomes necessary in such circumstances. It is also intended to sharpen the reader's general awareness of the strange things English-speakers actually say to one another.

■ PHRASAL WORDS

English is perhaps more of a phrasal language than is generally realized. In discussions of its vocabulary it is usual to place a great deal of emphasis on single words, with the distinction between words and phrases sharply defined. 'Man' is clearly a word, 'the man in the street' a phrase, and nothing could be simpler. The situation becomes more complex when 'man' becomes part of a compound word, such as **policeman, milkman, doorman**.

Each of these could be thought of not just as two words joined together, but as phrases in shorthand form. The meanings of the two individual words do not immediately indicate what is meant by the compound. There is certainly no regular pattern which makes clear the relationship between them. The fact that a policeman is a member of a police force does not make a milkman a member of a milk force. That a milkman delivers milk does not mean that a doorman delivers doors. If we come across an unusual compound word such as

pocketman – used in criminal slang, according to James Morton in *Low Speak* – we have no way of knowing that it condenses the idea: 'a member of a gang who holds the proceeds of a crime until the shareout takes place'.

Similarly, 'room' is a simple concept in itself, but compounds such as **bedroom, boardroom, classroom, cloakroom, courtroom, darkroom, grillroom, guardroom, saleroom, showroom, stateroom, storeroom** and **strongroom** again imply underlying phrasal constructions of very different kinds. In some cases we may be in doubt as to whether these compounds really are single words. We signal their phrasal nature by writing them with a hyphen, as in **waiting-room, changing-room, consulting-room, dining-room**. If we wonder whether the hyphen should be present or not and consult a dictionary for advice, it is well to consult only one. The lexicographers who compile the dictionaries often disagree among themselves. There are also national differences, with British dictionaries favouring hyphens more than their American counterparts.

To them a bedroom was a room with a bed and a wardrobe and a hard-backed chair, and its one purpose was sleep. You read and wrote and talked and listened to the wireless in the living-room. It was as if the names of the rooms were taken quite literally.

John Braine *Room at the Top*

In this book compound nouns, whether hyphenated or not, have not been treated as 'phrases', though many of them are curious enough. Explanations of the theatrical **green-room, (with)drawing-room** and the like would be justified. There are also words such as **elbow-room, leg-room, head-room** which become momentarily curious when seen out of context, suggesting rooms where elbows, legs and heads are kept. **Mushroom** is a genuine curiosity, a 'room' only by etymological accident: it is from French *mousseron*, originally a variety of mushroom which grew in 'moss'.

■ HYPHENATION

Hyphenation allows us to create different types of words which are obviously of a phrasal nature. We describe someone as a **baby-sitter** or **cradle-snatcher** or talk of someone's **stock-in-trade**. We use adjectives such as **common-or-garden** and **out-of-the-way**. These are fixed expressions, but ad-hoc conversion from phrase to hyphenated word can occur at any time. Poets sometimes create what Archbishop Trench called 'poems in miniature', as with Milton's 'golden-tressed', 'flowry-kirtled', 'vermeil-tinctured'. A novelist such as Dickens, in *The Pickwick Papers*, is imaginative in a different way. He writes of a 'touch-me-not-ishness in the walk, a majesty in the eye, of the spinster aunt'. Earlier in the novel he describes 'a little man with a puffy Say-nothing-to-me,-or-I'll-contradict-you sort of countenance'. J.I.M. Stewart, in *The Last Tresilians*, has: 'Leech was decidedly not one of your Christian-name-dropping dons.'

Wouldn't they feel gratified, Henry and Estelle, wouldn't they we-told-you-so if she were to tell them?

Truman Capote *Master Misery*

These hyphenated groups provide visual evidence that a required meaning cannot always be conveyed by a single word. More frequently, however, nouns are simply placed next to one another to form a single sense-unit, as in 'World Health Organization'. When such word groups are frequently used, there is often a tendency to shorten them in some way. Acronyms have become popular in modern times, reducing 'young urban professional', say, to **yuppie**. Some dictionaries now list **posslq** (pronounced possell-cue) as a word, saying that it is used in the USA for a 'person of the opposite sex sharing living-quarters'.

Acronyms, and the similar blends, quickly become established if they cater for a genuine linguistic need. Their origin is soon forgotten and they are thought by succeeding generations to be normal words. It is probably only older people, for instance, who remember that **radar** was coined by reducing the phrase 'radio detection and ranging'. The unwieldy 'light amplification by stimulated emission of radiation' became **laser**.

'You've made a conquest, you lucky s.o.b.'

Stanley Price *A World of Difference*

Initials may also be left as such and pronounced separately. The most-used phrasal expression of this type is **OK**, which is sometimes extended to **A-OK**. Other expressions have not achieved the same currency, but the war-time British radio show ITMA (pronounced as a single word and based on the phrase 'It's that man again') made **T.T.F.N.** a popular catch-phrase. The initials stood for 'Ta-ta for now'. Partial reduction to initials occurred in **Jolly D**, a colloquial form of 'jolly decent' which was formerly in vogue.

In older English phrases, ellipsis has often occurred as another way of shortening a phrase. **O'clock** does duty for 'of the clock', **goodbye** for 'God be with ye'. A phrase may also be reduced to a single word. This happens especially with Cockney rhyming slang, where a phrase like **butcher's hook** replaces 'look', but a speaker then says: 'Take a butcher's at that.' **High as a kite**, referring to 'tight' in the sense of 'drunk', is likewise reduced to 'high'. 'Use your loaf' means 'use your **loaf of bread**' – your

head. As Julian Franklyn points out, in *The Cockney*, the truncated form may subsequently be adopted by speakers who are unaware of the full phrase. Those who talk of giving someone a 'raspberry', for example, may not realise that it is derived from **raspberry tart**, rhyming on 'fart'.

This economy with words is a point of pride with many working-class speakers. Once a phrase such as 'I haven't the **foggiest idea**' becomes well-established, it can be reduced to 'I haven't the foggiest'. 'He hasn't an **earthly chance**' ('a chance on earth') becomes 'He hasn't an earthly'. 'Put him under!' – a manager's exhortation to his players – can be heard at any Saturday afternoon football match. The full form, 'Put him **under pressure**', would now sound strange in such an environment.

■ PHRASAL VERBS

Most native English-speakers make use without thinking of various kinds of phrasal words. To the envy of foreigners who are trying to learn English, they use in a similar casual way what have been described since Dr Bradley's time as 'phrasal verbs'. Such verbs were first noted, though not described as such, by Samuel Johnson in his famous *Dictionary*. He saw that the meanings of basic verbs were changed in some way, made more specific perhaps, when they were combined with adverbs and prepositions. To **look at** something is not the same as to **look for** it. To convey the specific meaning, both parts of the phrasal verb must be used.

A phrasal verb may in fact have several meanings, none of which it is possible to deduce from the meanings of the separate words that form it. A foreigner who was familiar with both 'look' and 'up' would not automatically be able to translate sentences like: Things are looking up; I'll look it up in the directory; We looked him up when we visited New York. These distinct meanings of **look up** have to be dealt with individually in a dictionary and learnt separately. Compare the use of **put up** in this further quotation from Stewart's *The Last Tresilians*. A university teacher says of the students: 'To me the interesting question is not how we put the little brutes up but how we put up *with* them.'

He asked if she would like to wash. But what he actually said was: 'Do you want to wash up?' And though it took only half a second for her to guess what he meant, she was so thrown by everything else that she embarked on an absurd explanation that in English this meant something different. 'I thought you meant . . . in England it means the plates. Wash the plates.' 'Oh', said Dolly, his wife, 'do the dishes. How fascinating.'

Penelope Gilliatt *A State of Change*

As we shall see later, our 'curious phrases' are often metaphors or other figures of speech. That is true of many phrasal verbs. In the group based on 'look', for example, **look down on** someone in the sense of having a low opinion of him is clearly metaphorical.

The English language makes great use of these verbal groups, variations in each case on a theme suggested by the main verb. In relaxed conversations they are usually preferred to single-word verbs which have roughly the same meaning. 'Seek' appears to be a synonym of 'look for', but no one would talk of 'seeking' the bunch of keys he had mislaid. The single word mainly survives in fossilized sayings. 'You are a man, a young man, and brought up, I suppose, as almost everybody is nowadays, with a view to seeking your fortune.' So says a character in Nathaniel Hawthorne's *The House of the Seven Gables*. Today a young woman could be addressed in similar vein, but the fortune would still be 'sought' rather than 'looked for'.

'Metaphor comes from the power of seeing things in the inside of your head,' said the unconscious disciple of Aristotle – 'seeing them so vivid that you see the likeness between them. When Bauldy Johnston said "the thumb-mark of his Maker was wet in the clay of him," he saw the print of a thumb in wet clay, and he saw the Almighty making a man out of mud, the way He used to do in the Garden of Eden lang syne. So Bauldy flashed the two ideas together, and the metaphor sprang! A man'll never make phrases unless he can see things in the middle of his brain.'

George Douglas *The House with the Green Shutters*

Imaginative speakers and writers, constantly aware of literal as well as metaphorical meanings, occasionally have fun with phrasal verbs as they do with other kinds of set phrases. We talk of **running up** a bill, for instance, when we allow it to accumulate. Dickens long ago pointed out, in *The Pickwick Papers*, that a bill was 'the most extraordinary locomotive engine that the genius of man ever produced. It would keep on running during the longest lifetime, without ever once stopping of its own accord.'

■ PHRASAL 'YOU'

The tendency in English to refine the meaning of a basic word by combining it with other words to form a phrase can be seen elsewhere. We increasingly form the comparatives and superlatives of adjectives by prefixing them with 'more' and 'most', rather than by inflecting the words concerned with '-er' and '-est'. A similar analysis could be said to occur in the pronoun system. While all grammarians recognize phrasal verbs as a feature of the English language, that is not yet true of phrasal pronouns, or more specifically, phrasal 'you'. A strong case for it can nevertheless be made.

As anyone who has studied a foreign language knows, languages other than English normally have at least two words for 'you'. The different 'you' words allow certain distinctions to be made, to show, for example, whether one person is being addressed or several. The specific 'you' word that is used may also reveal the relationship between speaker and hearer, whether it is one of social and professional equality or inequality.

At one time, these distinctions could be made in English. In the early stage of the language known as Old English there were three words for 'you': a single person was addressed as 'thou'; the dual form 'yit' was used for two people; 'ye' was the more general plural. This system was gradually simplified until 'thou' and 'you' were the only words used. 'Thou' was used affectionately to a family member or close friend. It was also used to a servant or social inferior, anyone to whom it was not necessary to show respect. 'You' was both the plural and respectful form.

Sir Andrew: Will either of you bear me a challenge to him?
Sir Toby: Go, write it with a martial hand; be curst and brief; it is no matter how witty, so it be eloquent and full of invention. Taunt him with the license of ink; if thou thou'st him some thrice, it shall not be amiss.

William Shakespeare *Twelfth Night*

The system was subsequently simplified still further. Although 'thou' lives on in certain English dialects, as well as in prayers and poetry, 'you' is now the single term used in standard modern English. Most grammarians, therefore, tend to echo the view expressed by Professor Joshua Whatmough in his *Language, A Modern Synthesis*: 'Those languages which distinguish a second person singular from the plural when addressing a single individual, especially a child or close relative or a servant, clearly pay attention to certain social relationships no longer linguistically distinguished in English.'

As for being able to distinguish between one person and several, Bergen Evans had this to say in his *Comfortable Words*: 'The disuse of *thou* has left a gap in our speech, because there are many times when we want to make it plain whether we are speaking to one person present or to several. We no longer have a standard word that makes this desirable distinction.'

■ RELATIONSHIP DISTINCTIONS

Standard *word* we may not have, but English-speakers are easily able to make precise relationship distinctions in direct address. A wife might make use of an intimate phrasal 'you' to ask: 'Are you ready, darling?' A friendly phrasal 'you' form of the same question could be: 'Are you ready, John?' The shop assistant's polite phrasal 'you' form would be: 'Are you ready, sir?' The *darling*, *John* and *sir* which have been added are known as vocatives or terms of address. They clearly link with *you* to modify its social meaning.

Social relationships, then, *can* be distinguished linguistically in English when an individual is being addressed. The terms of address are not as invariable as the prepositions and adverbs which form part of phrasal verbs; each is merely recognized in context as belonging to an intimate, friendly, polite, neutral, unfriendly or insulting group. 'You', which may be present or implied, is modified accordingly. The vocative terms themselves may be conventionally recognized, or spur-of-the-moment conversions. As for Mr Evans's point about being able to show that several people are the intended audience, the problem is easily solved: 'Are you ready, *you two*?'; 'Are you ready, *all of you*?'; 'Are you ready, *gentlemen*?'

'How's the old horse thief?'
'All right, I guess. How're you, you poor shrimp?'
'I'm first rate, you second-hand hunk of cheese.'
Reassured thus of their high fondness, Babbitt grunted, 'You're a fine guy, you are! Ten minutes late!'

Sinclair Lewis *Babbitt*

Many of the terms of address used to form a phrasal 'you' would qualify as curious phrases in themselves. Earlier this century one might have heard a speaker say: 'Are you ready, old socks?' 'Old' was merely affectionate, 'socks' was probably a deliberate corruption by humorous schoolboys of Latin *socius* 'chum'. **Old socks** was by no means confined to English public schools, as its use by one character to another in *Martin Arrowsmith*, by Sinclair Lewis, makes clear.

Such phrases have not been included in this book since they are fully dealt with in the present author's *Dictionary of Epithets and Terms of Address* (Routledge 1990). The Introduction to that book also argues the phrasal 'you' theory in considerably more depth. It is mentioned here as part of a general thesis: that in English the use of phrases of one kind or another is more significant than is generally recognized.

■ PROVERBS

Amongst the more traditional phrases we distinguish those which are felt to embody general truths as 'proverbs', 'adages' or 'maxims'. Lord Chesterfield was of the opinion that 'a man of fashion never has recourse to proverbs and vulgar aphorisms'. There may still be some people who share that view, though it

is difficult to see the justification for it.

All true, those old and wrinkled maxims, proverbs, clichés.

Judith Guest *Ordinary People*

Isaac Disraeli was more reasonable on the subject, though as a typical 19th-century gentleman he was equally patronizing. In his *Curiosities of Literature* ('The Philosophy of Proverbs') he says: 'The home-spun adages which remain in the mouths of the people are adapted to their capacities and their humours. Easily remembered, and readily applied, these are the philosophy of the vulgar, and often more sound than that of their masters. The proverbs of the street and of the market, true to nature, and lasting only because they are true, are records that the populace of Athens and at Rome were the same people as at Paris and at London, and as they had before been in the city of Jerusalem.'

Printed collections show that many phrases which at one time were considered to have achieved proverbial status have dropped out of use. The distinguished antiquarian William Camden, for instance, in his *Remains Concerning Britain*, gives examples of proverbs that might have enlivened a 16th-century conversation: **It is not good to have an oar in every man's boat; Better an old man's darling than a young man's warling; Trust is the mother of deceit; The more ye stir a turd, the worse it will stink**.

In *Lawnswood Chronicles*, David Gunston mentions several country proverbs which have fallen out of use: **Labour is light where Love doth pay; A closed mouth catches no flies; It is hard to wive and thrive both in a year**.

Such sentiments may still be valid, but the sayings are no longer familiar. Novelists, however, clearly assume a shared knowledge with their readers of many proverbs that are still widely known. Nina Bawden, in *George Beneath a Paper Moon*, has: 'I obliged the lady. Not just the one night, you know, but several nights running. No point in spoiling the ship for a ha'p'orth of tar.' 'All's well that ends well,' says someone in Evelyn Waugh's *Vile Bodies*. 'He might as well be hanged for a sheep as for a lamb' is in Upton Sinclair's *World's End*; 'practice makes perfect' in Ivy Compton-Burnett's *A House and Its Head*. 'Never put off till tomorrow what you can do today' is quoted in all seriousness by a mother to her son in Jetta Carleton's *The Moonflower Vine*. 'Better late than never' occurs on the next page. Thomas Hardy also quotes this in *Fellow-Townsmen*.

As far as Norman was concerned, what the eye didn't see the heart didn't grieve over.

Somerset Maugham *Flotsam and Jetsam*

Mary McCarthy has a character in *The Group*

whose special fondness for proverbs is remarked upon. He is made to prove the point by saying such things as 'beggars can't be choosers' and 'pride goeth before a fall'. It was probably the author herself who was proverbially-minded. Other characters in the novel quote proverbs, and Miss McCarthy is content to open a chapter with the words: 'It was an ill wind that blew nobody good.'

'Pride comes before a you-know-what.'

Barry Oakley *A Salute to the Great McCarthy*

Some proverbs are well enough known to be left unfinished or merely alluded to in passing. 'If the job's worth doing – !' says a character in Warwick Deeping's *Sorrell and Son*. 'All work and no play – ' says another character in the book. In both cases the reader is left to supply the missing words. 'All's fair in love' occurs in Mary Webb's *Gone to Earth*. Monica Dickens, in *The Fancy*, has: 'He still made mistakes, but then to err was human, as he frequently told Wendy Holt when she made one of her muddles with the rockers.' James Branch Cabell plays with this idea of suggesting the conclusion to a phrase in *Jurgen*. He quotes: 'When in Rome', setting up an expectation of 'do as the Romans do'. Instead he completes the sentence with 'one must be romantic'.

'I was just going to bed,' he said. '"Early to bed and early to rise," but I don't mind stopping a minute for such a one as you.'

Thomas Hardy *The Withered Arm*

'Fools rush in' is often quoted without the following 'where angels fear to tread', but the proverb can be alluded to in a different way. In Ruth Rendell's *Talking to Strange Men* a character says: 'You'd rushed in where angels fear to tread before I even got into the room.' E.M. Forster, in *Howards End*, has: 'My dear Miss Schlegel, I will not rush in where your sex has been unable to tread.'

'We've spared the rod. Maybe we were wrong.'

John Steinbeck *East of Eden*

Other Men's Wives, by Alexander Fullerton, has a remark about a man on his way to meet a woman for the first time. He thinks she will be unattractive and tries to 'reassure himself by recalling old adages about grey cats'. The reader is presumably meant to recognize an allusion to 'in the dark all cats are grey'. This in turn means that a woman's looks are not important once the bedroom light has been switched off.

Punning references are possible. In Vera Caspary's *Laura* 'a bull in a china shop' is said of a detective who is clumsily handling rare china. The pun is on 'bull', which in American slang has long referred to a policeman. In *Moses*, Susan Barrett has the exchange: 'The

last straw.' 'That breaks the camel's back?' 'The camel's back? I didn't know she'd been away.'

Playful variations can also be introduced. Fay Weldon, in *Down Among the Women*, has: 'The client, he suspects, would rather go home to his wife but can hardly look a gift lay in the teeth.' This makes the innocent **look a gift horse in the mouth/teeth** rather more bawdy: a saying which is earthy to begin with can be euphemistically toned down. In a Radio 4 documentary 'The Prostitutes' (March 1992), a contributor quoted: 'A standing whatsit has no conscience.' Similarly, in her novel *Pleasure Man*, Mae West has: 'Rising passion has no conscience, to put the old saying less vulgarly.' The vulgar version of the 'old saying', **a standing prick has no conscience**, is described by Partridge as 'virtually a proverb' and dates from the 19th century.

Aldous Huxley, in his *Brave New World*, adapts familiar proverbs to the needs of the society he describes: 'A gramme (of soma) in time saves nine' for **A stitch in time saves nine**; 'Never put off till tomorrow the fun you can have today' for **Never put off till tomorrow what you can do today**; 'Cleanliness is next to fordliness' instead of **Cleanliness is next to Godliness**. In real life, changes to the wording of proverbs tend to come about slowly and by accident as they pass from generation to generation by word of mouth.

As with terms of address, proverbs are worthy of a separate study and have not been fully dealt with in this book. Many of them would certainly qualify as 'curious'. Quoted above is 'spoil the ship for a ha'p'orth of tar', which seems to be a straightforward reference to the days of wooden ships. As it happens the original version of this proverb was to 'lose a sheep for a ha'p'orth of tar'. Tar was used medicinally by shepherds. Shakespeare refers to the practice in *As You Like It*, when Corin says: 'Our hands are hard, and they are often tarr'd over with the surgery of our sheep.'

◼ QUOTATIONS

Proverbs are a form of unattributable quotation. Quotations from known sources also form part of an educated person's vocabulary. They constitute another kind of self-contained phrasal unit which can be used in speech or writing. Shakespeare and the Bible are well-mined sources, and quotations or allusions to them are easily found in novels.

'Sometimes they tell me I get too worked up about what we can do, but what the hell. The world's our oyster. So many new things we can develop.'

Derek Jewell *Come In No.1 Your Time Is Up*

Pistol's remark in *The Merry Wives of Windsor*, for instance – 'Why, then the world's mine oyster, which I with sword will open' – is found in Trollope's *Doctor Thorne* as: 'The world was his oyster; but he knew it was not for him to open it with his lancet all at once. He had bread to earn, which he must earn wearily.' It is there again in John Dos Passos, *The Great Days*, when two men discuss having a good time: 'This time we'll make the world our oyster.'

Iago's brutal comment to Brabantio in *Othello* – 'Your daughter and the Moor are now making the beast with two backs' – occurs in Barry Oakley's *A Salute to the Great McCarthy* as: 'Again the beast with two backs is attempted, this time with her in the ascendant.' Mary McCarthy, in *The Group*, has it as: 'In an idle moment I played the beast with two backs with her.'

Mrs Leivers stuck unflinchingly to this doctrine of 'the other cheek'. She could not instil it at all into the boys. With the girls she succeeded better, and Miriam was the child of her heart. The boys loathed the other cheek when it was presented to them. Miriam was often sufficiently lofty to turn it. Then they spat on her and hated her.

D. H. Lawrence *Sons and Lovers*

Biblical quotations, by people other than those whose lives are based on daily Bible readings, tend to be of the **eye for eye**, **tooth for tooth** variety, often slightly misquoted. References to **turning the other cheek** occur regularly. Margaret Drabble, in *The Middle Ground*, writes: 'If one has decided to turn the other cheek, one might as well do it with a good spirit.'

There is a special significance when Edward Blishen says, in *A Cack-handed War*: 'So much angry talk revolved around that phrase about turning the other cheek.' The whole novel is about the experiences of conscientious objectors during World War Two. The quotation referred to is from the New Testament, Matthew 5.39 – 'Resist not evil: but whosoever shall smite thee on thy right cheek, turn to him the other also.' The average person would, like Blishen, merely allude to those words, but novelists sometimes portray lay evangelists whose speech is heavily punctuated with actual biblical quotations.

'It may even come to pass' – he liked to flavour his talk with biblical and other clichés – 'that, the said Hunt not being among those present, old Scrymgeour will have to do a hand's turn of work himself.'

Christopher Dilke *Freddie and Son*

Other sources are drawn upon according to the whim of the individual writer. E.M. Forster expects his readers to share the joke when he varies Nelson's message at Trafalgar: 'England expects every man to open his heart once.' In the same novel, *Howards End*, he alludes to a quotation that is usually attributed to the Duke of Wellington: 'There was nothing finicking

about their politeness: it had the Public School touch, and, though sedulous, was virile. More battles than Waterloo have been won on our playing fields, and Margaret bowed to a charm of which she did not wholly approve.' *The Concise Oxford Dictionary of Quotations* remarks in passing that the 7th Duke refuted the attribution to him of **The Battle of Waterloo was won on the playing-fields of Eton**. It suggests instead that a Frenchman called Montalembert was responsible for it.

In *Down Among the Women*, Fay Weldon sprinkles quotations or allusions to them as she goes along. Amongst many others there is the famous comment from the diary of Lady Caroline Lamb about Lord Byron: 'They are frightened of Wanda, they think she is mad, bad and dangerous to know.' Wanda herself is made to quote 'the snows of yesteryear', from Rossetti's translation of François Villon.

Bernard Wolfe plays with these same words in *The Late-Risers*. An American press agent says: 'Where are the snow jobs of yesteryear? Remember the halcyon days, when you could get a cheesecake shot of any shipoopi into any paper by announcing that she had just been chosen Girl I'd Most Like To Be Snowed Up With In An Igloo by the Eskimo Rotary Club of Upper Baffin Bay?'

Penelope Gilliatt, in *A State of Change*, makes the briefest of references to Thomas Gray's 'Full many a flower is born to blush unseen, And waste its sweetness on the desert air.' One of her characters says: 'I don't suppose you'd be tramping the streets looking for work if you wanted to blush unseen, would you?'

The heroine of Anita Brookner's *Hotel du Lac* begins a letter to a friend, 'A cold coming I had of it,' knowing that the intended recipient, at least, will recognize the allusion to T.S. Eliot's 'Journey of the Magi'. The same letter includes the words 'Not drowning, but waving', a reversal of Stevie Smith's well-known: 'I was much too far out all my life. And not waving but drowning.' The author's allusive style is shown even more clearly in a remark about two women that the heroine is observing: 'Butter wouldn't melt, thought Edith.' This is enough to trigger in the reader's mind a quotation from the 18th-century comedy *The Man of the World*, by Charles Macklin: 'She looks as if butter would not melt in her mouth.'

There are many people who love poetry and literature and who greatly value these reminders of favourite works. The ability to introduce apt quotations occasionally into a conversation has long been seen as a mark of intelligence and a good education. Proverbial allusions, as it happens, may be equally apt, but they do not carry the same prestige. Perhaps it is assumed that the proverbs are picked up in conversations with ordinary people, not acquired by study.

'It's just a slight case of our old friend the little green monster, eh, Donny?'

Monica Dickens *The Fancy*

Some quotations have themselves reached proverbial status, perhaps in a slightly altered form. Thus it could be said that there is now an English proverb, **discretion is the better part of valour**, derived from the Shakespearean comment in *Henry the Fourth*, Part One: 'the better part of valour is discretion'. Other quotations are simply not recognized as such. There must be many speakers who refer to jealousy as 'the green-eyed monster' without realising that they are quoting from *Othello*. Nor, perhaps, would the phrase 'a rare bird' call Juvenal to mind.

■ FOREIGN PHRASES

The 'rare bird' example brings us to another feature of educated English conversation. Those speakers and writers who *were* aware of Juvenal might refer instead to *rara avis*, or quote the full *rara avis in terris, nigroque simillima cycno* 'a rare bird on earth, and very like a black swan'.

Novels which are set in other countries or have foreign characters may use snippets of the language concerned to provide local colour. This is not at all the same thing as a conversation between two English-speakers which includes phrases and quotations from Latin or Greek, or modern European languages, especially French. The educational background of such speakers makes it possible for them to draw on extended linguistic reserves. They may feel that a foreign phrase expresses a thought more precisely than is possible in English, but other factors come into play. Just as membership of a particular group is often reinforced by the use of language, whether it be slang or professional jargon, so a polyglot conversation makes a flattering comment in itself on the educational background, and perhaps the social standing, of the participants. The foreign phrases display membership of an élite club.

Chris: The great roué.
Keller: What is that, roué?
Chris: It's French.
Keller: Don't talk dirty. (They laugh)

Arthur Miller *All My Sons*

Proponents of a classical education might well express things differently. There are perhaps still those who believe in the innate superiority of Latin and Greek language and literature, that snippets of those languages will raise the tone of an English 2conversation. That was probably the view of Richard Chenevix Trench, who says in the Introduction to his *Select Glossary*: 'In the present condition of education in England, the number of those enjoying the inestimable advantages, mental and moral, which more than any other languages the Latin and the Greek supply, must ever be growing smaller. It becomes therefore a duty to seek elsewhere the best substitutes within reach for that discipline of the faculties which these languages would better than any other have afforded. And I believe, when these two are set aside, our own language and literature will furnish the best substitutes; which, even though they may not satisfy perfectly, are not therefore to be rejected.'

That reluctant admission that English language and literature might have something to offer was made in 1906. The decline in the teaching of Latin and Greek, mentioned by Dr Trench, has continued. Some would say that there have been corresponding advances in the teaching of modern languages. This is no doubt reflected in the relative frequency of quotations in French, say, as opposed to Latin and Greek, that now occur in English conversations.

Novelists are obliged to be careful about their use of foreign phrases if they wish to appeal to a wide audience. Clearly there can be no guarantee that readers will understand what is being said. Few writers today would dare make a character speak as obscurely as Dr Middleton, say, in Meredith's *The Egoist*. The good doctor's classical allusions, of which he is immensely proud, mean much to him but little to the average person. Some writers employ the device of having a character who professes ignorance and demands translations of anything that is not said in English, but it is difficult to see what this achieves. It certainly implies in passing that the person who used the foreign phrase was insensitive or snobbish, unable or unwilling to adapt his speech to his audience.

'I give you carte blanche, *Mr Keith,' Lady Mercy replied. 'But use your discretion.'*

Eric Linklater *Poet's Pub*

Some foreign phrases are used so often that they are listed in English dictionaries, in normal alphabetical order rather than in an appendix, often without being italicized. Such is the case with 'tête-à-tête' and 'sang-froid', for instance, though many English-speakers would be puzzled by the diacritics of the first and pronunciation of the second. Similar French phrases are 'pied-à-terre' and 'fait accompli'. Presumably the dictionary-compilers feel that these have been absorbed into the language, but on the basis merely of frequent use, a phrase like *cherchez la femme*, which originated with Alexandre Dumas, could probably now be counted as English. *Au revoir* is well-enough known to have its own jokey English version, 'au reservoir'.

Mary McCarthy, in *The Group*, includes a light scattering of foreign expressions throughout the book. They are mainly of the frequently-used variety quoted above, plus slightly rarer French phrases such as *idée fixe* 'fixed idea, obsession'; *succès fou* 'tremendous success'; *de trop* 'superfluous'; *beau geste* 'gracious gesture'. *Mirabile dictu* 'wonderful to tell', *ne plus ultra* 'nothing further, perfection' are amongst the Latin phrases that occur. *Hoi polloi* 'the many, the rabble' appears to be Miss McCarthy's sole use of Greek, but once again this is familiar enough to be listed in even a medium-sized English dictionary.

■ SET PHRASES

Apart from a vocabulary of normal words, then, the linguistic armoury of a native English-speaker includes words of a phrasal nature, proverbs, quotations and foreign expressions. In addition there is a considerable stock of fixed phrases. These are variously described as idioms, collocations, catch phrases, slogans, colloquialisms and clichés. Each of these descriptions makes some kind of comment on their nature according to their form or function. An 'idiom', for example, as the original meaning of the word implies, is supposedly the 'private property' of a particular language, a linguistic idiosyncrasy. The phrase concerned cannot be translated word for word in order to convey its meaning. Many people use the word in a rather narrower sense to describe phrases which are especially picturesque or curious. It is probably more accurate to refer to these as metaphorical idioms and to phrasal verbs and the like as grammatical idioms. Both types can be combined in an expression such as 'get off scot free'.

He said, to Leila, 'What's your poison?' – a phrase he never used normally and only used now, it seemed to George, because he imagined it might be her idiom.

Nina Bawden *George Beneath a Paper Moon*

The description 'collocation' merely comments on the fact that the words in an idiomatic phrase consistently occur together. There are, for example, many two-word collocations in English, usually consisting of a preposition and a noun or adjective: **in fact**, **for instance**, **of course**, **by chance**, **at length**, **on hand**. So close is their association they are sometimes written as single words: **indoors**, **downstairs**, **outside**, **forever**, **offshore**. **All right** hovers between the two, with many arguing strongly that this should be written **alright** on the analogy of **always** from **all ways**.

So-called 'doublets' are also collocations: **free and easy**, **bright and breezy**, **pride and joy**, **down and out**, **safe and sound**, **heart and soul**, **now or never**, **sooner or later**, **rough and ready**, **high and mighty**, **null and void**, **ways and means**. As Logan Pearsall Smith pointed out, in his *Words and Idioms*, some of these expressions merely repeat a word emphatically: **again and again**, **neck and neck**, **over and over**, **round and round**.

Some writers use the word 'doublet' to describe a different kind of collocation, one in which a particular adjective is almost invariably associated with a particular noun. Rather literary examples cited by Professor Weekley, in his *Adjectives – And Other Words*, include **learned counsel**, **gallant officer**, **reverend gentleman**, **providential escape**, **speedy recovery**, **filthy lucre**.

'Catch phrase' describes a phrase originally associated with one person, perhaps an entertainer who used it frequently. It may then have 'caught on' and been taken temporarily into general use. During World War One, for example, a cartoon by Bruce Bairnsfather, along with its caption, became especially famous. It showed Old Bill, a walrus-moustached veteran soldier, in a water-logged shell-hole with another soldier. Bill was saying: 'Well, if you knows of a better 'ole, go to it.' Few today would recognize the allusion. Alexander Fullerton misquotes it as 'Show me a better 'ole, I'll go to it' in his *Other Men's Wives*, applying it to a man who wants to change his job.

A slogan is a phrase deliberately brought into being for advertising purposes, linked to a person or product. Slogans may become known to a wide public, but they are rarely absorbed into the language on a permanent basis. 'Colloquialism' draws attention to the fact that such a phrase is more likely to occur in relaxed, subjective speech than in formal, objective writing.

■ CLICHÉS

As for 'cliché', the word has a complicated etymology and is difficult to define. It was originally technical French for an embossed metal plate from which copies could be made. Early photographers then borrowed the word to describe the negative from which prints were taken. In a more general sense the word came to mean a banality, something commonplace and much copied. In English, cliché is now a subjective description, usually applied by a speaker to a word or phrase which he considers to be hackneyed and over-used. The word is sometimes used metaphorically, as when Peter Benchley writes, in *The Island*: 'It had been thrilling to live the life of the clichéd roué, to awaken in strange beds beside women whose names he had forgotten.'

Professional men cannot avoid knowing what they are supposed to be like – a thousand novels, a thousand motion pictures have typed them – until it is impossible for them to be other than a cliché of a character in some work of fiction.

Edward Hyams *Sylvester*

The question of whether a word or set phrase can rightfully be called a cliché creates many difficulties. Frequency of use cannot in itself be the only criterion. There are many phatic, formulaic phrases of the type **Good morning, How do you do?, Merry Christmas, Many happy returns of the day** which are universally used. They are prompted by specific circumstances and their correct use demonstrates a knowledge of social and linguistic conventions. Less formulaic, but arguably almost as conventional, are a great many other phrases which are also prompted by situations that regularly occur. The children's misbehaviour once again makes it necessary to **read the Riot Act**. An approaching examination means that one must **keep one's nose to the grindstone**.

It is phrases of this type which some would call clichés. Others see them as the linguistic equivalent of philosophical shrugs, an acceptance that familiar circumstances, albeit unpleasant ones, have once again arisen. The familiar words that are used can be rather comforting to both speaker and listener. The underlying message is: at least we are not dealing with the unknown; this is a well-enough known human situation to have its own linguistic convention.

Studies of children's speech, such as *Lore and Language of Schoolchildren* by Iona and Peter Opie, make it clear that children learn at an early age a number of set phrases which enable them to cope with recurring situations. **Finders keepers!** traditionally establishes ownership of something found by chance. If they are taunted in the playground because they are too clever or too stupid, too tall or too small, too fat or too thin, cry too easily, have red hair, wear glasses or generally offend others by being different in some way, they need to be able to respond quickly with a suitable retort.

Sticks and stones may break my bones but hard words cannot hurt me. His mother had taught him that when he was a little kid and had been subject to verbal bullying in the school playground.

Ruth Rendell *The Tree of Hands*

This may be no more than **Same to you with knobs on, Do me a favour – drop dead** or **Sticks and stones may break my bones, but names will never hurt me**. The accusation that **little things please little minds** may be met with **and little drawers fit little behinds**. Only the verbally gifted will be able to rely on the inspiration of the moment and say something original. The average child will be content to use any appropriate phrase which deflects the verbal attack and perhaps gives him the last word.

Situational phrases, then, are seen to be useful from a very early age. In adult life the playground taunts are not usually needed, though they may still surface. 'Am ah comin' dahn tonight? You tell the lads Ah'll be dahn there with knobs on,' says a man in James McCormick's *Heads I Win*.

What may turn a situational phrase into a cliché is the fact that the phrase concerned is too recognizably part of a speaker's idiolect, a personal saying which he uses regularly. The listener's irritation may then be caused as much by the predictable behaviour as the phrase itself.

'It's enough to make anyone puke the way you go on. Clichés and small talk. You're programmed, did you know that? You're a floppy disk the Great Computer Programmer has put a file of words and phrases on. Two hundred for average daily use. That's a good name for you, floppy disk. I think I'll call you that. It implies feebleness and learned responses in the right proportions. Christ, no wonder that wife of yours left you. What did you say every night before you went to bed, floppy? "It's going to be a fine day tomorrow. Me for Bedford. Up the wooden hill"?'

Ruth Rendell *Talking to Strange Men*

Most of us have a personal stock of words and idioms. For a situation where a number of different phrases might be used we will have made a choice from the available formulae. One person will always **clean his teeth**, others invariably **wash** or **brush** them. To toast a drinking companion, one man's **Bottoms up!** or **Cheers!** will be another's **Down the hatch!** or **Good health!** A promised telephone call becomes **I'll give you a bell** for one person, **I'll give you a tinkle** or a **buzz** to another. We notice such verbal habits in the mouths of others: it can be far more difficult to be aware of one's own favourite phrases. There are some, however, who quite deliberately begin to use expressions which they think that others will notice and associate with them. Nina Bawden creates a character in *George Beneath a Paper Moon* who consciously adopts 'quaint phrases'. They include **doncha know, shouldn't wonder**, the **wireless** and **old boy**.

His ideas are always referred to as 'germs'; his figure estimates are 'in the ball park'. Clichés. They jump out at you from everywhere, but you never see your own.

Judith Guest *Ordinary People*

The worst clichés are probably those which contribute no psychological comfort to speaker or hearer and nothing to the meaning of what is being said. There are those speakers who preface a sentence with **I must admit that, I must confess that, To tell you the truth, The fact is, As a matter of fact, Let's face it**, or turn a simple **now** into **at this moment in time**. There are others whose speech is constantly punctuated by **sort of** or **you know**. The phrases become verbal tics which distract and irritate the listener. The latter may stop listening in any real sense and begin counting the number of times the offending phrase occurs.

■ FASHIONABLE PHRASES

Clichés of this type are immediately apparent to any sensitive user of the language. It is more difficult to say whether a metaphorical idiom is a cliché or not. A phrase may slowly have come into general use, having been seen to be both vivid and useful, and then get spoilt for a while by its own popularity. There are fashions in set phrases as there are in words. Fashion in any area, however, implies change and movement, and what is fashionable today will not be so in future.

The word 'cliché', for example, is connected etymologically with English 'click' – a word which itself qualified as a cliché for a time. When P.G. Wodehouse was writing *The Clicking of Cuthbert*, 'click' in the slang sense of striking up a successful relationship with a girl was very much in fashion and was over-used. The word is still heard in that sense, but not frequently enough to offend the purists. As for phrases, **to blow someone up**, meaning to scold someone, was clearly very popular in the early 19th century. Dickens uses the phrase at least four times in *The Pickwick Papers*. It had become a cliché in his day; it is certainly not one today.

Right about this time everybody was saying 'out of this world', probably the crummiest popular phrase that ever hit the country. Everything was 'out of this world'. Everybody said it constantly and they all thought they were being bright and clever. Whenever anybody was real hot on something, whether it was some new disc by Armstrong or a new kind of pickle relish or auto chains, they just gave up any idea of using their goddam brains to give an accurate description and burbled, 'Oh, it's out of this world'.

Richard Bissell *The Pajama Game*

Certain types of writing are commonly said to be cliché-ridden. Romantic fiction is said to have almost a cliché language of its own. Frank Sullivan gave examples of it in *The Cliché Expert Testifies On Love*. He described typical heroes as dark, handsome chaps who have **sown their wild oats**, do not **play fast and loose** with girls' affections, **have hearts of gold** and are **diamonds in the rough**. They fall madly in love with **the Only Girl**, **pop the question**, **plight their troth** and **walk on air**. It is difficult to imagine any writer using such banal phrases today without being aware of their well-worn nature and deliberately making a joke of them.

Journalese also comes under fire, though perhaps it is to be expected that writers who have little time to read and revise their work should make heavy use of overworked, ready-made phrases. If too many occur in close context, they certainly become very noticeable. A short 'Open File' article about life-insurance which appeared in *The Observer* (8.3.1992), for instance, included the following remarks: 'She was proud of having kept up the policy **through** thick and thin.' 'Times were desperately hard in the Thirties.' 'Complaints have risen 77 per cent to more than 4000 – the **tip of a much larger iceberg** of dissatisfaction.' 'The public is gradually realising **it has been taken for an expensive ride.**' 'At the other end of the scale...' 'The life companies have **fought tooth and nail** to prevent disclosure of costs and commissions.'

He was no longer the public spirited countryman; he was cards-on-the-table brass-tacks and twenty-shillings-in-the-pound treat-him-or-mind-your-step Metcalfe, Metcalfe with his back up, fighting Metcalfe once again, Metcalfe who would cut off his nose any day to spite his face, sink any ship for a ha'p'orth of tar that was not legally due, Metcalfe the lion of the Rotarians.

Evelyn Waugh *An Englishman's Home*

A similar density of set phrases sometimes occurs in general fiction, usually in colloquial dialogue. 'I shall have to **strain every nerve** to find a replacement,' says a character in *Getting it Right*, by Elizabeth Jane Howard. 'Meanwhile we'll just have to **take the rough with the smooth.** But Gavin, keep them **up to the mark.**' 'We shall have to bring it all **into the open** and explain **in so many words** why we've been **keeping it dark**,' says someone in C.P. Snow's *The Affair*. Many of Snow's characters speak in this way. Elsewhere in the novel one of them describes a solicitor who is 'not the man to let **the grass grow under his feet.** If I tell him you're our man, you'll get a letter from him **before you can say Jack Robinson.** So I can't give you long to make up your mind. That's **as plain as a pikestaff**, isn't it?'

■ CLICHÉ COLLECTIONS

Some writers on language have bravely, or rashly, attempted to make a general list of clichés, but often they can do no more than say that at a particular time, in a particular part of the English-speaking world, certain phrases were being intensively used. The subjective nature of cliché classification becomes quickly apparent when a work like Eric Partridge's *Dictionary of Clichés* is consulted. He includes, for example, the proverbial **the more the merrier**, but when a friend arrives unexpectedly at a house already filled with visitors, this is a very acceptable situational phrase. The welcome implied by the words more than compensates for their familiarity.

Eric Partridge speaks of clichés with horror, but his attitude is roundly attacked by Nicholas Bagnall in his *Defence of Clichés*. Mr Bagnall's thesis – to paraphrase it considerably – is that there is a long literary tradition of alluding to phrases used by great writers. For ordinary speech, writers and speakers of the past have created a body of set phrases which form a kind of linguistic inheritance. This can justifiably be used if a writer or speaker is consciously aware of what he is doing. Mr Bagnall quotes from writers such as P.G. Wodehouse to show how effective the use of so-called clichés can be.

Ignorance could be bliss – Lord, as you grew older, how the truth of the old clichés came thundering home!

Nina Bawden *George Beneath a Paper Moon*

In *Don't Say It*, by Alan S.C. Ross, words and phrases are labelled by such descriptions as U, non-U, overworked, cliché. It is clearly implied that anything Professor Ross considers to be a cliché should never be uttered. One such phrase is **Elementary, my dear Watson!** This is certainly heard from time to time, but always as a joke. There is a considerable difference between the unconscious use of hackneyed expressions and their deliberate comic use. Perhaps more of a cliché, in modern times, is the remark that will now always be made when 'Elementary, my dear Watson!' is quoted. Someone is bound to point out: 'Sherlock Holmes never actually said those words, you know.' Someone else in the company is then likely to mention **Play it again, Sam**, the words never spoken by Humphrey Bogart in *Casablanca*.

The highly prescriptive attitude adopted by Professor Ross towards phrases that he considers to be clichés does not find an echo in this book. Speakers and writers can rescue a phrase from clichédom at any time by being aware of its established nature and using it in a controlled way. Humour often plays its part. In one of his 'And Moreover' columns in *The Times* newspaper, for instance, (5.2.1992) Alan Coren writes: 'The words I type are meaningless, and when I've finished typing them, I press the key which deletes them, but Keith doesn't know this, he just thinks I'm working my fingers to the bone. . . . I want Keith to know this writing game is not all beer and skittles.'

Eric Partridge lists both **work one's fingers to the bone** and **not all beer and skittles** in his *Dictionary of Clichés*, but it would be absurd to say that Alan Coren should not have used them. His article comes across as conversationally relaxed and friendly, and no literate reader doubts for one moment the writer's control of language. The touch of exaggeration adds to the fun as he comments humorously on the embarrassment felt by those who work mainly with their minds in the presence of those who labour physically.

Quotations throughout this book show imaginative writers making fun of well-worn phrases. In Victorian novels, for instance, a cad or scoundrel had to be 'thrashed within an inch of his life'. E.M. Forster uses the phrase in all seriousness in *Howards End*. Elizabeth Jane Howard, in *Getting it Right*, has: '"I thought I'd mow the lawn first." She liked the lawn mown within an inch of its life, so this suggestion found favour.'

This renewal of old phrases is as pleasing to the average reader as the sudden introduction of a verbal novelty, something which is made fun of in its turn by the novelists. In *The Incomparable Atuk* Mordecai Richler has the exchange: '"There's nothing. I'm clean as a seal's tooth." "Seal's tooth. Very good. Colourful. I want you to stick to that sort of idiom in public, Atuk." "Shit. You're not talking to a stage Eskimo. Like I don't rub noses any more."'

'I'm pretty good at inventing phrases – you know, the sort of words that suddenly make you jump, almost as though you'd sat on a pin, they seem so new and exciting even though they're about something hypnopaedically obvious. . . . Words can be like X-rays, if you use them properly – they'll go through anything. You read and you're pierced.'

Aldous Huxley *Brave New World*

The above discussion is meant to demonstrate that a 'cliché' defies easy definition. It is not a matter of formal characteristics. Intensive, unthinking usage by an individual or set of people at a particular time can cause any proverb, quotation, foreign expression, grammatical or metaphorical idiom to become a cliché. Even then, the classification may remain subjective and localized. Expressions like 'I've been **killing adders** (busy) all morning' and **Indeed in the double deed** (preceding a lie or cock and bull story) are perhaps clichés in Pembrokeshire (both are listed in *Place Names and Dialects of Pembrokeshire*, by P. Valentine Harris), but would be verbal novelties elsewhere.

■ FORMAT PHRASES

It would be far more satisfactory to classify phrases according to observable linguistic criteria. Thus Nigel Rees, in his *Dictionary of Popular Phrases*, usefully identifies the 'format phrase', which he describes as being 'capable of infinite variation by the insertion of new words'.

Such phrases *must* vary, since they are incomplete in themselves and can only be used when appropriate names or words are inserted. Examples are: 'Any friend of . . . is a friend of mine'; 'If you've seen one . . . you've seen them all.' Thomas Tryon, for example, in *All That Glitters*, writes: 'I guess I needn't describe the "Community Room". Seen one community room, seen 'em all.' In the same novel occurs: 'Belinda Carroll had a middle name, but you never saw it in print or on a theatre marquee. Her middle name was trouble with a capital "T".' This same format phrase occurs in *Women and Thomas Harrow*, by John P. Marquand: 'Emily's middle name is Loyalty. Emily Loyalty Harrow. She added it the moment she dropped her maiden name.'

Sinclair Lewis, in *Main Street*, has: 'Like fishing?' 'Fishing is my middle name.'

'You wouldn't know neatness if it was your middle name.'

Margaret Laurence *The Diviners*

These format phrases are similar in one way, but can easily be differentiated. The 'friend' of the first example allows substitution of one or two equivalent words. Evelyn Waugh, in *Vile Bodies*, has the idiom as: 'Any pal of Ginger's is a pal of mine.' 'Mate' and 'buddy' could equally well be used. In the second example it would have been enough to have 'community room' mentioned in the first sentence only. 'Seen one, seen them all' becomes meaningful if what is referred to is in close context. The 'middle name' example allows restricted substitution of the possessive: 'my/your/his/her/ John's/Emily's middle name.' With some idioms, plural pronouns could also be used, sometimes with a logical change of the noun, sometimes not. We would probably say that something was **above their heads**, but **they put their foot in it**.

Set phrases vary considerably as to whether they allow substitutions. Many are invariable, others might be described as paradigmatic, allowing forms such as: 'I'm tied to my mother's apron strings', 'you're tied to your mother's apron strings', 'he's tied to his mother's apron strings', 'we're tied to our mothers' apron strings', and so on.

It can be left to the academic linguists to arrive at a detailed classification system of phrases, with suitable labels for each category. A dictionary of idioms for foreign students would be inadequate without such labels, plus further notes about British and American usage, whether a phrase is still considered to be slang, and so on. Native-speakers are fortunate in having an in-built knowledge of such matters.

The present work adopts the philosophy that we should have a more positive attitude than is normally the case to old phrasal friends, who constantly prove their worth in daily speech. Banalities and platitudes, needless to say, should always be avoided, but a large number of grammatical and metaphorical idioms have an essential part to play in spoken and written English. This book attempts to show that metaphorical idioms, especially, are as interesting as they are useful; that they can be used imaginatively by good writers and speakers; that the stories which lie behind their origins reveal much about our social and linguistic history. We should, so to say, be tickled pink about our rich stock of curious phrases.

■ ACTING UP

'Teacher, this woman has been caught in the act of adultery.'

New Testament, John 8.4

To be **caught in the act** uses 'act' in its basic sense of an action or deed, one which in this case is usually immoral or illegal. The phrase is the equivalent of legal Latin *in flagrante delicto* 'in blazing crime'. *Flagrare* 'to blaze' leads to English words such as 'flagrant' and 'conflagration'. *Delicto* 'crime' looks as if it is connected with 'delicious'; 'delinquent' is in fact the nearest English word. Another legal phrase is **act of God**, which relates to storms and natural events over which man has no control.

'Sara, what a meal!' Marty says. 'This is a tough act to follow, dear.'

Judith Guest *Ordinary People*

A **tough act to follow** began as theatrical language but has come into general use. Originally it referred to taking the stage after a performance that had just received great applause, putting the onus on the next performer to maintain the high standard. Other frequently used phrases from the same source include **getting in on the act**, **do a disappearing act**, **put on an act** and **get one's act together**. To 'get in on the act' is to become a participant in something, although one was not initially concerned with it. If the others say that someone is 'getting in on the act', it probably indicates that they resent the newcomer's intrusion.

To 'do a disappearing act' is to disappear in a surprising way, especially when someone is looking for you. 'Putting on an act' is behaving falsely, hiding one's true feelings. To 'get one's act together' is to organize and manage one's life in a proper way. The American army equivalent is **have one's ducks in a row**, referring to a duck with a flotilla of ducklings sailing along behind her.

■ ADAM AND EVE

'Arthur does not know you from Adam.'

Warwick Deeping *Sorrell and Son*

In English we can insist that we have no idea who someone is by saying that we **don't know him from Adam**. The phrase is normally used of a man. French is less sexist, since *ne connaître ni d'Eve ni d'Adam* 'not know someone from Eve or Adam' can easily be applied to a man or woman. Perhaps in the French version of the saying lies the explanation for its use – the speaker does not even know whether the person concerned is a man or woman.

Speculation is necessary because nothing is known for certain about the origin of this phrase. We can only hope, however, that Charles Earle Funk, in *A Hog on Ice*, has his tongue firmly in his cheek when he refers to an 'ancient argument' about whether Adam had a navel or not. Artists usually portray both Adam and Eve with navels, as if they were born in a conventional way. Strictly speaking they should be shown without them. Dr Funk, who occasionally indulges in flights of fancy in the explanations he offers for well-known expressions, says that art critics with an eye for anatomical detail began to insist on correct representation. Otherwise, he imagines the critics saying, it would not be possible to tell ordinary people from Adam.

In Jetta Carleton's *The Moonflower*

Vine a young girl tells her mother that 'if I met him in the middle of the road I wouldn't know him from Adam!' Her sister is much amused, since the two of them had come across the man concerned while he was bathing naked in a pool. Some speakers do perhaps link the idea of not knowing a man from Adam with not knowing what he looks like in an undressed state.

■ ALEXANDER THE GREAT

'We're simpletons, you smart Alecs can twist us round your little fingers like bloody chewing-gum, can't you?'
Alexander Fullerton *Other Men's Wives*

The phrase **smart Alec** 'know-it-all, smugly clever person' was in use in America by the 1860s. The first name Alexander, of which Alec(k) is the normal diminutive, was popular there at that time, but soon went out of fashion. It is possible that the rapid spread of this phrase temporarily affected the name's popularity.

In the early 1990s Alexander has returned to favour, even though 'smart Alec' is widely known and used. The association of the phrase with the name, however, has obviously been weakened, since 'Alec(k)' now often appears in print as 'alec(k)'. *Dover One*, by Joyce Porter, has: 'If MacGregor was going to develop into a real smart alec, life was going to get very uncomfortable.' Similarly in Kate O'Brien's *Pray for the Wanderer* we read: 'A smart alec from literary London has only to step your way to have you crying.'

'Don't you take any smart-aleck stuff from any of that lot, there. They're only muck the same as any of us.'
Margaret Laurence *The Diviners*

No one has ever been able to trace a specific Alec whose behaviour gave rise to this saying. This is in spite of the efforts of many competent linguists. One is therefore led to wonder whether there ever was such a person. 'Smart Alec' was possibly a euphemism for **smart ass**. The phrase has led to an adjectival form, **smart-alecky**, used by American but not yet by British speakers of English.

■ ALL EARS

Ears are featured in a number of expressions which have curious literal meanings. We are **all ears**, or **give ear/ lend an ear** to someone if we pay attention to what he is saying. The injunction from Brutus to the crowd to 'lend me your ears' in *Julius Caesar* is one of the best-known Shakespearean quotations. It sticks in the mind because the notion of lending one's ears to someone else is rather odd. We think nothing, though, of **lending someone a hand** 'giving him some assistance'. In *Measure for Measure* Mariana says to Isabel 'lend me your knees', meaning 'kneel beside me, join me in supplication'.

Mrs Paradise, I am tired of explaining these things. I explained to you the badgers; it went in one ear and out the other.'

Nigel Dennis *Cards of Identity*

We **listen with half an ear** if we are not very attentive, which may cause us to be told later that what was said **went in one ear and out the other**. The latter phrase sounds modern, the sort of thing a parent complains about daily, yet the expression is recorded in the 15th century. Although it is normally used as an accusation that someone is, or has been, inattentive it can also be used to mean 'I refuse to listen to what you're saying.' 'It goes in one ear and out the other by me,' says someone in Margaret Laurence's *The Diviners*.

We have some justification for paying scant attention if someone is **bending our ear** 'insisting on talking to us at great length'. We may also force someone to listen by metaphorically **pinning back his ears**. In *Dover One* Joyce Porter writes: 'He'd pin Mr High-and-Mighty Bartlett's ears back for him with a few home truths about the collection of mental deficients posing as a police force.' This could also be described as **giving someone an earful** or **an earbashing**. When somebody, by contrast, says something that we are delighted to hear, we may say that it is **music to our ears**. This phrase could also be used of sounds other than speech.

I have it on good authority. Friend of mine got it from a friend of his, Indianapolis man, who has his ear close to the ground in Washington.'

Richard Bissell *The Pajama Game*

To **have/keep one's ear to the ground** is to pay close attention to what is happening. The image evoked is of plainsmen listening for the sound of horses' hooves. 'You fellows certainly do keep your ears to the ground' is said to a stock-broker in *The Quiet American*, by Graham Greene. If professional men of that type indulge in confidential conversations, they have a **word in someone's ear**. The need for caution is commented on in the proverbial **walls have ears** 'listeners are everywhere'.

'If I did try to do something I'd only get sent off with a flea in my ear.'

Kingsley Amis *Lucky Jim*

Sending someone away with a flea in his ear involves scolding him so sharply that he feels as if his ears are being bitten by a flea. This is another expression which dates from the 15th century yet is still frequently used today. 'Didn't I come to your door this morning, Harry, and get sent away with a flea in my ear?' asks a man in *Henry's War*, by Jeremy Brooks. The reply is: 'I didn't send you away with a flea in your ear, Charlie. You came at a bad moment.' The phrase is alluded to in a slightly different way in *Theirs Was the Kingdom*, by R.F. Delderfield: 'If I were in your shoes I'd own up to it. You may even come off with a flea in your ear. My father has overlooked worse.'

'You know one or two of these mugs. Bite one of their ears.' So I took aside a chap I knew and bit his ear for ten bob.

Henry Lawson *Stifner and Jim*

When a human, rather than a flea, **bites someone's ear** he is trying to borrow money from him. The person approached might decide to **turn a deaf ear** to the request. 'He had turned a deaf ear to the pleas of both Dover and Sergeant MacGregor' is in Joyce Porter's *Dover One*. Mary McCarthy, in *The Group*, has: 'She was too much of a liberal to "turn a deaf ear" to a hungry baby.' This 'deaf ear' can be as useful as the 'blind eye' which we all decide to turn on occasion.

If that fella's ears didn't burn after he'd taken her away, they must have been made of asbestos.

L.A.G. Strong *The Nice Cup o' Tea*

When Monica Dickens writes, in *The Fancy*: 'The names they called each other made your ears burn' she appears to mean that the names were embarrassing to anyone else who overheard them. Normally a comment that **someone's ears are burning** is a reference to an old belief that somewhere, someone is talking about him. Often there is an implication that what is being said is adversely critical. 'She held her head very high these days, as though her pretty ears were burning' writes Mary McCarthy, in *The Groves of Academe*.

The people who are doing the talking and causing the ears to burn are not **within earshot**. As we perhaps more often say, they are **out of earshot**. 'While your new admirer is out of earshot, let me give you some advice' says someone in James Purdy's *Eustace Chisholm and the Works*. 'Earshot' is formed on the analogy of 'gun shot, pistol shot' and literally means within or outside the sound of a shot.

'I'm up to the ears with work, I'm completely booked for tonight.'
C.P. Snow *The Masters*

Some expressions are concerned merely with the position of the ears on the body rather than their hearing function. To be **up to one's ears** is clearly to be almost submerged. **Head over ears** can be used with a similar meaning. In his short story *Episode*, W. Somerset Maugham writes: 'He was so easy, so gay, so full of high spirits, and above all so obviously head over ears in love with Gracie, that Mrs Carter soon succumbed to his charm.' The meaning is that he is 'over head and ears' in love with her, submerged in his love. Many writers would use **head over heels** in this context.

Mrs Reed soon rallied her spirits; she shook me most soundly, she boxed both my ears, and then left me without a word.
Charlotte Brontë *Jane Eyre*

The **boxing of someone's ears**, frequently administered to children and servants in former times, seems to have been more like slapping someone round the face than **giving him a thick ear**, as another expression puts it. The latter refers to punching the ear hard enough to make it swell and become a **cauliflower ear**.

Pique was eighteen. Only. Not dry behind the ears.

Margaret Laurence *The Diviners*

Other 'ear' expressions include **wet behind the ears** or **not dry behind the ears** 'immature and inexperienced', like a young child who has to be reminded to dry behind his ears after washing. **Out on one's ear** refers to sudden dismissal from a job, as if with one's face on the ground after being thrown from the premises. A person may then have to **play it by ear** 'respond to a situation as it develops, not following a pre-determined course of action'. Metaphorically a person is playing a tune after hearing it, without having studied the score.

■ ALL SHOOK UP

Shaken and not stirred is a catch-phrase associated with James Bond, who liked his Martinis prepared in that way. Had Ian Fleming written the Bond books a few years later, he would probably have stipulated 'stirred and not shaken'. The *Savoy Cocktail Book* comments on the change in thinking that has occurred since 1930. It is now correct, say the editors, to stir a clear cocktail and shake only those that contain a fruit juice or are cloudy. Be this as it may, Bond's form of the phrase will no doubt live on. In reality, there are probably few drinkers with a good enough palate to detect exactly how their Martini has been prepared.

'Shake a leg, we don't have all day.'

Barry Oakley *A Salute to the Great McCarthy*

People are likely to shake hands when meeting, parting or reaching agreement. They may literally shake their heads to mean 'no', though in some parts of the world this action displays agreement with the speaker. **Shake a leg**, by contrast, is a metaphorical idiom, not something that anyone actually does except as a joke. It originally meant to begin dancing, then 'make a start' in a more general way. The phrase is now most frequently used as an imperative to mean 'Hurry up!', though this meaning is curiously missing from the 1990 edition of *The Concise Oxford Dictionary*.

Shake down has various meanings, especially in US slang. 'To shake someone down' is to blackmail him or obtain money by extortion. Metaphorically, money is being shaken from his pockets. The police may also 'shake a place down' when they conduct a thorough search. Their activities, figuratively speaking, make the whole building shake. A friend who is asked to provide 'a shakedown' knows that a night's lodging is needed in the form of a couch or other makeshift bed. Perhaps rather dated now are expressions like **no great shakes** 'of little value', originally used in dicing to refer to a poor throw. **All shook up**, the phrase seized on by Elvis Presley, smacks of the 1950s. At the time it was used by American teenagers to mean 'very happy, exhilarated'.

Even more old-fashioned is the idea of **shaking the dust from one's feet**. You do this if you leave a place in anger, vowing never to return. The phrase alludes to the New Testament,

Matthew 10.14: 'And if any one will not receive you or listen to your words, shake off the dust from your feet as you leave that house or town.'

'He served me a very wizened portion of silverside, which I consumed in two shakes of a lamb's tail.'

Dane Chandos *Abbie*

When Jetta Carleton writes, in *The Moonflower Vine*: 'I'll have 'em done **in two shakes**', meaning 'very quickly', it seems as if the speaker is not bothering to complete the longer version: **in two shakes of a lamb's tail**. We have become familiar with the latter form, but it is probably no more than a later, fanciful extension of 'in two shakes', or 'a brace of shakes'. 'The whole business world will know what's happened in a brace of shakes' says the hero of *Freddie and Son*, by Christopher Dilke.

These expressions were in use by the beginning of the 19th century and may once again have been a reference to dicing. As for the longer version, those who are familiar with the rapid way in which lambs shake their tails know that two shakes occupy a very short time indeed – less time than it takes to say 'in two shakes of a lamb's tail'.

■ APPLE-PIE

Webster's New Collegiate Dictionary waxes lyrical on the subject of 'apple-pie'. It defines the term as an adjective which means 'excellent, perfect', then continues: 'of, related to, or characterized by traditionally American values (as honesty or simplicity)'. Curiously, these two definitions come from very different sources. The second relates to the real apple-pie which any visitor to the US is glad to sample. The first derives from the phrase **apple-pie order**, which means 'extremely neat and tidy'. This possibly had nothing to do originally with apples or pies.

There is another phrase **apple-pie bed**, which refers to a bed made with a single sheet, folded back half-way down. Apple-pie beds are a common joke at scout camps and in boarding schools. The victim thinks he is getting between two sheets, then finds that the folded sheet prevents him from stretching his legs. As with 'apple-pie order', the first words may be a corruption of French *nappe pliée*. *Nappe* is 'table-cloth', and occurs in our word 'napkin'. *Pliée* means 'folded'. A schoolboy translation might easily turn *nappe pliée* into 'folded sheet', since *nappe d'eau*, for instance, is a 'sheet of water'. Folded table-cloths – *nappes pliées* – could also have suggested tidiness, or 'apple-pie order'.

He had an heir of his own as well as the squire; one also who was the apple of his eye.

Anthony Trollope *Doctor Thorne*

The apple of one's eye is someone who is highly cherished. The saying is an ancient one, found in the Old Testament, Deuteronomy 32.10: 'He cared for him, he kept him as the apple of his eye.' A child who wishes to be the apple of his teacher's eye traditionally takes a shiny apple to the classroom as a gift. The practice was formerly so common that it led to the American term **apple-polisher**, a toady. **Apple-polish** is flattery, and someone who uses it is said to **polish (shine) up the apple**.

To **upset someone's apple-cart** is used in both America and Britain in the sense of 'upset someone's plans'. It

appears to be a straightforward metaphor, conjuring up a chaotic image of apples rolling in all directions. In Britain, the man pushing such a cart might still be called a **coster-monger**. This was earlier **costard-monger**, a seller of costard apples. The 'costard' was so-called because it was heavily ribbed – Latin **costa** 'rib'.

Costards are no longer seen, but at a time when they were common, 'costard' was also a slang word for 'head'. Children would chant 'cowardy cowardy costard' at a child who would not accept a dare. When the costards disappeared, the children amended the chant to 'cowardy cowardy custard', using a word that was more familiar to them. It was probably the 'custard' reference that then helped to associate yellowness with cowardice.

■ ARM IN ARM

'I told you on the telephone that I never wanted to see Roy again. It wasn't true – I'd give my right arm to see him again.'

John Stroud *On the Loose*

When we have a strong desire for something to happen we are likely to say that we would **give our right arm** to have it occur. The statement is an example of hyperbole, or exaggeration. We are stressing the importance of our need, saying that it means as much to us as our right arm.

'Right arm', at least, is what is usually mentioned. In *The Beautiful and Damned*, by F. Scott Fitzgerald, a character says: 'I'd **give my right hand** to save you one little moment's pain.' Edward A. Rogers, in *Face to Face*, leaves it to his readers to complete the phrase: 'I'd sure give my right you-know-what to go back with him.' Writers in the 19th century sometimes said in similar circumstances that they would **give their ears**.

Those same early writers might also have described their most reliable assistant and chief helper as their **right arm**. The modern expression is usually **right-hand man**. Both phrases acknowledge the overwhelming importance to the average person of the right arm and hand.

I used to ride alone mostly, chancing my arm to save an hour...

Ian Jefferies *Thirteen Days*

That same arm is no doubt referred to in **chance one's arm** 'take a big risk'. Criminals who 'chance their arm' may come up against the **long arm of the law**, by which phrase we refer to the extent of legal authority. Other 'arm' expressions, such as **keep someone at arm's length** 'not allow a friendship to develop', greet someone **with open arms** 'effusively', tend to be straightforward metaphors. In modern times **shot in the arm**, clearly derived from the idea of injecting a drug, is used in a general way of something that provides a stimulus. The result of an opinion poll provides a shot in the arm to a party's election campaign; reduced taxes are a shot in the arm for industry.

She had placed her arms akimbo, like some stage version of herself in low comedy.

Michael Innes *Honeybath's Haven*

A phrase of great interest to etymologists is **with arms akimbo**, which is used to describe someone standing with hands on hips, the elbows pointing outwards. George Douglas, in *The House with the Green Shutters*, refers to the 'gossips gathered at the pump, with their big, bare arms akimbo'.

The peculiar word 'akimbo' is thought to derive from 'can bow', where 'can' means a vessel such as an urn, and 'bow' refers to the bow-shaped handle on either side of its neck. The person standing 'with arms akimbo' is forming a shape similar to that of a two-handled pot. An old-fashioned French phrase is *faire le pot à deux anses* 'make a pot with two handles', formerly used of someone standing in this way.

■ AT ONE'S HEELS

'Officially, she will have to perform the tasks I allot to her. She will come to heel, and that will be very good for her.'

E.F. Benson *Trouble for Lucia*

To make someone **come to heel** forces that person to submit to one's commands like an obedient dog. If the person refuses to submit, he may be **digging in his heels**, which changes the metaphor to a tug-of-war contest and a competitor who is trying to prevent himself from being dragged forward. Another way of avoiding submission would be to **take to one's heels** 'run away'. The raised heels of a runner make them more noticeable.

With fewer people reading the Classics, references to a person's **Achilles' heel** have become rarer. The phrase means a serious fault in someone's character that is likely to cause his downfall in spite of his other advantages. According to legend, Achilles, chief hero on the Greek side in the Trojan War, was plunged by his mother into the Styx while he was still an infant. This rendered him invulnerable, except in the heel by which he was held. Achilles was eventually killed when Paris, who had been told by Apollo of this vulnerability, shot an arrow into his heel.

Those who are thought to be rich may still be described as **well-heeled**. There appears to be a simple link with **down at heel** (formerly 'down at the heel'), used of someone who is clearly impoverished. The latter expression refers to shoes that are worn down, but earlier phrases commented on hosiery which had holes at the heels. In *King Lear* Shakespeare has Kent remark that 'A good man's fortune may grow **out at heels**.'

The sense development of 'well-heeled' indicates that it was not originally prompted by the existence of 'down at heel'. The earlier American meaning of 'well-heeled' was 'armed with a suitable weapon'. This seems to support the view that the expression came from cock-fighting and referred to the metal spurs worn by the cocks. Only later was there a change of meaning to 'affluent', no doubt influenced by 'down at heel'.

■ AT THE WHEEL

'You must be quite a big wheel.'

John le Carré *The Spy Who Came In From The Cold*

A **big wheel** is a person of some importance in an organization. 'Big wheels here tonight, eh?' says a student at a party in Malcolm Bradbury's *Eating People is Wrong*. He means that professors, such as the one he is addressing, are present. Exactly what kind of wheel is meant in this expression is not clear; it is 'big' which carries the sense. The

allusion may be to machinery, since there is a corresponding saying used by someone in a lowly position: 'I'm only a **cog in the machine**.'

'Big wheel' is modern, but many speakers would instead use **big shot** in the same sense. This in turn derives from **big gun**, used in the 19th century and alluding to the importance of a ship which carried such guns. (See also page 48 for the possible derivation of 'big cheese' from a Hindi word.)

I saw a wheel upon the earth beside the living creatures, one for each of the four of them. As for the appearance of the wheels and their construction: their appearance was like the gleaming of a chrysolite; and the four had the same likeness, their construction being as it were a wheel within a wheel. When they went, they went in any of their four directions without turning as they went.

Old Testament, Ezekiel 1.15

The saying **wheels within wheels**, which hints at a complex network of forces and motives, also sounds, like modern business terminology, based on the analogy of complicated machinery. It is surprising, therefore, to find the phrase in the Old Testament, as quoted above. Ezekiel the priest is relating his visions of God.

He supposed it was his duty, in these times, to put his shoulder to the wheel.

Mary McCarthy *The Group*

To **put one's shoulder to the wheel** 'work hard at a particular task' is a clear reference to wagon-drivers who were often obliged to put their shoulders to a wheel when the latter became stuck in a rut or mud. The men joined their own forces to that of the horses. Less logical is the phrase **to put a spoke in someone's wheel** 'prevent someone from carrying out his plans'. Since wheels usually need spokes, it would make more sense if putting a spoke in someone's wheel helped them in some way.

There is an old Dutch expression *een spaak in't wiel stecken* which means the same as 'put a spoke in someone's wheel', though a correct English translation would be 'put a bar or pole in the wheel'. The reference was to putting a bar or pole between the spokes of a wheel to act as a primitive brake and stop it turning. It is easy to see how Dutch *spaak* could be mistakenly translated as 'spoke', and this is what appears to have occurred.

'Put a spoke in someone's wheel' tends to be used by British rather than American writers. Josephine Tey demonstrates its use in *The Franchise Affair*: 'We can join forces to put a spoke in the wheel of this moppet.'

■ BACK SLANG

'I shouldn't talk too much in public about your plans. People might think you were too ambitious. We don't want to put their backs up.'

C.P. Snow *The Masters*

Observation of the natural world has led to some of our 'back' expressions. We are all familiar with the cat's habit of arching its back when angry; for at least two centuries we have carried over the idea of a raised back indicating human irritation. To **get one's back up** is to become angry, though more often we speak of **putting someone's back up**. People obviously do not literally arch their backs, but they have their own ways

of showing us that we have given offence.

'Time and again I warned him, but it was water off a duck's back.'

John Stroud *On the Loose*

We also notice when our complaints or warnings make no impression on the listener. **Like water off a duck's back** again borrows a natural image to describe something that makes no impression, though a far older saying refers to words that have **gone in one ear and out the other**. Children, past-masters at ignoring what is said to them, quickly get accustomed to hearing such phrases, with parents continually exclaiming that they might as well be **talking to a brick wall**.

Dumby: It's no use talking to Tuppy. You might just as well talk to a brick wall.
Cecil Graham: But I like talking to a brick wall – it's the only thing in the world that never contradicts me!

Oscar Wilde *Lady Windermere's Fan*

Another expression related to childhood is **piggy-back**, which originally had nothing to do with pigs or the word 'back'. The earlier form was **pick-a-back**, which earlier still was **pick-pack**, a reduplication of 'pack'. The original idea was that a child who was being carried piggy-back was being carried like a pack, but since he was always on someone's back, the change from 'pick-pack' to 'pick-a-back' soon followed. Children themselves no doubt transformed 'pick-a' into 'piggy'.

'Now that I'm working, maybe she'll get off my case.'

Steven Bauer *The River*

To **be on someone's back** in a different sense is to be a considerable nuisance to him. The irritated request to **get off my back!** 'stop annoying me!' now sounds a little dated, the more recent version being **get off my case!** This began as American slang and is based on the idea that someone who is **on your case** is making judgements about you as if he were in a court of law. Telling him to 'get off your case' is a reminder that he has no right to act in that way. Another more specialised American slang expression is to **get the monkey off one's back** 'to overcome an addiction to drugs'.

Behind her back Mr Schneider had been supplying him.

Mary McCarthy *The Group*

Other 'back' phrases are mostly simple metaphors. Something done **behind one's back** is deliberately done without one's knowledge. To **turn one's back on** someone or something is an obvious way of ignoring it. To **put one's back into** a task is to exert all one's efforts, something we promise to do when we say that we will **bend over backwards** 'do everything in our power' to help someone. We mean that we will not think about our personal dignity or comfort. In Ruth Rendell's *The Tree of Hands*, a woman who is fond of set phrases uses three in quick succession to say: 'You know I'd bend over backwards to give you a helping hand. But if it means giving in my notice, I have to draw the line.'

An ironic remark about not **breaking your back** might be made to a workman who is making little effort, though he might reply that he has **broken the back of** what he has to do if he has already done most of it. **Mind your backs!** is another way of saying 'Get out of the way!'

Scratch my back and I'll scratch yours was first suggested to someone in the 17th century. No doubt the person concerned understood that this was not to be taken literally, that a favour was being requested that would then be reciprocated. The expression is a kind of acknowledgement in advance that **one good turn deserves another**.

'Surely middle-class children like this . . .'
'Middle-class my backside!'

Leslie Thomas *Tropic of Ruislip*

In use before the 'scratch my back' expression was the word **backside**, which is still used colloquially for the buttocks. 'Backside' is a word that 'many people find unduly hearty' – the extraordinary comment of Professor A.S.C. Ross in *Don't Say It*. It is certainly a word that has always been difficult to take seriously. The first literary occurrence, as noted by *The Oxford English Dictionary*, is in a tale about Robin Hood written at the beginning of the 16th century. It tells us: 'with an arrowe so broad, he shott him into the backe-syde'. Somehow this does little for Robin's reputation as a marksman.

■ BAGS OF BEANS

'She's strong and well and full of beans.'

W. Somerset Maugham *Here and There*

Full of beans was originally applied to a well-fed horse. In Shakespeare's *A Midsummer Night's Dream* Puck says:

> *I jest to Oberon, and make him smile*
> *When I a fat and bean-fed horse beguile,*
> *Neighing in likeness of a filly foal.*

'Bean-fed' horses were later described in slang as 'beany' or 'full of beans'. They had plenty of energy and were ready to be exercised. From this developed the additional notion of general good health and high spirits. 'How was Rufe Little? All alive and full of beans?' asks a character in *Face to Face,* by Edward A. Rogers. Bernard Wolfe, in *The Late-Risers,* has: 'Pop was full of beans that day.'

The phrase has acquired a second possible meaning in the USA, where it is used as a synonym for **full of prunes**, or **full of hops**. Beans, prunes and hops all have laxative qualities, and these are euphemisms for **full of shit** or **crap** 'wrong, mistaken, talking nonsense'. **Full of bull** also occurs, where 'bull' is for 'bullshit'. With **full of it** the listener or reader is allowed to decide for himself which word could replace 'it'.

'We'll drink a health to the day dear father gets the knighthood he wants so much, because that's the day I shall spill the beans.'

Angus Wilson *Anglo-Saxon Attitudes*

The meaning of **spill the beans** 'reveal a secret' is well-known, but its origin is a mystery. Although beans were used in ancient elections, votes being cast by beans being placed in one container or another, there is little chance that this phrase refers to such practices. Had that been so, the expression would have come into use centuries ago, whereas it occurs only in modern times. It may link with the popular activity at local fairs, where the number of beans in a jar must be guessed. Only when the jar is opened and the beans are spilled is the truth known, which certainly fits the meaning of the phrase. 'Tell me the truth,' a woman says, in Eric Linklater's *Poet's Pub,* 'Spill the beans!'

Several other expressions mention beans. **Not to have a bean**, in an expression like 'I haven't a bean', meaning 'I haven't any money at all', is a simple allusion to the low value of a bean. A person who hasn't a bean hasn't enough money to buy one. This aspect of beans, that they are worth little or nothing, was commented on centuries before 'bean' acquired a slang meaning of 'a guinea coin', or 'beans' became a reference to 'cash'.

A **bean-feast** (or **beano**) is a 'a good meal, an occasion of merry-making', but both words are old-fashioned and are now rarely used. Various explanations have been offered for 'bean-feast', all variations on the theme of someone who annually offered his employees or neighbours a feast of beans and bacon. The benefactor was presumably English, since neither 'bean-feast' nor 'beano' was ever used by Americans.

Old bean, used as a friendly term of address to form a 'phrasal you' (see Introduction, page 9) was also decidedly British when it came into early 20th-century use. John Galsworthy commented on the expression in *To Let* (1921). He talked of young girls 'bare-necked, visible up to the knees . . . with their feet, too, screwed around the legs of chairs while they ate, and their "So-longs" and their "Old Beans" and their laughter – girls who gave him the shudders whenever he thought of Fleur in contact with them'.

'Old bean' would now only be used jokingly as a vocative, in a suitably 'posh' accent. As for its origin, it was presumably connected with the slang use of 'bean' meaning 'head'. It could also have been a shortening of 'bean-pole', a common generic nickname for a tall person.

'I was a fool, I was, and didn't know how many beans made five. I was born yesterday, I was.'

B.L. Farjeon *Miser Farebrother*

While 'old bean' was in vocative use, one might have heard references to someone who **knew how many beans made five**, someone, that is, who was 'alert, street-wise.' The expression was a watered-down version of knowing how many blue beans made five white ones. The answer was five – once the skins had been removed.

■ BARGAINING POSITIONS

'I've no business to bore you with my dreary psychological hang-ups. That's not what you bargained for, is it?'

Nina Bawden *George Beneath a Paper Moon*

Bargain-hunting is a universal sport, practised in every society. Obtaining something for less than its value is one of the great pleasures in life. This makes it all the more curious that we are usually not pleased when we metaphorically **get more than we bargained for**. A conversation in J.I.M. Stewart's *The Last Tresilians* runs: 'Luke,' she said, 'I didn't mean quite all this.' 'You've got more than you bargained for, all right.' You've got more than you expected, in other words, and the extra something was not welcome.

For fifteen cents they call you 'sir' even, into the bargain.

Garson Kanin *Moviola*

We also talk metaphorically of getting something **into** or **in the bargain**. 'In the bargain' is an American form of the phrase: in Britain it is now always 'into', though 'to the bargain' was once used. Once again there is a suggestion of something added that is not necessarily wanted. 'Everything would stay there and be hopelessly creased into the bargain,' writes Anita Brookner, in *Hotel du Lac,* of clothes in her suitcase.

When we 'strike' a bargain we are referring to the striking of hands, a kind of primitive handshake, that showed that agreement had been reached. In modern times we usually talk of **striking** or **driving a hard bargain**, being forced to buy at a high price or sell at a low one. The deal might still be concluded with a handshake: another common practice in former times was for buyer and seller to ratify it with a drink. This was known as a **wet** or **Dutch bargain**, but both terms are obsolete.

Also obsolete is the 17th-century proverb **to be beloved is above all bargains**. There was another, more world-weary saying of the same time that we still use, and which for some is almost the philosophy by which they live – **make the best of a bad bargain**.

■ BARKING DOGS

Mr Jordan gave a little grunt, not unamiable. Paul divined that his master's bark was worse than his bite.

D.H. Lawrence *Sons and Lovers*

There was a 16th-century proverb **barking dogs seldom bite**. It referred to people as much as to dogs, and was based on simple observation of human behaviour. Then, as now, a person who displayed his anger by ranting and raving seldom followed it with violent physical action. 'A great prater, a weak performer', as R. Cotgrave explained it in 1611.

The idea of someone's **bark being worse than his bite** developed from this notion. 'His' here is used grammatically, and includes 'her'. Indeed, the phrase is often applied to women. Mary McCarthy writes, in *The Group:* 'Her bark was worse than her bite, they used to reiterate to each other. But they were afraid that some man, who did not know the old dear as they did, would take her at her word.' Vera Caspary, in *Laura,* has: 'Don't take Mrs Treadwell too seriously. Her bark is worse than her bite.' David Walker's *Geordie* applies the phrase in a rather unusual way: 'Even an eagle has a worse bark than a bite. Dad said a missel-thrush was fiercer at the nest than an eagle.'

Another 16th-century proverb was: **Don't keep a dog and bark yourself**. The idea behind it, that it is foolish to employ someone to do something, then do it yourself, is still valid, but the expression is little used. Nor do we speak of someone **barking at the moon** if he is doing something ineffectual, though dogs continue to indulge in this practice. Perhaps the idea lingers on in the modern British slang terms **barking** or **barking mad**, if these do not simply refer to mad dogs.

'You're barking up the wrong tree. The reason you don't find a girl is that you don't want a girl. You want a lovely young quean.'

Elizabeth Jane Howard *Getting it Right*

The Americans lay claim to the phrase **bark up the wrong tree**. It occurs in American literature from the 1830s, referring specifically in one early instance to a 'coon dog'. This was a dog used to hunt raccoons, which live mainly in trees. The dog was supposed to find a tree which lodged a raccoon, then bark to attract its master's attention. If it 'barked up the wrong tree' it was 'mistaken, following the wrong course of action'.

A tree itself has a 'bark', of course, but this is a coincidence. Three different words led to 'barks' of different kinds. Tree bark comes from an Old Norse word which seems also to have led to 'birch'. The bark of the dog probably imitates the actual sound. Latin *barca* 'ship of burden' gave us 'bark, barque', though we are more familiar with the later form 'barge'.

■ BATSMEN AND BATMEN

'And this junior officer sees fit, off his own bat, and without reference to higher authority, to assist the Special Branch officer.'

Frederick Forsyth *The Day of the Jackal*

To do something **off one's own bat** 'to do something on one's own initiative' is a metaphor from cricket. It is only the batsman who can hit the ball, no one can do it for him. 'I should like to start something – something off one's own bat – that's what I should like,' says a character in Virginia Woolf's *Night and Day*. **Right off the bat** looks similar but has a different meaning and origin. In a sentence like 'You can tell right off the bat that they're foreigners' it means that you can tell 'immediately'. The expression is American and derives from baseball. The same game gives rise to **bat something around**, discuss an idea or proposal.

If you must ponder it, then do it alone at isolated periods with long intervals in between, so as not to drive yourself bats.

Judith Guest *Ordinary People*

These phrases refer to the 'bat' used to hit a ball, related to Old French *batte* 'club' and *battre* 'strike'. To have **bats in the belfry** 'be eccentric or crazy' clearly alludes to the mammal. In one sense this is not a 'bat' at all: the word was altered from its original form 'bakke' during the 16th century. Nor, for that matter, should 'belfry' be spelt in that way; in Old French it was *berfrei*. The spelling change is, of course, easily understood given the strong association of a belfry with 'bells'. 'Bats in the belfry' is sometimes alluded to by saying that someone is 'bats' or 'batty'.

The mammal also features in **like a bat out of hell** 'extremely fast', formerly a popular colloquial phrase. Its source has not been traced, though it appears to have been in use by 1900. A satisfactory explanation as to why a bat should want to escape from hell faster than anything or anyone else has not yet been noted.

There was at one time another kind of bat, or more properly *bât*, from a French word meaning 'pack-saddle'. A **bat-horse** carried such saddles, which often contained military equipment, and a 'batman' looked after them. Later he became a servant to an officer in a more general sense. All this was before Bob Kane invented Bruce Wayne, the man who donned his bat-suit to become Batman in a comic-strip series of 1939.

Finally there is the phrase **not bat an eyelid** 'show no emotion or reaction'. We should really say 'not bate an eyelid'. In falconry a hawk was said to be 'bating' when it was beating its wings impatiently and fluttering away from the fist or perch.

■ BEATING EVERYTHING

'You've had some daft ideas but this beats the band. I've never heard of anything so ridiculous.'

Margaret Forster *Georgy Girl*

Something **beats the band** when it is better, or worse, than everything that has gone before, even the band that led the parade. This is the most plausible explanation, though other reference sources mostly talk about making more noise than a band. F. Scott Fitzgerald appears to use the phrase in that sense in *The Great Gatsby*. Myrtle says: 'I lay down and cried to beat the band all afternoon.'

Charles Earle Funk, in *A Hog on Ice,* has a different view. He comments on the over-popularity of this phrase in the USA in the 1930s, then explains it in terms of arriving at a spot before the head of the parade reached it. He imagines father whipping up the horses to get there in time, or a small boy running 'on the wings of the wind'.

'Beat the band' became popular in the USA because of its pleasing alliteration and the American fondness for marching bands. That persists, as anyone who has stood amongst the crowd to watch Macy's Thanksgiving Day Parade in New York can testify, but this phrase is now used less frequently, unless it happens to be an idiolectal favourite. It appears to be a pet-phrase of Margaret Forster, for instance, who assigns it in *Georgy Girl* to different characters in the space of a few pages.

Beat the Dutch is an earlier Americanism with much the same meaning as 'beat the band'. It looks suspiciously like one of the many anti-Dutch allusions in English, referring to ancient hostilities between the two nations, but there are those who see it as a back-handed compliment. Dutch settlers in the New World quickly became successful merchants, following ancestral traditions. They offered goods of excellent quality at fair prices. Something that 'beat the Dutch' may conceivably have been metaphorically better than anything the Dutch traders could offer.

It's what Eunice has done to Marge that really takes the cake. She has turned that girl against me.

Truman Capote *My Side of the Matter*

Something that **takes the cake** also 'beats the band' or 'Dutch' by being surprising or remarkable. Some speakers would use **take the biscuit** with the same meaning. The original idea of 'taking the cake' was presumably winning the cake that was offered as a prize, as in the famous **cake-walk** of the American Negro. The cake-walk was popular at the end of the 19th century and was a competition in which couples walked as gracefully and stylishly as possible. From this was developed a dance performed on stage, characterized by high prancing steps and a backward tilt to the body. The 'biscuit' version of the saying seems to have been a British variant, where the specific significance of the cake as a prize was less obvious.

With all these sayings, ironic usage now predominates. The speaker is commenting on something that beats everything else, takes the prize, for being worse than what has gone before. Children do not always grasp that point. 'Billy, you do take the cake!' says an adult in Michael Rumaker's *The Pipe*. 'And I eat it, too, I like it,' is the reply.

■ BEDSIDE MANNERS

He might have just got up 'on the wrong side of the bed', as Mother said; Daddy was cross too, sometimes, in the morning.

Mary McCarthy *The Group*

There was a superstitious belief in the early 19th century that a bed had a right side and a wrong side, and that it was important to get out of it every morning on the right side. It was assumed that someone who was grumpy and bad-tempered, obviously not enjoying his day, had made the mistake of **getting out of (on) the wrong side of the bed**.

Few people now are even aware of such a superstition, but they allude to it regularly. Bernard Wolfe, in *The Late-Risers*, has: 'Mort Robell was groggy. He'd gotten up on the wrong side of the bed, definitely.' 'Got out of the wrong side of bed this morning, did we?' says someone in Tom Sharpe's *Porterhouse Blue*. It's a question which is asked every day in homes and at work.

Someone who is more permanently in a bad mood may be discovering that life is not always a **bed of roses** 'delightful place', as some down-to-earth friend will remind him. When his problems, especially if they happen to be marital problems, are thought to be of his own making, he is also likely to be told: **you made your bed and you must lie on it**. Such words of comfort are, of course, much appreciated.

Miss Letitia Piper had actually been brought to bed of a fine boy and girl.

Richard Brinsley Sheridan *The School for Scandal*

To **go to bed with someone** is a modern euphemism for having a sexual relationship with that person. Few people would now speak, though, of a woman being **brought to bed** 'delivered of a child'. John Fowles writes in *The French Lieutenant's Woman*: "'E gave me money for when I was brought to bed', but the novel is set in the 19th century when the phrase was still in regular use. It is slightly more surprising that Fay Weldon should choose to head a chapter in *Down Among the Women*: 'Scarlet is Brought to Bed.'

Early to bed and early to rise, makes a man healthy, wealthy and wise has been a much-quoted proverb since the 16th century. Now that most people are aware that individuals have different sleep-patterns and bodily rhythms, fewer people believe this particular piece of folk-wisdom. Parents still tend to see it as a useful part of their armoury, however, when dealing with young children. Perhaps some also inflict on their children old jokes about **going (up the wooden ladder) to Bedfordshire** or **going to sheet alley**.

A similar joke refers to **the land of Nod** 'sleep', punning on a place-name which is mentioned in the Old Testament, Genesis 4.14. After Cain killed his brother he 'went away from the presence of the Lord, and dwelt in the land of Nod, east of Eden'. No such country has been identified. Cain may have spent the rest of his life as a vagabond, since scholars connect Nod with Hebrew *nad* 'wanderer'.

To **take to one's bed** 'go to bed and remain there because of illness' is now old-fashioned, but a person confined to bed for a considerable time is still described as **bed-ridden**. This is a metaphorical description which was earlier **bed-rid**, as when Berowne refers in Shakespeare's *Love's Labour's Lost* to the 'decrepit, sick and bed-rid' king of France. Earlier still, a 'bed-rid' was the person himself, a 'bed-rider', someone mounted on a bed instead of a horse.

■ BELL-RINGING

Don Pedro: He hath a heart as sound as a bell, and his tongue is the clapper; for what his heart thinks, his tongue speaks.

William Shakespeare *Much Ado About Nothing*

Shakespeare's **sound as a bell**, quoted above, lives on with the sense 'in perfect condition', alluding to the pure tone of a finely-tuned bell. His reference to the tongue as the 'clapper' also entered into slang usage in former times. Modern British slang makes it possible to refer to someone who is speaking **like the clappers**. There is no specific allusion to the tongue in that case; 'like the clappers' means 'very quickly' and could equally well be applied to a fast-moving person or vehicle. The allusion is presumably to the rapid movements of clappers inside an electric bell.

'It's by Ed Banion. That name ring a bell?'
'Vaguely.'

Edward A. Rogers *Face to Face*

It is normally a name which **rings a bell**, revives a memory, in other words, which is buried deep in our minds or simply 'sounds familiar'. 'The name rang an immediate bell' writes Ruth Rendell, in *Talking to Strange Men*, using that curious construction which the English language allows. 'Immediately rang a bell' is meant. Elsewhere in the same novel someone else says: 'The name does ring a bell, though.' The name concerned is calling attention to itself, as it were. The same idea was formerly to be met with in the colloquial expression **ring one's own bell** 'boast about one's own accomplishments'.

'Leave James Joyce to blow his own trumpet.'
'He's dead.'

Edna O'Brien *The Country Girls*

The more familiar way of describing boastfulness is to talk of someone **blowing his own trumpet**. George Douglas, in *The House with the Green Shutters*, writes: 'They felt it was a silly thing of Gourlay to blow his own trumpet in this way.' The author adds the interesting comment: 'Being boys, they could not prick his conceit with a quick rejoinder. It is only grown-ups who can be ironical; physical violence is the boy's repartee.'

A flourish of trumpets has long been used to draw attention to an important person or to introduce a proclamation. It has always been considered distasteful, however, for someone to draw attention to himself in a noisy way. The New Testament, Matthew 6.2, has: 'When you give alms, sound no trumpet before you, as the hypocrites do in the synagogues and in the streets, that they may be praised by men.' This is one of the earliest instances we have of someone being advised not to blow his own trumpet.

'It gets my goat when a fellow gets stuck on himself and goes round tooting his horn merely because he's charitable.'

Sinclair Lewis *Babbitt*

A pleasant American alternative phrase with the same meaning as 'blow one's own trumpet' is **toot** or **blow one's own horn**. 'Hold your gab!' says someone in *The Lyre of Orpheus*, by Robertson Davies, 'Priest Simon doesn't want to hear you blow your horn.' American speakers might also talk of **shooting off one's bazoo** 'talking in an exaggerated and boastful way'. 'Bazoo' is a corruption of a Dutch word meaning 'trumpet'.

■ BEWARE OF THE BULL

'You didn't believe that cock-and-bull story, did you?'

Joyce Porter *Dover One*

Many cock-and-bull stories are told about the origin of the phrase **cock-and-bull story**. One of them concerns two English inns, The Cock and The Bull, both at Stony Stratford, in Buckinghamshire. It is said that stage-coach horses were changed at both while the passengers exchanged jokes and stories, thus giving rise to the expression 'cock-and-bull stories'.

The coach passengers may well have exchanged jokes, but the origin of this saying, which was in use well before the stage-coach era, is to be found elsewhere. Professor Weekley long ago pointed out that there was once a word 'cockalane' in English derived from French *coq à l'âne* 'cock to the ass'. The reference was to an incoherent story which wandered from one subject to another. The basic idea rather than the French expression was taken into English with the slightly changed meaning of 'a ridiculous story told as if true'.

Charles Dickens, in *The Pickwick Papers*, has: 'He was bribed by that scoundrel Jingle, to put me on a wrong scent, by telling a cock-and-bull story of my sister and your friend Tupman.' The phrase remains a popular one in more recent novels. 'D'you think I believe that cock-and-bull story?' asks someone in *A High Wind in Jamaica*, by Richard Hughes. 'You don't go for that cock-and-bull story about their colonel having been kidnapped by Russian agents?' asks a character in Mordecai Richler's *The Incomparable Atuk*.

Truncated forms of 'cock-and-bull story' are seen in the British slang use of 'cock' in expressions like 'that's a load of cock', meaning 'that's nonsense'. The American equivalent would probably be 'that's a load of bull' or 'bullshit'.

She took the bull by the horns and said she wanted him to let her have a chance at reporting on a French or an Italian novel.

Mary McCarthy *The Group*

To **take the bull by the horns** is to face a dangerous or difficult situation with boldness. The allusion is as obvious as that in the description of a clumsy person as a **bull in a china shop**. Josephine Tey alludes to the latter phrase in *The Franchise Affair*: 'Robert had pictured him as a bull-in-a-china-shop type'. (For a punning use of 'bull in a china shop' see Introduction page 11.)

■ BIRTHRIGHT

To some men, born silver-spooned, a seat in Parliament comes as a matter of course.

Anthony Trollope *Doctor Thorne*

Trollope clearly alludes, in the above quotation, to the expression **born with a silver spoon in one's mouth**. It was formerly the custom to present a child at its christening with a spoon. A child born into a wealthy family could expect that spoon to be made of silver, or even of gold. Upton Sinclair, in *World's End*, prefers the 'gold' version of the saying and paraphrases its meaning when he has someone say: 'Life has been easy for you. You were born with a gold spoon in your mouth.' In *Jaffery*, William J. Locke creates a further variant: 'You have to be born, like Uncle Adrian, with a golden pen in your mouth.' Uncle Adrian supposedly has great gifts as a writer.

Another reference to the circumstances of a person's birth occurs in the old-fashioned euphemism **born on the wrong side of the blanket**, used of an illegitimate child. Modern cynicism leads to the saying **there's one born every minute** 'there are a lot of gullible people about'. The person who makes this statement may well say that he himself **wasn't born yesterday** 'doesn't suffer from lack of experience'.

■ BLOODY COLD

George felt a chill run through his veins like iced water. His blood running cold, he thought, intellectually appraising the truth of this cliché.

Nina Bawden *George Beneath a Paper Moon*

It was generally believed in the Middle Ages that the temperature of someone's blood could change considerably, and that the changes were linked to his or her emotional state. Someone whose emotions were roused, whose **blood was up** as one phrase expresses it, was thought to be hot-blooded. Lack of emotion, or fear, was thought to be reflected literally in a cooling of the blood.

These early beliefs survive in various

phrases which relate the intensity of human emotions to an imaginary temperature scale. We still say, of something that makes us very angry, that it **makes our blood boil**. As we experience fear we say that our **blood runs cold**. Richard Hughes, in *A High Wind in Jamaica*, has: 'Tabby pranced up and down, exclaiming in a tone of voice the children had never heard him use before and which made their blood run cold.'

Looking back at it in cold blood, I think I should have shot the mare.

Geoffrey Household *Watcher in the Shadows*

We do something **in cold blood** when we do it without emotion, unaffected by the passion of the moment. 'I'd marry her in cold blood . . .' says a character in Penelope Gilliatt's *A State of Change*, making it sound as if he were thinking of committing a crime. The phrase has become associated with ruthless **cold-blooded** criminals, amoral and lacking in normal human sympathy. The more positive aspect of 'cold-bloodedness' is often referred to by the French phrase **sang-froid**. This literally means 'cold blood' but is used figuratively of coolness and composure, especially when maintained in a difficult situation.

Owen Roberts was used to hard stares and cold shoulders.

Jeremy Brooks *Henry's War*

We also speak of being 'cold' or 'cold-hearted' towards other people when we are unfriendly. We may even **give them the cold shoulder** 'deliberately ignore them'. In the early 19th century people spoke of **showing someone the cold shoulder**, where the reference was clearly to turning one's

back on someone in a cold manner. The 'shoulder' reference is an ancient one. In the Old Testament, Nehemiah 2.29 we read: 'Yet they acted presumptuously and did not obey thy commandments, but sinned against thy ordinances, by the observation of which a man shall live, and turned a stubborn shoulder and stiffened their neck and would not obey.'

Wits in the 19th century turned 'show the cold shoulder' into 'give the cold shoulder of mutton', explaining that this was what one did to a guest who was not welcome. Some writers have taken this humorous reference to the left-overs of yesterday's meal in all seriousness and offer the 'mutton' explanation as a true one.

'You have the devil's own luck. They have cold feet.'

John Fowles *The French Lieutenant's Woman*

To **have cold feet** 'suffer from a loss of nerve or confidence' is recorded only from the beginning of the 20th century. Professor Kenneth McKenzie of Princeton University drew attention some years ago to a reference in Ben Jonson's play *Volpone*: 'Let me tell you: I am not, as your Lombard proverb saith, cold on my feet.' The proverb concerned apparently had the figurative meaning 'to be without money'. Professor McKenzie connected it with a card-player quitting a game with the excuse that his feet were cold. This could easily have been interpreted, he said, as a wish to pull back from a difficult position, thus leading to 'having cold feet' in the modern sense.

The theory is ingenious but irrelevant. No figurative reference to having cold feet, in either the Italian or English sense, has been found in the literature of the 18th or 19th centuries. The proverb cited by Jonson in 1606 remained purely Italian; the similarity of the later English phrase was coincidental. The latter was probably suggested by the natural reaction of someone who steps into cold water and instinctively retreats.

■ BRASS BAND

'Let's get down to a few brass tacks! How did they do it, and where's the body?'

Joyce Porter *Dover One*

Julian Franklyn, in *A Dictionary of Rhyming Slang*, has no doubt that the 'brass tacks' in the phrase **get down to brass tacks** are there to rhyme on 'facts'. He believes that the expression originated with London Cockneys, but was established in the USA by the beginning of the 20th century. T.S. Eliot made use of the rhyme in *Sweeney Agonistes* 'Fragment of an Agon':

> *Birth, and copulation, and death.*
>
> *That's all the facts when you come to brass tacks.'*

'Get down to brass tacks' is well-used by American writers. 'Roy thought he better get down to brass tacks' is in Bernard Malamud's *The Natural*. Mary McCarthy, in *The Group*, has the interesting exchange: '"Do *come down to brass tacks*." "'The Brass Tack',," Norine said, frowning. "Wasn't that your name for a literary magazine at college?"'

Because of such usage, many linguists have searched for an American origin of this expression. Some suggest that it related to the cleaning of sailing-ship decks and the exposure of brass nails, but this is less convincing than the rhyming slang explanation. Meanwhile, the phrase continues to prove its worth. A speaker in Henry Cecil's *Brothers in Law* who is rather fond of set phrases says: 'Now let's get down to brass tacks. No beating about the bush. All fair and above board. In for a penny, in for a pound. Who laughs last, laughs loudest.'

Fred Bullock told old Osborne of his son's appearance and conduct. 'He came in as bold as brass.'

William Thackeray *Vanity Fair*

From the 16th century 'brass' was commonly used as a symbol of hardness and endurance, but also of lack of sensitivity and effrontery. As it happens, the metal referred to in earlier times as 'brass' was any alloy of copper: Shakespeare's 'brass' (e.g. 'Can any face of brass hold longer out?' *Love's Labour's Lost*) was probably what we would now call 'bronze'. We retain the metaphorical senses of the word when we describe someone as **brassy** 'showy and impudent' or **brazen** 'shameless'. **Brazen hussy** would now probably be applied to a woman only as a joke, but **bold as brass** could still describe a cheeky young person.

A name – if the party had a voice
What Mortal would be a Bugg by choice,
As a Hogg, or a Grubb or a Chubb rejoice,
Or any such nauseous blazon?
Not to mention many a vulgar name
That would make a doorplate blush for shame
If doorplates were not so brazen.

Thomas Hood

In the *Old Curiosity Shop* Dickens creates the disreputable attorney Sampson Brass and Sally, his sister. He then has fun with what he calls their 'melodious' surname. Sally is described by Quilp as 'hard-hearted as the metal from which she takes her name. Why don't she change it – melt down the brass, and take another name?' The same speaker later addresses her brother as 'You brazen scarecrow'.

Modern humorists allude coyly to **brass-monkey weather**, expecting others to be aware of the phrase **cold enough to freeze the balls off a brass monkey**. The latter phrase is a straightforward joke of Australian origin, but the 'tribe of ingenious etymologists', as Ernest Weekley once called them, cannot resist trying to make it more complicated. They prefer an explanation which involves stacks of cannon-balls on warships.

The Oxford English Dictionary does mention that a type of small cannon was known in the 17th century as a 'brass monkey'. The term is labelled 'obsolete' since no further references to it after 1663 have been discovered. It is also true that the boys on warships who carried powder to the guns were known as 'monkeys'. In Royal Navy slang, 'monkey' has long been used to describe anyone or anything small. There is no evidence of any kind, however, to support the fanciful statement sometimes made that cannon-balls were stacked on something called a 'brass monkey', from which they fell when frozen.

■ BRICKWORK

Steerforth approved of him highly, and told us he was a brick. Without exactly understanding what learned distinction was meant by this, I respected him greatly for it.

Charles Dickens *David Copperfield*

'Stella, you're a brick,' says a man to a woman in John Sherwood's *The Half Hunter*. A curious compliment, on the face of it, but to **be a brick** is to be solid and dependable, loyal and generous. The phrase had only recently come into use when Dickens made the remark quoted above in *David Copperfield* (1849–50).

A **gold-brick**, by contrast, in American military slang, is someone who shirks the work he has been assigned. This sense is an extension from 'swindler', one who deals in counterfeit gold bricks, things which appear to be valuable but are worthless.

'Sound of falling bricks,' she muttered, when Mr. LeRoy remained silent.

Mary McCarthy *The Group*

Someone who **drops a brick** makes a social error by saying or doing the wrong thing. He or she is metaphorically dropping a brick on to his own foot. Also present is the idea of attracting attention to oneself for the wrong reason, as seen in the alternative expression **drop a clanger**, where 'clanger' is anything that makes an unpleasant noise. Both phrases are relatively modern. Typical usage of 'drop a brick' occurs in Elizabeth Jane Howard's *Getting it Right*: 'He'd have her safely under the dryer so that she would be unable to hear any more bricks that Minnie dropped.' Monica Dickens, in *The Fancy*, has: 'That was a pretty good brick you dropped.'

They'd be down on me like a ton of bricks . . .

Alan Sillitoe *Saturday Night and Sunday Morning*

Bricks also feature in straightforward similes. To **come down on someone like a ton of bricks** is to criticize him with great force or violence, to crush him with a verbal assault. In *The Group*, Mary McCarthy chooses to use the phrase in a more physical sense: 'She knew that he ought not to have gone to sleep like a ton of bricks on top of her.' Another well-known simile is **like a cat on hot bricks**, used since the 17th century to describe someone who is restless and nervous. Many a child has been told by a parent: 'For heaven's sake sit still, you're like a cat on hot bricks.'

■ BRIDGING THE GAP

Well, it was all water under the bridge now.

Elizabeth Jane Howard *Getting it Right*

References to 'bridges' in popular phrases allude to both past and future. **Water under the bridge** is often quoted as a reminder that what is in the past will not return and cannot be altered. In the background is the thought that a river, like time, flows on. A speaker in Derek Jewell's *Come In No.1 Your Time Is Up* says: 'It's a while back. A few millions shakily invested in an ex-colony. Water under the bridge.' John Le Carré, in *The Honourable Schoolboy*, has: 'No one minds how bad it is. It's water under the bridge, I promise you.'

She would have liked to have burned every bridge that linked her to the old life.

R.F. Delderfield *Theirs Was the Kingdom*

To **burn one's bridges** is to make it impossible to go back to a previous situation. It involves doing something, accidentally or deliberately, that permanently affects one's circumstances. A woman in Mary McCarthy's *The Groves of Academe* says: 'I might exercise the proverbial woman's privilege and change my mind. I hold it safer to burn my bridges.' She has decided to resign from her job and does not want to be able to withdraw her resignation if she later has moments of doubt.

'You remember Cortez, the fellow who burnt his boats? I've burnt mine . . . I stole that car . . . It's too late even to go back.'

Graham Greene *A Drive in the Country*

'Burn one's bridges' is an obvious metaphor, as is the alternative **burn one's boats**. This phrase only came into use in the 19th century, but whoever coined it may have been thinking specifically of ancient invaders who burned their boats when they landed on foreign shores. They were making a statement that victory or death lay in store for them because they would never retreat. Metaphorically, as in reality, to 'burn one's boats' deliberately is to take an irrevocable step.

In *Self* Beverley Nichols writes: 'She must be sure of her next move before she burnt her boats.'

'Daddy told him to take it calmly and cross his bridges as he met them.'

Kate O'Brien *Pray for the Wanderer*

A 'bridge' is mentioned again in the proverbial advice **Never cross a bridge till you come to it** 'deal with something if it happens, don't worry about it beforehand'. The proverb dates only from the 19th century and is obviously of restricted application. It would presumably not be a good idea to base business practice on such a philosophy. The underlying message of the proverb is that some of the things we worry about in advance do not happen. 'I'm not concerned with publicity and scandal,' says someone in R.F. Delderfield's *Theirs Was the Kingdom*. 'We'll cross that bridge when we come to it.' In the event she is not obliged to do so. The same writer makes another character say: 'We'll jump that ditch when we come to it.' This makes the basic point equally well, but it is likely that English-speakers will continue to cross bridges rather than jump ditches, if and when they need to do so.

■ BRUNT-BEARING

'You bore the brunt for all of us.'

James A. Michener *Chesapeake*

'Brunt' is a word of mysterious origin which at first had the meaning 'a sharp blow'. By the 15th century it had come to mean 'a violent attack, assault', as by enemy soldiers during a battle. A century later the word was being used in a more abstract way. It was possible to speak about the brunt of temptation or affliction. There was also a phrase **at the first brunt** which originally meant 'at the first charge' but became simply another way of saying 'at first'.

'At the first brunt' is no longer used, but we still talk about **bearing the brunt** 'receiving the main force or impact' of either a physical or verbal assault. The character who says 'I'll bear the brunt of it' in Anthony Trollope's *Doctor Thorne* is referring to her husband's anger when he learns that she has not done as he wished.

Ivy Compton-Burnett, in *A House and Its Head*, has 'You will bear the brunt of it' spoken to a woman whose father is about to marry again. She

replies: 'There will be no brunt from Cassie. And I am used to yielding my position as mistress of the house.' This appears to mean 'there will be no attack from Cassie', restoring to 'brunt' a meaning that became obsolete in the 17th century.

■ BRUSH MARKS

'You're all alike, you're all tarred with the same filthy brush, you're not men at all, you're a shower of dirty-minded little boys and there isn't one of you worth twopence.'

Alexander Fullerton *Other Men's Wives*

All tarred with the same brush (earlier **with the same stick**) means 'all sharing the same faults'. The allusion is probably to the use of tar by shepherds for medicinal or identification purposes – see Introduction page 11 for remarks about **spoil the ship (sheep) for a ha'porth of tar**. This was a common 17th-century practice, and was in the minds of Fletcher and Massinger in *The Spanish Curate*: 'I have nointed ye, and tarr'd ye with my doctrine, and yet the murren sticks to ye.'

Covering someone with tar and feathers was once a form of punishment. This might also have been in the minds of those who first spoke about people being 'tarred with the same brush', since those so treated were guilty in one way or another.

Colleen McCullough, in *An Indecent Obsession,* converts the saying into a format phrase: 'Speak for yourself, Captain. We are not all tarred with the troppo brush. You can call yourself barmy if you like, but there's nothing wrong with me.' The speaker means that prolonged duty in the tropics does not affect everyone in the same way.

■ BUCKING PEOPLE UP

'We're passing the buck to you.'

Mordecai Richler *The Incomparable Atuk*

To **pass the buck** 'pass responsibility on to someone else' was originally a term used by poker players. *Webster's Dictionary* says that 'buck' is an abbreviation for 'buckhorn knife', i.e. a knife with a handle made of buckhorn. It was formerly used in poker games to mark the next player to deal, so that during the game the buck was passed round the table, along with the responsibility for dealing. Mark Twain, in *Roughing It* (1872), has: 'I reckon I can't call that hand. Ante and pass the buck.'

'Buck' developed other meanings in American English. The noun could be used for anything that was used as a token or reminder. Nigel Rees therefore suggests, in his *Dictionary of Phrase and Allusion*, that it may have led to the slang use of 'buck' for a dollar (coin). The etymology of 'buck' in that sense certainly baffles American philologists. 'Buck' also became a verb, as in a sentence like 'He bucked the responsibility', where the meaning is the same as 'passing the buck' in its modern metaphorical sense.

President Truman had a sign on his desk in the Oval Office: 'The buck stops here.' The phrase seems to have been his own invention and has become almost as well-known as 'passing the buck' itself.

Other expressions which include 'buck' are related to the male deer and have sometimes changed their meanings considerably. The 'bucking' of a horse compares its action with the way a buck-deer leaps. Telling someone to **buck up**, now means that

he should become more cheerful or should make haste. In one sense it is like telling him to **buck his ideas up** 'become more alert', to **wake his ideas up** as another phrase expresses it. Originally 'to buck up' meant to get dressed up like a young buck, where 'buck' meant 'a dashing young fellow'.

■ BUSH-BEATING

There didn't seem much point in beating about the bush. In a way it was a relief to say it to someone.

John Welcome *Stop at Nothing*

To **beat about the bush** 'to approach a subject in a roundabout way and avoid getting to the point' has proved its worth as a metaphorical idiom since the 16th century. It is still frequently used, judging by the number of times it occurs in novels. 'Our Mr Catchpole was never one to beat about the bush,' is in *Lucky Jim*, by Kingsley Amis. 'Now, enough of this beating about the bush,' says someone in Zane Grey's *Betty Zane*. 'It's no good beating about the bush, Penn. You know what I'm after' says a villainous character in *The Penny Box*, by Alice Dwyer-Joyce.

A similar expression, to **beat the bush** 'to do work for the benefit of others', has not survived. Both this and 'beat about the bush' referred originally to 'bat-fowling', which involved hunting birds at night when they were roosting in bushes. The bushes would be disturbed by bats or clubs and the birds netted or stunned as they tried to escape. The beaters would no doubt disturb many bushes before lighting upon one that contained the birds. They would have been beating about the bush until they discovered the bush that really mattered. In bat-fowling it was a case of trial and error, but use of 'beat about the bush' in modern times often implies that a speaker is deliberately evading the issue. The proverbial **bird in the hand is worth two in the bush** clearly derives from the same source. Something already obtained is of more value than something merely promised.

Rosalind: If it be true that good wine needs no bush, 'tis true that a good play needs no epilogue. Yet to good wine they do use good bushes; and good plays prove the better by the help of good epilogues.

William Shakespeare *As You Like It*

Another proverb, **good wine needs no bush**, relates to the early custom of displaying a bush to indicate that liquor was for sale. In a more general sense, this saying means that anything of real quality is its own advertisement. In *The Honorary Consul*, Graham Greene is talking about the local brothel when he writes: 'There were no exterior signs to differentiate her establishment from the other houses in the respectable street. A good wine, Doctor Plarr thought, needs no bush.'

■ BY ALL MEANS

'The difference between you and Snaith is that he thinks the end justifies the means and you think the means justify the end. You'd never play a dirty card.'

Winifred Holtby *South Riding*

The end justifies the means is said when something good is achieved by dubious methods. An example might be the raising of a great deal of money for a worthwhile charity by means of a lottery. If the money raised was put to a good cause, even those strongly opposed to gambling in all its forms might be persuaded that 'the ends justify the means'. This is

not the same thing as being totally unscrupulous, being prepared to use **fair means or foul** to achieve one's purpose.

Winifred Holtby, quoted above, is rather fond of using a phrase followed by its mirror image, as in the example about 'ends justify the means and means justify the end'. Elsewhere in *South Riding* occur such sentences as: 'Alderman General the Honourable Sir Ronald Tarkington, K.C.M.G., D.S.O., of Lissell Grange was a fine figure of a man and a fine man for any figure.' There is also a conversation which runs: '"She may be all right and she may fly to pieces. I should say it's touch and go." "More go than touch, if you ask me," snapped Emma.'

Book reviewing, however, was only a means to an end.

Mary McCarthy *The Group*

A **means to an end** is something not important in itself which helps one to achieve something which is important. It is a kind of metaphorical stepping-stone. In the Mary McCarthy example quoted above, book reviewing is not what the woman concerned wants to do, but it keeps her in regular touch with publishers. That, in its turn, may lead to the publication of her own book.

'Means' refers specifically to money and other such resources rather than 'method' in phrases like **live beyond one's means** and **means test**. The first of these was described by Mr Micawber in *David Copperfield*: 'Annual income, twenty pounds, annual expenditure twenty pounds ought and six.' The result of 'living beyond one's means' even to this small extent was, as Mr Micawber well knew, misery. The 'means test' is an official enquiry to which those who apply for public funds are subjected.

■ BYGONE DAYS

He showed in his manner that bygones were to be bygones.

Mary Webb *Gone to Earth*

Let bygones be bygones 'let us forgive and forget past quarrels' is a proverb that has survived since the 17th century. 'Bygone' is a fossil-word of obvious meaning, though in normal modern English the order of its components would be reversed and we would talk of what has 'gone by'. Dr Johnson described 'bygone' in his dictionary as 'a Scotch word'.

In the 17th century 'bygone' often referred specifically, as it does in the proverb, to a sin or offence committed in the past. Shakespeare refers to 'bygone fooleries' in *The Winter's Tale*. His only other use of the word is in the same play, applied to the 'bygone day'. Typical modern usage is seen in the heading to a *Times*' article (24.2.1992) about barristers' wigs: 'Itchy symbol of a bygone age.'

■ CABIN CREWS

'Born troublemaker, probably in cahoots with his sister in Michigan.'

James A. Michener *Chesapeake*

To be **in cahoots** with someone is to be in league or partnership with him. It would be unusual to hear anyone other than an American use the phrase. Richard Bissell, in *The Pajama Game*, demonstrates typical usage when a character says: 'He's in cahoots with the union.' Alistair Maclean, in *The Dark Crusader*, has the alternative structure: 'Fleck and the professor are in cahoots. The professor and the Navy are in cahoots.' It is also possible to **go in cahoots with** or **cahoot with someone**, or more simply to **go cahoots** 'share equally'.

The fact that French *cahute*, German *Kajüte* and Dutch *kajuit* all mean a 'small hut' suggests that 'in cahoots with' derives from pioneer immigrants who shared a frontier cabin. There is no metaphorical phrase in any of those languages which could have been translated, but men 'in a cabin with' one another would have needed to collaborate closely in order to survive. As it happens, the same might be said of **cabinet ministers**. A political 'cabinet' takes its name from the small room which was originally set aside for meetings.

'In cahoots with' has been in use since the early 19th century. It could at first be used in a singular form but is now always plural.

■ CALL A SPADE A SWORD

'I ought to have known there was ideology behind this. That's the nigger in the woodpile.' 'The Negro in the woodpile,' murmured Domna and was instantly ashamed of the joke. The President threw back his head and roared. 'Touché!' he cried and grew thoughtful. 'It's an ugly thing how our language is defaced with expressions of prejudice. "Catch a nigger by the toe" – did you use to chant that as a boy, John? Sometimes I think we ought to make a clean sweep and invent a new world language.'

Mary McCarthy *The Groves of Academe*

The phrase a **nigger in the woodpile** 'a hidden cause of trouble or inconvenience' is little used now that 'nigger' is thought of as a highly offensive term for a black person. The word is a corruption of 'negro', which itself borders on being offensive. As for 'nigger in the woodpile', it referred originally to black slaves who were escaping and forced to hide from their pursuers in a woodpile or any other place of concealment.

In Maurice Edelman's *The Minister*, the man who makes the following speech is well aware that his remarks will cause offence: 'M'landa – he's the nigger in the woodpile. You will observe, sir, that my views on Africa are not shrouded by any sophisticated considerations. I don't feel any great compulsion to call the black members of our Empire our coloured brothers. I want to make it clear that when I speak of M'Landa and his ilk, I believe in calling a spade a Spade.'

To **call a spade a spade** is to speak openly and frankly, but the speaker quoted above in *The Minister* is deliberately playing on the slang meaning of 'spade', a black person. The word in this sense derives from the playing-card suit and the phrase **as black as the ace of spades**. As it happens, 'spade' in the playing-card sense is a mis-translation. The original is Spanish *espada* 'sword'.

'He's encouraged me to look things in the face, and call a spade a spade when necessary.'

R.F. Delderfield *Theirs Was the Kingdom*

'Call a spade a spade' is the result of another mis-translation. It came into English by mistake when Nicholas Udall translated Erasmus from Latin into English in the 16th century. Erasmus had himself translated Plutarch from Greek into Latin, making a mistake as he did so with this phrase. The Greek original had a word meaning 'bowl, trough, boat', found in many learned English words which begin with 'scapho-'. Erasmus confused it with a similar Greek word meaning 'to dig'. Udall followed Erasmus and invented an English idiom which has been well used ever since, though it should have been something like 'call a boat a boat'.

Mary Webb usefully glosses 'call a spade a spade' in *Gone to Earth*: 'You call a spade a spade, Mr Reddin; you are not, as our dear Browning has it, mealy mouthed.' This is after Reddin has announced that the woman living with him is his 'keep', or 'kept woman', not his wife.

A more emphatic form of the phrase occurs in W. Somerset Maugham's short story *Appearance and Reality*: 'Rabelais with his *gauloiserie*, which may be described as the ribaldry that likes to call a spade something more than a bloody shovel.' Similarly Ruth Rendell, in *Talking to Strange Men*, has: 'That was coming out into the open, Charles thought. That was what he had once heard his father say wasn't calling a spade a spade but a bloody shovel.'

There is an interesting allusion to the phrase in Derek Jewell's *Come In No.1 Your Time Is Up*. A woman is described as 'a believer in spade-calling, proclaiming to the world that she was no respecter of persons until they showed themselves worthy of respect'.

■ CASTING NASTURTIUMS

'After loafing here for three months does this runt have the audacity to cast aspersions in my direction?'

Truman Capote *My Side of the Matter*

It sounds rather pompous these days to talk about **casting aspersions**. 'You oughtn't cast aspersions like that,' says a character in Arthur Miller's *All My Sons*: you shouldn't make damaging comments that might harm someone's reputation.

The idea behind this expression seems to be that you are sprinkling something filthy that will soil or stain another person. 'Aspersion' derives from Latin *spargere* 'to sprinkle'. The same Latin word accounts for the 'sparge pipe' – a long pipe with holes in it at intervals – which is used to sprinkle water onto grass or crops.

Henry Fielding, in his famous novel *Tom Jones* (1749) says: 'I defy all the world to cast a just aspersion on my character.' Aspersions have been 'cast' ever since, until schoolboy humour came up with 'casting nasturtiums' as an alternative. Even in that form, says Professor A.S.C. Ross in *Don't Say It*, it's still a cliché.

■ CATALOGUE

'Far-fetched? Gawd, it's enough to make a cat laugh!'

Joyce Porter *Dover One*

A change of animal has occurred in **enough to make a cat laugh**, said of anything that is thought to be absurd. Daniel Defoe, in *Robinson Crusoe*, says 'it would have made a dog laugh'. Samuel Pepys uses the same phrase in his *Diary*. There was another expression with the same meaning – **enough to make a cat speak**. Dickens elaborates on that in *Nicholas Nickleby*, when the servant to Miss Squeers says of Matilda Price: 'It's enough to make a Tom cat speak French grammar, only to see how she tosses her head.' These phrases were merged by James

Robinson Planché in his *Extravaganzas, The Queen of the Frogs* (1879), who made of them 'it would have made a cat laugh'.

'If we 'ave a smaller 'ouse,' said Mrs Kipps, 'there won't be room to swing a cat.' Room to swing a cat, it seemed, was absolutely essential. It was an infrequent but indispensable operation.'

H.G. Wells *Kipps*

The saying about **not having enough room to swing a cat** does tend to make people ask why one would want to swing a cat in the first place. As Nina Bawden puts it, in *George Beneath a Paper Moon*: 'What do you think of the cottage? Not much room to swing a cat, I daresay, but then who wants to swing cats?' In *The Diviners*, Margaret Laurence has: 'The bathroom is so small you couldn't swing a cat in it (if you should ever desire to engage in such an activity – where do these phrases come from?)'

To answer Margaret Laurence's question, the generally accepted explanation of this phrase is that the 'cat' referred to is a **cat o' nine tails**, the whip that was used for punishment in the 17th century. It had nine pieces of rope, each about 18 in (45 cm) long, attached to a short handle. It was commonly called 'the cat', and had long been in existence when 'room to swing a cat' was first recorded in 1771. The theory that 'cat' was a Scottish word for a 'rogue' and that 'swing' meant 'hang from a gallows' has little to support it. It is always possible, though, that the phrase originally meant what it says, since swinging cats by their tails is said to have been a 'sport' in times past.

'We really have to watch him with the girls, and the trouble is they all think he's the cat's pyjamas.'

John Stroud *On the Loose*

'Pyjamas' ('pajamas' is the preferred American spelling) were introduced in the West as night-wear at the beginning of the 20th century. Earlier the word applied only to the loose trousers worn by both sexes in some Asian countries. By 1910 fashionable Americans were throwing pajama parties, the garments still having novelty value. By the 1920s, when the idle rich were amusing themselves by inventing slang expressions, a number of silly animal phrases came into use. The ones which have survived are **cat's pyjamas**, **cat's whiskers**, and **bee's knees**, all meant to convey the meaning of 'something excellent'.

'Cat's whiskers' appears to be justified, cats showing considerable pride in their whiskers, but 'cat's pyjamas' appeals to writers. 'You are feeling fine this morning, quite like the cat's pyjamas' says someone in Malcolm Lowry's *Under the Volcano*.

'He's so damned pleased with himself. Talk of a cat swallowing a canary.'

W. Somerset Maugham *The Facts of Life*

A cat which had managed to catch a bird would probably be licking its lips, looking as if it were pleased. The notion leads to the humorous comparison of someone's self-satisfied smugness with **the cat that swallowed a canary**. Another well-known comparison is made when someone has a broad fixed grin on his face: **grin like a Cheshire cat** has been used since the 18th century. The phrase was made far more widely known by Lewis Carroll in *Alice's Adventures In Wonderland*, where the grinning Cheshire cat belongs to the Duchess.

Wild guesses have been made as to the origin of this phrase but no theory can be proved. Partridge thought the reference was to a cat that was pleased with the cheese it had eaten, and that 'a cheeser cat' had become 'a Cheshire cat'. Others have said that Cheshire cheese was sold at one time moulded so as to look like a grinning cat.

When the cat's away is often quoted, leaving the listener or reader to complete it with **the mice will play**. The proverb dates from the 16th century and is one of many which mentions a cat. It alludes to children (or perhaps a husband) getting up to mischief when the woman of the house is not present. The woman in this case is not necessarily the spiteful woman who has been described as a 'cat' since the 13th century.

To **play cat and mouse** with someone is to torment him as a cat torments a mouse before killing it. Other miscellaneous 'cat' expressions include **wait to see which way the cat jumps**, which is the same thing as 'sitting on the fence' and refusing to make a decision. A **cat's paw** is a person who does something risky or unpleasant for someone else. A fable relates the story of a monkey who used the paw of his friend, the cat, to get chestnuts from the fire. **Catcalls**, dreaded by actors, were once whistles which emitted a squeaky sound. They could be purchased and taken to a theatre, to be used there by the audience if the play was disliked. Samuel Pepys recorded in his *Diary* in 1659 that he had bought a catcall for two groats. It must have been unnerving for actors of the time to know that the audience had such instruments with them, and were waiting for any excuse to play an active part in the evening's proceedings.

■ CHEESE-PARING

'You said half past six,' Lily said. 'I got cheesed off waiting.'

Clifford Hanley *The Taste of Too Much*

To be **cheesed off** is British slang and means to be bored and irritated. The phrase seems to have originated in the Royal Air Force during World War Two. It is probably only used by writers and speakers who lived through that period. The author Leslie Thomas belongs in that category, and in his *Tropic of Ruislip* a character says: 'I get cheesed off with the game.'

The expression is difficult to explain. **Pissed off** came into use at roughly the same time and with the same meaning, though **piss off** in the sense of 'go away' was already established. In the 1940s the word 'pissed' was not uttered in polite mixed company, and Chapman's *Dictionary of American Slang* records the softened-down forms **peed off** and **p o'd**. 'Cheesed off' may have been a euphemism for 'pissed off', inspired perhaps by too much cheese on military menus. The synonymous **brassed off** was also in military use and derived from brass-cleaning duties.

Older slang phrases referring to boredom are **browned off** and **fed-up**. The colour brown has long been associated with gloom, and those who were in a state of gloomy distraction were formerly said to be **in a brown study**. In *Service Slang*, J.L. Hunt and A.G. Pringle report that 'brown off' at one time could be used as a transitive verb: 'A Sergeant-Major has it in his power to "brown off" a junior N.C.O. or man who makes a nuisance of himself.' The meaning here is presumably 'to reprimand'.

To be 'fed up' implies that one has 'had enough' and is no longer interested in food. A person is metaphorically fed up when he has had enough of a situation and finds nothing of interest in his surroundings. A more intensive form of the phrase is **fed (up) to the teeth**. 'I'm merely fed to the teeth with myself, that's all' occurs in Malcolm Lowry's *Under the Volcano*. Evelyn Waugh, in *Work Suspended*, has: 'You get fed to the teeth with people making one get out of their way all the time.'

Cheese is mentioned in one or two other interesting expressions. **Cheese it!** was formerly criminal slang and meant 'Stop it, leave off, get away from here'. The 'cheese' in this case has been explained as a corruption of 'cease'. Someone who is described as a **big cheese** is an important person. Anglo-Indians, it is said, converted Urdu *chiz* 'correct thing' into 'cheese' and applied it to anything that was of good quality. Such usage is discussed by G. Subba Rao in his *Indian Words in English* and examples are to be found in the works of Thackeray.

■ CHICKEN FEED

The eldest Miss Larkins is not a chicken; for the youngest Miss Larkins is not that, and the eldest must be three or four years older. Perhaps the eldest Miss Larkins may be about thirty.

Charles Dickens *David Copperfield*

'Chicken' is now used for the domestic fowl, though originally it referred only to the young bird, what we now call a 'chick'. Just as a young girl can be referred to as a 'chick' in slang, so 'chicken' was formerly used of a young person. The word is still sometimes used affectionately to a child as a term of address. 'How would you like that, chicken?' is said by a mother to her daughter in *Mariana*, by Monica Dickens. 'Chicken' in its sense of 'young person' survives mainly, however, in the phrase **no chicken**, which is usually applied to a woman who is no longer young.

Don't count your chickens, he said to himself, there's a long way to go yet.

Ruth Rendell *Talking to Strange Men*

The folly of **counting one's chickens before they are hatched** has been commented on proverbially since the 16th century. This is another of those proverbs which rarely needs to be completed by a speaker because it is so well known: a reference to 'counting one's chickens' is enough to remind most people that they are taking success for granted but things could still go wrong. 'We shall be hot favourites' says a speaker in Derek Jewell's *Come In No.1 Your Time Is Up*. 'I'm glad,' is the reply, 'but don't count your chickens.'

Edward Blishen, in *A Cack-handed War*, varies the proverb to apply it to a man thinking about his future marriage: 'I'd walk about, smiling to myself, and counting our children before they were hatched.'

■ CHIPPING IN

'Chip off the old block, you know. Took me right back, hearing her rant on like that. I had much the same thing from Claire when she wanted to marry Sam.'

Nina Bawden *George Beneath a Paper Moon*

Chip off the old block is applied especially to a son who resembles his father in appearance and perhaps in character. Comparison of a man with a block occurs in *The House with the Green Shutters*, by George Douglas: 'Gourlay, a strong block of a man cut off from the world by impotence of speech.' As the Nina Bawden quotation above shows, 'chip off the old block' can also apply to a mother and daughter. The metaphor is self-explanatory; a small piece of wood chipped from a larger block has its same basic characteristics. When the phrase was first used in the 17th century, it was in the form **chip of the old block**. Careful speakers and writers might still use 'of' for 'off'.

Carpenters traditionally acquire the nickname Chips or Chippy amongst their workmates. This applies both to those who are wood-workers by trade and those who happen to bear Carpenter as a surname. A far more recent epithet, **chiphead**, is applied to a computer enthusiast, referring to his supposed love of the silicon chip and its integrated circuitry.

Other expressions with 'chip' allude to the plastic counter used to represent money in gambling casinos. **When the chips are down** means 'when the crisis-point is reached', as if the decision about where to place the chips has been made. In British slang it is still sometimes said of someone that he has **had his chips**. This can mean that the person concerned is dead or dying, or that he has been defeated. The first meaning is connected with **cash in one's chips** 'die', alluding to the end of a gambling session. In the sense of being 'defeated' the phrase refers to chips that have been gambled and lost. (For 'chip on one's shoulder' see page 193.)

■ CLEAR THINKING

The coast being clear, Peregrine came forth from his den . . .

Tobias Smollett *The Adventures of Peregrine Pickle*

The **coast is clear** originally meant that no coast-guards were in the vicinity, and smugglers could land or put to sea in relative safety. In a general sense the phrase is used to mean that people who are undesirable from the speaker's point of view are not around.

The phrase's range of use is demonstrated in the following: 'Mr Tupman and the rest of the gentlemen left the garden by the side gate just as he obtained a view of it; and the young ladies, he knew, had walked out alone, soon after breakfast. The coast was clear.' This is from *The Pickwick Papers*, and Dickens means that Jingle can now approach the spinster aunt and pretend to be her suitor. 'Look here, Meg, is the coast clear?' in E.M. Forster's *Howards End* simply means 'Have they gone?' 'You may have come to see whether the coast was clear' in *Getting it Right*, by Elizabeth Jane Howard, means: 'You may have come to see whether the other man in my life has gone so that you can take his place.'

■ CLOSE TO ONE'S HEART

My heart aches, and a drowsy numbness pains / My sense.

John Keats *Ode to a Nightingale*

Many of our 'heart' expressions, curious if their literal meaning is considered, derive from the ancient belief that the heart was the centre of thought, emotion and feeling. Since it was recognised that if the heart ceased to beat then life itself came to an end, it was natural to think that everything not experienced through the physical senses was linked to the heart.

What wew call **heartache**, then, is actually a mental anguish, or feeling of great disappointment. The word is not one that we use in daily conversation, nor would we frequently say something like 'My heart ached for the dear fellow', though this occurs in William J. Locke's *Jaffery*. Perhaps the words are best left in the immortal setting given to them by Keats, and before him by Shakespeare in *Hamlet*. The metaphorical meaning of 'heartache' first occurs in the 'To be or not to be' speech:

> *To die, to sleep –*
> *No more; and by a sleep to say*
> *we end*
> *The heartache and the thousand*
> *natural shocks*
> *That flesh is heir to. 'Tis a*
> *consummation*
> *Devoutly to be wished.*

'You're not in any way obliged to buy,' said Mr Isaacs rather haughtily, 'but I assure you that you'll regret it from the bottom of your heart if you don't.'

Evelyn Waugh *Vile Bodies*

Many other expressions naturally arise once the heart is seen as the repository of human feelings. Somebody can **break our heart** by distressing us greatly, perhaps after we have **given** or **lost our heart** by falling in love. Anything which is *deeply* felt is **from the bottom of one's heart**. 'I do pity you from the bottom of my heart' says a character in E.M. Forster's *Howards End*. The phrase remains in fairly common use, meant to emphasize that whatever feeling is being described is both sincere and intense.

His heart began to sink as he remembered who she was, and then plummeted.

Elizabeth Jane Howard *Getting it Right*

If that feeling is one of trepidation, then in popular belief we **have a sinking heart** or our **heart sinks**. 'His heart began to sink within him' writes Washington Irving, in *The Legend of Sleepy Hollow*. Monica Dickens, in *The Fancy*, has: 'He looked at her now with a sinking heart and hoped she wasn't going to make trouble with him.' If something **strikes fear into one's heart**, the heart supposedly sinks further still. It can be said that **one's heart is in one's boots**.

'That proves you have a wicked heart; and you must pray to God to change it; to give you a new and clean one; to take away your heart of stone and give you a heart of flesh.' I was about to propound a question, touching the manner in which that operation of changing my heart was to be performed, when Mrs Reed interposed.

Charlotte Brontë *Jane Eyre*

An unfeeling person **has no heart** and may therefore be asked to **Have a heart!** 'show some compassion'. Instead of being **heartless** he may be **hard-hearted** or have a **heart of stone**. Charlotte Brontë could not resist her heart-transplant joke, quoted above, though 'heart of flesh' was not a very imaginative substitute. Soon after *Jane Eyre* was published, in 1847, people began to talk about a **heart of gold**, which all those who had a generous nature were thought to possess. Such well-intentioned people, of course, also had their **hearts in the right place**.

Jane, even while her heart really warmed to him, went through the necessary fiction of welcoming surprise.

J.I.M. Stewart *The Last Tresilians*

'Hard-heartedness' may instead be described as **cold-heartedness**, so that by contrast a sympathetic person is **warm-hearted**. As feelings of friendliness and liking develop, we say that our **heart warms to someone**. This notion of 'warming' has blended with a former phrase which talked of **rejoicing** or **delighting the cockles of the heart**. George Douglas writes, in *The House with the Green Shutters*: 'The moment the whisky had warmed the cockles of his heart Gourlay ceased to care a rap for the sniggerers.'

'Cockles of the heart' came into use in the 17th century, and refers to the similarity in shape to a cockle shell and the heart. The resemblance is acknowledged in the zoological name of the cockle, *Cardium*, which is based on the Greek word for 'heart'.

'Look into your heart – into your heart of hearts.'

Anthony Trollope *Doctor Thorne*

'Heart' is used in a more general sense to describe the most important, innermost part of anything, **the heart of the matter**. One's **heart of hearts** refers to a place in the heart which guards one's most private thoughts and feelings. Mary McCarthy writes, in *The Group*: '"You used to like her best, Lakey. I think you still do, in your heart of hearts." Lakey smiled at the cliché.' Lakey's reaction is easy to understand; it is difficult not to smile at many of these 'heart' phrases, but they were not always clichés. As with 'heartache', 'heart of hearts', originally 'heart of heart', is again from *Hamlet*. The Prince says to Horatio:

> *Give me that man*
> *That is not passion's slave, and I*
> * will wear him*
> *In my heart's core, ay, in my*
> * heart of heart,*
> *As I do thee.*

'I'm going to have a heart to heart talk with that fellow,' he said grimly.

P.G. Wodehouse *Bill the Conqueror*

English people have been having **heart to heart talks** with one another, 'talks of great frankness and intimacy', since the end of the 19th century. Since that time it has also been possible for one person to tell another: **my heart bleeds for you** 'your misfortunes affect me deeply'. The allusion in both cases is clear.

Eat your heart out! sounds a very modern phrase, but it would have been readily understood in the 16th century. The phrase means 'be jealous, envy me' and is a rare use of the subjunctive: 'may jealousy eat your heart out'. In the 16th century it was usually longing or vexation that was said to eat someone's heart out.

At first, being little accustomed to learn by heart, the lessons appeared to me both long and difficult.

Charlotte Brontë *Jane Eyre*

To **learn something by heart** has been a way of talking about memorizing something since the 14th century. The French also talk about learning something *par coeur* 'by heart', and the English phrase may be derived from it. It is tempting to think that the original French phrase was *par choeur*, implying that something was learnt by a choral method, but there is no evidence to suggest that this was the case.

Such mistranslations do occur, as in the famous case of Cinderella's slipper. In the original French tale the slipper is made of *vair* 'fur'. This was heard as *verre* 'glass', and was so translated. The 'glass slipper' that was accidentally created in this way has appealed to the imagination of countless children.

■ CLOUD BANK

I was in Cloud-Cuckoo-Land again.

Alice Dwyer-Joyce *The Penny Box*

Cloud-Cuckoo-Land is an ideal, imaginary place, a dream land where one builds castles in the air. The phrase translates Greek *Nephelococcygia*, the name of an imaginary town in Aristophanes' comedy *The Birds*, supposedly built in the air by the birds to help separate the gods from men. 'Obviously you were away off in Cloud-Cuckoo-Land' says a teacher to a young girl, in *The Diviners*, by Margaret Laurence. 'Cloud-Cuckoo-Land' could well be a place for those who believe all too easily that **every cloud has a silver lining**, that something good will always reveal itself in what appears to be a disaster.

*'He's a bit up in the clouds. All this
Anglo-Catholicism makes him think we
can put the clock back.'*

Angus Wilson *Anglo-Saxon Attitudes*

Somebody whose **head is in the clouds**
or who is **up in the clouds** is not so
much a dreamer as a fanciful person
who is rather obscure and mystical.
His thoughts are a long way from
those that concern the normal person
going about daily life. He does not
give the impression that his **feet are
on the ground**, that he is dealing with
life in a practical way.

*'If one gentleman under a cloud is not
to put himself out of the way to assist
another gentleman in the same
condition, what's human nature?'*

Charles Dickens *The Pickwick Papers*

Clouds can be threatening and
forbidding, as well as airy nothings.
Someone whose gloomy mood has a
depressing effect on others is said to
cast a cloud over them. The metaphor
is commented on by Arnold Bennett,
in *Clayhanger*: 'Not a word at
breakfast. But a thick cloud over the
breakfast table! Maggie showed that
she felt the cloud. So even did Mrs
Nixon. The niece alone, unskilled in
the science of meteorology, did not
notice it.' Even worse is a cloud of
suspicion or disgrace. This is the one
we have in mind when we say that
someone is **under a cloud**.

■ COLOUR CODE

*The story that popped into her mind
was a bit off colour, but it would point
a moral to Nils.*

Mary McCarthy *The Group*

In the above quotation Mary
McCarthy uses **off colour** to mean
'not quite proper, suggestive of
obscenity'. The allusion is to
something which is not as 'white' or
pure as it should be. Applied to a
person, however, 'off colour' means
'unhealthy', with obvious reference to
the colour of the skin. 'Have you
noticed Graham off-colour for long?'
says a character in Richard Gordon's
The Face-Maker. The reply is: 'No.
Not at all. It's a bolt from the blue.'

*About this time a bolt came from the
blue or a bomb fell at our feet – the
metaphor doesn't matter so long as it
conveys a sense of an unlooked-for
phenomenon.*

William J. Locke *Jaffery*

As William J. Locke says above, **a
bolt from the blue** is something that
happens suddenly and unexpectedly,
as when a bolt of lightning strikes out
of a clear sky which gave no warning
of a storm. 'Bolt' compares the
lightning to the short, thick arrow
shot from a cross-bow. 'I have your
assurance that your changed
circumstances have come on you like
a bolt from the blue,' asks someone
in *The French Lieutenant's Woman*,
by John Fowles.

*Then, quite out of the blue, it occurred
to me to ring up Claudine and ask her.*

Peter Draper *A Season in Love*

Out of the blue is a watered down
version of this expression, putting
emphasis on the unexpectedness of
what happens, rather than its
devastating effect. 'I'm so sorry to
arrive out of the blue like this,' says
someone in Alexander Fullerton's
Other Men's Wives. Once again the
allusion is to a clear blue sky which

gave no warning signs of an impending change.

Max swore blue bloody murder as Roy howled with laughter.

Bernard Malamud *The Natural*

To **cry/shout/scream blue murder** 'cry out very loudly in fear and alarm' dates from the 19th century and is based on the much earlier French oath *Morbleu!* The latter appears to mean 'blue death' – *mort bleu* – but is in fact a euphemism for *mort Dieu* 'death of God'. *Bleu* was a meaningless substitution for a word of similar sound. The 'blueness' of 'cry blue murder' may later have become significant when attached to the Bluebeard legend. Typical modern usage of the phrase is seen in Angus Wilson's *Anglo-Saxon Attitudes*: 'A few of his utterances are liable to make our union chaps cry blue murder.' In *Surfeit of Lampreys* Ngaio Marsh has: 'He and Daddy have been yelling blue murder.'

Her room-mates were green with envy.

Mary McCarthy *The Group*

One of the best-known 'colour' phrases in modern English is **green with envy**. This would have perplexed speakers of English in the 16th century who associated jealousy with yellow. Shakespeare still made this association, which is why Nym says in *The Merry Wives of Windsor*: 'I will possess him with yellowness', meaning that he will make Page jealous.

Nevertheless, it seems to have been Shakespeare who was responsible for causing green to become the colour of envy, allowing yellow to switch later to cowardice. In *Othello* Iago makes a hypocritical speech to the Moor:

> *O beware, my lord, of jealousy;*
> *It is the green-ey'd monster which*
>   *doth mock*
> *The meat it feeds on.*

By 'green-ey'd monster' Shakespeare meant a cat, which plays with a mouse before it kills it and eats it, thus 'mocking the meat it feeds on'. Metaphorically, Shakespeare was comparing jealousy to a cat and saying that jealousy makes a mockery of love – even though it feeds on love. In the simplest possible terms, jealousy does to love what a cat does to a mouse. This was no doubt the thought that was uppermost in Shakespeare's mind when he wrote Iago's speech. His use of 'green-ey'd monster' for 'cat' accidentally linked greenness with the emotion he was describing.

'How many customers have asked you if you've got green fingers, Sharon?'

Ruth Rendell *Talking to Strange Men*

A person who has **green fingers** has a natural instinct for gardening. Plants seem to grow well when he or she plants them. The American equivalent of this phrase appears to be **green thumb**, as used by Bernard Malamud in *The Natural*: ' "I have that green thumb," he said huskily, "and I shoulda farmed . . ." '

'There was no sex in it, or rather no overt sex. She didn't give me the green light or anything like that.'

John Wain *The Contenders*

To **give someone the green light** is to give him a signal to begin or to continue. The green light of street traffic lights is obviously the most likely source for this metaphor, though similar signals are given in other situations. In a BBC radio studio, for example, a speaker will 'go ahead on a green', knowing that when the green light flashes the microphone is live.

'Red light' does not have a parallel meaning: one does not figuratively 'give someone a red light' to tell them to stop. A **red light district** 'an area where there are many sex-shops and prostitutes' is named for the red lights which are actually there, red lights having become associated internationally in modern times with such activities. Those who decide to **paint the town red** 'spend a boisterous night out' may visit a 'red light district', though the two phrases are not connected. It has plausibly been suggested that 'painting the town red' originally referred to behaviour that would lead to a certain amount of blood being splashed about.

It seemed incredible to him, not used to academic meetings, that they should have rushed off in chase of this red herring.

C.P. Snow *The Affair*

A very different type of 'red' phrase is **red herring** 'something irrelevant which is introduced into a conversation and which distracts speakers from the main topic of conversation'. 'Red herrings' are kippered herrings, and the important thing about them is that they have a strong smell. They were therefore used by huntsmen to train their hounds. A red herring drawn across a path would leave a strong scent; the hounds had to be trained to ignore it and continue to follow the scent of the fox.

'Something seemed to go off inside me – and I saw red'.
'So you can see red. Well – I shouldn't have thought it. It's rather – interesting'.

Warwick Deeping *Sorrell and Son*

To **see red** refers to another controversial sport, and the red capes which are carried into a bull-ring. There they are waved about in an effort to enrage the bull. A human being who 'sees red' is being compared metaphorically to a bull which is charging at its tormentor. From the same source comes **red rag to a bull**, something said to a person which will make him very resentful, angry or violent.

'What a red-letter day, dear!' she cried.
'Quaint Irene suddenly becoming so world-wide.'

E.F. Benson *Trouble for Lucia*

A **red-letter day** was originally one marked in red in an ecclesiastical calendar in order to give it prominence. The feast days of the most important saints and other major church festivals were so marked, so it is easy to see how 'red-letter day' came to mean 'an important, memorable day, one likely to be remembered'. The complete break with its religious meaning is seen in Mary McCarthy's *The Group*: 'But the red-letter day in Mr Andrews' life was the day he became a Trotskyite.' In Ruth Rendell's *The Tree of Hands* a woman about to fly home to her husband says: 'This is going to be a red-letter day for Daddy. Do you know we've never been separated so long in all our married life?'

She wasn't untruthful but she wasn't above telling a white lie so as not to spoil his evening.

Ruth Rendell *The Tree of Hands*

The person who tells a **white lie** knows that what he is saying is untrue, but believes that his behaviour is excusable. His action is motivated by kindness or politeness rather than malice or self-interest; he is lying for a very good reason.

'White lies' were identified as such in the 18th century and caused much debate. Strict moralists were of the view that lying of any kind could not be justified, that white lies soon led to black lies. It seems to have been the women of the time, especially those of social rank, who defended white lies. Mary Russell Mitford, in one of her *Our Village* sketches 'Admiral On Shore', was later to refer to the 'female privilege of white-lying'. Modern women usually claim that 'changing one's mind' is a **woman's privilege**.

Modern use of 'white lie' is seen in Stephen Vizinczey's *In Praise of Older Women*: 'I should have been relieved that she accepted my insincere white lie, but I was hurt.' *In Cards of Identity* Nigel Dennis has the exchange: ' "The truth is that the play is going to be an act of occupational therapy for Mr Towzer." "That is pretty much what I guessed." "But it was a *white* lie, wasn't it?" "White or black, you run along now." '

■ COMING CLEAN

'Haven't you got things you'd like to get off your chest? I'm sure you must have. You mustn't be inhibited about this, John. You can say anything to me.'

Ruth Rendell *Talking to Strange Men*

The *Daily Chronicle* (September, 1902), as quoted by *The Oxford English Dictionary*, said: 'The desire is either to deliver a message to the world or to express the individual personality – to **get it off your chest** is the horrid, vulgar phrase.' The expression was obviously a new one to whoever wrote those words. The idea of coughing in a chesty manner was foremost in his mind. In modern times most people think only of the metaphorical meaning, 'bring mental relief by saying something that one has wanted to say for a long time'.

Present-day writers appear to find the phrase neither vulgar nor disgusting. Penelope Mortimer, in *The Pumpkin Eater*, has: 'I had to write to you if only to get things off my chest.' Charles Webb writes, in *The Marriage of a Young Stockbroker*: 'If she'd wanted to get some problem off her chest I would have listened.' Later in the same novel someone says: 'She's getting some things off her chest.' James Purdy, in *Eustace Chisholm and the Works*, has: 'And another thing I got off my chest . . .'

'I can see that I'll have to make a clean breast of it. I never thought you'd get on to me.'

Mary Stewart *This Rough Magic*

It is difficult to know how much 'get something off one's chest' was influenced by the much older **make a clean breast of something** 'make a full confession'. 'I made a clean breast of it, and put myself in his hands' says someone in Arnold Bennett's *Clayhanger*. The expression dates from the 18th century and is based on the notion that the breast, like the heart, is the seat of the affections and emotions, as well as private thoughts and feelings. 'Chest' and 'bosom' were sometimes used for 'breast' in this sense. Spenser referred in the

16th century to courage creeping into a manly chest. We might still talk of a **bosom friend**, someone entrusted with one's innermost thoughts and secrets.

■ COUNTING ONE'S BLESSINGS

'I think I should go mad in prison. Didn't it embitter you against everything?'
'It was a blessing in disguise.'

Eric Linklater *Poet's Pub*

The name of James Hervey, born in 1714 at Hardingstone, near Northampton, is little known today. Hervey became rector of Weston Favell and was the author of *Meditations and Contemplations*, which had a great success at the time. He wrote many other religious works, described in *Everyman's Dictionary of Literary Biography* as 'characterized by overwrought sentiment, and overloaded with florid ornament'.

Only one of Hervey's 'ornaments' survives today, just three words from everything he wrote in his lifetime. In his *Reflections on a Flower Garden* (1746) he included a hymn 'Since All the Downward Tracts of Time'. It contained the words: 'E'en crosses from his sov'reign hand are blessings in disguise.' **Blessing in disguise** 'a seeming misfortune which is eventually revealed to be a good thing for the person concerned' caught the public's imagination and became part of the language. Not that everyone has thought the phrase itself a blessing. Eric Partridge quotes it with distaste in his *Dictionary of Clichés*.

The old-fashioned exclamation **Well, I'm blessed!** could be considered a phrase in disguise. It was a euphemism for 'Well, I'm damned!'

Also old-fashioned is the statement: **I haven't a penny to bless myself with.** The expression dates from the time of the silver penny, which had a cross on it.

■ CUTTING REMARKS

'That's cut and dried, is it? You're going to show up there.'

C.P. Snow *The Affair*

Individual words often change their meanings with the passing of time; phrases do the same. An example of the latter is provided by **cut and dried**, also found as **cut and dry** in previous centuries. The words originally referred to dried herbs sold by herbalists which lacked the freshness of those growing in the garden. Metaphorically they were used of ideas and language which were well-worn. A 'cut and dried' sermon, for example, was one based on generally accepted notions, offering no fresh ideas or interpretations. In modern times, something which is 'cut and dried' is agreed on, without the need for further questions. It is 'clear-cut.'

'With Jo leaving, and so suddenly, I shall have my work cut out.'

Susan Barrett *Moses*

'Cut' features in many phrasal verbs, metaphorical idioms, sayings and proverbs. To **have one's work cut out**, for instance, is to face a lot of work that must be done in a short time. The reference is to tailoring, where skilled workers cut out materials that are assembled by seamstresses who work under pressure. Clothes that are 'well-cut' lead to phrases such as a **cut above**, originally used of people who were superior to others because they were better dressed. 'Cut above' can now be used in a more general way to indicate noticeably good quality in any sphere of activity.

The world of tailoring also led to the proverbial **cut one's coat according to one's cloth** 'to adjust oneself to circumstances, live within one's means, attempt to do only what is practicable'. Ngaio Marsh, in *Surfeit of Lampreys*, deliberately mixes this saying with another expression, to **cut a caper** 'to dance about in a foolishly happy way'. The mixture emerges as: 'We must use our cunning and cut our capers according to our cloth.'

To **cut and run** is to take oneself away quickly from a situation that is becoming difficult. The expression was originally nautical and referred to those occasions where there was no time to weigh anchor. Instead the anchor cable was cut and the ship set sail. Another nautical idiom, now very seldom used, made it possible to refer to the **cut of someone's jib**. Sailors would say that they liked or disliked the 'cut of someone's jib', meaning that they reacted positively or negatively to his general appearance. The reference was to a sailing-ship's prominent jib-sail.

'We might want to use it some day against those damned Jews in the Third Ward. Cut them down to size.'

James A. Michener *Chesapeake*

To **cut someone down to size** has the obvious meaning of 'to make him realize that he is not as important (big) as he thinks he is'. One way of doing this socially, perhaps, is to **cut someone dead** 'act as if he did not exist'. 'Cutting' people in this sense has been occurring since the 17th century. Angry fathers from that time

onwards were also **cutting off with a shilling** their errant sons. They were actually disinheriting them: a shilling or other small sum was mentioned in the will to show that the act was intentional, that the son had not accidentally been overlooked.

Keller: What ice does that cut?

Arthur Miller *All My Sons*

American speakers rather than British are likely to announce that something **cuts no ice** with them, though Josephine Tey, in *The Franchise Affair*, has an Englishwoman ask: 'How much ice will this cut?' The phrase is usually a negative statement – 'that cuts no ice with me' – often of something that has just been said, to mean that it makes no impression on the speaker. The image evoked is that of a ship trying to proceed through ice-bound waters and not succeeding. By contrast, someone who **cuts a dash** makes a strong impression because of his dress and manner.

'P'raps I must say I von't pay, and cut up rough.'

Charles Dickens *The Pickwick Papers*

We may **cut up rough** 'act angrily and violently', as Sam Weller jokingly threatened to do with his father. We can **cut corners** to achieve something quickly, not allowing rules and regulations to bother us too much. We can **cut it fine** if we arrive on the platform five seconds before the train departs. We can promise to **cut a long story short**, though leaving out irrelevant detail often proves to be more difficult than we anticipated.

'But that's very stupid, surely,' said a visitor once, who thought of entering into competition. 'It's cutting off his

nose to spite his face! Why is he so anxious to be the only carrier in Barbie that he carries stuff for next to nothing the moment another man tries to work the roads?'

George Douglas *The House with the Green Shutters*

Each of us also has the right to **cut off his nose to spite his face**. A reference in a 17th-century French document says that Henri IV realized that to destroy Paris was *comme on dit, se couper le nez pour faire dépit à son visage* 'as they say, to cut off the nose to spite one's face'. The saying was clearly in circulation by that time, probably derived from a European animal fable that has not survived. The phrase has continued in use to mean 'injure oneself materially in taking revenge on someone', though it conveys that message in a far more vivid way.

■ DAY BY DAY

At six o'clock I called it a day.

Dashiell Hammett *The Dain Curse*

'Day' occurs in many metaphorical phrases where the allusion is fairly straightforward. The 'day' referred to in **call it a day**, for instance, can be a period of time ranging from a few hours to many years. The original use of the phrase occurs when, at the end of the working day, someone signals that he is about to go home by saying 'I think I'll call it a day', but the expression can also be used in a more general sense to mean 'bring something to an end that has been going on for a long time'. The man who says, in W. Somerset Maugham's *The Lotus Eater*: 'Don't you think after twenty-five years of perfect happiness one ought to be satisfied to

call it a day?' means that one ought to be content to die.

'The travelling secretary of a birth control society called to ask for her support as alderman. Mrs B. replied: "I've had five children already, and I was seventy-two last birthday. Aren't you a bit late in the day for me?"'

Winifred Holtby *South Riding*

Late in the day can also refer both to the late evening hours of a particular day, or to a time which is near the end of a far longer period. The quotation above shows the phrase being used to mean something like 'fifty years late', but it could equally well be used to mean someone who comes calling at a relatively late hour. **At the end of the day** is now almost exclusively used in its metaphorical meaning of 'all things considered', based on the assumption that everything has indeed been considered by evening.

To **have had one's day** is also purely metaphorical, referring to a loss of power and influence, an end to a successful period. A person who has 'had his day' might look back to the **good old days**, a time in the past which is remembered with affection, when things were better. He will tell his friends that **those were the days** 'that was a happier and better time'. **Days of yore** also refers to the distant past: 'yore' means 'of years (ago)'.

An object which is old-fashioned can also be said to have 'had its day'. If it is looking rather battered it might be described as having **seen** or **known better days**.

'We can put a bit by now for a rainy day.'

W. Somerset Maugham *Gigolo and Gigolette*

Many people like to feel that they have 'a little tucked away', 'a nest-egg', 'something for a **rainy day**'. The 'rainy day' is a time of trouble or misfortune when extra money will be needed, and has been referred to in this way since the 16th century. Abraham Tucker, in *Light of Nature Pursued*, told his readers at the end of the 18th century: 'It behoves us to provide against a rainy day while the sun shines.'

With luck, the figurative 'rainy day' never comes. Another day that may never arrive is **one day** or **one of these days**, when we must get together with an old acquaintance, clear out the attic or do something equally worthwhile. The emptiness of 'one of these days' has long been recognized. Dickens, in *The Old Curiosity Shop*, had this to say about the phrase: '[Mr Brass] so overflowed with liberality and condescension, that in the fulness of his heart he invited Mr Swiveller to partake of a bowl of punch with him at that remote and indefinite period which is currently denominated "one of these days".'

His father's son was as good a man as Mr Noddy, any day in the week.

Charles Dickens *The Pickwick Papers*

'Any day in the week' is another phrase that has survived from Dickens's time to the present day, though in slightly altered form. **Any day of the week** is now the usual wording, still heard in verbal jousting matches. The phrase adds nothing to the sense of the words that precede it, but allows an emphatic tone to be used.

'You'll have to ask her to name the day.'

H.G. Wells *Kipps*

In **name the day**, 'day' normally refers specifically to 'wedding day'. The quotation above means that Artie Kipps should ask Ann whether she will marry him. If that question has already been settled, 'naming the day' merely specifies on which day the wedding will occur. 'We will tell Betty you have named the day for your wedding' says someone in Zane Grey's *Betty Zane*.

The phrase has been used in this specialized way since the early 19th century, but it can also be used in a non-marital context. In Joseph Heller's *Good as Gold* a character who says: 'You name the day. We'll go any time you say, after the holidays' means 'say when we should leave on a trip'.

'Grenfell, your days are numbered – you and that rag of yours.'

Barry Oakley *A Salute to the Great McCarthy*

To say that **someone's days are numbered** can mean that the person will soon die, or that his time in a particular job will soon come to an end. The notion that every individual has a certain number of days allotted to him in advance is mentioned from the 14th century onwards. Shakespeare alludes to the idea in *King Henry the Sixth*, Part Three. The Duke of York says:

> *The fatal followers do pursue,*
> *And I am faint and cannot fly their fury;*
> *And were I strong, I would not shun their fury.*
> *The sands are numb'red that make up my life.*

'How long did it take you?'
'About a month of Sundays.'

Judith Guest *Ordinary People*

Specific days are little mentioned in set phrases, though 'Sunday' occurs in **one's Sunday best** 'one's best clothes' and **a month of Sundays**. The latter phrase has been used colloquially since the end of the 19th century to mean 'a very long time'. A far older expression, used if someone feels that he is being falsely accused of taking too long to do something, is the proverbial **Rome wasn't built in a day**. The reference is to Rome rather than another city because the proverb was translated from Latin.

'Are you judging today?'
He shook his head. 'Busman's holiday.'

Muriel Spark *The Fancy*

A **busman's holiday** involves doing in your leisure time what you do for a living. In the quotation above, the reference is to a man who is visiting a rabbit show for pleasure, when normally he is at such shows in a professional capacity.

'Busman's holiday' appeared in print at the very end of the 19th century and is rumoured to refer to conscientious London busmen. It is said that they would ride their own buses on their day off to make sure that their horses were not ill-treated. Perhaps a story was in circulation in the 1890s about a particular busman who behaved in this way, but it has not been traced.

■ DEAD LANGUAGE

Frank: That boy's going to be a real doctor; he's smart.
Jim: Over my dead body he'll be a doctor.

Arthur Miller *All My Sons*

Never say die is a proverbial saying that means 'never give up hope'. Some people seem to interpret it literally, using euphemistic phrases such as **pass away** and **pass on** for 'die'. 'Dead' is also avoided, though the phrase that replaces it may be irreverent. Joseph Heller, in *Good as Gold*, has: 'Now he ain't pushing around people. He's **pushing up daisies**. A suicide.'

The verb 'die' is thoughtlessly used, however, when someone expresses a strong desire by saying that he is dying to do this or that. A hyperbolic reference to death also occurs when someone states his strong opposition to something by saying that it will happen **over his dead body**. The word 'only' is implied – only if the opposer is dead will it happen. The speaker usually applies the expression to himself, but it can occur in the third person. 'Take over McCarthy's Motors,' says a man in Barry Oakley's *A Salute to the Great McCarthy*. 'Over my father's dead body' is the reply.

'I'd like to have a piece of cake,' he said patiently.
'Well, it's your funeral.'

John Steinbeck *The Wayward Bus*

We also cheerfully tell someone that **it's his funeral** if he decides to pursue a particular course of action – the consequences will be felt by him alone. The literal meaning of the phrase is quite striking, but it is often applied to trivial matters such as getting fat if one eats too much cake, as in the Steinbeck quotation above. 'Go on, it's your funeral' is said to someone who is taking a risk which may lead to punishment in *Thirteen Days*, by Ian Jefferies. *Sorrell and Son*, by Warwick Deeping, has: 'I'm not worrying. It's not my funeral.'

'If I muddled them, it would be the death of me.'

Nigel Dennis *Cards of Identity*

We **nearly die laughing** or say that someone or something **will be the death of us** in further exaggerations. We mean by the latter phrase that we will be caused great worry, but do not really expect such worry to have fatal results. Nor, usually, has someone who has **got away with murder** escaped from justice, though he may have bent the rules considerably without being punished. If he has **made a killing** on the stock market or suddenly gained a lot of money in some other way his friends will congratulate, not condemn, him.

Dead as a door-nail has been in use since the 14th century, but has had a number of variants. They include **dead as a herring**, **dead as a dodo**, **dead as mutton**, **dead as Julius Caesar**, **dead as a tent-peg**. Eric Partridge explained both the 'door-nail' and 'tent-peg' expressions by saying both were 'constantly being hit on the head'. As for herrings, they are said to die very quickly when removed from the sea.

D.H. Lawrence, in *Sons and Lovers*, has the following interesting exchange: '"Tha'd drop down stiff, as dead as a door-knob." "Why is a door-knob deader than anything else?" asked Paul, curious. "Eh, I dunno; that's what they say," replied his father.'

■ DEMON PHRASES

By nature warmly emotional enough to 'burn her fingers' over Robin Adair . . .

Berta Ruck *Ancestral Voices*

To **burn one's fingers** is the simplest of phrases, describing an experience which is clearly very painful. When used metaphorically the phrase becomes more complex. We 'burn our fingers' if we invest unwisely in a business and suffer financially. We also use the expression about relationships that cause emotional pain because our love or trust is betrayed. The words imply that we are to some extent to blame for our own suffering. We should have listened to our heads, not our hearts. We should have known that putting our hand in the fire was a dangerous thing to do.

In *The Groves of Academe* Mary McCarthy gives the phrase a more interesting, abstract definition. She describes a college president whose support for a member of staff has proved to be a mistake. Another member of the faculty tells him: 'You won't persuade anybody that he was let go for budgetary reasons. It will be assumed, as a matter of course, that you had your eyes opened, got your fingers burned, learned a thing or two, tasted your own medicine – all the ugly phrases coined by the demon in us to describe the deceit and disappointment of the spiritual by the material factor.'

These are fine words, but 'tasted your own medicine' can hardly have been what was meant here. To have a **taste of one's own medicine** is to suffer the same ill-treatment that one has been imposing on others. It is a practical example of poetic justice. The college president probably **took his medicine**, 'accepted the punishment meted out by fate or his fellows'. 'I do not care about myself, I'll go and take my medicine' says a young hero in Zane Grey's *Betty Zane*. The meanings of the two phrases do occasionally overlap. William Trevor, in *The Old Boys*, has: 'Surely you know that we must take our medicine? We are at the receiving end now. Our son may call the tune and we must dance.'

■ DONKEY WORK

'Talk the hind leg off a donkey, Saul would,' Colin said. 'Very excitable sort of chap.'

Frederic Raphael *The Limits of Love*

A person who can talk at great length without pausing is said to be able to **talk the hind leg off a donkey**. John Le Carré, in *The Honourable Schoolboy*, prefers the plural form: 'As long as Sam thought he was leading Smiley from the scent, he would talk the hindlegs off a donkey.'

The phrase has had many different forms in the past, 'bird', 'cow', 'dog' and 'jackass' often being used instead of 'donkey'. If the talker is a great charmer he is said instead to be able to **charm the birds off the trees**. This phrase occurs, for instance, in James Mitchell's *When the Boat Comes in*: 'Charm the birds off the trees, Jack would, but he's got no heart at all.'

The only active duty the army had seen in donkey's years was when two divisions were hired out to one Hymie Slotnick to make a Western.

Mordecai Richler *The Incomparable Atuk*

Donkeys are not especially renowned for living to a great age, in spite of Sam Weller's comment in *The Pickwick Papers* that some people believe them to be immortal. The explanation for **donkey's years** 'a very long time' must be sought elsewhere. It is in fact 'donkey's ears' which are especially long, and which were originally referred to. The change from 'ears' to 'years' was natural in view of their closeness in sound and the meaning of the phrase. 'I'm beginning to think that life resembles something I haven't experienced for donkey's years – it's like Saturday night in an old-fashioned public-house.' So says the hero of Richard Gordon's *The Face-Maker*, adding by way of explanation of his last remark: 'It gets better towards closing-time.'

Many speakers would use **for ages** instead of 'donkey's years', using the hyperbole which is also present in the expression **never in a million years**. This is merely an emphatic way of saying 'never'. Mary McCarthy demonstrates the use of the phrase in *The Group*: 'But the group would never believe, never in a million years, that Dottie Renfrew would come here, with a man she hardly knew, who made no secret of his intentions.'

■ DREAMLAND

The allegorical poem *Roman de la Rose* was composed in the 13th century by Guillaume de Lorris and Jean de Meung. It had a great influence throughout Europe and was partly adapted into English by Chaucer and others. The English version contains a reference to **castles in Spain**, translating *châteaux en Espagne*, referring to idle day-dreams that are unlikely to be made reality.

'As a girl she built the usual castles in the air; but all her girlish hopes and aspirations have long been dead.'

Henry Lawson *The Drover's Wife*

French writers of the time also referred to castles in Asia or Albania, an indication that 'Spain' was of no particular significance. It was simply an alien, Moorish country where a Christian would have no right to build anything at all. By the 15th century English writers were also using **castles in the skies**, but Sir Thomas North, in his translation of Plutarch (1676), wrote: 'They built castles in the air, and thought to do great wonders.' **Castles in the air** has since been the usual English form, though some writers and speakers still refer to 'castles in Spain'. Modern French retains *châteaux en Espagne*.

The expression is so well known that a reference to 'building castles' is enough to suggest day-dreaming. Another way of alluding to the phrase is shown by Dickens in *The Old Curiosity Shop*: 'The glare and hurry of broad noon are not adapted to idle pursuits like mine; a glimpse of passing faces caught by the light of a street lamp or a shop window is often better for my purpose than their full revelation in the daylight, and, if I must add the truth, night is kinder in this respect than day, which too often destroys an air-built castle at the moment of its completion, without the smallest ceremony or remorse.'

There is another well-known 'castle' expression to the effect that **an Englishman's home is his castle** 'in his own home an Englishman is secure and private and has the right to do as he wishes'. In an age where the re-possession of Englishmen's homes by building societies and banks has become commonplace, the phrase is less often heard.

■ DROPPING IN

'I call this something!'
'A drop in the bucket.'

Carson McCullers *The Heart is a Lonely Hunter*

A drop in the bucket is a very small, insignificant quantity. It is often being compared to a much larger amount, especially that needed for a specific purpose. Truman Capote, in *My Side of the Matter*, uses the phrase rather differently: 'It's not a drop in the bucket to what came later that same evening.' In this case, 'it's nothing to

what came later' would have been synonymous.

The 'drop in the bucket' image is used in a modern translation in the Old Testament, Isaiah 40.15: 'Behold, the nations are like a drop from a bucket, and are accounted as the dust on the scales.' In the 14th century Wyclif had translated the phrase as 'drop of a bucket'. Dickens elaborated this idea in *A Christmas Carol* (1844), making Jacob Marley's ghost say: 'The dealings of my trade were but a drop of water in the comprehensive ocean of my business.' Since that time **a drop in the ocean** has been frequently used.

■ DUBIOUS PRACTICES

'Well, Mr Doubting Thomas?'

Mordecai Richler *The Incomparable Atuk*

Mordecai Richler, in the quotation given above, creates a nonce name (coined for the occasion) based on the phrase **doubting Thomas**. The Thomas referred to is the Apostle, of whom we read in John 20.24: 'Now Thomas, one of the twelve, called the Twin, was not with them when Jesus came. So the other disciples told him, "We have seen the Lord." But he said to them, "Unless I see in his hands the print of the nails, and place my finger in the mark of the nails, and place my hand in his side, I will not believe."'

The *Temple Dictionary of the Bible* comments: 'Thomas's refusal to credit the news of the resurrection was only the disbelief of a broken heart, and a withered hope. It was "too good news to be true".' Nevertheless the words uttered by Thomas have meant that his name has for centuries been associated with scepticism.

'Doubt' occurs also in **give someone the benefit of the doubt** 'assume innocence in the absence of clear proof of guilt'. The 'b' in 'doubt' has always been silent in English, the verb having been borrowed from French *douter*. The 'b' was artificially restored by lexicographers on the basis that the word derived from Latin *dubitare* and a 'b' should therefore be present. The same thing was done with *debt*, from French *dette*, ultimately from Latin *debere* 'to owe.' Dictionary-makers no longer try to control the language in this way, knowing full well that if they tried to do so they would be ignored by the public.

■ EASY MEAT

'The old boy's woman-crazy: he'd be duck soup for a woman like you.'

Dashiell Hammett *The Dain Curse*

Duck soup is American slang for something easy, 'a piece of cake' (see page 105). The phrase probably derives from **sitting duck** 'an easy target'. The 'sitting duck' soon ends up in the hunter's bag and may well provide the 'duck soup'. The duck will, as it were, be **in the soup** both literally and metaphorically. 'In the soup' meaning 'in trouble' is probably a fanciful alteration of **in hot water**, used in the same sense.

To take to something like a duck to water is to respond to something in a totally natural way, as if one were born to it. Other 'duck' metaphors are less cheerful. A **lame duck** is a person or organization in difficulties, needing outside help. It is on its way to becoming a **dead duck**, something that will certainly fail.

Even 'duck and drake', the innocent children's game which involves skimming flat stones across water,

long ago acquired a more sinister meaning. The game was named in the 16th century and to **play duck and drake with something** (later **ducks and drakes**) soon came to mean to spend money or time in a careless way, as if throwing coins rather than stones into the water. The idiom is found in literature but is no longer used in speech.

A well-known verbal 'duck' is the **Bombay duck**, a jokey corruption by English sailors in the 18th century of the fish called 'bummalo', **bombila** in its native form. The allusion to 'duck' parallels that of 'rabbit' in 'Welsh rabbit' (see page 186). The sailors were implying that the fish was a poor man's substitute for meat.

The 'duck' in cricket derives from **duck's-egg**, the shape of which resembles the '0' entered against the player's name.

■ END TO END

'I'm at a loose end, when I'm not rehearsing there's nothing to do at all, is there?'

Margaret Drabble *The Garrick Year*

At a loose end was sometimes 'at an idle end' in the 19th century. Metaphorically, one is like a boat which is drifting, not tied to a particular place or thing. There is no special task to perform and one is not quite sure what to do with one's time. Also nautical in origin is **to the bitter end**. This is now applied to completing an unpleasant job that one would rather abandon: originally the reference was to a rope or cable wound round the bitts, or posts on the deck of a sailing ship. When the cable was paid out 'to the bitter end', none remained on the bitt itself. Landlubbers understandably interpreted the phrase differently, assuming that 'bitter' meant 'unpleasant'.

'There was a bit of debt and with one thing and another it got bigger. Oh well, we didn't make ends meet.'

Edna O'Brien *The Country Girls*

The 'ends' referred to in **make (both) ends meet** 'live within one's income' are the two ends of the year. The phrase is based on the idea of getting through the entire twelve months without running into debt. The English phrase has been in use since the 17th century and matches the French **joindre les deux bouts de l'an** 'join the two ends of the year'.

'I don't blame her in the least for going off the deep end, refusing to listen to a word I said.'

Alexander Fullerton *Other Men's Wives*

Go off the deep end 'become extremely angry or emotional' is a fairly modern expression, apparently connected with the deep end of a swimming pool. A more recent phrase still which has the same meaning is **go ape**. The allusion here is easy to understand, human behaviour being compared to that of the animal; the swimming pool allusion is more mysterious. Perhaps angry gesticulations suggested the frantic body movements of a non-swimmer in deep water.

To **throw someone into the deep end** is another modern phrase derived from a swimming pool. It is applied especially to people who are new to a job and are very quickly faced with its most difficult aspects, instead of being exposed over a period of time to increasingly difficult tasks. Metaphorically, they are thrown into deep water to see whether they can swim or not.

■ EYELINES

He took all opportunities of being particular with his eyes, through which he conveyed a thousand tender protestations. She saw, and inwardly rejoiced at the humility of his looks; but, far from rewarding it with one approving glance, she industriously avoided this ocular intercourse.

Tobias Smollett *The Adventures of Peregrine Pickle*

We are all thoroughly familiar with 'ocular intercourse', as Smollett chooses to call it in the above quotation. Elsewhere in *The Adventures of Peregrine Pickle* he also refers to 'the silent rhetoric of tender looks' and discusses 'the subject of love, upon which he expatiated with great art and elocution, using not only the faculty of speech, but also the language of the eyes, in which he was a perfect connoisseur'.

'She's been giving us the eye ever since we came in.'

Michael Rumaker *The Bar*

Eye language is certainly much used for amorous purposes. A person who **gives someone the eye** is making it clear by facial gestures that a closer acquaintanceship would not come amiss, that the person being given the eye arouses sexual interest. The fuller form of this expression is to **give someone the glad eye**, where 'glad' appears to have its obsolete sense of 'shining'.

'All the bronzed young foremen would make eyes at me, and I would be spoilt. But if she was there she could glare back at them and turn them to stone.'

John Sherwood *The Half Hunter*

To **make eyes at someone** also expresses a sexual interest in a person. Once again there is a fuller form of the phrase, to **make sheep's eyes at someone**. In the 16th century the phrase is usually found as **cast** or **throw a sheep's eye at** or **upon someone**, a sheep seemingly having the ability to suggest when it looks at a person that it is dying of love. Jonathan Swift amused himself with the phrase in his *Polite Conversation*: 'I have often seen him cast a sheep's eye out of a calf's head at you.'

When amorous glances were mutually exchanged, 17th-century writers talked of two people **changing** or **mingling eyes**. In *The Tempest* Prospero fondly remarks of his daughter Miranda and Ferdinand, who have instantly fallen in love: 'At the first sight / They have chang'd eyes.' In the more modern idiom, they **only have eyes for** one another.

Shakespeare was the first to suggest another metaphor which describes the delight that a lover feels when he is looking at the object of his affections – he **feasts his eyes upon** her. Sonnet 47 begins:

> Betwixt mine eye and heart a
>   league is took,
> And each doth good turns now
>   unto the other.
> When that mine eye is famish'd
>   for a look,
> Or heart in love with sighs himself
>   doth smother;
> With my love's picture then my
>   eye doth feast,
> And to the painted banquet bids
>   my heart.

'Feast one's eyes on' is used less poetically in ordinary conversation. 'Feast your eyes on that' can mean little more than 'take a good look at that', though there is a clear implication that what is referred to, whether it be an object or a person, is **easy on the eye** 'pleasant to look at'.

Her husband tried to catch her eye with a pleading expression.

Clifford Hanley *The Taste of Too Much*

The language of the eyes is not only a language of love. We might try to **catch someone's eye** 'make eye contact with someone' for a variety of reasons. 'Catching' seems to be an odd word to use, suggesting that an eye is being tossed around like a tennis ball, but the verb is used in its basic sense of stopping something, holding it in a fixed position. We have 'caught someone's eye' when they look at us directly and are able to see and respond to our facial gestures, to know what we are thinking without our having to put our thoughts into words.

The fact that we have to 'catch someone's eye' correctly implies that a person will normally be looking from one person or one object to another, constantly changing the direction of his gaze. To some extent, then, everyone has a **roving eye**, though we reserve that description for someone who is constantly looking for new sexual partners.

'You did not meet his eye. What did you expect in return?'

William Trevor *The Old Boys*

Someone may be well aware that we are trying to 'catch his eye' but deliberately avoid direct eye contact. He refuses to **meet our eye**, as we express it. This describes a visual sensation in terms of touch, an example of a device frequently employed in poetry and known as a synaesthetic metaphor. It is much the same as Shakespeare's mixing of the sensual references in the opening speech of *Twelfth Night*, with its 'sweet sound / That breathes upon a bank of violets / Stealing and giving odour'.

We extend 'meet someone's eye' into the fixed phrase **more than meets the eye**, by which we imply that a person or thing has hidden depths that need investigation. In *Getting it Right* Elizabeth Jane Howard remarks that art 'is for showing people that there is a lot more to things than usually meets the eye'.

'Cats and birds do not see eye to eye.'

William Trevor *The Old Boys*

Metaphorically, to **see eye to eye** with someone is to agree with him. 'The only time we ever do see eye to eye with women is when we're layin' inside them' says a male chauvinist in Leslie Thomas's *Tropic of Ruislip*. John Braine, in *Life at the Top*, has: 'I have worked for your father-in-law. We never saw eye to eye.'

The original reference to 'seeing eye to eye' is in the Old Testament, where in Isaiah 52.8 we are told: 'Hark, your watchmen lift up their voice, together they sing for joy; for eye to eye they see the return of the Lord to Zion.' It seems to have been from this idea of a number of people seeing the same thing that the figurative sense of being in agreement arose.

'You don't expect me to turn a blind eye to murder, do you?'

Joyce Porter *Dover One*

To **turn a blind eye to** 'pretend not to notice' tends to be applied to actions rather than people or objects. The phrase has its counterpart in 'turn a deaf ear to' something. Allusions to either phrase are possible, rather than quoting them in their full form. Alexander Fullerton, for example, in *Other Men's Wives*, has: 'In regard to what Serge had done, blind eyes seemed to be the order of the day.'

'Keep your eyes skinned for an officer of the law, dear boy, they're everywhere.'

Dane Chandos *Abbie*

The opposite thought to 'turning a blind eye' can be expressed if someone has genuinely failed to observe something. He can **have his eyes opened** by someone else. He can also be warned to **keep his eyes open**, or more graphically, to **keep his eyes skinned** or **peeled**. The latter phrases originated in the USA in the early 19th century and refer to peeling back the eyelid, which covers the eye with 'skin', in order to keep a sharp lookout. 'Got your eyes skinned to-night?' asks someone in Eric Linklater's *Poet's Pub*.

Substitution of a slang equivalent of 'eyes' is possible. A character in Geoffrey Wagner's *Sophie* is referring to customs officers when he says: 'We shall jus' keep our peepers skinned then, shan't we?'

To **clap eyes on** someone or something is to catch sight of a person or object suddenly. Dickens was one of the first to talk about 'clapping eyes on someone' in *Oliver Twist*. The only connection with the sound made by clapping the hands together is in the suddenness of the movement. The same image is evoked when we talk of someone being 'clapped in prison'.

'Didn't I have a chance to learn it with my own two eyes?'

Michael Rumaker *The Pipe*

Many other well-used expressions refer to the eyes, with metaphorical allusions of varying complexity. We affirm the truth of an assertion that something has happened by swearing that we have **seen it with our own (two) eyes**. If we observed it with great attention, mixed perhaps with astonishment, we may say that we were **all eyes** for what was going on. The phrase implies that our eyes were wide open, dominating our face more than usual.

'A sight of you is good for sore eyes; and my eyes have been sore enough too since I saw you.'

Anthony Trollope *Doctor Thorne*

A **sight for sore eyes** is someone or something that we are relieved to see, such as a person who has come to help us when we are very busy. The phrase has been in use since the 18th century and extends the idea of relief to sore eyes to feelings of relief in general. The person who comes to help is especially welcome if we are **up to our eyes** in work, almost submerged in it.

The delicacy of the eyes, and the extreme pain caused by injury to them, underlies a phrase like **do someone in the eye** 'hurt or humiliate someone' by metaphorically punching him in the eye. The same thought is present when we say that a defeat or rejection will be **one in the eye for** the person who suffers it.

To **have eyes bigger than one's stomach** is a modern phrase, often directed at greedy children who have piled a great deal of food onto a plate, only to find that they cannot eat it all. To **cry one's eyes out** is hyperbole typical of the 17th century, when the expression began to be used. It suggests that someone's eyes have been washed out of their sockets by

floods of tears. **In the twinkling of an eye** is an out-dated and rather coy phrase which refers to something that happens very quickly.

Shakespeare, as usual, can be relied upon to suggest a more impressive phrase. It is thanks to him that we speak about seeing something **in our mind's eye** when we picture it in our imagination. The phrase occurs in *Hamlet* during a memorable exchange:

> *Hamlet: My father – methinks I see my father.*
> *Horatio: Where, my lord?*
> *Hamlet: In my mind's eye, Horatio.*
> *Horatio: I saw him once; 'a was a goodly king.*
> *Hamlet: 'A was a man, take him for all in all, I shall not look upon his like again.*

■ FEATHER-BRAINED IDEAS

'Never expected anything of the sort . . . When this here old Bean told me, you could have knocked me down with a feather.'

H.G. Wells *Kipps*

You could have knocked me down with a feather means 'I was amazed'. The expression has been current since 1850 and was probably introduced by Charles Dickens. In *David Copperfield* Dr Chillip says: 'You might have knocked me down on the flat of my back, sir, with the feather of a pen.' Judith Guest says in *Ordinary People*, of a young man who is surprised: 'He looks like we could knock him over with a feather about now!' Josephine Tey also uses 'over' rather than 'down' in *The Franchise Affair*: 'She picked up the man at the next table. You could have knocked me over with a feather.'

Wilson had recognised a match in him the moment he came to Barbie, and had resolved to act with him if he could, but never to act against him. They had made advances to each other – birds of a feather, in short.

George Douglas *The House with the Green Gables*

Birds of a feather flock together is still often quoted, though speakers rarely bother to complete the sentence. 'Birds of a feather' refers to 'people of similar interests', but there is a strong implication that those interests are not legal. There was an alternative version of this proverb in the 17th century which was even more alliterative: **Fowls of a feather flock together**.

To **feather one's nest** stems from the idea of a bird making itself comfortable, but the human who indulges in this practice is often doing so at someone else's expense. The expression remains in common use, whereas it would now be unusual to hear someone being accused of **showing the white feather** 'showing fear, signs of cowardice'. The white feather was amongst the tail feathers of a game bird and showed that it was of inferior quality. To present a man with white feathers, in the days when a man had to be a man, was a dreadful insult. Their significance would probably no longer be recognized.

■ FIDDLE-FADDLE

'How's yourself, Ruth?'
'Fit as a fiddle,' she answered gaily.

E.M. Forster *Howards End*

'I'm as fit as a fiddle' says a character in **W. Somerset Maugham's** *Flotsam*

and Jetsam. As a way of saying that a person is in good health, **fit as a fiddle** is a curious expression. Some writers believe that it refers to the healthy tone of a finely-tuned fiddle, others that it originally referred to the fiddler rather than the fiddle. Fiddlers are often very active physically as they perform, and have to be in good health.

'I'm not worried about it, no,' she said. 'I've become rather used to playing second fiddle to the work that men do, even at my tender age. We haven't got a chance really, have we? The wars you fight are far more fulfilling than the relieving of a slight irritation in the loins.'

Derek Jewell *Come In No.1 Your Time Is Up*

Expressions where the fiddle itself is definitely referred to include the one applied to someone who looks miserable; he is told that he has a **face as long as a fiddle**.

To **play second fiddle** is to take a secondary role, not to be leader. Upton Sinclair extends the metaphor in *World's End* when he says: 'Was Lanny going to play second fiddle in some fashionable chamber concert?' The allusion is to a man marrying a titled woman who might rather over-shadow him.

Fiddle-de-dee and **fiddlesticks** are old-fashioned exclamations which mean 'nonsense'. The words are perhaps connected with **fiddling** in a phrase like 'fiddling about'. This in turn refers to the rapid finger movements involved in fiddling. There may also be an allusion to manual dexterity in being **on the fiddle**, which involves doing something illegal, cheating someone.

Fiddler's Green is traditionally the sailor's paradise, where all old sailors find their resting-place. Fiddlers provide the entertainment there by day and night. Wilfred Granville adds, in his *Dictionary of Sailors' Slang*: 'Being Elysium, Fiddler's Green has lasses, suitably responsive, and glasses, suitably filled.'

■ FINGERS AND THUMBS

A number of 'finger and thumb' phrases are simple figures of speech, readily understood. A clumsy person is said to be **all fingers and thumbs**, or if his clumsiness involves letting things slip from his fingers, he is a **butter-fingers**. The person who denies hitting someone else says vehemently that he didn't **lay a finger on him**. In Ruth Rendell's *The Tree of Hands* a man who is thought to have murdered a child insists: 'I never laid a finger on him, I never touched him.'

'You think you can hector me, and do as you like because you had me under your thumb in other days.'

Anthony Trollope *Doctor Thorne*

References are frequently found in literature to relationships where one person is **under someone's thumb** 'under that person's influence or control'. 'She's got you under her thumb like a husband' occurs in *The Mackerel Plaza*, by Peter de Vries. Muriel Spark, in *Memento Mori*, writes: 'She has poor Lisa right under her thumb.' Anthony Powell, in *Casanova's Chinese Restaurant*, has: 'She was two years older than George, now to all appearances completely under her thumb.' Francis King implicitly demonstrates the meaning of the phrase in *The Needle*: ' "He has been rather under your thumb ever since his return." "Not at all! He's been totally free." '

Someone who is bored is likely to

twiddle his thumbs. Apart from the tuning dials of radios, thumbs seem to be the only things that English people do 'twiddle'. Something which is over-conspicuous is said to **stick out like a sore thumb**. The phrase evokes an image of a throbbing thumb heavily wrapped in bandages, amusing as long as the thumb belongs to someone else.

'He wouldn't lift a finger for any of us.'

C.P. Snow *The Masters*

Not making the slightest effort to help is often described as **not lifting a finger**. The opposite attitude is attributed to a man in *Self*, by Beverley Nichols: 'He would **work his fingers to the bone** for her.' This shows the normal form of the expression which refers to working very hard, usually without thanks. Elizabeth Jane Howard, in *Getting it Right*, talks instead of 'wearing my fingers to the bone'.

The faintest shadows under the cheekbones. Nothing you could put your finger on, but it all added up to someone who certainly wasn't James Bond.

Ian Fleming *Diamonds are Forever*

To **put the finger on** someone is a slang expression for 'giving information to the police about a person's criminal activities'. If the accusation is made openly then one is said to **point the finger at** him. To **finger someone** refers to either of these actions. The person concerned may be **light-fingered** or **sticky-fingered**, 'have a tendency to steal'. He may even have his **fingers in the till**, 'be stealing from his employer'.

We can also **put our finger on**

something rather than someone if we identify it precisely, though in both cases the phrase may derive from an identification parade and the identification of a suspect in this way. 'In what way has she changed?' asks someone in Nina Bawden's *George Beneath a Paper Moon*. 'Hard to put a finger on,' is the reply. 'Just growing up, I suppose.'

'It will be incumbent on me to know what Tilling is thinking and feeling. My finger must be on its pulse.'

E.F. Benson *Trouble for Lucia*

If we are closely aware of what is happening in any given situation we **have our finger on its pulse**. We are metaphorically monitoring it by listening to its heart-beat. E.F. Benson's Lucia points out in *Trouble for Lucia* that Catherine the Great 'always had her finger on the pulse of her people'. Knowledge of a different kind is referred to when we **have something at our fingertips**. We can readily call necessary information to mind.

He never fussed; he was not like this new man who wanted to have his finger in every pie.

W. Somerset Maugham *The Verger*

We now talk of someone who wants to have **a finger in every pie** or **a finger in the pie** where a 16th century speaker would have said have a 'hand' in it. In both cases the implication is that the finger or hand should not be there. The person who insists in having something to do with whatever is going on is meddling where he is not wanted. In Shakespeare's *King Henry the Eighth* the Duke of Buckingham is talking about the Cardinal of York when he says: 'The devil speed him! No man's

pie is freed / From his ambitious finger.' There is usually someone in a modern business organization to whom those words could be applied.

'I wish I had been your child,' said Flick wistfully. 'How simple everything would have been then, wouldn't it?' 'If you mean that you would have twisted me round your finger even more easily than you do at present, you are probably right.'

P.G. Wodehouse *Bill the Conqueror*

Twist someone round one's (little) finger 'manipulate a person so that he does exactly what you want him to do' dates from the 18th century. The image may be drawn from equestrianism, the idea being that one has complete control over a horse even though the reins are held with only one finger. In *King Henry the Fourth,* Part One Sir Richard Vernon praises Prince Hal, who 'vaulted with such ease into his seat / As if an angel dropp'd down from the clouds / To turn and wind a fiery Pegasus, / And witch the world with noble horsemanship.' In the 'turning and winding of the fiery Pegasus' is the notion inherent in twisting a person around one's little finger.

The phrase seems to have been applied at first to masterful men, but writers often have womanly wiles in mind. In *Barnaby Rudge* Dickens has Gabriel say: 'There's my weakness. I can be obstinate enough with men if need be, but women may twist me round their fingers at their pleasure.' William J. Locke, in *Jaffery*, has: 'Of the two, Doria seemed to have unquestionably the stronger will-power. "Surely," said I, "you can twist him round your little finger."' In modern German one can say: *Ich kann ihn um den (kleinen) Finger wickeln* 'I can wind him around the (little) finger'.

'You keep your fingers crossed with a girl that age, it's all you can do.'

Nina Bawden *George Beneath A Paper Moon*

Another German phrase is *den Daumen halten* (or *drücken*) 'hold or clasp one's thumb'. In English this becomes **cross one's fingers** or **keep one's fingers crossed**. 'I've been keeping my fingers crossed' says a character in C.P. Snow's *The Affair*. Mary McCarthy, in *The Group*, has someone say 'We all had our fingers crossed'. This is one of those interesting phrases derived directly from a physical action, though the modern person who literally crosses his fingers is no longer consciously making a sign of the cross to ward off evil. He is merely hoping for good luck to come to him or to someone he has in mind.

He dropped a hint once that she need not go to quite such length in describing a novel that she was turning thumbs down on.

Mary McCarthy *The Group*

Other physical gestures have verbal equivalents. Barry Hines, in *The Blinder*, has: 'Lennie gave them **V signs** all round.' Later there is a reference to giving 'Frank and Bill the **thumbs up**'. The latter gesture, along with **thumbs down**, relates to the signals given at Roman gladiatorial games. A thumb held upwards meant that a gladiator had fought well and his life should be spared. The downward-pointing thumb conveyed a less happy message. In modern times men's lives are not at stake when these gestures are made: approval or disapproval is being shown in a more general way.

In *Life's Little Oddities* Robert Lynd has an essay called 'Thumbs Up' in which he discusses the increased use of the gesture during World War Two. 'The gesture of "thumbs up", which has recently (1940–1) spread in England, is up to a point a gesture of defiance, but it differs from all the other gestures of defiance that I know in being good-humoured. Soldiers and sailors who have been through the furnace, when they hold their thumbs up, are always smiling. Thumbs up, indeed, might be described as a manual smile.'

The V sign is a rude gesture made with the middle and index fingers extended, the other fingers being curled inwards towards the speaker's body. If the curled fingers face away from the body, the sign becomes the **V for victory**. In Britain the V sign appears to be in the process of being replaced by the extension of the single middle finger, described in American slang as **giving someone the finger**. The insult lies in the implied destination of the finger concerned, sometimes hinted at in the words which accompany the gesture: **up yours!**

There is a similar implication in the modern injunction **get/take/pull your finger out!** The phrase, which means 'stop slacking, get on with the job, work more quickly' is now used by many speakers who do not bother to ask themselves from where exactly the finger needs to be removed. American slang offers two possible answers to that question. A lazy person may be told not to **stand around with your finger up your ass**. The euphemistic version says **with your finger in your ear**.

■ FIRE ALARMS

Chapter XXXVIII. How Mr Winkle, when he stepped out of the frying-pan, walked gently and comfortably into the fire.
Charles Dickens *The Pickwick Papers*

The expression **out of the frying-pan into the fire** 'from a bad situation to one even worse', has been in regular use since the early 16th century. In ordinary speech it is not usually necessary to go beyond 'out of the frying-pan'. The listener will complete the saying for himself. Novelists can play with the idea as they will. G.B. Stern writes, in *The Matriarch*: 'He'd divorce her and you'd have to marry her, and sweat like anything to keep her for ever in humdrum rooms. Hebe in the frying-pan is happier than she'll ever be in the fire. She's got her luxuries; she's got you.'

By morning the fat was in the fire.

Mordecai Richler *The Incomparable Atuk*

Another domestic image is conjured up by **the fat is in the fire**, meaning that a great deal of trouble has been incurred and there is little now that can be done about it. Metaphorically, fat has dripped from the meat into the fire and is spitting dangerously in all directions. Perhaps the trouble has arisen because someone **played with fire** 'took foolish risks'. This idiom seems to be applied frequently to relationships which have become more intimate than was wise. 'Michael knew what he was doing,' writes Iris Murdoch in *The Bell*, of someone on the verge of an unwise relationship. 'He knew that he was playing with fire.'

'They'd have got on' –
'– like a house on fire!' My sister, as it at times happens, literally took the words out of my mouth.

Berta Ruck *Ancestral Voices*

Another expression which refers to relationships is **get on like a house on fire**. Robertson Davies, in *The Lyre of Orpheus*, uses the variant: 'We shall get on like a house afire.' The phrase dates from the early 19th century, when house-fires were more common and spread more rapidly than they do today. While the complete phrase is normally applied to 'warm' feelings which rapidly develop between two people, some make use of 'like a house on fire' as a synonym for 'with great force, vigorously'. In *The Natural* Bernard Malamud is talking of a baseball player when he writes: 'You will soon snap into your form. From there on in you will hit like a house on fire.'

People who have **many irons in the fire** are engaged in a number of business activities simultaneously. They are being likened to a busy blacksmith of old. Because of the energy they display they may be described as **balls of fire** or **fireballs**. They are progressing meteorically through life.

If everybody was going to set the world on fire, it would be a pretty hot, unpleasant place to live.

Denison Hatch *The Stork*

Such people are also those who are said to **set the world on fire**, or **set the Thames on fire** 'do remarkable things', though these phrases are often used negatively or ironically. *You All Spoken Here*, by Roy Wilder, Jr, reports that this is also the case in the southern United States. 'He'll never set a river a-fire with a split match' is used there to mean 'he won't amount to much'.

The 'setting a river on fire' metaphor is a common one, not restricted to English, nor to the Thames. *Er hat den Rhein und das Meer angezündet* 'he has set the Rhine and the ocean afire' dates from the late 16th century. *Brewer's Dictionary of Phrase and Fable* quotes a similar Latin tag that mentions the Tiber. The idea of setting a river alight clearly appealed to the imagination of our ancestors as a marvellous achievement.

Attempts have nevertheless been made to explain 'set the Thames on fire' in a more ingenious way. The existence of a dialectal word 'temse', meaning a 'sieve', especially one used in brewing, was enough to convince a writer to *Notes and Queries* in the 19th century that a lazy worker might be told ironically that 'he would not set the temse on fire'. For this one must award full marks for imagination, but the truth, as so often, is simpler than fiction.

There was a moment's silence. Delver had hung fire.

J.I.M. Stewart *The Last Tresilians*

One or two other 'fire' expressions allude to the firing of a gun. A fire-arm is said to **hang fire** if it is slow in firing. When a person metaphorically 'hangs fire' while speaking, he pauses for a moment, uncertain how to continue. Someone who is literally **in the firing line** during a battle is in a position where he can be shot; metaphorically he is in a position where he is exposed to criticism and blame.

John answered them all, 'I baptize you with water; but he who is mightier than I is coming, the thong of whose sandals I am not worthy to untie; he will baptize you with the Holy Spirit and with fire.

New Testament, Luke 3.16

Baptism of fire refers to any initial experience which is extremely trying. The phrase is often used of a young soldier, taking part in his first battle. This is in imitation of Napoleon III, who gave *recevoir le baptême du feu* 'receive the baptism of fire' that sense in the war of 1870. The phrase is often used in other contexts, such as someone's first hectic day in a new job, and was originally suggested by the passage from Luke quoted above. An article in the *Temple Dictionary of the Bible*, edited by Ewing and Thomson, assumes that St John was referring to the 'fire of zeal'.

■ FLESHING IT OUT

'What can you want to do now?' said the old lady, gaining courage.
'I wants to make your flesh creep,'
replied the boy.
This sounded like a very bloodthirsty mode of showing one's gratitude; and as the old lady did not precisely understand the process by which such a result was to be attained, all her former horrors returned.

Charles Dickens *The Pickwick Papers*

Dickens amuses himself in the above quotation with the idea of **making someone's flesh creep**. The news that is supposed to have this effect on the old lady is that Mr Tupman has been seen kissing the maiden aunt. Usually, what we have in mind when we use this expression is something rather more horrifying or repugnant. Our fear and loathing produces a physical sensation, one which has been likened since the 14th century to that of unmentionable creatures creeping over our skin.

The phrase is often used conventionally to mean little more than 'causing nervousness'. 'He gave a laugh which made my flesh creep' occurs in Zane Grey's *Betty Zane*. In

Richard Gordon's *The Face-Maker* a woman says that she wants to be aware of what is happening to her during an operation. 'The surgeon looked doubtful. "We've got some pretty frightening-looking toys up there." "Now you're trying to make my flesh creep."'

How he had yearned for the flesh-pots of Toronto.

Mordecai Richler *The Incomparable Atuk*

In other expressions 'flesh' is used for the body. **Sins of the flesh** include lechery and gluttony, catered for in the **flesh-pots** of the world. 'Flesh-pots' were once literally pots in which meat was cooked. They were associated with places where one could live luxuriously by the reference to 'the flesh-pots of Egypt' at Exodus 16.3: 'And the whole congregation of the people of Israel murmured against Moses and Aaron in the wilderness, and said to them, "Would that we had died by the hand of the Lord in the land of Egypt, when we sat by the flesh-pots and ate bread to the full; for you have brought us out into this wilderness to kill this whole assembly with hunger."'

■ FLITCH IN TIME

For many centuries pig-meat, in the form of pork or bacon, was the meat normally eaten in English rural areas. Bacon, in particular, was so closely associated with peasants that Shakespeare has Falstaff say, in *King Henry the Fourth,* Part One: 'On, bacons, on! What, ye knaves!' By 'bacons' he meant men who were later to be called 'chaw-bacons', rustics who were constantly chewing bacon. They were 'bacon-fed knaves', as Falstaff also calls them.

'I think you might offer me some sort of explanation.'
'For saving your bacon?'

Alexander Fullerton *Other Men's Wives*

References to **saving one's bacon** occur only after Shakespeare's death, but he would have understood the phrase to refer to **saving one's skin**, **hide** or **neck**. To 'save someone's bacon' is to save him from injury, loss or danger. The 'bacon' is his own 'bacon-fed' body, not a flitch of bacon that he happens to be carrying. It has even been suggested that 'bacon' in this context originally referred to the buttocks. The idea is appealing, even though there is no evidence to support it. As it happens, the words 'bacon, buttock and back' are all closely linked etymologically.

To 'save someone's bacon' continues in fairly regular use. It can even refer to several people at once. 'Help will come but not in time to save our bacon,' says a speaker in Alistair Maclean's *The Dark Crusader*. In Josephine Tey's *The Franchise Affair* an Englishman says to a Dane: 'You have saved our bacon', and is obliged to explain what he means. Had the novel been written more recently there would no doubt have been a joke about Danish bacon.

Americans seem to have more fondness for the phrase to **bring home the bacon**. It can mean 'to succeed with one's projects' or 'earn enough to support oneself and the family'. *Bailey's Dictionary* of 1720 defines the cant meaning of 'bacon' as 'the Prize, of whatever kind which Robbers make in their Enterprizes'. He makes no reference, however, to 'bringing home the bacon', which is modern and appears to have been launched in the USA.

That fact makes it extremely unlikely that the phrase could have anything to do with the famous Dunmow Flitch, awarded every four years at Great Dunmow in Essex, to a married couple who can prove that they have not quarrelled for a year and a day. American commentators must surely be correct in citing the practice at rural fairs of holding pig-catching contests, the pig being covered with grease. Whoever manages to catch the pig 'brings home the bacon'.

■ FLY-PAST

But in every ointment there is a fly, in every good thing a catch of some sort.

P.G. Wodehouse *Cocktail Time*

The 'ointment' referred to in **fly in the ointment** was that used by the ancient Hebrews after washing. It was made of oil and various sweet-smelling substances and could be used on the hair and beard as well as the skin, which it was thought to keep soft. To put ointment on ('anoint') the feet of a person was to pay him special honour.

There are many references to ointment and anointing in the Bible, including the passage at Ecclesiastes 10.1: 'Dead flies make the perfumer's ointment give off an evil odour.' The passage continues: 'So a little folly outweighs wisdom and honour.' In modern times we think in a different way of the 'fly in the ointment'. It is whoever or whatever spoils an otherwise satisfactory situation.

J.I.M. Stewart uses the phrase in *A Use of Riches* and seems to imagine flies of different sizes causing smaller or greater problems: 'He felt a little bad, perhaps, that he and poor old Hugo Petford-Smith belonged to the same regiment. Still, it was only a small fly in the ointment.' In *Exit*, Harry Farjeon is more concerned with how many flies there are: 'That, from my point of view, is the one fly in the ointment.'

O. Henry, in *The Love-Philtre of Ikey Schoenstein*, says: 'The fly in Ikey's ointment (thrice welcome, pat trope) was Chunk McGowan.' 'Pat' here means 'apt', while 'trope' refers to the figurative use of a word or phrase. The 'fly in the ointment' expression is apt because Ikey is a pharmacist.

He didn't like people to think he was brutal. He had the name of being a gentleman, a decent man who wouldn't hurt a fly.

Edna O'Brien *The Country Girls*

In *Tristram Shandy*, Laurence Sterne says of his uncle Toby: 'He was of a peaceful, placid nature, no jarring element in it, all was mixed up so kindly within him; my uncle Toby had scarce a heart to retaliate upon a fly. Go, says he, one day at dinner, to an over-grown one which had buzzed about his nose, and tormented him cruelly all dinner-time, and which after infinite attempts he had caught at last, as it flew by him; I'll not hurt thee, says my uncle Toby, rising from his chair, and going across the room, with the fly in his hand, I'll not hurt a hair of thy head: – Go, says he, lifting up the sash, and opening his hand as he spoke, to let it escape; go, poor devil, get thee gone, why should I hurt thee? – This world surely is wide enough to hold both thee and me.'

Sterne goes on in this famous passage to speak with great feeling about the influence this childhood incident had on him. The phrase **would not hurt** (or **harm**) **a fly** no doubt alludes to it. Edna O'Brien, in *Girl with Green*

Eyes, writes: 'You know me,' Tim Healy said, 'I wouldn't hurt a fly.' John Updike, in *Rabbit Redux*, has: '"I did tell him what a gentle brother you were." "Never hurt a fly if he could help it, used to worry me."'

He winked at Roger, plainly indicating that there were no flies on Mr Alec Blake.

Henry Cecil *Brothers in Law*

No flies on someone was originally a metaphor drawn from flies buzzing around a horse. It has been influenced by the slang meaning of 'fly', which is 'artful, knowing', and has come to have roughly that meaning. 'Mum was awful fly, much flier than dad' writes David Walker, in *Geordie*. Also slangy is **bar-fly**, describing someone who is constantly in bars and pubs.

One other modern phrase is **fly on the wall**, used to describe a hidden or unnoticed observer. The expression is much-used in connection with a certain kind of television documentary, though in normal conversation one might say: 'I wouldn't mind being a fly on the wall when he tells the boss he's leaving.'

■ FOOTNOTES

If Isidore put his foot down and made it clear what marrying such a fellow entailed, the whole thing would blow over.

Frederic Raphael *The Limits of Love*

To **put one's foot down** now means to be firmly insistent about something, usually something that one does not want to happen. Typical usage is seen in William J. Locke's *Jaffery*: 'You must put your foot down. You mustn't let him do it.' Even when one

appears to be 'putting one's foot down' for a positive reason, as in J.I.M. Stewart's *The Last Tresilians*: 'I put my foot down, I insisted that the whole thing, lock, stock and barrel, should be by Leonard Benton Curry,' there is an implicit suggestion of something else that is being prevented.

The earlier forms of this phrase, which came into use in the 19th century, always referred to putting one's foot down *on* something. Metaphorically, a person was holding something down with his foot or crushing it underfoot and destroying it. When the preposition does survive, writers are not always clear about where to place it. Upton Sinclair, in *World's End*, has: 'This is one thing on which I have to put down my foot.' Mary McCarthy, in *The Group*, has the equally clumsy: 'You did not have your relations to live with you if you wanted your marriage to succeed; it was the one thing on which you put your foot down.'

I was rested by not having to think of things to say by myself, so I put my best foot forward.

Ian Jefferies *Thirteen Days*

Put one's best foot forward is grammatically curious as it stands, but could be thought of as a jumbled form of 'put one's foot forward as best one can'. In the 17th century 'better foot' was used, and the phrase had a literal meaning of walking somewhere as quickly as possible. In Shakespeare's *Titus Andronicus*, Aaron says:

> Come on, my lords, the better foot
>   before;
> Straight will I bring you to the
>   loathsome pit
> Where I espied the panther fast
>   asleep.

'Put one's best foot forward' could still have the meaning of going somewhere on foot as quickly as possible, but it is more often employed metaphorically. In the Jefferies quotation above the meaning is 'made the best effort I could to carry on a conversation'. Ivy Compton-Burnett, in *A House and Its Head*, has: 'We can best repay him by throwing up our heads, facing the four winds squarely, and putting our best foot foremost out of the morass.' The meaning here is 'do our best in every possible way'. This quotation also demonstrates the fixed form of the phrase: a plural subject does not cause a change to 'putting our best feet forward'.

'He obviously gets off on the wrong foot with his colleagues.'

Angus Wilson *Anglo-Saxon Attitudes*

Along with the notion of a 'better' or 'best' foot, we commonly talk about having a 'wrong' foot. We **get off on the wrong foot with someone** when our relationship begins badly because of a tactless remark or misunderstanding. 'We got off on the wrong foot, you and I, Sergeant,' says a soldier in Ian Jefferies' *Thirteen Days*. Kingsley Amis, in *Lucky Jim*, has the similar: 'Afraid I got off on the wrong foot with you last night.' *To Kill a Mockingbird*, by Harper Lee, has: 'You're starting off on the wrong foot in every way.'

This phrase is optimistic in that it assumes that the relationship concerned could become much better. It has simply got away to a faltering start. The people involved are temporarily out of step with one another, but by being more careful when they start to move forward again, all will be well. The image brought to mind is of a couple in a three-legged race who have fallen over because of uncoordinated movements. Both remain convinced that they will make good progress once a minor problem has been solved.

Should I have declared that I'd never set foot in the place before (which I had), or should I have pretended I ate there all the time?

Margaret Drabble *The Middle Ground*

English speakers have referred to **setting foot in** a place since the 15th century. The phrase is still in common use with the meaning 'enter, go inside', especially, as the Margaret Drabble quotation suggests, when there is a negative emphasis. 'I won't set foot in that place again' makes its point more firmly than 'I won't go in there again'.

'A haulier should get his foot in the door of every warehouse in the area.'

R.F. Delderfield *Theirs Was the Kingdom*

To **get one's foot in the door** is often used metaphorically to mean 'establish close contact with someone'. This may be a business contact, as in the above quotation, or a more personal one. A young man is said to 'have his foot in the door' when he has been invited to a girl's house and met her parents.

A less happy situation is referred to if somebody has **one foot in the grave**. The phrase came into use in the 19th century and originally meant that someone was at the point of death. It is now sometimes used humorously by a person who is getting on in years and jokingly says of himself that he has 'one foot in the grave'.

It is unlikely to be such a person who **plays footsie** with someone. This involves surreptitiously touching the foot of someone who is sitting nearby with one's own foot as a way of indicating sexual interest. The response may be negative, in the form of a kick, or positive in the form of a returned pressure. The latter may lead the people concerned to **play kneesie**.

They were dragging their feet really, Barry knew, because after that, unless someone came in with an order in the next couple of days, there'd be nothing.

Ruth Rendell *The Tree of Hands*

The expressions discussed above all make use of 'foot', which remains invariably singular. A number of other phrases mention 'feet'. To **drag one's feet**, for instance, is used purely figuratively and means to be slow or ineffective in whatever one happens to be doing. There is often a suggestion that the slowness is deliberate, that it is meant to sabotage someone else's efforts or cause annoyance.

'Later, they will have to decide for themselves, find their own feet.'

J.I.M. Stewart *A Use of Riches*

Those who **find their feet** learn to become independent, confident in their own abilities. The allusion is to a toddler who gradually learns how to walk unaided. Adults placed in a strange environment metaphorically become infants again, needing constant help. They 'find their feet' as they become familiar with their surroundings, with what needs to be done, and so on. 'What Baba doesn't know is that I'm finding my feet' occurs in Edna O'Brien's *Girl with Green Eyes*. Ruth Rendell, in *Talking to Strange Men*, has: 'I think you've all settled in pretty well, don't you, and found your feet.' 'Found y'feet yet, have you?' asks someone in

Alexander Fullerton's *Other Men's Wives*.

He was bitterly disliked in Warsaw. He had fallen on his feet too many times.

Penelope Gilliatt *A State of Change*

To **fall on one's feet** is to be lucky, to obtain a successful result even in circumstances where disaster would have seemed a more likely outcome. The allusion is to a cat, famed for its capacity for survival and reputed always to land on its feet no matter how it falls. A typical person who 'falls on his feet' is sacked from his job unexpectedly, but soon afterwards – because he is now immediately available – is able to take up a much better post.

'It'll be funny not having you under my feet all day.'

James Mitchell *When the Boat Comes in*

It tends to be a housewife who talks about having her children and husband **under her feet** if they are around the house all day. They are near her all the time so that she seems to tread on their toes whenever she turns around.

Another domestic image is created by **put one's feet up** 'relax in a chair'. Originally the person relaxing would have put his feet on a footstool, or would have supported his feet in some other way. The emphasis in the phrase is no longer on this specific raising of the feet, merely on resting. Leslie Thomas's *Tropic of Ruislip* has: 'When you get in from the City it must be very nice just to put your feet up for a few minutes.' 'Just you put your feet up' is spoken by an elderly housewife to her husband in James Mitchell's *When the Boat Comes in.*

'Poor thing,' said Mrs Mark. 'I've walked you off your feet.'

Iris Murdoch *The Bell*

A person may need to 'put his feet up' because he has been 'walked off his feet'. To **walk someone off his feet** is to tire him out by making him walk too far or too fast. He is almost literally forced off his feet by being obliged to rest. A romantic young lady might prefer to be **swept off her feet** 'overwhelmed with love'. The phrase manages to suggest a man who literally lifts a woman in his arms and twirls her around, so that she hardly knows what is happening. The expression is metaphorical, however, and a man can also be swept off his feet if he suddenly falls in love.

She had taken Kay up for all she was worth, because Kay, as she said, was 'malleable' and 'capable of learning'. Now she claimed to have detected that Kay had feet of clay, which was rather a contradiction, since wasn't clay malleable?

Mary McCarthy *The Group*

Mary McCarthy amuses herself in the above quotation with the phrase **feet of clay**. To find that someone who is greatly admired has 'feet of clay' is to discover that he has a basic weakness or fault. The allusion is to the Old Testament, Daniel 2.31, where Daniel first correctly describes and then interprets a dream that has been troubling King Nebuchadnezzar. The king had dreamed of an image, the head of which 'was of fine gold, its breast and arms of silver, its belly and thighs of bronze, its legs of iron, its feet partly of iron and partly of clay.'

Daniel interpreted the feet of iron and clay as a divided kingdom brought about by marriage. It would not hold together, 'just as iron does not mix with clay'. A statue made of the strongest metals in its upper parts would still be toppled if there was a weakness at its base; a kingdom would likewise collapse if a fundamental weakness was introduced.

■ FOOTWEAR

'In this case, I think perhaps the boot's rather on the other foot.'

Angus Wilson *Anglo-Saxon Attitudes*

'Don't think I'm doing anything for you in putting you up,' writes W. Somerset Maugham in *The End of the Flight*, 'the boot's on the other leg'. This looks like one of Maugham's typically personal versions of well-known expressions, since most people would say or write **the boot's on the other foot** to mean that the situation is now reversed. **On the other leg**, however, was the earlier version according to *The Oxford English Dictionary*. Nina Bawden, in *George Beneath a Paper Moon*, has: 'Don't say listen Leila, listen Leila, to me anymore; it's time the boot was on the other foot, don't you think? I'm older than you, George.'

He was getting too big for his boots.

Ruth Rendell *Talking to Strange Men*

Too big for one's boots is also found as **too big for one's breeches**, as in Upton Sinclair's *World's End*: 'All our working men have got too big for their breeches.' The basic idea in both versions of the phrase is that the person concerned is getting an inflated or swollen idea of his own importance. Someone accused of excessive servility is said to be a **boot-**

licker, prepared to **lick the boots** of anyone who is senior in the hierarchy. The coarser version of this phrase refers to **arse-licking**, alluded to in its turn in **brown-nosing**.

Tough as old boots, that woman, for all her performances.

Margaret Laurence *The Diviners*

The simile as **tough as old boots** has been applied to people since the 1870s. **Put the boot in** 'behave in a ruthless manner' is a modernism, alluding to the unpleasant habit of thugs administering a brutal kicking to a victim. **Boot-legging**, with reference to the smuggling of alcohol, especially during the Prohibition period in the USA, was so-called because smugglers hid bottles in the tops of knee-length boots.

Pull oneself up by one's own bootstraps compares someone who improves his position in life by his own efforts to someone who uses the bootstrap – the loop sewn on to the back of a boot – to pull on his own boots. This phrase in turn suggested **boot up** to computer designers as a term which could refer to the automatic loading of programs when the machine is switched on.

'I wouldn't accept, if I were in your shoes.'

Richard Gordon *The Face-Maker*

One or two 'shoe' phrases exist alongside those that feature 'boots'. To **shake in one's shoes** is to be afraid. **If I were in your shoes** is a long-winded way of saying 'if I were you'. The idea of putting oneself in someone else's shoes also gives rise to **dead men's shoes**, jobs that are taken over only when those who previously did them retire or die. The phrase is used of a situation where promotion

is unlikely to occur other than in such circumstances. Raymond Williams, in *Border Country*, has: 'They stop me crawling about in the world, looking for dead men's shoes.'

■ FOR WHOSE SAKE?

'For Pete's sake, sit down,' Max hissed.

Bernard Malamud *The Natural*

Writers are not sure whether they are talking about a person when they use the exclamatory phrase **for Pete's sake**. Some give 'Pete' a capital letter: 'What on earth did they *think* you were made of, for Pete's sake?' says a woman in Elizabeth Jane Howard's *Getting it Right*. Others treat 'pete' as a word rather than a name: 'Watch, for pete's sake, watch!' is in Judith Guest's *Ordinary People*. Michael Rumaker, in *Exit 3*, has: 'For pete's sake, don't start that again.'

The phrase is obviously the equivalent of **for God's sake**, **for Christ's sake**, **for heavens' sake**, **for goodness' sake** and the rarer **for mercy's sake**. **For pity's sake** was also much used in former times, and it seems likely that this was transformed, deliberately or accidentally, into 'for pete's sake'. In that case, 'pete' is indeed a word and should be written with a lower-case 'p'. It seems most unlikely that the allusion is to Saint Peter. Saints are not generally referred to by diminutive forms of their names.

Nevertheless, the saint's name theory cannot be totally abandoned. In *Under the Volcano*, by Malcolm Lowry, a woman says: 'For Pete's sake have a decent drink.' Elsewhere in the novel, however, someone says: 'Shut up, Geoff, **for the love of Mike!**' The more pious forms of this would be **for the love of God** or **for the love** of **Christ**, but **for the love of Pete** is also found. This may be the 'Pete' who evolved from 'pity', but 'Mike' in that case remains a mystery. A complex solution would involve the substitution of 'Mike' for 'Pete' because it was a more usual name among Roman Catholics, who in turn might have been more likely to use exclamations of this type.

■ FORTY WINKS

She was sleeping like a log.

W. Somerset Maugham *The Facts of Life*

To **sleep like a log** is so familiar an expression that it seems always to have been with us. Iris Murdoch, in *The Bell*, makes a character say: 'I'm so dead tired these days I sleep like the proverbial log. The last trump wouldn't wake me.' As it happens, 'to sleep like a log' is not *proverbial*. The phrase appeared only towards the end of the 19th century, but quickly replaced the earlier **sleep like a top**, first used in Sir William Davenant's play *The Rivals* in the 17th century. The allusion there was to the way a top remains motionless when it is spinning very quickly.

To **sleep like the dead** is another variation that has been used in the past, but 'sleep like a log' clearly leads the field in modern times. 'They're all very tired. They'll sleep like logs' is in Malcolm Bradbury's *Eating People is Wrong*. William J. Locke, in *Jaffery*, has: 'You've slept like a log all night, but Liosha and I need rest.' James Purdy varies the phrase slightly in *Eustace Chisholm and the Works*: 'He'll rest the way he always rests – like a log pile.' 'Log' has no special significance, of course, it is merely an example of something which shows no sign of life.

'I didn't sleep a wink.'

William Trevor *The Old Boys*

Those who habitually sleep like logs might say that getting to sleep is **as easy as falling off a log**, where a log that is floating in the river is meant. Insomniacs tend to claim that they **did not sleep a wink**, or **did not get a wink of sleep,** a dramatic statement to the effect that not even one eye was shut for a brief moment. Mary Webb says unkindly, in *Gone to Earth*: 'Mrs Marston had what she called "not a wink of sleep" – that is to say, she kept awake for half an hour after getting into bed.'

The brief nap referred to as **forty winks** may have been humorously linked originally (in the pages of *Punch* magazine) with the Thirty-nine Articles, the points of doctrine assented to by those taking orders in the Church of England. Monica Dickens alludes to the phrase in an unusual way in *The Fancy*. A man who has been woken slightly earlier than necessary tells his wife: 'I'm going to have another wink.'

■ FUSS AND FEATHERS

'Palimpsest,' says one of them to Miss Russell, 'could you give us the meaning?'
Great Scott! My heart sank for her, what a word!

Barry Oakley *A Salute to the Great McCarthy*

Great Scott! is a euphemism for **Great God!** The phrase was first used in the USA in the mid-19th century and was presumably suggested by the fame at the time of someone called Scott. Sir Walter Scott had died in 1832; the explorer Robert Falcon Scott was not born until 1868. The best-known Scott when this phrase came into use, especially in America, was undoubtedly General Winfield Scott (1786–1866), otherwise known as 'Old Fuss and Feathers'. The nickname alluded to his notorious vanity and pomposity. This in turn may have led to 'Great Scott!' being used ironically, as if 'Scott' was a synonym for 'God'.

'Great Scott!' is now not often heard but occurs in literature. Stephen Vincent Benét, in *Everybody was Very Nice*, has: 'Great Scott, I can remember when I was just a kid and the Prentisses got divorced. They were pretty prominent people and it shook the whole town.'

The other Scott who has entered the language, for the moment, at least, is Lieutenant Commander Scott of the Starship *Enterprise*. In the American television series 'Star Trek', first shown 1966–9, Captain Kirk would usually at some stage issue the command **Beam me up**, **Scottie**. He would then disintegrate and magically reappear on board the *Enterprise*. 'Beam me up, Scottie' is sometimes used jokingly to mean 'Get me out of here' and is kept alive by ardent 'Trekkies' at numerous conventions.

■ GAMESMANSHIP

'If you play ball with me, we'll play ball with you.' (Honest to God, you'd have thought it was going to be one long tennis match.)

Alan Sillitoe *The Loneliness of the Long-Distance Runner*

Ball games of various kinds have led to a number of expressions. To **keep the ball rolling** 'to keep a communal activity going' would have been expressed as **keep the ball up** in the late 18th century. To **set the ball rolling** 'begin an activity' could also at that time have been **open the ball**, though in that wording the reference was to a formal social occasion where dancing took place. 'Ball' in that sense is connected with 'ballet' and 'ballade' and derives from Old French *baler* 'to dance'. The spherical 'ball' is a different word entirely, derived from Old Norse. Traced back far enough, it links with Latin *follis* 'bellows' and Greek *phallós* 'penis'.

Modern phrases such as **to play ball with someone** 'cooperate', **keep one's eye on the ball** 'pay attention to the matter in hand' and **the ball's in your court** 'it's your turn' are self-explanatory. 'That put the ball back in Programming's court' occurs in *Face to Face*, by Edward A. Rogers. The same novel has: 'Dale remained silent. This was Rufus Little's party. Let him carry the ball.' The specific meaning here is 'let him decide which way the conversation should proceed'. **Carry the ball** 'take on the chief role' is used in the USA but not in Britain.

To be **on the ball**, meaning to be quickly responsive and aware of everything that is happening, stems from the same idea of having one's eye on the ball. In modern soccer commentaries the player 'on the ball' is the one who has it at his feet, but this is recent usage and would not have led to the metaphor.

'I really would like to talk about the script,' said Don. 'The rushes today were a balls up.'

Penelope Gilliatt *A State of Change*

To **have a ball** or 'enjoyable time' is clearly another reference to dancing. Slang expressions such as **make a balls of** 'make a mess of' and **balls-up** 'mess, disaster' are more difficult to explain. The latter may be a British form of the American phrase to **ball** up 'to confuse, lead astray', which in turn leads to **balled-up**. There is a tendency to associate such phrases with **balls** 'testicles', but a more innocent explanation is possible. In the 19th century, when horse-drawn transport was normal, a horse was said to be 'balled-up' when it accumulated snow and ice on its hooves.

'He knows bloody well he's got us by the short hairs . . .'

John Braine *Life at the Top*

No convenient euphemistic explanation can be offered for **have someone by the balls** (**by the short and curlies**, in the modern version, refers to pubic hair). The first of these has been in use, according to Partridge's *Dictionary of Historical Slang*, since the late 19th century. The meaning given there is 'to have utterly in one's power, especially of women over men'. Needless to say, these are still phrases that could cause offence in polite circles.

■ GETTING ONE'S KICKS

'Nobody ever leaves for good,' he said, 'unless they kick the bucket somewhere.'

Alan Sillitoe *A Tree on Fire*

Kick the bucket 'to die' has often been explained in terms of a suicide kicking away the bucket on which he has stood in order to leave himself suspended. The explanation is not very convincing. The phrase seems always to have been applied to those dying naturally as well as unnaturally. Even amongst suicides, only a small proportion hang themselves, and there is no reason to think that they always choose to stand on a bucket rather than a stool or chair.

The alternative explanation is more complicated but probably nearer the truth. It depends on the fact that 'bucket' has in the past had another meaning besides 'container for liquid'. Shakespeare, for instance, uses the word to mean 'the beam of a balance or crane' in *King Henry the Fourth*, Part Two. Falstaff refers to 'he that gibbets (hangs) on the brewer's bucket'. The word in this sense is said to have survived in dialect for the beam from which pigs were suspended when slaughtered. While in that position their heels could be said to be 'kicking the bucket'.

There was a phrase **kick the beam** in use in the 18th century, the time when 'kick the bucket' began to be used. 'Kick the beam' referred literally to a scale of a balance which was so lightly loaded that it flew up and hit the cross-beam when the weight was put on the other side. Figuratively, it meant to 'fly in the air'. One can speculate that the soul of a person 'kicked the beam' in that sense when he died.

Speculation of any kind is unsatisfactory, but there is no doubt that 'bucket' formerly had the secondary meaning 'beam'. Modern French has *trébuchet* for a pair of scales used to weigh delicate objects. The *-buchet* of this word is from the same source as 'bucket' in its sense of 'beam'.

'Kick the bucket' is not an elegant phrase, but it is well used colloquially. Literary examples are also relatively common. 'I haven't finished making all my false moves yet, and I dare say I won't until I kick the bucket' is in Alan Sillitoe's *The Loneliness of the Long-Distance Runner*. James Purdy, in *Eustace Chisholm and the Works*, has: 'Should old Maureen kick the bucket, you go call on Reuben.' An earlier example is in Trollope's *Doctor Thorne*: 'You wouldn't do as young Hatherly did, when his father kicked the bucket.'

'We shall only be kicking our heels at the station.'
'Better to run no risk of missing our train,' she said.

E.F. Benson *Trouble for Lucia*

Another expression which once meant 'to die' was **kick up one's heels**. This is now mostly used to refer to having a good time, the allusion being to dancing in a vigorous way. To **kick one's heels**, by contrast, is to wait about in an irritated and bored manner, with nothing to do in theory except kick one's own heels. If the waiting is imposed by someone else, then one is being forced to **cool one's heels**. The person responsible for the waiting-period ironically supposes that one's heels have become heated by walking, and that they need to cool down. 'Turtle came in late. He kept us cooling our heels' says someone in William Trevor's *The Old Boys*.

'It's no fun any more. I used to get a kick out of playing because I knew it maddened McLeod. But now nobody cares if I play or not.'

W. Somerset Maugham *Sanatorium*

The ambiguity of 'kick' phrases is seen again in **get a kick** 'derive a pleasurable experience' out of something and the older **get the kick**, which meant to be dismissed from a job. In a job context it has been possible since the 1820s to talk of **kicking someone upstairs**, removing someone who is causing problems by theoretically promoting him. In reality his influence is restricted in his new post.

It is usually young people who are said to **kick over the traces**. The 'traces' here are part of a horse's harness, straps which attach the horse to a cart or carriage. A horse literally kicks over (above) its traces in order to kick out more freely. Figuratively the phrase means to 'refuse to accept discipline or control, to throw off the usual restraints'.

■ GETTING RATTY

He saw life, values, his relationship with Janet, slipping away in the rat race.

Edward A. Rogers *Face to Face*

The rat race is now a much-used expression, referring to an individual's daily competitive struggle in professional life. It is a marathon race where one has to keep up with the others or be overtaken. It is also a race where one is forced to be a rat, 'someone who behaves in an unpleasant or despicable way'. C.P. Snow uses 'rat race' in a rather special way in *The Affair*: 'Once more the useless rat race of anxiety went on in my mind.'

'Rat race' is modern, but 'race' itself has been used since the 16th century to refer to the course of life, or part of it. Dryden talks of 'the race of life'; William Cowper, in *Tirocinium* (1784), has: 'The well-known place / Whence first we started into life's long race.'

As for rats, man's continuing hatred of them is reflected in opprobrious words which we apply to nasty people: someone is a 'rat', a 'ratbag', a 'ratfink'. 'Rat' is especially applied to someone who disappears at times of difficulty, an allusion to the old superstition that rats desert a ship which is doomed to sink on its next voyage. 'Ratfink' is used in American slang, both parts of the word meaning a scab who works during an official strike. 'Rats!' itself is for some people an expression of disgust.

They know we hate their guts and smell a rat if they think we're trying to be nice to them.

Alan Sillitoe *The Loneliness of the Long-Distance Runner*

To **smell a rat** 'sense that there is dirty work afoot' and **like** or **as wet as a drowned rat** have also been in use since the 16th century. Other similes which were in use at that time, such as **drunk as a rat**, **poor as a rat**, **weak as a rat** are no longer in common use, though the first of these has been resurrected in modern times as **rat-arsed**. 'Smell a rat', however, has always been a popular expression and is still found on all sides. 'He had some other strongish reason – I don't know what – to smell a rat' is in Geoffrey Household's *Watcher in the Shadows*. Angus Wilson, in *Anglo-Saxon Attitudes*, has: 'He smelt a rat, but he kept mum.' 'He only got what he deserved. He should have smelt a rat' is in W. Somerset Maugham's *An Official Position*. 'I smelled a rat and he smells to high heaven!' is said by a character in Truman Capote's *Jug of Silver*.

Given the long-standing and widespread hatred of rats, Kenneth Grahame's achievement in making Ratty a sympathetic character in *The Wind in the Willows* seems the more remarkable. There is a human Ratty in Samuel Lover's *Handy Andy*, though the boy concerned explains that his name is really Horatio.

■ GETTING STONED

Being very anxious to leave no stone unturned, I waited until Mr Spenlow came in, and then described what had passed.

Charles Dickens *David Copperfield*

Picturesque Expressions, edited by Laurence Urdang, assigns a classical origin to **leave no stone unturned** 'do everything possible to accomplish one's aim'. The expression is said to be the advice 'purportedly given by the Oracle of Delphi to Polycrates the Cretan when he asked where he could find the treasure believed to have been hidden by Mardonius, a Persian general whom he had defeated at the Battle of Plataea (477 BC). Upon following this advice, Polycrates located the treasure beneath the stone floor of Mardonius' tent'.

There are problems with this explanation: the Battle of Plataea took place two years earlier than stated, and it was Pausanias, not Polycrates, who defeated and killed Mardonius. Nevertheless, the Greeks were no doubt familiar with the idea contained in this phrase, which has been used in English metaphorically since the 16th century. Early writers sometimes referred to 'moving' or 'rolling' every stone, but none makes mention of an oracular pronouncement. There is probably no need to do so – the meaning of the phrase is self-evident. Modern use of the phrase is seen in William Golding's *Free Fall*: 'I can't take any risks at all. No stone unturned, Sammy, no avenue unexplored.'

'There is – there was – a range of stables, a stone's throw from the villa.'

J.I.M. Stewart *A Use of Riches*

Other popular phrases which feature

'stones' are also mostly self-explanatory. Something that is within a **stone's throw** is obviously only a short distance away. To say that trying to get money, sympathy, help or whatever from someone is like trying to get **blood from a stone** also makes it clear that the task is impossible. In the 17th century, the connection between 'blood' and 'money' was well established. Getting someone to part with a substantial sum of money was commonly referred to as 'bleeding him'. We might still today talk of **bleeding someone white** 'getting someone to part with all his money'. 'They've all bled poor Lisa white,' says Muriel Spark in *Memento Mori*, meaning 'they have all sponged on her'.

You cannot get blood from a stone is proverbial. Other proverbs include **People in glass houses should never throw stones** 'no one should criticize others if he is open to the same criticism himself', and **A rolling stone gathers no moss** 'a person who never settles avoids taking on responsibilities'.

The modern phrase to **get stoned** 'be heavily under the influence of alcohol or narcotics' appears to allude to the primitive punishment of stoning someone. It may therefore be based on the idea of self-inflicted punishment. The phrase was first applied in the USA to getting drunk on wine.

■ GIFT ELEPHANTS

'Perhaps, Provost, before we break up, you will give us some idea of where this monstrous white elephant is to be accommodated?'

J.I.M. Stewart *The Last Tresilians*

There are two familiar phrases in English connected with the ancient kingdom of Siam (now Thailand). One of them is **white elephant** 'a possession that is nominally valuable but is of little practical use or worth'. It is likely to absorb its owner's money in maintenance costs. The 'white elephant' referred to in the above quotation, for instance, is a collection of coins and art which will need a special building to house it. In this instance, use of the 'white elephant' phrase causes the same speaker a little later to substitute 'elephant' for 'cat' and ask: 'Have I let the elephant out of the bag?'

The story that gave rise to the figurative use of 'white elephant' was that the King of Siam, if he took a dislike to one of his courtiers, would present him with a white elephant. Such animals were venerated and not allowed to work. The courtier who received the gift could not, as it were, look a gift elephant in the mouth. He was obliged to keep the animal and pay for its upkeep over a long period, with no hope of getting anything in return.

Evelyn Waugh has fun with the phrase in *Work Suspended*: 'It was a large canvas at which he had been at work intermittently since 1908. Even he spoke of it, with conscious understatement, as "something of a white elephant". White elephants indeed were almost the sole species of four-footed animal that was not somewhere worked into this elaborate composition.'

The second familiar phrase is **Siamese twins**, so-called because of Chang and Eng, born in Siam in the early part of the 19th century. The twins were joined together at the waist. For many years, until they died in 1874, they were a famous exhibit in Barnum's Circus. In allusion to the twins there was at one time a **Siamese coupling**, which referred to a method of joining fire-hoses.

■ GOBBLEDEGOOK

The companies were suspicious he might be a flash in the pan. 'By the end of the season, if you keep on like you're going, they'll be ready to talk turkey, then we'll put the heat on.'

Bernard Malamud *The Natural*

Talk turkey is American slang for 'talk bluntly and plainly'. One can also **talk cold turkey**, which means 'make a frank statement, especially about something unpleasant'. The 'cold turkey' image is based on the idea of the meat being eaten without any fancy accompaniments. 'Talking turkey' may derive from the same idea, though American linguists insist on repeating an absurd story about a discussion between a native American and a white man about hunting spoils. The discussion supposedly centred on which of them was to have a crow and which a turkey. In J.I.M. Stewart's *The Last Tresilians* occurs: 'I wanted to talk, and have her talk, straight turkey.' Later in the same novel is: 'Meanwhile, that turkey had to be talked!'

American drug addicts are sometimes subjected to a **cold turkey cure**. This involves having all supplies of a drug stopped abruptly, rather than the quantity gradually being reduced. Once again 'cold turkey' is used as an image of plainness and lack of subtlety.

The menus are in hectographed handwriting. Nelson's face tightens, studying it. 'It's all in gobbledygook.'

John Updike *Rabbit Redux*

People who use pompous and unintelligible professional jargon could be said to be 'talking turkey' in a different kind of way. **Gobbledegook**

(also spelt **gobbledygook**), is derived from the guttural gobbling sound made by a male turkey. The word is used by some speakers, as in the Updike quotation above, in the more general sense of 'unintelligible language'.

■ GOING DUTCH

'Do you think I can't work without Dutch courage?'
'Scatcherd, I know there is brandy in the room at this moment, and that you have been taking it within these two hours.'

Anthony Trollope *Doctor Thorne*

Dutch courage 'a false courage induced by drinking alcohol' used to be known in English as **pot-valour**. The rivalry between the Dutch and the English in the 17th and early 18th centuries caused many derisive remarks to come into being, of which 'Dutch courage' is one that remains current. The obvious inference is that the Dutch themselves were only valiant after they had been drinking. Another possibility, however, is that English soldiers who went to the Netherlands made use of spirits such as gin to bolster themselves. The phrase 'Dutch courage' continues to be well used. Richard Gordon's *The Face-Maker* has: 'The coming interview had blunted his appetite for food while sharpening it for the drink, leaving him flushed and muzzy. Not that he needed Dutch courage, he told himself. After all, he had been through the experience once already.'

I hit upon the idea of talking Double Dutch to him. You know – Twinkle Twinkle Little Star becomes Twimginkle Twimginkle Limgittle Starmgar. I learned it in the wimgink of an eye.

Dane Chandos *Abbie*

Double Dutch 'gibberish' has been used only since the 19th century. Any foreign tongue sounds like gibberish if one has no knowledge of it, and it is not unusual for it to be interpreted as nonsense. 'Double Dutch' is heard very infrequently in modern times: the speaker who uses it in the above quotation makes use of a far more current expression when she says to her nephew 'We'll go Dutch, darling boy'.

Going Dutch 'paying for one's own meal or paying an equal share of the bill in a restaurant' is now more usual, women having established their right to be independent. The phrase came into use at the beginning of the 20th century in the form **Dutch treat**. The original reference was to parties to which everyone brought some food. Truman Capote, in *Shut a Final Door*, has: 'The bar was closing. They went Dutch on the check and, while waiting for the change, neither spoke.'

'If he ain't got enough out on 'em, Sammy, to make him free of the water company for life, I'm one Dutchman, and you're another, and that's all about it.'

Charles Dickens *The Pickwick Papers*

I'm a Dutchman is a phrase which is always preceded by a conditional statement – if such is the case, then I'm a Dutchman. This says in a roundabout way that the speaker is convinced that the condition does not apply, since he clearly is not a Dutchman. In his short story *The Unconquered*, Somerset Maugham writes: 'If that didn't mean that his colouring had made an impression on her he was a Dutchman.' English football managers appear to have adopted the phrase recently, making remarks like: 'If that wasn't off-side, then I'm a Dutchman.'

When he talked to her today like a Dutch uncle, it was because he was trying to teach her the trade.

Mary McCarthy *The Group*

Don't give me the Dutch Uncle just because I made a joke,' says a character in Len Deighton's *Funeral in Berlin*. He means: 'Don't lecture me in a severe way.' The Dutch, especially in Pennsylvania, had the reputation of being disciplinarians, though a 'Dutch uncle' would be expected to mix severity with avuncular kindliness.

To **talk to someone like a Dutch uncle** remains more American than British. A British phrase, by contrast, is **my old Dutch** 'my wife', made famous by a song of the same title, composed and sung by the music-hall star Albert Chevallier (1861–1923). It includes the lines: 'There ain't a lady livin' in the land/As I'd swop for my dear old Dutch.' Chevallier himself said his wife's face reminded him of a Dutch clock, which was why he used the phrase. It was already in existence, however, having begun as **duchess of Fife**, Cockney rhyming slang for 'wife'.

■ GOING STRAIGHT

'Shall we join the lady?' he said roughly, already making a beeline for the door.

Richard Hughes *The Fox in the Attic*

Pollen-bearing bees are believed to return to the hive by the shortest possible route. To **make a beeline** for someone or something is therefore to go in a direct line to the person or object. The expression was introduced by American writers at the beginning of the 19th century but is also used in Britain. In *The Half Hunter*, John

Sherwood imagines a rather unusual insect when he writes: 'More likely she would slip out of the flat on some pretext and make a jet-propelled beeline for the police station.'

As the crow flew, we were doing better than if we had stuck to the main road.

Joanna Jones *Nurse is a Neighbour*

The other common phrase that refers to travelling in a straight line is **as the crow flies**. In Charles Webb's *The Marriage of a Young Stockbroker*, a man is measuring the distance between two places on a map and announces that it is less than fifteen miles. 'Not by the roads,' he is told. 'You're doing it as the crow flies.'

A Dictionary of English and Folk-Names of British Birds, by H. Kirke Swann, remarks in its article on the crow (or 'carrion-crow' as it is more fully known): 'The saying "as a crow flies" refers to the rook, which flies straight across country on its homeward journey, and not to this species.' Both crow and rook belong to the genus *Corvus*, as do the raven and jackdaw: any one of these birds is likely to be referred to by laymen as a 'crow'.

'Stone the crows,' said Lester Ince.

C.P. Snow *The Affair*

Stone the crows is a meaningless exclamation of surprise or disgust. The idea of disgust is also present in to **eat crow** 'be forced to do something distasteful or humiliating, eat humble pie, back down'. The phrase is usually explained by reference to an incident in the American War of 1812. It is said that a soldier who shot a crow for sport was forced to eat part of it by the land-owner, though he afterwards compelled the landowner to eat the rest of it. 'Are you eating crow?' asks someone in *Cards of Identity*, by Nigel Dennis. In this instance a bystander comments: 'A direct apology would not be in keeping with Shubunkin's distinctive identity. Like all sexologists, he must be permitted the fullest ambiguity.'

'Mr Gourlay! I've had a crow to pick with you for more than a year.'

George Douglas *The House with the Green Shutters*

To **have a crow to pick/pluck/pull with someone** is based on the idea of animals fighting over their prey and means to have something disagreeable to settle with someone. Most speakers today would prefer to use 'have a bone to pick with someone' to express this idea (see page 199), but the 'crow' version has a long history. In the 17th century people also spoke of **pulling/plucking a crow together** if they were going to settle a dispute. *The Comedy of Errors* has: 'If a crow help us in, sirrah, we'll pluck a crow together.'

The first part of this typically Shakespearean pun refers to breaking into a house with the help of a **crowbar**. Opinions differ as to how the latter tool got its name. It was known simply as a 'crow' until the 19th century. Some scholars say it was named because one end is shaped like a crow's beak. Others say that it is a separate word, derived from Old French *cros de fer* 'iron hooks'. The latter theory is supported by the earliest references to the tool in the 14th and 15th centuries, when it was always 'crows of iron'.

■ GOING TO THE DOGS

She had led Gerrard a dog's life, but had always refused to give him his freedom.

W. Somerset Maugham *The Social Sense*

Phrases which mention dogs are very common in English. The appearance and behaviour of the animals is alluded to in detail for metaphorical purposes. Phrases which refer to their life-style in former times may look odd in a modern context, but they have not always been as pampered as they tend to be today.

To **lead someone a dog's life**, for instance, was first used in the 16th century and means to make that person's life a misery. 'Watch Committees can be devils. You've got to be top dog or they'll lead you a – er a dog's life,' says a character in Joyce Porter's *Dover One*. The author has the grace to add: 'There was a pause while both men pondered over the infelicity of this metaphor.' The 'infelicity' comes from the mixing of the two 'dog' sayings, **top dog** referring to someone who is the leader of a group in the way that one dog always emerges as leader of a pack.

'These new novels make me tired. If it's true to life, which I don't believe, the next generation is going to the dogs.'

F. Scott Fitzgerald *The Beautiful and Damned*

To **go to the dogs** 'to destruction, ruin' also dates from the 16th century. The sense is hinted at in *Macbeth*: 'Throw physic (medicine) to the dogs – I'll none of it.' There was another saying in Shakespeare's time

not to have a word to throw at a dog 'to have nothing to say'. In *As You Like It* Celia says: 'Why, Rosalind! Cupid have mercy! Not a word?' 'Not one to throw at a dog,' replies Rosalind. Celia then jests: 'No, thy words are too precious to be cast away upon curs; throw some of them at me.'

'These people are invincible,' said Mr Wilson as he introduced their next opponents to them after tea. 'I'm afraid you haven't a dog's chance.'

Martin Armstrong *Calf Love*

Not have a dog's chance 'have no chance at all' dates only from the 19th century. Earlier references to **dog-chance** are to the lowest or losing throw at dice, otherwise known as the **dog-throw**. The phrase in that sense translates Latin *canicula*. 'Not have a dog's chance' may derive from it, having begun as 'have only a dog-chance' and changed its form later.

'I hope you won't decide that sleeping dogs are best left.'

Josephine Tey *The Franchise Affair*

The fondness of dogs for sleeping leads to expressions like **dog-tired**, to **lie doggo** and the proverbial **let sleeping dogs lie**. 'Dog-tired' is 'very tired'; 'lie doggo' simply means to lie very still, like a dog; the -o ending is of no particular significance. The sleeping-dog proverb is recorded from the 14th century. It has survived because it can be so aptly applied to peaceful situations which are likely to become troublesome if someone interferes with them.

Dogs are also well-known for fighting. In World War One an aerial combat between opposing fighter planes was known as a **dog-fight** because of the constant twists and turns of the opposing aircraft. A man and woman having a dispute are said to **fight like cat and dog**, while the ruthless competition of the modern business world is sometimes described as **dog eat dog**.

The reference to 'eating' serves as a reminder that before the advent of specially-prepared tinned dog food, dogs more normally ate whatever scraps remained after a meal. This led to the use of **dog's breakfast** or **dog's dinner** to describe a muddle or mess, though in Royal Navy slang the phrase became a **monkey's breakfast**. Modern **doggy bags** supplied by restaurants now mean that even 'scraps' can be fairly luxurious.

It is humans, of course, who eat **hot dogs** 'frankfurters'. 'Dog' in wartime military slang was a 'sausage', perhaps with specific reference to a dachshund. 'Hot dog' is thought by *Webster's Dictionary* to derive from the exclamation. It seems more likely that 'Hot dog!' meaning 'Great!' derived from the food, which made use of the dog-equals-sausage equation.

'And now for God's sake, hock and soda-water,' laughed the very handsome curly-haired youth who had spoken at this morning's session. Anna knew her Byron and knew what this meant; it was the locus classicus *of the hair of the dog in literature.*

Mary McCarthy *The Groves of Academe*

Specific parts of a dog are mentioned in sayings. To **have a hair of the dog that bit you** now refers to having a little more of the same drink that made you drunk the night before in order to shake off a hangover. Originally it had a far more literal sense. It was believed in medieval times that if a mad dog bit you, a hair plucked from the same dog and laid across the wound would cure it. The belief was of course nonsensical. Many drinkers have discovered that 'a hair of the dog' in the alcoholic sense is equally useless.

In the quotation given above, Mary McCarthy's character is thinking of *Don Juan*, where Lord Byron several times comments on his own favourite hang-over cure of hock and soda-water. Canto Two, for instance, has:

> *Ring for your valet – bid him quickly bring*
> *Some hock and soda-water, then you'll know*
> *A pleasure worthy Xerxes the great king;*
> *For not the blest sherbet, sublimed with snow,*
> *Nor the first sparkle of the desert spring,*
> *Nor burgundy in all its sunset glow,*
> *After long travel, ennui, love, or slaughter,*
> *Vie with that draught of hock and soda-water.*

To mark the place where she had wearied of instruction she had slipped in the Treasury Note; a thing she often did, being prejudiced against dog's ears.

Eric Linklater *Poet's Pub*

What we normally call a **dog-eared page** in a book was formerly a **dog's ear**, in obvious allusion to the similarity between the turning over of a page-corner and the bend in a dog's ear. In Washington Irving's *The Legend of Sleepy Hollow* Ichabod Crane disappears. His estate is found to contain 'a book of old psalm tunes, full of dog's ears'.

Golfers also talk of a **dog-leg** 'a sharp bend'. William J. Locke, in *Jaffery*, mentions golf in a different context: 'Jaffery with a **hang-dog** expression came with me to the golf course.'

Hang-dog now means little more than 'ashamed'. It formerly referred to the kind of despicable person who was fit only to be hanged like a dog.

'Give a dog a bad name, and all that, but we may as well be prepared.'

Iris Murdoch *The Bell*

Hanging a dog is also mentioned in the full form of the proverb **give a dog a bad name and hang him**. Few speakers today would bother to quote the last three words. This saying does not refer to calling a dog Primrose instead of Butch; 'name' is used in the sense of 'reputation'. The full meaning is that once someone has acquired a bad reputation he might as well be hanged, since even if he genuinely reforms, few will believe that he has changed his ways.

'Give a dog a bad name' is still in current use. In the same way, a dog's tail could be alluded to in a conversation which had nothing to do with canine matters, yet no one would think it odd. Businessmen might say, for instance, that a single department of a company was having far too much influence on the company's policies as a whole. The situation could be described as an example of **the tail wagging the dog**.

Also heard in a business context these days is the saying **you can't teach an old dog new tricks**. A modern interpretation of this seems to be that employees should be encouraged to retire as early as possible because they will not be able to cope with changing methods and situations.

'There are frustrated people who don't want others to have what they can't get themselves.'
'Dog in the manger,' said Westercote.

'Exactly – Aesop put it much better than I can.'

Maurice Edelman *The Minister*

Dog in the manger, attributed to Aesop in the above quotation, certainly derives from a medieval fable, but scholars have long doubted whether Aesop was responsible for the collection of animal tales attributed to him, or whether such a person existed. The originator of the phrase may be uncertain, but it accurately identifies the unpleasant attitude of those who only begin to want something when someone else shows an interest in it. Kate O'Brien, in *Pray for the Wanderer*, has: 'You're inventing it now so as to get out of your dog-in-the-manger scene with some kind of flourish! You never wanted me until he did!'

It was raining cats and dogs and do you think anyone came to meet us?

Truman Capote *My Side of the Matter*

Raining cats and dogs is perhaps the best-known English idiom amongst foreign students of the language, who are always struck by its oddity. Strange things are said to fall from the sky, however, when it rains heavily in other countries. *Il pleut des hallebardes* in French literally means 'it's raining halberds', a halberd being the long-handled weapon which is a cross between a spear and an axe. More commonly, French people speak about bad weather as *un temps de chien*, literally 'dog-weather'. *Es regnet Heugabeln* in German is 'it's raining pitchforks'.

The origin of 'raining cats and dogs' ('pissin' cats an' dogs' in Alexander Fullerton's *Other Men's Wives*) is not known. Jonathan Swift seems to have been the first to make use of the phrase, in his satirical *Complete Collection of Polite and Ingenious Conversation* (1738). In this he was making fun of society 'wits' and the absurdity of their conversation. 'Raining cats and dogs' may have been no more than an over-the-top example of what such people said in their search for novelty.

Other explanations that have been offered include the suggestion that heavy rain in earlier times could quickly cause floods. This would drown a number of cats and dogs in a city, so that after torrential rain it would look as if cats and dogs had fallen from the sky. Those who have seen the effect of flash-floods in a city like Bangkok will probably be receptive to this idea.

Dr Brewer preferred a link with Norse mythology and the storm god Odin, often portrayed with cat and dog. The latter were said to influence the weather. Dr Brewer did not go on to comment on the likelihood of such an erudite reference suddenly becoming an everyday expression in English. Even more bizarre is the suggestion made by Edwin Radford (in *Crowther's Encyclopaedia of Phrases and Origins*) that an obsolete French word *catadoupe* 'waterfall' led to the expression. Perhaps more acceptable would have been a suggestion that Greek words such as *cataclysm* 'violent disaster such as a flood' and *cataract* 'waterfall' became associated with 'cats' in the minds of uneducated people, but that would still not explain the extension 'to cats and dogs'.

'I want to see a man about a dog,' he said.
'What dog? I have no dog, I say,' she shouted, but he pushed past her.

Edna O'Brien *Girl with Green Eyes*

To **see a man about a dog** is still used by men who feel they need to announce, albeit euphemistically, that they are going to the lavatory. Monica Dickens, in *The Fancy*, has: 'Mr Bell had left them to see a man about the proverbial dog, ha-ha.' The phrase demonstrates the usefulness of 'dog' expressions in a wide range of social situations and contexts. One thinks of men wearing **dog-collars** or **dog-tags**, who are **dogsbodies** or have offended their wives and are **in the dog-house**. 'Dogsbody' has even become an adjective. Robertson Davies, in *The Lyre of Orpheus*, has: 'There are plenty of dogsbody jobs associated with art and music which wealthy volunteers are graciously permitted to do by the professionals.'

The Dog-day sun in its decline reached the low ceiling with slanting sides . . .

Thomas Hardy *A Tragedy of Two Ambitions*

Further expressions include **dog days**, the hottest and unhealthiest days of the year, so-named because it was believed in former times that Sirius, the dog-star, added its heat to that of the sun during this time, and **Doggone it!** 'God damn it!' where 'dog' reverses the letters of 'God'. In rhyming slang **dog and bone** is for 'telephone'. With such a wide range of phrasal reference, it does seem as if, from a linguistic point of view, **every dog has its day**.

■ GOING TOO FAR

'I consider you a viper. I look upon you, sir, as a man who has placed himself beyond the pale of society, by his most audacious, disgraceful, and abominable public conduct.'

Charles Dickens *The Pickwick Papers*

A person who does or says something which is **beyond the pale** goes further than convention allows with regard to decency and propriety. He breaks the unwritten laws of society. Metaphorically he is going past a boundary which is marked by a 'pale', a fence made of palings, Latin *pālus* 'stake'. 'Beyond the pale' has been the usual form of this expression since Dickens, but Ivy Compton-Burnett, in *A House and Its Head*, has: 'You have put yourself outside the pale of other men.'

■ GOING WRONG

'I don't feel grave, that's all I can say; you're going quite on the wrong tack.'

E.M. Forster *Howards End*

One meaning of 'tack' is the direction in which a sailing ship is moving, as determined by the position of the sails in relation to the wind-direction. Figuratively, 'tack' has long been used to mean 'the course of action a person is taking'. **On the wrong tack** is frequently applied metaphorically to someone who is thought to be going in the wrong direction. Changes of policy can be referred to using the same image. J.I.M. Stewart, in *The Last Tresilians*, has: 'She went off **on another tack** – and it was the personal tack I'd been banking on.' *A High Wind in Jamaica*, by Richard Hughes, has: 'Then he went off **on a fresh tack.**' In *Doctor Thorne* Trollope has someone say dismissively: 'He goes on every tack, just as it's wanted.'

'You're really on the wrong track there.'
'I don't believe it for an instant.'
'Truly you're wrong – '

C.P. Snow *The Affair*

Some speakers and writers use on **the wrong track** instead of 'on the wrong tack'. They may be thinking of a railway track or the kind of track that is a path, but they could instead have in mind the idea of tracking in the sense of 'following' someone or something. It is easy to see how the two phrases overlap at times in meaning, but a slight change of emphasis is present. To be on a certain tack is to be going in that direction but not necessarily because one is involved in an investigation.

'You've got a one-track mind, Marty. Strike me pink, you have.'

C.P. Snow *The Affair*

Other 'track' expressions exist, using the word in both its 'trail' and 'trace' sense, or referring specifically to a railway track. The latter leads to **one-track mind**; for an explanation of this, see under 'Keeping Count' on p.132. In America to come from the **wrong side of the tracks** is to live in the poorer district of the town. The phrase suggests that railway tracks cut across the middle of the town and create a rich area on one side, a poor area on the other. The real allusion is to where people live in relation to the noise and squalour of the freight yards and industrial areas.

'I've been on the track o' the thing for a while back, but it was only yestreen I had the proofs o't.'

George Douglas *The House with the Green Shutters*

'Track' is a 'path' or 'trail' in **off the beaten track** 'in seclusion, away from well-trodden paths'. **Make tracks for** somewhere is to start in that direction, as when workers make tracks for home at the end of the day. To be **on the track of** is to be in pursuit of something or someone, perhaps someone who is trying to **cover his tracks** 'leave no evidence of what he has been doing and where he has been'. Here 'track' is almost synonymous with 'trace'. In a more general sense we talk of **keeping track** or **losing track** of people and events, 'being aware or not of what is happening to individuals and in the world at large'.

■ GOOD TIMES

'If that's what you want, call the case and you'll have a whale of a time.'

Henry Cecil *Brothers in Law*

Whale of a time was considered to be an exclusively American phrase in the early 20th century. It has since taken a firm hold in Britain. The 'whale' is used as a symbol of both excellence and quantity, so that the phrase is a synonym of **no end of a good time** or **the time of one's life**. 'Jesus, we're having a whale of a time' is said by Baba in Edna O'Brien's *The Country Girls*. The same character says, in *Girl with Green Eyes*: 'I'm having a whale of a time.' 'Out every night.'

■ GOOSE-COOKING

'One direct question from either of you, and Maynard's goose would have been cooked. You had him on the ropes and you didn't know it.'

Mary McCarthy *The Groves of Academe*

Nobody has been able to offer a satisfactory explanation of why **cook somebody's goose** means to ensure that person's failure. There is a story about townspeople derisively hanging out a goose for the king of Sweden to shoot at when he arrived with only a few soldiers. He then announced his intention of 'cooking their goose'.

One problem with this tale is that it applies to a king who lived in the 16th century, yet the expression appeared only in the 19th century. Nor do the Swedes themselves talk about metaphorically cooking someone's goose. Partridge and others seem keen to point out that **settle someone's hash**, a phrase of roughly similar meaning, had come into use in English some time before the 'goose' expression, but the relevance of this is not obvious.

Whatever the reason for its original use, the image evoked by 'cooking someone's goose' seems to appeal, since the phrase is widely used. 'He's cooked his own goose, all right' is in J.I.M. Stewart's *The Last Tresilians*. W. Somerset Maugham, in his short story *Lord Mountdrago* has: 'I thought it a very good opportunity to cook his goose, and by God, sir, I cooked it. I tore his speech to pieces. . . . If ever a man was made a fool of I made a fool of Griffiths.' Nigel Dennis writes, in *Cards of Identity*: 'The emergence of a tough young rival has cooked his charming and irresponsible goose.' O. Henry, in *The Caliph, Cupid and the Clock*, has: 'I ought to have known at 8.31 that my goose was cooked.'

'The wife's posse is breathing down my neck hard. Don't give out this address, or my cook is goosed.'

Bernard Wolfe *The Late-Risers*

The 'cook is goosed' reversal, quoted

above, is possible because to **goose someone** has its own slang meaning of 'prod someone unexpectedly between the buttocks'. Enraged geese are said to attack the groin area of human beings. The upturned thumb of the person who 'gooses' someone else has also been compared to a goose's neck.

'You say Robert is – 'she began and made a curious gesture, as if throwing something away. It meant, 'Robert is off on his eternal wild-goose chase.'

John Wain *The Contenders*

A **wild-goose chase** is a foolish or obviously unproductive quest. Once again the phrase is in common use. 'He'd found himself on a wild-goose chase' is in Malcolm Lowry's *Under the Volcano*. 'Afraid it was a wild goose chase, doc,' is said by a character in Penelope Gilliatt's *A State of Change*. In John Le Carré's *The Honourable Schoolboy* the phrase is alluded to briefly: 'They've got it all wrong. It's a goose-chase.'

The simplest explanation of the phrase is probably to be drawn from greylag geese in flight. They fly in V-shaped formation and remain at the same distance from one another, making no attempt to overtake the goose they appear to be 'chasing'. A 'wild-goose chase' is thus one which appears never to succeed, one goose never 'catching' another.

'What a woeful day it was for the soft little creature, when you first came in her way – smirking and making great eyes at her, I'll be bound, as if you couldn't say boh! to a goose!'

Charles Dickens *David Copperfield*

Geese have a reputation for being both stupid and timid. Someone who **cannot say boo to a goose** is therefore very timid indeed. The saying is not frequently heard, but Joyce Porter uses her own version of it in *Dover One*: 'She was a sickly, unattractive, dowdy individual who hadn't enough spirit to say boo to a gosling.'

What's sauce for the goose is sauce for the gander 'what's good for one is good for another' is usually applied to husbands and wives. The proverb was first recorded in 1670, and has its equivalent in German: *Was dem einen recht ist, ist dem andern billig* 'what is right for one is fair for the other'.

'He's your boy-friend. I'm just a dear old gooseberry.'

Penelope Mortimer *The Pumpkin Eater*

Etymologists are agreed that the gooseberry has nothing to do with 'goose', but how the fruit got its name is something of a mystery. John Ayto, in his *Glutton's Glossary*, mentions that gooseberries were frequently used to stuff geese in Tudor and Elizabethan times. He thinks that connection gave rise to the name of the fruit. Professor Weekley, however, pointed out that one of the gooseberry's dialectal names was grozell, which clearly links with French *groseille* 'gooseberry'. The French word in turn derives from German *kraus* 'curly', a reference to the hairs on some varieties of gooseberry. It is perhaps this *kraus*, then, that ultimately became the 'goose' of gooseberry.

To **play gooseberry** is to be the unwanted chaperon to a pair of young lovers. 'She's probably ditched us' says one young man to another in Clifford Hanley's *The Taste of Too Much*. 'What do you expect?' he adds pointedly, 'when she's stuck with a gooseberry?' 'Gooseberry' in this sense is sometimes said to derive from a person who ostensibly gathered gooseberries while ensuring that a young couple were not left alone. Another explanation is possible. 'Gooseberry' had already acquired the meaning of 'fool' before the idea of 'playing gooseberry' emerged in the 1830s, and the phrase could therefore have meant 'playing the role of a fool'.

The 'fool' meaning had come about because of the dessert called a 'gooseberry fool'. This in turn was named because light desserts are 'foolish things'. The word 'trifle' applied to a dessert shows a similar thought pattern.

There is, of course, a jokey custom of telling inquisitive young children that babies are found under gooseberry bushes. This has arisen only in recent times and cannot be connected with 'playing gooseberry'.

■ GRASS LANDS

'A fine solicitor he is. Not the man to let the grass grow under his feet. If I tell him you're our man, you'll get a letter from him before you can say Jack Robinson.'

C.P. Snow *The Affair*

Not let the grass grow under one's feet is recorded in 1707 in its present-day meaning of 'not waste time, do something immediately'. The phrase speaks for itself. Virginia Woolf, in *Night and Day*, has: 'We have to take the enemy by surprise,' he said. 'They don't let the grass grow under their feet.' The author refers to the phrase again later: 'She was striking a blow against the enemy, no doubt, who didn't let the grass grow beneath their feet. Mr Clacton's words repeated themselves accurately in her brain.'

'Are you interested in Jane, because if so I advise you to keep off the grass.'

Christopher Dilke *Freddie and Son*

Keep off the grass, the sign commonly seen in public parks and gardens, is now interestingly used as a warning to keep away from a person in whom the speaker is interested. *Lucky Jim*, by Kingsley Amis, has the exchange: '"He was trying to persuade me to keep off the grass." "As far as she's concerned?" "Yes."' The 'grass' is unimportant in the metaphoric sense, the whole message being conveyed by the 'keep off'. A treacherous friend who ignored such a warning might well be called a **snake in the grass**.

Grass widows 'women whose husbands are away from home for long periods' were discarded mistresses in the 16th century. They were certainly not the 'grace-widows' that some writers try to make them. Similar expressions occur in Dutch and German, the latter language referring to 'straw widows' and 'straw widowers'. 'Grass widowers' would be unusual in English, and it is interesting that Stephen Vincent Benét, in *Everybody was Very Nice*, refers instead to 'grass-bachelors' when talking about divorced men.

'How could she live with him knowing about his boy-friend?'
'It's happened before. You don't have to roll in the hay to stay married.'

Derek Jewell *Come In No.1 Your Time Is Up*

The 'grass' in the original 'grass widow' probably referred to the bed of grass or straw used by a man and his mistress for **romps in the hay**, the modern **roll in the hay**. An Elizabethan expression which euphemistically referred to robbing a girl of her chastity was **give a girl a green gown**, the 'greenness' being imparted by the grass in which she lay. In Germany, chopped straw was laid before the door of an unchaste woman. It has also been said that a bride who had very obviously, in the words of Professor Weekley, 'anticipated conjugal life', carried a wreath of straw at her wedding instead of a bouquet of flowers.

Being **put out to grass** occurs rather later in life, when one is forced to retire. Those to whom this happens tend to use this expression with some bitterness, not appreciating the comparison between themselves and elderly horses, turned into a field and allowed to graze.

To **grass on someone** in British criminal slang is to inform the police of his activities. The phrase is commonly said to derive from rhyming slang, 'grass-hopper' rhyming on 'copper'. Equally possible is the use of 'grass in the park' rhyming on 'nark, police spy'. 'Nark' in turn represents Romany *nak* 'nose'.

■ GRINDING AXES

Every one of them had his own ax to grind here, a thing Domna made abundantly clear, but joyously, as though self-interest were a newly discovered cardinal virtue.

Mary McCarthy *The Groves of Academe*

Charles Earle Funk, in his book about the origins of phrases *A Hog on Ice*, defines to **have an ax to grind** as 'to flatter a person or to be obsequious when seeking a favor from him'. *Webster's New Collegiate Dictionary* is rather more accurate when it talks of having 'an ulterior often selfish purpose to further'. Other dictionaries tend to agree with that definition, and *Collins Cobuild English Language Dictionary*, which is primarily for foreign students of English, expands it to: 'If you **have an axe to grind**, you have a particular belief or a desire to make something happen, which you keep telling people about in order to persuade them that you are right or that something must be done.'

Dr Funk's explanation is based on the events of the story which launched the phrase in 1811. The story was called 'Who'll turn the grindstone?' and was written by Charles Miner. It appeared first in the Wilkes-Barre *Gleaner* but was later reprinted in *Essays from the Desk of Poor Robert the Scribe*. That book in turn seems to have been confused with *Poor Richard's Almanack*, the more famous work of Benjamin Franklin. Many reference books (such as *Brewer's Dictionary of Phrase and Fable*) therefore attribute the story to Franklin.

The story is about a young boy who is flattered about his intelligence and strength by a stranger. As a result, the boy willingly grinds an axe for him. The stranger's manner then changes abruptly and he tells the boy to get off to school. The author's comment on this was: 'When I see a merchant over-polite to his customers, begging them to taste a little brandy and throwing half his goods on the counter – thinks I, that man has an ax to grind.'

In *Howards End* E.M. Forster writes: 'I can't stand those people who run down comforts. They have usually some axe to grind.' Ngaio Marsh, in a *Surfeit of Lampreys*, considers who might have committed a murder: 'A servant? A lunatic? Somebody with an axe to grind?'

'You would have the inside story of my getting the ax.'

Mary McCarthy *The Group*

To **get the ax** is an Americanism meaning to lose one's job abruptly, to **get the sack** as a British speaker would probably say. The 'ax' image needs no explanation; the 'sack' would have contained at one time the tools which a workman took from one job to the next. To **get the boot** and **get the bullet** are other possible ways of talking about sudden job loss. A conversation in *The Blinder*, by Barry Hines, runs: '"There's talk of 'em laying men off." "It won't be t'face men who'll get t'bullet."'

'Ax' itself looks American to British eyes, to whom 'axe' is the more usual form. The original editors of *The Oxford English Dictionary*, who also attributed the story about 'having an axe to grind' to Benjamin Franklin, had this to say on the subject: 'The spelling *ax* is better on every ground, of etymology, phonology, and analogy, than *axe*, which has of late become prevalent.' Those words were written in the 1880s. Recent Oxford dictionaries have conceded defeat, admitting that it is only the Americans who use the 'better' spelling.

■ GUNNERS

'They're saying that a man who says one thing in private should stick to his guns in public.'

Maurice Edelman *The Minister*

The soldier who **sticks to his guns** during a battle continues to fire at the enemy when he comes under attack himself, he does not immediately abandon his position and retreat. Metaphorically someone who 'sticks to his guns' does not easily abandon his beliefs. 'If you really believe that, why don't you stick to your guns?' says someone in Mary McCarthy's *The Groves of Academe*.

Someone who is **going great guns** is doing something vigorously and successfully. The allusion is to 'an all-out attack', a full-scale bombardment by heavy artillery. To **spike someone's gun**, on the other hand, is to stop someone's progress towards his goal. In the 17th century a spike was literally driven into the touch-hole of an enemy's cannon to make it unserviceable. To **jump the gun** 'anticipate the official starting time' is a more recent phrase which is less warlike. The allusion is to the athlete who starts to run before the starting-gun has been fired.

'You'll learn, young son of a gun!' said Big James.

Arnold Bennett *Clayhanger*

Son of a gun is used by some speakers as a variant of 'son of a bitch', but as a term of address it is vaguely commendatory. The origin of the phrase was explained in a *Sailor's Word Book* of 1867: 'applied to boys born afloat, when women were permitted to accompany their husbands to sea'. Some writers claim that this is a euphemistic version of the tale, that the women allowed on board during the 18th century were not necessarily wives, and when a child was born it was not always clear who had fathered it. The birth would be entered in the log-book as 'son of a gun', a canvas having been stretched between guns to provide a makeshift lying-in room. The latter version of the story would be more meaningful if log-books containing such entries were available for inspection.

■ GUT FEELINGS

*'You've got a well-known stomach
complaint. No guts.'*

Ruth Rendell *The Tree of Hands*

'Guts' are not something one talks
about in polite circles; the word has a
rather coarse tang. References to a
person's 'gut' or 'guts' in phrases like
beer gut and **greedy guts** are to his
stomach. Both phrases are concerned
with over-indulgence, the first
commenting on the distended
stomach produced by large quantities
of beer, the second on having an
over-healthy appetite for food and
drink in general. The 'stomach'
meaning leads to more positive
applications. We speak of someone
having or not having the 'guts' or
'courage' to do something – having
the 'stomach' for it or not.

*We both hated each other's guts by
that time.*

J.D. Salinger *The Catcher in the Rye*

The expression **hate someone's guts**
intensifies the idea of hating someone,
using 'guts' to mean – if indeed it has
a specific meaning in this context –
the innermost part of a person. **Gut
feeling** plays on the same idea of
something buried in one's innermost
self. Perhaps the nearest equivalent is
to feel something 'in one's bones', but
whereas the latter phrase might be
used by a woman, it is more likely to
be a man who refers to a 'gut feeling'.
Similarly, a woman would probably
be content to say 'I hate him'; it has a
more masculine ring to say 'I hate his
guts'. Barry Hines has a man use the
phrase in *The Blinder*: '"That's him
who's always on at you, isn't it?" "He
hates my guts."'

*'I'm just about sick of toadying round
the Management, and sweating my
guts out for a lousy lot of bastards like
you.'*

Monica Dickens *The Fancy*

To **sweat one's guts out** 'do work of a
hard nature to one's utmost limit' is
also masculine. It is certainly
attributed to a man rather than a
woman in the above quotation from
Monica Dickens. An alternative
version sometimes found is **slog one's
guts out**. Both phrases make use of
the kind of hyperbole, or
exaggeration, seen in 'cry one's eyes
out', 'laugh one's head off'.

*'Manzoni wants you. Wants your guts,
I think.'*
'What?'
'For garters.'

Alexander Fullerton *Other Men's
Wives*

Announcing that one wants to **have
someone's guts for garters** is a lurid
way of saying that one wants to do
something unpleasant to the person
concerned. The phrase would
typically be used by an army sergeant
referring to one of his men. 'Guts'
here has the specific meaning
'intestines'. It is also these which have
theoretically been removed when a
person talks about **feeling gutted**
'deeply disappointed'.

■ HAIR-LINES

*'I do not ask you to lie. I would not do
such a thing.'*
*'I would be lying by inference, by what
I leave out.'*
'Come, you are splitting hairs.'

William Trevor *The Old Boys*

'Hair' expressions are well-used in English. English-speakers have been referring, for instance, to **splitting hairs** 'making over-fine, unnecessary distinctions' since the 17th century. The phrase is still in common use, and has given rise to nouns such as **hairsplitting**. Mary McCarthy, in *The Group*, has: 'It would be just like Harald to start hairsplitting now.' Ian Jefferies, in *Thirteen Days*, avoids 'hairsplitter' by writing: 'Look boy, I don't want to sound like a splitter of hairs but that's *my* wagon lying all over the road and that's *your* gun with the hot barrel.'

'To split hairs' has always been purely metaphorical, but is interpreted more literally by Vera Caspary in *Laura*. She is referring to detectives when she describes 'the cold, dry, scientific kind who split hairs under a microscope'. There was, incidentally, a 19th century variant of the phrase – to **split straws** – used for instance by Disraeli and Dickens. 'Well, my dear sir, we won't waste time in splitting straws' says the lawyer who is negotiating with Jingle about the spinster aunt in *The Pickwick Papers*.

There was one youngster that used to rather get in my hair.

Stephen Vincent Benét *Everybody was Very Nice*

To **get in someone's hair** is to annoy that person. The phrase is used unthinkingly in modern times, though what is literally being said is decidedly unpleasant. The person who is 'in someone's hair' is being compared to head-lice. Upton Sinclair writes in *World's End*: 'It would be better if you didn't have anything to do with this fight. You see, Molly Jessup and Esther have been in each's hair of late.'

'I don't mind telling you, since I've been rather letting my hair down.'

Kingsley Amis *Lucky Jim*

To **let one's hair down** 'relax, especially after previously having been rather formal' alludes to women allowing their hair to return to a natural state instead of keeping it up artificially in elaborate arrangements. Metaphorical application of the phrase can have a wide range of meanings. It can refer to being rather more frank in what one says, as is the case in the *Lucky Jim* quotation above, or to unrestrained merry-making.

'What is it, Elliott?' she asked a little peevishly.
'You'll find out, just keep your pretty hair on, little girl.'

John Steinbeck *The Wayward Bus*

Telling someone to **keep his** (or **her**) **hair on** is a slangy way of saying 'don't tear your hair out', which is what people in a rage are alleged to do. A more polite way of expressing the thought would be: 'There's really no need to worry.' 'Keep your hair on, darling. I've no intention of going,' said by a character in Iris Murdoch's *The Bell*, is meant to be rude.

'Have you read any of her books? Enough to make your hair stand on end. I saw a few dicey things when I was seconded to the Commandos during the war, but it was nothing to some of the things she describes.'

Joyce Porter *Dover One*

Something that **makes one's hair stand on end** is usually something horrifying, something that has an 'electrifying effect' on the person concerned. To **make one's hair curl** would be used by some writers with similar meaning. The effect that great fear can have on the hair of the body has long been recognized. Job 4.14 has: 'Dread came upon me, and trembling, which made all my bones shake. A spirit glided past my face; the hair of my flesh stood up.' Anthony Trollope appears to have been a little sceptical, however. In *Doctor Thorne* he writes: 'Mr Moffat at once saw his fate before him. His hair doubtless stood on end.'

Fear, it seems, is not the only emotion that can produce such an effect. *Getting it Right*, by Elizabeth Jane Howard, has: 'She said it was the best piece of music she had ever heard in her life. "It made my hair stand on end." "It *is* on end," he said, and found himself wanting to touch it.'

'You wrote The Diamond Gate without turning a hair. Why should you worry yourself to death about this new book?'
William J. Locke *Jaffery*

Not to turn a hair 'to remain cool and unruffled' was first used of horses who did not show sweat by the roughening of their hair. To have seen **neither hide nor hair of someone** is to have seen no trace of him at all. 'Hide' is normally of an animal's skin but is jokingly applied to a human in this expression. A rather more literary phrase is **hairbreadth escape**, suggested by Shakespeare's Othello. He told Desdemona's father: 'Of moving accidents by flood and field; / Of hairbreadth scapes i' th' imminent deadly breach.' Such accounts helped to make Desdemona fall in love with him, starting a chain of events that were to end in tragedy.

■ HALF-BAKED CAKES

Kate thinks Judith cannot have her cake and eat it.
Margaret Drabble *The Middle Ground*

J. Heywood's *A Dialogue containing the number in effect of all the Proverbs in the English Tongue* (1546) mentions **You cannot eat your cake and have it**. This makes perfect sense, both literally and metaphorically. If it is necessary to choose between two courses of action which are mutually exclusive, it is impossible to enjoy the benefits of both.

At some point between the 16th century and the present day, the words of this saying have been reversed. All modern dictionaries agree that **you cannot have your cake and eat it** is now the usual form, a view supported by examples of the phrase found in contemporary literature. Mordecai Richler, in *Joshua Then and Now*, has: 'You decided to have your cake and eat it too. You would cover your ass and make Kevin the patsy.' 'I understand', says Mrs Renfrew in Mary McCarthy's *The Group*, 'that you want to have your cake and eat it too.'

This makes rather less sense, since it is possible to have one's cake for quite a time before eating it. One could enjoy having it there on the sideboard, anticipating with pleasure the moment when one would eat it. In the end, of course, the same point is reached whether the eating comes first or not. The cake cannot simultaneously be both kept and eaten.

'You'll find the second job's easier after you've done the first. And the third's a piece of cake.'

Derek Jewell *Come In No.1 Your Time Is Up*

Cakes do tend to be eaten rather than kept, especially when fresh, hot out of the oven. Since the end of the 19th century we have said of a popular product that it sells **like hot cakes**. In modern idiom we could also say that selling such a product is a **piece of cake**, by which we mean as easy as eating a piece of cake. Someone who wants to share benefits or profits wants **a slice of the cake**. This popularity of cakes was long ago attested by the 16th-century phrase **cakes and ale**, symbolic of 'pleasant living'.

On the negative side, at one time a businessman whose product failed to sell like hot cakes might have said **My cake is dough**. In Shakespeare's *The Taming of the Shrew* Gremio uses this common 17th-century expression that meant 'my project has failed'. Earlier in the same play he says 'our cake's dough on both sides' with the same meaning. The expression, now obsolete, was a reminder that even hot cakes only sell well if they are properly cooked.

■ HALF TIME

'Come and see how the other half lives.'
'Other half of what?' asked Treece.

Malcolm Bradbury *Eating People is Wrong*

An informal invitation to visit someone may conclude with a humorous remark about seeing **how the other half lives**. The implication is that the person being invited will see the life-style of people who, depending on the context, are either much richer or poorer than himself. The answer to the question posed by Treece, then, in the Bradbury quotation above, is the other half of society. Had the invitation been to meet someone's **better half**, then in theory a wife or husband could have been meant. In practice it tends to be men who use this expression, with strained jocularity, of their wives.

Yes, that fair neck, too beautiful by half,
Those eyes, that voice, that bloom, all do her honour:
Yet, after all, that little giddy laugh
Is what, in my mind, sits the best upon her.

Leigh Hunt *On the Laugh of Madame d'Albret*

Too . . . **by half** is a format phrase which means 'far too . . .'. In the Leigh Hunt quotation above, the remark that Madame d'Albret is 'too beautiful by half' can only be taken as a compliment, but often this phrase is used in anything but an admiring way. When Arnold Bennett says in *Clayhanger* that Orgreave was 'too clever by half' he means that his cleverness makes him dangerous to others.

'You can't half swim.'

William Golding *Lord of the Flies*

It is often said that the British have a special love of understatement. Rhetoricians would certainly find examples of litotes and meiosis being used in daily speech, especially in Scotland, it seems. David Walker comments in *Geordie* that 'I don't mind' is 'Scottish for I'd like to'. A little later, when someone says 'Not bad,' he adds that the speaker is 'concealing his pleasure; for understatement is next to Godliness in these parts'.

Not half is used by some speakers to make an emphatic assertion. 'Do you like ice cream?' 'Not half!' Those who use that expression might also combine 'not half' with 'is', 'can' and 'do' to create emphatic forms of those verbs. 'You can't half swim', quoted above, means 'you really can swim'. Another boy in the book says: 'You don't half look a mess,' meaning 'you look a terrible mess'. 'It ain't 'alf 'ot' might be said by a Londoner on a very hot day.

R.M. Ballantyne, in *The Coral Island*, has a character who says: 'I don't half like it. It seems to me that we'll only have hard fightin' and no pay.'

In earlier times 'half' was used for emphasis in uneducated speech without being negated. In *The Pickwick Papers* Dickens has Mr Pickwick express astonishment at the way voters are gathered for a particular party at an election. Sam Weller says: 'Lord bless your heart, sir, why where was you half baptised? – that's nothin', that ain't.'

Another way of using 'half' for emphasis is seen in Zane Grey's *Betty Zane*: 'These rods have been made by a lover of the art. Anyone **with half an eye** could see that.' Modern stallholders who tell potential customers that something would be **cheap at half the price** are also trying to be emphatic, though 'cheap at twice the price' is presumably meant.

In the modern colloquialism 'You don't know **the half of it**', the implication is that you do not know the most important facts. It might be more prudent to say 'You only know the half of it', since the form normally used allows the riposte – 'No, I know all of it.'

'Here, 'alf a mo', said Brother Collister.

Monica Dickens *The Fancy*

'Half' is also commonly added to words like 'minute' and 'second' to speak about a very brief period of time. Someone will be asked to wait **half a minute, half a second, half a tick, half a jiffy**. Sometimes the halving principle seems to operate on the accompanying words, as in **half a mo', half a sec, half a jiff**. In *Abbie*, by Dane Chandos, 'half' is curiously used, effectively cancelled out by what follows: 'We will be with you in half a brace of shakes.'

■ HAPPIEST DAYS

'Thought I'd take an afternoon off from the office.'
'Playing hookey, eh?'

Mordecai Richler *The Incomparable Atuk*

Since the 15th century 'to hook it' has meant to turn around suddenly and go away. From this meaning of 'hook' comes to **play hookey**, disappear from school or work without permission. Playing hookey is much talked about in *Huckleberry Finn* as one of the young hero's favourite occupations. Mark Twain's story no doubt helped to popularize the expression.

'My misfortunes all began in wagging, Sir; but what could I do, exceptin' wag?'
'Excepting what?' said Mr Carker.
'Wag, Sir. Wagging from school.'
'Do you mean pretending to go there, and not going?' said Mr Carker.
'Yes, Sir, that's wagging, Sir.'

Charles Dickens *Dombey and Son*

The Lore and Language of Schoolchildren, by Iona and Peter Opie, mentions a number of local British terms which refer to truancy. They include **playing (the) wag, hopping the wag, wagging school, bobbing school, fagging off, fanagin, jigging it, jouking, playing the kipp, playing the tick, playing lag, miching/mitching, playing (the) nick, plunking, sagging, skiving, ticking school, twagging, hopping it, bunking off school**. These are of obscure origin, though the references to 'wag', formerly widespread, may imply that the truant was being waggish, 'mischievously impudent'.

■ HAT TRICKS

Some purists maintain that a **hat trick** should only be applied to the taking of three wickets with consecutive balls in the game of cricket. That was certainly its first sporting connection, towards the end of the 19th century. These days, of course, the phrase is commonly used in other sports, applied to the scoring of three goals by the same person in a single match.

As Professor Weekley points out, in his *Etymological Dictionary of Modern English*, the original allusion was clearly to the kind of trick performed by the conjuror who pulls a rabbit from a hat. Performing a hat trick, in that context, is doing something remarkable – something that seems to be impossible. This comparison of the bowler with the conjuror would be enough in itself to explain the saying, but it is commonly said that the bowler concerned was entitled to receive from his club a new hat, or its equivalent in money terms.

There seems to be no evidence to show that new hats really were presented in such circumstances or, as others have suggested, that a collection for the bowler was made by passing the hat round amongst the spectators. No one seems to have suggested that the phrase may also have been a simple pun, based on the fact that a 'bowler' is both a cricketer and a kind of hat. Surely that made the comparison of the sporting achievement with the conjuror's feat all the more suitable?

'You have told us about the dispositions of your Berlin organisation. That, if I may say so, is old hat.'

John Le Carré *The Spy Who Came In From The Cold*

Eric Partridge reports on another pun which concerns the phrase **old hat**. Before this assumed its modern meaning of anything which is boringly familiar it was used in the coarse slang of the late 17th century to refer to the female pudenda. The allusion was to 'something that was frequently felt'. This may well explain why we still talk about old hat rather *an* old hat. Now that the meaning of the phrase has changed, modern writers on language usually assume that a specific old hat is meant and explain the phrase by referring to changing fashions. Derek Jewell illustrates usage of the phrase in *Come In No.1 Your Time Is Up*: '"Giles Lymington's contacts in Whitehall and Parliament remain valuable." "But old hat. The younger men scarcely know him."'

Asking someone to **keep something under his hat** seems to be reasonably straightforward. What is under someone's hat is his head, and the phrase humorously suggests that the information that has just been passed on should be kept inside the head – memorized – not written down or repeated in speech. At least one writer, however, has speculated that letters and other objects might literally have been secreted beneath a messenger's hat. That can hardly have been relevant if the information was merely spoken in the first place.

'Did you hear what that bastard said to me?'
'Sometimes he talks through his hat.'

Bernard Malamud *The Natural*

More mysterious is the comment that someone is **talking through his hat**. At the end of the 19th century, in the USA, the phrase appears to have meant that someone was bluffing or blustering. It quickly came to mean that he was talking nonsensically. The original allusion may have been to the pompous speech of men wearing imposing top hats. The phrase quickly seems to have conjured up an image of someone doing something ridiculous, while perhaps muffling his speech so that it could not be understood.

'He's not a diamond merchant, Sir,' he said, 'or I'll eat my hat.'

Ian Fleming *Diamonds are Forever*

Also curious is the assertion that in certain specified circumstances, the speaker will **eat his hat**. The 'clerical gentleman', a prisoner in the Fleet who is confronted with the innocence of Mr Pickwick, goes so far as to say that 'if I knew as little of life as that, I'd eat my hat and swallow the buckle whole'.

The Pickwick Papers was published in 1837, and Dickens appears to have been the first to record this phrase in its modern form. Earlier speakers had referred to **eating Old Rowley's hat**, 'Old Rowley' being a nickname for Charles II. They also talked, as we still do, of **eating their words** if they were forced to retract a statement.

Those who talk of eating their hats if some particular thing happens are supremely confident that they will not need to do so. The phrase reflects that confidence. The speaker is merely saying: 'I can promise to do anything, however silly, because I am quite certain that what I have said will never happen.' When everyone regularly wore hats, the phrase must have had rather more force than it does today. A young speaker using it now might be asked by friends whether he had a hat that was his to eat.

The following passage from *The Great Days*, by John Dos Passos, is not linked to the origin of the expression but is relevant: 'Sanchez' chief attraction for his lady friends when everything else failed was a cousin who ate straw hats. Juanito was a sappy looking sawed off fat man who made a hobby of it.

'It took a good deal of rum to get him started but suddenly, when the evening was far enough advanced, he would start breaking off little pieces of the brim of someone's straw hat and chewing on them and before you knew it the straw hat was gone. The girls were enchanted. Usually they fell into Sanchez' arms on the strength of it. Nobody ever thought of falling into Juanito's arms. He looked too repulsive.'

Hats off to Max Weiler for his beautiful order from Halle Bros., in Cleveland!!

Richard Bissell *The Pajama Game*

In ordinary speech hats can still be dropped, taken off to someone or thrown into a ring. We do something **at the drop of a hat** because in former times that was frequently the signal for a fight or a race to begin. **To take one's hat off to someone**, metaphorically speaking, is to express admiration for something which that person has done. In French one need merely say *Chapeau!* 'Hat!' 'I take my hat off to you' will be understood.

The phrase is a reminder of the days when gentlemen regularly paid respect to ladies they met in the street by raising their hats to them. In *The Fancy*, Monica Dickens writes: 'It's surprising how they take to engineering work. There's an older woman too; I must say I take my hat off to her. It must be very tiring.' Nigel Dennis, in *Cards of Identity*, has: '"A damned good start," the captain whispered to Beaufort: "I take my hat off."'

A politician who **throws his hat into the ring** becomes a candidate for office. The 'ring' is the boxing-ring, originally formed by a circle of spectators, and the man who threw in his hat was once accepting the challenge of a prize-fighter.

'On my honour, gentlemen, my hand upon my heart, you will find no bad hats among my passengers.'

Graham Greene *The Heart of the Matter*

It is probably only speakers of a certain age who would refer these days to **bad hats**, meaning people who are disreputable, not to be trusted. Completely obsolete is the 19th-century Cockney catch-phrase: 'what a shocking bad hat!' which was applied to any objectionable person. The phrase was sometimes attributed to the Duke of Wellington, though Eric Partridge, a great expert on such matters, found no evidence to support the claim. 'Hat' has never been a slang word for a person, so 'bad hat' remains something of a mystery.

One might still hear it said that something or someone is **knocked into a cocked hat** by someone or

something else. In the 1870s this phrase was defined as 'being altered beyond recognition' by being knocked about. The underlying idea seems to be that something or someone is thoroughly beaten by being knocked into a peculiar and unnatural shape, namely that of the three-cornered hat that was commonly worn in the late 18th and early 19th centuries. Some have tried to connect the phrase with the game known as cocked-hat, a variation of ninepins. This uses only three pins, set up to form a triangle.

'Cap' phrases exist as well as those that refer to 'hats'. To go **cap in hand** to someone, for instance, is to approach that person humbly. This is not the same thing at all as 'taking one's hat off to someone', which is a voluntary act of recognition. The image brought to mind by 'cap in hand' is that of a lowly working-man approaching his employer. In former times he would have been under considerable obligation to show respect to a superior.

When the ladies had retired after dinner, the wily old fellow said to his son, 'Have a care, Joe; that girl is setting her cap at you.'

William Thackeray *Vanity Fair*

For centuries a different kind of cap, often a light covering of muslin, was worn indoors by a lady. It was also known as a 'mob-cap', sometimes as a 'mob'. When she went outside she was likely to retain it beneath her bonnet. By the 18th century, it was being playfully said of a woman who showed interest in a particular man that she was **setting her cap** at him.

Commentators on word and phrase origins invariably assume that this expression meant that a woman put on her most becoming cap in an effort to attract the man concerned.

The 'setting' of the cap is perhaps interpreted as being similar to the setting of a trap. A more interesting interpretation of the phrase was suggested in the 1920s by Ernest Weekley, who pointed to the French expression *mettre le cap sur*, 'to turn the head (of a ship) towards'. Professor Weekley believed that the English equivalent of this nautical phrase was applied to young women who were seen, as it were, to be sailing in a particular direction. There was then a natural confusion with the article of clothing and a reinterpretation of meaning.

Women no longer wear mob-caps, but some huntsmen might still follow a centuries-old tradition by putting **a feather in their cap** to celebrate a kill. Even those who detest the idea of killing birds and animals might say without thinking that something is a feather in someone's cap. They would mean that it was an achievement which deserved congratulation. The phrase has been used in that way since the 16th century, though at one time feathers in the cap were also associated with foolishness. 'What plume of feathers is he that indited this letter?' asks the Princess of France, in Shakespeare's *Love's Labour's Lost*, when she hears what Don Adriano de Armado, the fantastical Spaniard, has written.

'She was always a crank. Got a bee in her bonnet about Mussolini later on.'

Angus Wilson *Anglo-Saxon Attitudes*

Finally there are two useful hat-related expressions which are likely to occur in any conversation. **If the cap fits, wear it** is so well-known as a proverb that it rarely needs to be said in full. It can even be alluded to negatively. 'I don't say the cap fits you and John Middleton,' says a character in Angus Wilson's *Anglo-*

Saxon Attitudes. The statement, in other words, doesn't necessarily apply to you two.

As for someone who has a strange fixed idea about something, a whim, we now say that such a person has **a bee in his bonnet**. The phrase in its modern form is pleasingly humorous. It is found earlier as **bees in the head** or **bees in the brain**, though it was not always bees which were buzzing around. In the 17th century a speaker might well have conjured up the unpleasant image of a **maggot in the head** or **brain**. In German one would speak instead about a 'grass-hopper (*Grille*) in the head'.

To have 'a bee in one's bonnet' is first recorded in the works of Thomas De Quincey, 1845. The phrase was probably in general spoken use by that time, and has remained so ever since. Its familiarity allows it to be alluded to in shortened form, as when a man says of his son, in Sinclair Lewis's *Babbitt*: 'Ted's new bee is he'd like to be a movie actor.' The expression serves a useful purpose, helping us to talk about other people's peculiarities. 'Everyone's got some bee in his bonnet,' says a character in C.P. Snow's *The Affair*, and he may be right.

■ HEADLINES

'I attended a lecture of yours once, Professor Gay,' he said.
'I congratulate you,' said Gay.
'It was a bit above my head.'

C.P. Snow *The Affair*

'Heads' are featured in many metaphorical expressions. In some the literal meaning easily suggests the figurative sense, as in a phrase like **above** or **over one's head** 'too difficult to understand'. The spoken or written words are 'beyond one's reach', as it were, pitched at too intellectual a level. 'It flies too high over men's heads' is found in the early 17th century in the works of Lord Bacon. References occur even earlier to promoting someone **over the head** of a senior colleague.

What someone is unable to do, when something is 'above his head', is **get it into his head**. The latter phrase is often used by frustrated speakers who are trying to make someone understand a simple proposition. 'Can't you get it into your (thick) head?' is frequently asked at such moments.

'This is just off the top of the head, see? It's in a tentative spirit.'

Bernard Wolfe *The Late-Risers*

Off the top of one's head is a useful phrase, peculiar though it is in its literal meaning, to make it clear that we have not given what we are saying a great deal of thought. Penelope Gilliatt, in *A State of Change*, applies the phrase to a wider range of decisions: ' "When I direct a film," said Hug, "I'm going to do it off the top of my head." "People should only do that when they've made a lot of films," said Kakia.' Mordecai Richler, in *The Incomparable Atuk*, shows the more usual way of using the phrase as a disclaimer: 'Speaking off the top of my head, well, no.' Margaret Laurence, in *The Diviners,* has: 'I don't think well off the top of my head.'

'You shouldn't say such things in front of the child, George. She'll get swollen-headed.'

Penelope Mortimer *The Pumpkin Eater*

The humorous notion that conceit is an affliction which causes a person to become **swollen-headed** arose in the late 19th century. In 1884, according to a contemporary newspaper, the New York term **big bug** was synonymous with **swellhead** as used in Washington. By 1891 Kipling was writing, in *The Light that Failed*: 'Dick, it is of common report that you are suffering from swelled head.'

Long before this, from the 14th century onwards, a person was said to be 'inflated' or 'puffed up' with pride. This has some basis in reality, since an arrogant person is likely to throw out his chest as if there is more air in his lungs than usual. Pretending that a person's head had swollen, enabled jokers to offer sarcastic condolences. We retain the image in modern times, though references to a **big head** rather than a 'swollen head' would now be more usual. We might instead say that success has **turned someone's head**. This seems to suggest that he now turns away from old friends, but the original idea was that his success had made him giddy.

'I thought you were wonderful.'
'One mustn't let things like that go to one's head. Henry said it didn't really mean a thing.'

Henry Cecil *Brothers in Law*

Another way of alluding to big-headedness is to say that something has **gone to someone's head**. The metaphor in this instance is probably drawn from the effects of alcohol, which someone might say has 'gone straight to his head'. He would mean that it has affected his powers of reasoning, made it difficult for him to think properly. Conceit or pride is likened to alcohol because it similarly distorts normal thinking. 'Power might go to the Eskimo's head,' says a character in Mordecai Richler's *The Incomparable Atuk*. F. Scott Fitzgerald, in *The Beautiful and*

Damned, has: 'Education's a great thing, but don't let it go to your head.'

At thirty-four, he wanted to know what it was like to hold his head high, even though he wouldn't be able to afford the price of too many hair-cuts.

Denison Hatch *The Stork*

To **hold one's head high** is not to be conceited, it is simply to avoid feeling inferior to others and ashamed of one's background. The allusion is based on the simple fact that people who are worried about their social standing or feel humbled by others who are present, tend to look downwards. To 'hold one's head high' is to avoid an attitude of humility and quietly state one's right to be among equals.

In certain circumstances, of course, it is more prudent to **keep one's head down**. If the boss is in a furious mood and looking for an argument, it is better to keep out of the way and avoid trouble. 'Keep one's head down' in this sense alludes to a battlefield, where bullets are flying around. In a working context, though, the phrase is sometimes applied to doing a sustained piece of work, keeping one's attention fastened on it and not allowing oneself to be distracted.

Roger looked out of the window again and then blood suddenly rushed to his head. When blood rushes like that to a man's head he may win a VC, commit suicide, marry the girl or say something he will regret or be proud of for the rest of his life.

Henry Cecil *Brothers in Law*

A rush of blood to the head is our unscientific explanation for an impulsive action. The phrase usefully describes a phenomenon which most people have experienced – a sensation that caution is about to be thrown to the winds and one is going to take a great risk. This realization causes a physical reaction, as do fear and exhilaration, both of which operate together at such a moment.

'We must simply keep our heads and take the right line with Gabriel.'

Ngaio Marsh *Surfeit of Lampreys*

At such times we try to keep our heads. 'We must keep our heads' says someone in Edward Hyams's *Sylvester*. 'Are you implying that I've lost mine?' is the reply. Both phrases, to **keep one's head** and **lose one's head**, are elliptical for 'keep control of' or 'lose control of' one's powers of reason. 'We rather lost our heads' is said by a character in E.M. Forster's *Howards End*. In Vera Caspary's *Laura*, a man is told: 'Don't lose your head. She's not for you.' Here it is love which is causing the loss of control.

Both of these phrases are commonly used without much thought, but occasionally the literal meaning, especially that of 'losing one's head', makes itself felt. A sub-editor at *The Times* amused himself with a headline: 'Boy held after losing his head' (19.2.1992). The story that followed concerned 'a football supporter who disguised himself in a gorilla suit and breached a court curfew to see Middlesbrough play'. When his team scored, 'he threw the gorilla head in the air and was spotted by a police officer'. The youth was arrested and was later remanded in custody for having broken his bail conditions. It is unlikely that the tale would have merited the space it occupied had it not been for the 'losing his head' pun.

'If I had ever suggested to my daughter that she should go about in that state she'd have laughed her head off.'

Elizabeth Jane Howard *Getting it Right*

There are other ways in which we can 'lose our heads.' Humorous exaggeration leads to **laugh one's head off**, where at least it is our own action which brings about the loss. Another person can be responsible for the head removal by **talking one's head off**, using a great deal of non-stop chatter.

'I'm the one in the wrong. I bit your head off.'

Kingsley Amis *Lucky Jim*

A more aggressive person may **bite someone's head off** by saying something in a curt and angry way. 'Biting' has been used to describe unpleasant speech since the 14th century, mainly in 'backbiting', and the earlier form of 'bite someone's head off' was **bite** or **snap someone's nose off**. Shakespeare's *Much Ado About Nothing*, for instance, has Claudio talking about having 'had our two noses snapp'd off with two old men without teeth'.

'Bite one's head off' is a relatively modern expression which is well used. In *The Great Days* John Dos Passos has: 'The great man was very nice to us. Asked us over to his table and everything. Everybody said he'd bite our heads off.' John Updike writes, in *Rabbit Redux*: '"Pop, I *told* you we couldn't make it, we took the kid out to eat and then to a movie." "O.K., don't bite my head off."'

A person who is really angry may not be content with the use of biting words, he will threaten to **knock someone's head off**. A slang substitute for 'head' is possible in this case, so that it may be one's 'block' which is going to be knocked off.

'It's my head on the block, not yours,' said Smiley.

John Le Carré *The Honourable Schoolboy*

The person who says that **his head is on the block** is saying graphically that if things go wrong, it is he who will metaphorically be beheaded, suffer most. In a similar way, the general warning that **heads will roll** if certain circumstances arise, means that a number of people will be punished, perhaps by losing their jobs.

'You seem to have your head screwed on the right way. Would you mind if I asked your advice on something?'

Kingsley Amis *Lucky Jim*

To **have one's head screwed on the right way** seems to imply that even if one's head does roll, it is possible to fix it back on again. The humorous allusion, of course, is to a diver's helmet, which by popular mythology could be screwed on the wrong way if he was careless enough to allow such a thing to happen. The phrase merely means that the person concerned appears to have common sense. 'Mr Penezzi always 'ad 'is 'ead screwed on 'is shoulders the right way' says a character in W. Somerset Maugham's *Gigolo and Gigolette*.

'You must have been living with your heads buried in sand.'

Ruth Rendell *Talking To Strange Men*

A very popular 'head' phrase stems from the belief that ostriches bury their heads in the sand in times of danger. Being unable to see what is threatening them, it is said, they think themselves safe. If ostriches really were to bury their heads in the sand, their situation would quickly become very dangerous indeed; they would begin to suffocate. What they actually do, according to experts, is lie on the ground with their necks stretched out in a sensible effort to avoid detection.

Even those who are well aware of what ostriches actually do are likely to go on talking about people who **bury their heads in the sand**. It is a useful way of describing those who hope that by ignoring a problem it will solve itself. The phrase is so well established, and so closely associated with the supposed behaviour of the ostrich, that allusions to it are possible in various ways. In *The Limits of Love*, for example, by Frederic Raphael, there is a reference to 'head in the sand Utopianism'. Elsewhere in the novel the author has: 'The trouble is, most people think they can be ostriches until the last minute.'

'Ostriches' are frequently mentioned. Jeremy Brooks, in *Henry's War*, writes: 'It may prise a few ostrich heads out of the sand.' John Sherwood, in *The Half Hunter*, has: 'Why does Stella try to keep it from her? That sort of ostrich policy always ends in disaster.' *Abbie*, by Dane Chandos, has: 'She was the ostrich with its head being pulled out of the sand.'

Gilbert, when drunk, was full of wondrous stories and elaborate leg-pulls. He decided to give him his head.

Angus Wilson *Anglo-Saxon Attitudes*

It is the horse, rather than the ostrich, to which we refer in **give someone his head** 'allow a person to go ahead as fast as he wishes'. We could refer instead to **giving someone free rein**, 'allowing him to make his own decisions'. More mysterious is the animal alluded to in **sex rears its ugly head**. 'Ugly' is normally included, presumably with reference to moral ugliness, but Mary McCarthy, in *The Group*, writes: 'Has sex reared its head here?'

As Nigel Rees puts it, in his *Dictionary of Popular Phrases*, there is a suggestion of a Loch Ness Monster type of creature. By chance this phrase came into use a year or two before the *Inverness Courier* had revived the monster story in the early 1930s, but there does seem to be a connection. The phrase has all the appearance of a quotation, but no one has yet identified a source.

Miscellaneous 'head' phrases include **banging one's head against a brick wall**, which is what a speaker may claim to be doing if he continues to fail after many attempts. To **keep one's head above water** is to stay out of debt. If this is something one can do easily, then one can **do it standing on one's head**.

Putting two heads together is in response to the proverbial **two heads are better than one** 'a joint opinion is better than that of one person'. Mary McCarthy, who can always be relied upon for an example of a set phrase, has someone say in *The Group*: 'There must be *something* you and Jim could do with him, if the two of you put your heads together.'

Not be able to make head nor tail of something is not to be able to discern any sense in something. *Picturesque Expressions*, edited by Laurence Urdang, explains this in terms of a tossed coin that lands in such a way that neither 'heads' nor 'tails' can be called. This is not the case. The citations for the phrase given in *The Oxford English Dictionary* make it clear that the original allusion was to not being able to distinguish the beginning from the end of an unsatisfactory story or line of argument.

■ HEARING AID

Mr Jingle uttered a patronizing 'Hear, hear' which was responded to by the remainder of the company.

Charles Dickens *The Pickwick Papers*

Hear, hear! is now normally used to congratulate someone on what he has said and express agreement with it. The phrase is a shortened form of **Hear him, hear him**! used in the British House of Commons at the end of the 17th century to draw attention to what a member had said. The exclamation at that time was by no means always intended as a compliment. Said in a particular tone of voice it could mean 'just listen to what this idiot is saying'. Those who use the phrase in modern times may have such thoughts at the backs of their minds, but in theory they are expressing approval.

■ HIDDEN TALENTS

She had put Helena, who was not one to hide her light under a bushel, on the board of the literary magazine.

Mary McCarthy *The Group*

Someone who **hides his light under a bushel** is too shy or modest to reveal his talents and good qualities to others. The 'bushel' referred to is a wooden container used to measure a bushel (equivalent to eight gallons) of grain or fruit. Two thousand years ago it would have been a familiar every-day object.

The phrase became well-known because of its use in the New Testament. According to Matthew 5.14, Jesus told his disciples in the Sermon on the Mount: 'You are the light of the world. A city set on a hill cannot be hid. Nor do men light a lamp and put it under a bushel, but on a stand, and it gives light to all in the house. Let your light so shine before men, that they may see your good works and give glory to your Father who is in heaven.'

The image occurs again at Mark 4.21: 'Is a lamp brought in to be put under a bushel, or under a bed, and not on a stand? For there is nothing hid, except to be made manifest; nor is anything secret, except to come to light.' Luke 11.33 has: 'No one after lighting a lamp puts it in a cellar or under a bushel, but on a stand, that those who enter may see the light.'

In modern times 'hide one's light under a bushel' is often phrased negatively. Derek Jewell, in *Come In No.1 Your Time Is Up*, has: ' "Is he as much of a financial genius as they make out?" "The best finance director in the country. He doesn't exactly hide his light under a bushel." '

There was formerly another phrase that referred to **measuring other people's corn by one's own bushel**. It was a rather long-winded way of talking about judging others by one's own standards. Bishop Joseph Henshaw, in his *Horae Succisivæ*, or *Spare Hours of Meditations* (1631) remarks that 'men usually measure others by their own bushels: they that are ill themselves, are commonly apt to think ill of others'.

■ HIGH HORSES

'She was quite nice as well, a bit toffee-nosed, though, no offence.'

Clifford Hanley *The Taste of Too Much*

People who act in a supercilious way are universally unpopular. They are described by a number of metaphorical phrases, many of which expand the idea of **looking down on others**. They may **look down their noses**, for instance, which they are said to do when they assume an expression of disdain. Those who do this will sometimes tilt their heads backwards, as if confronted by a bad smell. For a moment they will have their **noses in the air**. This action can easily be directed *at* a specific person. 'Catherine had **turned up her nose at** him' writes Rumer Godden, in *The Lady and the Unicorn*.

Habitual behaviour of this kind may well lead to the accusation, in Britain at least, that such a person is **toffee-nosed**. 'Toffee-nosed young bugger!' says a policeman, in Joyce Porter's *Dover One*. The 'toffee' was perhaps suggested by another British slang term, 'toff', used of a well-dressed upper-class person. 'Toffee-nosed' may also carry the idea of being **stuck-up**, an older term with much the same meaning. The Opies, in *Lore and Language of Schoolchildren*, reported that 'toffee-nosed' was being well-used by British schoolchildren in the late 1950s to describe a **swankpot**. Perhaps it was children who converted old-fashioned 'toff' into 'toffee' and linked it with expressions such as 'look down one's nose'.

A male toff of the past frequently wore a 'high hat'. The hats themselves are seldom seen today, but **high-hat** lives on to describe snobbish behaviour. 'That'd put a stop to all her high-hat nonsense before it's too late' occurs in Kate O'Brien's *Pray for the Wanderer*. American speakers might instead say that a person is a **high-hat** or **high-hatter** and use **high-hatted** as the adjective. Another construction again is used by Mae West in *Pleasure Man*: 'I asks him civil if he catches our act, and he turns the ice on me; gives me the high-hat.'

---

*'Would you care to be back at Jordan's?' he asked Clara.
'I don't think so,' she replied.
'Yes, she would!' cried her mother; 'thank her stars if she could get back. Don't you listen to her. She's for ever on that 'igh horse of hers.'*

D.H. Lawrence *Sons and Lovers*

Another way in which a person looks down on others is from a 'high horse'. He may be described as **on his high horse** or be told to **get off his high horse**. The allusion is an obvious one, and it is surprising that such phrases have only been used since the beginning of the 19th century. 'High horse', incidentally, is not a description that would be used by horsemen. *The Horseman's Dictionary*, by Lida Fleitmann Bloodgood and Piero Santini, makes no mention of it, but does have an interesting entry under 'High School' (*Haute École*). The first sentence reads: 'The training of horses to execute a series of highly complicated movements known as "airs".'

'What if I talked white-folks' talk at church, and with my neighbours? They'd think I was puttin' on airs to beat Moses.'

Harper Lee *To Kill a Mockingbird*

By coincidence, **putting on airs** is another way of acting in a superior way. The phrase was earlier **give oneself airs** but seems to have merged with **putting on side**, which once meant much the same thing (the metaphor being derived from putting side on a billiard ball). C.P. Snow demonstrates the use of the modern phrase in *The Masters*: 'Do you think I'm going to vote for a man who's taking it for granted he's been elected and is behaving like the Master before the present one is dead? And whose wife is putting on airs about it already?'

The artificial movements of horses were presumably called 'airs' because they described doing something with a certain air, in an airy manner, gracefully and delicately. The 'airs' that a person is said to put on are based on a similar idea, though that is not to suggest that the phrase referring to superciliousness is derived from *Haute École* terminology.

■ HILL COUNTRY

Men reach their sexual peak at sixteen and decline thereafter. Brian was twenty-four. No doubt he was over the hill. Eight years over the hill.

Erica Jong *Fear of Flying*

A person can be **over the hill** in the sense that a crisis has been passed, as in a severe illness, so that he is now getting better. In a different sense the phrase means that he is past his prime and beginning to decline. John Le Carré, in *The Honourable Schoolboy*, has: 'Senility, Jerry told himself. You're over the hill, sport, no question.'

Not everyone would define a man of twenty-four as being 'over the hill', as does Erica Jong in *Fear of Flying* even when thinking of him purely in terms of sexual activity, but Miss Jong is entitled to her view. Even she would not say that anyone of that age is **as old as the hills**, using the commonest simile applied to age. Angus Wilson writes, in *Anglo-Saxon Attitudes*: 'Fifty-five must seem as old as the hills to a girl like you. And anyway,' Rose added, 'I *look* as old as the hills.'

A **hill of beans** is an American term for anything of insignificant value. The implication is that even a huge pile of beans, long used as symbols of valueless objects, would be worth little or nothing. **Not worth a hill of beans** and **doesn't amount to a hill of beans** are commonly found, as is the comment that someone **doesn't know beans** about a subject. **Hill-billy** is also an American term for a rustic, someone who comes from a backwoods area. 'Billy' is merely the pet-form of William used as a generic name.

■ HOGGING THE SHOW

Nevertheless, as he received no salary, he felt that his independence was secure. Independent as a hog on ice, he thought, in one of the Old Loyalist Ontario expressions which popped up, unbidden, in his mind when least expected.

Robertson Davies *The Lyre of Orpheus*

Charles Earle Funk explains in the Foreword to *A Hog on Ice* that it was curiosity about the origin of **as independent as a hog on ice** which led to his interest in popular sayings. The expression is unknown in Britain; in spite of this, Dr Funk eventually concluded that the expression originated in Scotland with the game of curling. A stone that stops short is known as a 'hog', and it is certainly on ice, but it is difficult to see how this can relate to a phrase which means 'cockily independent'. It is more likely to be an ironic reference to a real hog trying to walk on ice, something it is quite unable to do. The hog soon gives up the attempt and waits to be dragged away. A sarcastic reference to a hog on ice being independent, when the very opposite is true, can easily be imagined.

Between my wife's natural desires, my exotic wishes, and the contractor's inherent culpability, we went hog-wild.

Carl Sterland *Chuck*

Another purely American expression is to **go hog-wild**. It means to 'become over-excited' as hogs apparently do when aroused. The phrase is often applied, as it is in the quotation above, to spending money too freely. It is recorded in print from 1904 but was no doubt in colloquial use before that time.

I thought I might as well go the whole hog – I might as well die for a pound as a penny, if I had to die.

Henry Lawson *Stiffner and Jim*

In Britain to **go the whole hog** 'do something completely, thoroughly' is a more familiar phrase, though this is said to have originated in America at the beginning of the 19th century. A 'hog' in slang meant a ten-cent piece, just as in Britain it later meant either a shilling or a sixpence. The coin-names would have come about because of the representation of a hog-like animal on them. 'To go the whole hog' would have meant to spend all one's money at once, to invest everything. 'We ought to have gone the whole hog and struck his name off the books' is in C.P. Snow's *The Affair*.

The phrase is sometimes used to mean 'have sexual intercourse' as in 'I have tried all sorts of erotic things, but my girl-friend refuses to go the whole hog'. This occurs in a letter of desperation written to an agony aunt by the young hero of *The Growing Pains of Adrian Mole*, by Sue Townsend.

The Oxford English Dictionary prefers a more literary explanation of 'go the whole hog', quoting a poem by William Cowper 'Hypocrisy Detected'. Cowper's theme is that Mahomet banned his followers from eating only part of a hog, not specifying which part:

> *But for one piece they thought it hard*
> *From the whole hog to be debarr'd.*

By the use of sophistry, says Cowper, Mahometans manage to convince themselves that each part in turn is acceptable, and 'eat up the hog'. This explanation of the phrase is ingenious but is probably what Americans graphically know as **hog-wash** 'nonsense'.

■ HOLED UP

We shall generally find that the triangular person has got into the square hole, the oblong into the triangular, and a square person has squeezed himself into the round hole.

Sydney Smith *Sketches of Moral Philosophy*

The clergyman and wit Sydney Smith (1771–1845) was the first to apply the differently-shaped hole metaphor to people who find themselves in positions unsuited to their abilities and training. His lecture, quoted above, was published in 1806. By the end of the 19th century a **square peg in a round hole** had become almost proverbial, a recognition that Smith had identified a widespread human phenomenon.

Writers appear to appreciate the phrase. Elizabeth Jane Howard, in *Getting it Right*, combines it with an echo of Shakespeare: 'Boredom might be a kind of evil, ubiquitous secret that people called by any other name that suited their nature and view of themselves. Discontent, dissatisfaction, being a square peg in a round hole, envy . . .'

W. Somerset Maugham, as so often, creates a personal version of a standard phrase. In *The Lotus Eater* he says: 'Most people lead the lives that circumstances have thrust upon them, and though some repine, looking upon themselves as round pegs in square holes, the greater part accept their lot.'

Edward Blishen, in *A Cack-handed War*, elaborates on Sydney Smith: 'He was, in every sort of profound sense, an outcast. In his case, the phrase about a square peg in a round hole was laughably inadequate. The labour force at the Quarry was full of pegs merely square. The War Ag knew how to hammer these down, most of the time, into their ill-fitting holes. But it would not be easy to name the shape of peg that might suggest Leonard's unsuitability and crazy awkwardness – and his unhammerability.'

'Top hole,' said the English peer.

W. Somerset Maugham *Gigolo and Gigolette*

'Holes' occur in a few other English expressions. **Top hole** used to be an exclamation which meant 'excellent', but it became associated with aristocratic idiots and would only be used now as a joke. It probably referred to some method of scoring, as on a cribbage-board. A much older saying of similar origin was **take someone a hole lower** 'humble or humiliate someone'. This has been replaced by **take someone down a peg or two** in the same sense. Monica Dickens, in *The Fancy*, has: 'He had had to change his policy towards Sheila recently. She used to be one of the ones who had to be taken down a

peg, countering each reminder of a black mark with stubborn hauteur.'

To **pick holes in** 'find fault with' someone was earlier **find holes in**, and more specifically, **find a hole in someone's coat**. Shakespeare's *Henry the Fifth* provides an example when Fluellen says of Bardolph: 'I do perceive he is not the man that he would gladly make show to the world he is; if I find a hole in his coat I will tell him my mind.'

To be **in a hole** is to be in an awkward situation, perhaps financially embarrassed. This could have come about because of expensive purchases which have **made a hole** in one's resources. The person to whom this will most likely happen cannot help spending money as soon as he gets it, described in the vivid phrase: **money burns a hole in his pocket**.

■ HOLLOW VICTORIES

After all, he reflected a shade impatiently, not every young woman had the privilege of being deflowered by a dissector of the entire female pelvis. But there were sighs and tears, regrets and recriminations. He felt he had won a hollow victory.

Richard Gordon *The Face-Maker*

A **hollow victory** originally meant that one person had 'beaten the other hollow'. *The Times* (July 1894) reported: 'The Prince's cutter steadily left her opponent and gained a very hollow victory.' This is 'hollow' in the sense of 'complete, thorough'. Dickens uses the word in that sense in *Bleak House* when Mr Guppy describes the house he has bought in Lambeth as 'a hollow bargain'.

When Tom Wolfe writes in *The Bonfire of the Vanities*: 'He had run right over her, but it was a hollow victory' he clearly means something else. He does not say *and* it was a hollow victory. His meaning is that the victory had no real significance. The 'hollowness' is easily understood in this case, suggesting as it does an outer casing which has nothing solid inside it. The question is whether to **beat someone hollow** therefore means that one somehow extracts everything that is inside one's opponent, leaving only the outer shell.

'You women beat me all hollow!'

Zane Grey *Betty Zane*

As it happens, things as well as people can be 'beaten hollow'. Dickens once again provides an example of such usage. In *The Pickwick Papers* there is a discussion about gifts to electors which help persuade them to vote for a particular candidate. A man says: 'Five-and-forty green parasols, at seven and sixpence a-piece. Beats stockings, and flannel, and all that sort of thing hollow.'

'Hollow' acquired its senses of 'complete, completely' in colloquial speech rather than literature. This lends support to the suggestion reported by Ernest Weekley that 'hollow' in this phrase is a corruption of 'wholly'. 'Beaten wholly' would have been said by educated speakers. It could easily have been mis-heard by the uneducated as 'beaten hollow' and understood to be a reference to beating someone until he had nothing left inside. The modern use of 'hollow victory' interestingly restores 'hollow' to its original meaning of emptiness.

■ HOLY WRIT

'She was a holy terror. Any man in the South Riding was scared of her.'

Winifred Holtby *South Riding*

'Holy' was used in its Old English form to translate Latin *sacer* 'sacred'. Historically the word links with 'whole', as well as 'health' and 'heal'. To 'hallow' something is to make it holy, safe from profanity. None of this has prevented creators of slang from using the word 'holy' as they will, though to describe someone as **a holy terror** is perhaps justifiable. 'Holy' here means 'awesome, beyond belief'.

Gil straightened up, galvanized. 'Mort! Holy! Holy jumping! Come here, quick!'

Bernard Wolfe *The Late-Risers*

Use of the word 'holy' in a number of exclamations is more difficult to explain. Slang dictionaries record such expressions as **Holy cats!**, **Holy cow!**, **Holy gee!**, **Holy Mackerel!**, **Holy Moses!**, **Holy shit!**, **Holy Smoke!** 'Holy gee!' is clearly a euphemism for 'Holy God!' The other terms could also be considered euphemistic in that they avoid 'Holy Christ!'

None of these exclamations is much used in Britain, though they are readily found in American and Canadian novels. Mordecai Richler's *Joshua Then and Now*, for instance, uses 'holy shit!' and has the exchange: '"You could have seen me in *Thunderball*. You know, the Bond film." "Holy cow. Were you really in that?"' Most American of all is the extraordinary **Jesus H. Christ!**, where 'Holy' is treated as if it were a middle name and reduced to an initial.

'I believe I'm bleeding.'
'Holy Smoke, so you are!'

H.G. Wells *Kipps*

It is possible that some of these 'holy' expressions were coined as mild insults to particular religious groups. 'Holy cow!' would have mocked Hindus, for whom that animal is sacred. 'Holy Mackerel!' would have been aimed at the Roman Catholics who ate fish every Friday, just as 'Holy Smoke!' would have been a comment on their use of incense. Supporting the fish theory is the fact that **Holy Cod** was once a nickname for Good Friday. 'Holy Moses!' would have been anti-Semitic, since Moses was frequently used as a generic nickname for a Jewish male.

The professional Holy Joes, in and out of the pulpits, make a lot of noise about their rescue societies and good works, but Keate's charity proved the more practical in the long run.

R.F. Delderfield *Theirs Was the Kingdom*

Holy friar 'liar' was at one time a rhyming slang term. **Holy Joe** is a nickname used in third person reference, mainly by military personnel, to describe a padre or chaplain. In the Royal Navy, according to Wilfred Granville's *Dictionary of Sailors' Slang*, the chaplain is also known as the **Sin Bosun**. *Service Slang*, by J.L. Hunt and A.G. Pringle, says that **sky pilot** is a Royal Air Force equivalent.

'What in the name of all that's holy are we goin' to do wi' it?'

Margaret Barrington *The End of a Hero*

Novelists sometimes amuse themselves with phrasal exclamations as they do with metaphorical idioms. In *The Mackerel Plaza* Peter de Vries creates a reverend hero whose surname is Mackerel. We are told that he hates to be addressed as 'Brother' or 'Reverend', preferring 'Mr Mackerel'. The author continues: 'The familiarity of "Hi, there, Mackerel" would not have unduly alarmed him. Just beyond that, however, lay the comic marshlands of "Holy Mackerel", a nickname under which he had smarted in student days and which he lived in cold fear of some local wit's reviving.'

In Susan Barrett's *Moses*, there comes a moment when a man realizes that he is the father of a baby to whom the mother has already given the name Moses. As the truth strikes him, he utters the inevitable 'Holy Moses!' The author claims for this 'a Freudian aptness'.

■ HOME THOUGHTS

'Lord, I shall be glad when we get to Dover. Home, sweet home, eh?'

Evelyn Waugh *Vile Bodies*

John Howard Payne was born in New York in 1791. By the age of eighteen he was on stage as an actor, billed as The American Juvenile Wonder, but he was already writing plays as well as acting in them. He also wrote musical dramas, including *Clari, The Maid of Milan*. In this was included a song 'Home, Sweet Home' which had an outstanding success. It introduced the phrase **home, sweet home** into the language as well as **there's no place like home**. The latter phrase occurs in the verse:

Mid pleasures and palaces though we may roam,

Be it ever so humble, there's no
place like home;
A charm from the skies seems to
hallow us there,
Which, seek through the world, is
ne'er met with elsewhere.
Home, home, sweet, sweet home!
There's no place like home! there's
no place like home!

Payne was American consul in Tunis
1843–5 and went there again in 1851.
He died in Tunis in 1852.

'He's a home bird as you know, sir.'

Margaret Forster *Georgy Girl*

Home comforts are alluded to **make
oneself at home**, which is to act in
someone else's house as if one were in
one's own home, to make that place a
home from home, as it were. One is as
comfortable there as in one's own
home. A **home bird** is now someone
who appreciates such comforts and
likes to spend as much time as
possible at home. The 'bird', however,
was possibly suggested by 'hen-
pecked', since 'home bird' at the end
of the 19th century was applied to a
hen-pecked husband.

Charity begins at home has been
proverbial since the 14th century.
Nothing to write home about 'of little
interest' came into use in the 19th
century and would have had a literal
meaning to soldiers serving abroad.
Far more recent is the ironic question
who's he when he's at home? which
implies 'presumably the people he
lives with know who he is, but no one
else knows'.

Another jocular colloquial phrase is
till the cows come home 'for a very
long time'. It is often used in a
statement like: 'You can tell him till
the cows come home, but he still
won't understand you.' The
expression has been used in English
since the early 17th century. 'I

warrant you lay a Bed till the cows
came home,' quoted by Jonathan
Swift in his *Polite Conversation*,
clearly refers to cows coming in from
the fields in the evening.

'It's time somebody told you a few
home truths,' said Doris.

Margaret Forster *Georgy Girl*

References to 'home' in set phrases
are not always allusions to pleasant
comforts. **Home truths**, for example,
are unpleasant facts that come **close
to home**, as another saying expresses
it. They are truths which directly
concern the person at whom they are
aimed. Any remark which is 'close to
home' is embarrassingly relevant to
the person who hears it said.

'You've been a bad mother for bloody
years and now it's coming home to
roost.'

Fay Weldon *Down Among the Women*

Things which **come home to roost**
'return to their source, the person
responsible for them' are always
unpleasant. The phrase appears to
have originated with Robert Southey,
in *The Curse of Kehama* (1810):
'Curses are like young chickens; they
always come home to roost.' Lord
Lytton, in *Alice*, has: 'The curse has
come home to roost.' The phrase is
no longer restricted to curses, but
applies to mistaken behaviour of any
kind. John Fowles demonstrates
modern usage in *The French
Lieutenant's Woman*: 'A certain past
cynicism had come home to roost.'

Polixenes: *I'll have thy beauty
scratch'd with briers and made
More homely than thy state.*

William Shakespeare *The Winter's
Tale*

For a British speaker of English, to
hear a woman described as **homely**
tends to conjure up an image of a
motherly figure who devotes herself
to looking after the home and family.
American speakers usually mean that
the woman concerned is plain and
unattractive, if not downright ugly.
Shakespeare and his contemporaries
would have understood 'homely' in
this sense. 'To see such lovers,
Thurio, as yourself; / Upon a homely
object Love can wink' says Valentine,
in *The Two Gentlemen of Verona*,
meaning that Thurio is an ugly brute.
The word provides a good example of
the preservation in American English
of an early meaning lost in Britain.

■ HORSE SENSE

*'I don't think you're very interested in
girls, are you, Peter?'
'Oh, I don't know.'
'Oh, I bet you're a dark horse all
right.'*

Clifford Hanley *The Taste of Too
Much*

It is natural that some of our 'horse'
phrases should derive from horse-
racing. Typical is a **dark horse**
'little-known person who suddenly
achieves prominence'. The allusion is
not to the colour of the horse but to
one whose performance has been kept
'dark', or secret. Typical illustrations
of use occur in C.P. Snow's *The
Affair* – 'Martin's a dark horse. I
should like to know what he wants
for the college' – and Elizabeth Jane
Howard's *Getting it Right*. In the
latter novel a young man comes home
with a young titled lady, though he
normally has no girl friends at all.
His sister says: 'Well, Gavin, I think
you're a very dark horse.'

To have information **straight from the
horse's mouth** is to have it from the
best authority, the one person above
all others who can state the facts. In
Aldous Huxley's *Brave New World*
the phrase is quoted several times in
the opening chapters as students note
down what the Director of Hatcheries
and Mustapha Mond say to them. To
back the wrong horse is to give one's
support to a candidate who
subsequently loses in any kind of
election.

*'I don't want to look a gift-horse in the
mouth, which is not a gracious thing to
do.'*

Charles Dickens *David Copperfield*

To **look a gift-horse in the mouth** is to
refuse or criticize a gift. The allusion
to 'looking a horse in the mouth'
refers to what one does when buying
a horse. An examination of its teeth
helps to assess its true age. The 'gift-
horse' phrase can be used in an
abstract sense of a favour granted, as
in Len Deighton's *Funeral in Berlin*:
'Don't look a gift-horse in the mouth,
peach blossom. Take off.'

*Harald had merged in it the story of
his father's life with some of the story
of Alexander Meiklejohn at Wisconsin,
not admitting to himself that this
father and Meiklejohn were horses of a
different colour.*

Mary McCarthy *The Group*

In Shakespeare's *Twelfth Night* Maria
says at one point: 'My purpose is
indeed a horse of that colour,'
meaning that her purpose is
'something of that kind'. **A horse of a**

different colour therefore is simply something or someone very different.

To **eat like a horse** is to eat a great deal, while to say that one **could eat a horse** emphasizes one's hunger. To **flog a dead horse** is to persist with something when it is clearly useless to do so.

'When I was a child I heard a grown-up man telling someone "wild horses weren't going to drag him" to some party. I was dying to hear about them and where they dragged people . . . Nobody ever told me.'

Berta Ruck *Ancestral Voices*

Miss Ruck complains in the quotation above that no one would tell her as a child about the wild horses. They were perhaps being kind, not wishing to fill her mind with images of horses attached to someone's arms and legs, pulling in different directions. This was a way of torturing people in the Middle Ages to extract information from them. The phrase, however, appeared only in the 19th century.

Mary Webb has a character in *Gone to Earth* who makes much of the **wild horses wouldn't drag it from me** expression. 'Wild 'orses shanna drag it from me, nor yet blood 'orses, nor 'unters, nor cart-'orses, nor Suffolk punches!' he proclaims. Later he repeats this formula. The author comments: 'When he had made a good phrase, he was apt to work it to death.' The phrase occurs again without authorial comment in Alice Dwyer-Joyce's *The Penny Box*: 'Wild horses would never have dragged such words out of her.'

Now they are thinking of changing horses in mid-torrent.

Dane Chandos *Abbie*

Folk-wisdom talks about the folly of trying to **change horses in mid-stream** 'make major changes in the middle of an undertaking'. The 'mid-torrent' version quoted above is used by the idiosyncratic Aunt Abbie, who says elsewhere in the novel: 'Hold your horses, dear, lest you repent at leisure.' To **hold one's horses** is simply to pause for a moment. Margaret Laurence, in *The Diviners*, has: ' "I was a preacher." "What? You? And what's so – ?" "Hold your horses. Let me finish." '

First achieve balanced development; then specialize. Don't put the cart before the horse in other words.

David Walker *Geordie*

Proverbs still quoted in modern times include **you can take a horse to water but you can't make it drink**, used to remind someone that a person who is given an opportunity may still decide not take advantage of it. **Locking the stable door after the horse has bolted** is doing something too late, such as trying to take out an insurance policy on a house that has burned down. To **put the cart before the horse** is to reverse the logical order of things.

■ HOWLERS

It was one of his jokes that art criticism, which for years had kept the wolf from the family door, was a racket.

J.I.M. Stewart *The Last Tresilians*

In the expression **keep the wolf from the door** it is famine which is personified as a wolf. Poverty and distress are likened to a ravenous animal which is always beyond the door, anxious to enter. Earning enough money, by any legal means, keeps the wolf away. 'Keep the wolf from the door' has been in use since the 15th century (the last wolf to be killed in the wild in England, according to *The Language of Field Sports*, by C.E. Hare, was in 1682) and still serves a useful purpose, though those who use it probably no longer have a picture in their minds of a malignant animal. Penelope Mortimer, in *The Pumpkin Eater*, refers to '. . . a story about Jake taking up script-writing to keep the wolf from the door'.

'They knew that if you testified openly, I'd be the one they'd throw to the wolves.'

James A. Michener *Chesapeake*

To **throw someone to the wolves** 'fail to protect someone from severe treatment at the hands of others' also makes use of the wolf's reputation for ferocity. The person 'thrown to the wolves' will be metaphorically pulled to pieces or severely mauled. In modern times it is often the media who are perceived as a pack of wolves, waiting to tear apart an innocent victim.

'I never had any close pal,' Jules says lightly. 'Lone wolf, that's me.' Cliché. But true. It is him. He is distant, distant from the town, from Morag, from everything, perhaps even from himself.

Margaret Laurence *The Diviners*

Other 'wolf' expressions include **lone wolf**, a reference to a person who is mostly content to go his or her own way without needing the company or support of others. It is said that although wolves normally live and hunt in packs, there are some who choose to lead a separate existence.

The **wolf whistle** which is supposed publicly to express admiration for someone, usually of the opposite sex, refers back to 'wolf' in the sense of 'predatory or ravenous male looking for sexual gratification'. This over-states the case, however, since amongst groups of workmen a wolf-whistle is often an automatic response and not a genuine expression of admiration. It merely signals to one's fellow-workers in a conventional way that the man doing the whistling retains a lively interest in the opposite sex.

'Beware of false prophets, who come to you in sheep's clothing but inwardly are ravenous wolves.'

New Testament, Matthew 7.15

To **cry wolf** is constantly to say that there is danger when there is none. The ancient fable warns that the shepherd-boy who cried wolf too often merely to attract attention was not believed when finally a wolf appeared. A **wolf in sheep's clothing** 'someone who appears friendly but is an enemy in disguise' is also frequently attributed to a fable, but the New Testament, in the passage quoted above, was probably responsible for making the metaphor well known. An interesting reversal is suggested in Derek Jewell's *Come In No.1 Your Time is Up*: '"His cynicism hides a heart of gold." "A sheep in wolf's clothing you'll be telling me next."'

■ ICE-BREAKING

Mrs Cluppins having once broken the ice, thought it a favourable opportunity for entering into a short dissertation on her own domestic affairs . . .

Charles Dickens *The Pickwick Papers*

To **break the ice** 'do or say something to remove the uneasy tension that may be present amongst people who do not know one another', has been a popular phrase since the 17th century. It occurs very commonly in literature. '"I've broken the ice now," she thought, as he walked away. "I think he was only shy"' is in W. Somerset Maugham's *Winter Cruise*. Ngaio Marsh, in *Surfeit of Lampreys*, has: 'You'll be able to break the ice by telling her that you recognized her at once from her likeness to your father.' 'They'd met before; the ice had been broken, one might have said, pre-prandially' is in *Other Men's Wives*, by Alexander Fullerton.

Occasionally the phrase is used in its earlier sense of 'make a beginning', where a developing relationship is not involved. The man who says 'Good! I did the breaking of the ice' in E.M. Forster's *Howards End* means only that he has started an idea in someone's head. The phrase can also be used with reference to preparing the way for someone else, acting as an ice-breaker for other ships, as it were.

Other 'ice' expressions include **skate on thin ice** 'talk about a subject that is controversial and may at any moment provoke an argument'. For **cut no ice** see page 58. To have something **on ice** is to have it in reserve, as if in a refrigerator.

■ IF ONLY

'If, and this is a big if, we have some product for you to throw in which they'll swallow.'

Edward A. Rogers *Face to Face*

A big if now occurs with some frequency in conversations. It makes the point that the condition introduced by 'if' is an important one and may not easily be met. In the background is the thought that this small two-lettered word is somehow capable of expanding. 'If you can keep your head when all about you / Are losing theirs and blaming it on you' writes Kipling in his famous poem, as one of many conditions that will make a boy a man. Kipling called the poem 'If'; 'A Big If' would have been even more appropriate.

A body could go crazy pondering the ifs of life – or of history. As Bink's grandfather, the President, once said impatiently to a questioning Cabinet officer, 'If, if, if! If a bullfrog had wings, he wouldn't bump his arse so much!'

Denison Hatch *The Stork*

In Shakespeare's time 'and' could be used to mean 'if.' 'No more of that, Hal, and thou lovest me', says Falstaff. 'And' with this meaning was frequently reduced to 'an' and survived in that form until the 19th century. Children then would recite: 'If **Ifs and Ans** were pots and pans there'd be no trade for tinkers.' **Ifs and buts** is the modern phrase, referring to the complications that cast doubt on a proposed undertaking. They make it **iffy**, as we also say, proving that 'if' can indeed be expanded.

■ IN AGREEMENT

'She's nothing much on looks,' I said quickly. 'You can say that again,' she said.

Richard Bissell *The Pajama Game*

Eric Partridge, in his *Dictionary of Historical Slang*, records that **Say it again**! was a catch-phrase used by tailors from 1870. It meant 'I heartily agree with you.' The modern equivalent, **You can say that again**, is certainly not restricted to tailors and is current in all English-speaking countries. 'You know how the phone scares you sometimes,' says someone in *Tropic of Ruislip*, by Leslie Thomas. 'And you can say that again,' replies another.

The phrase inevitably causes some people to amuse themselves by pretending to think it is a genuine instruction to repeat the words. The joke for most people has worn rather thin. Alexander Fullerton, in *Other Men's Wives*, has: ' "Must have been a very amusing thought." "You can say that again." Serge decided not to.'

■ IN SO MANY WORDS

'I should like to have a word with you,' said Ralph.
'As many words as you like, sir,' rejoined Squeers.

Charles Dickens *Nicholas Nickleby*

Singular forms of nouns are sometimes used collectively in English phrases. A person who wants to **have a word with you** (a **word in your ear** if confidential) will undoubtedly want to have more than one word. In a similar way, the person who says 'Why not come and **have a bite** with us?' in Francis King's *The Needle* is not thinking of offering his guest a single bite. In the case of 'word' it is of course possible to **have words with someone** in a different sense. 'Harald and Kay were in the bedroom, having "words", she supposed,' writes Mary McCarthy in *The Group*, and we know that the words were definitely not friendly ones.

'If I may get a word in edgeways, I'd like to tell you about another part-time marriage.'

Berta Ruck *Ancestral Voices*

Not to be able to get a word in edgeways is a humorous expression that came into general use towards the end of the 19th century. Some speakers would use 'edgewise' for 'edgeways', but the image remains the same. There is no logic about the saying when it is applied, as it always is, to spoken language, but it makes its point. The speaker is simply commenting on how difficult it is to break into a discussion.

'Word' is sometimes used for 'word of honour', or solemn promise. We **give someone our word** that we will do something, and are said to be **as good as our word** if we do it. **On my word of honour** is sometimes brought into use to emphasize that we are telling the truth. 'On my word of honor', says Keller, in Arthur Miller's *All My Sons*, 'there's a jail in the basement'.

He must know that a good word put in for him by Scarlet would do him no end of harm.

Fay Weldon *Down Among the Women*

To **put in a good word for someone** again shows the collective use of 'word'. The 'good word' consists of any number of positive and admiring comments. We use the phrase again when we say that we **haven't a good word to say for someone**. We really can't think of anything pleasant to say about him. It is possible to be more emphatic about our dislike by employing the format phrase X **isn't the word for him**. 'He's harmless', someone says, and we say contemptuously: 'Harmless isn't the word for him.' We may then go on to specify which word we consider to be more suitable, or we leave it to our companion's imagination.

'Mum's the word.'

Mary Webb *Gone to Earth*

Some idiomatic phrases specify a particular word, as in **from the word go** 'from the very beginning', or really do mean a single word, as when someone **leaves without a word** or tells us **not to breathe** (or **say**) **a word about something**. In the latter case he could have said instead: **Mum's the word**. 'Mum' here is connected with an inarticulate sound such as a mumble, and has nothing to do with the familiar word for 'mother'. It often occurs in the phrase to **keep mum**. 'You're to keep mum as usual,' says a character in Geoffrey Wagner's *Sophie*, referring to criminal activities. Mary McCarthy, in *The Group*, has: 'Whatever was said about the Apartment, she was going to keep mum; let the others talk.'

If we are not prepared to argue with someone we may let him or her **have the last word**, though once again 'word' may be stretched to many sentences. 'Having the last word' is considerably less enjoyable if the person to whom we are speaking has indicated his lack of interest in what we are saying. 'I'll **take your word for it**' is one way of doing that.

'I shall not bandy words with you.'

Nathaniel Hawthorne *The House of the Seven Gables*

The person who is prepared to 'take our word for something' is not prepared to **bandy words with us**. This phrase was popular with the Elizabethans, who played a game called bandy which was similar to tennis. Something which was **bandied about** was metaphorically sent to and fro like the ball in that game. The phrase was applied especially to repartee. 'Well bandied both,' says the Princess to Katharine and Rosaline in *Love's Labour's Lost*, 'a set of wit well play'd'. Another application is shown in *King Lear*: 'Do you bandy looks with me, you rascal!' says the king to Oswald.

In modern times it is usually words or names that are bandied. 'I did not bandy words with him . . .' says the formidable aunt in Dane Chandos's *Abbie*. In *Laura* Vera Caspary has: 'Men were bandying her name in pool parlors . . .' Frederick Forsyth, in *The Day of the Jackal*, has a similar 'Don't you think it a rather odd procedure to bandy a man's name and reputation about in this manner?'

'Well, what a shock, this is certainly eat your words department.'

Roger Longrigg *Daughters of Mulberry*

We do other curious things with words apart from bandying them about. We **put words into someone's mouth** when we tell him what to say or claim that he has said something he did not in fact say. We **take the words out of someone's mouth** if we say what he was going to say before he has a chance to say it. Sometimes we are forced to **eat our words** and admit that we were wrong.

Conversational phrases are suitable for use in social intercourse, at gatherings where strangers are present, and where we weigh our words before uttering them.

James Main Dixon *English Idioms*

Other odd verbal behaviour consists of **weighing one's words** 'considering them carefully before speaking', and **twisting someone's words** to make them mean something other than what was intended. 'He suspects her of trying to send him mad, by twisting his words' writes Fay Weldon, in *Down Among the Women*. Someone who doesn't **mince words** metaphorically makes no effort to make them easier to digest. He says what he has to say bluntly. As with many of these 'word' phrases, the metaphorical implications are straightforward, yet vivid. Their meanings would be relatively easy to guess if we were not familiar with them.

I could not commit the gross indelicacy of saying 'My poor friend, where do you come in?' or words to that effect.

William J. Locke *Jaffery*

There are many other 'word' phrases. **Words to that effect** 'other words which convey the same general meaning' is a useful saving formula for someone who feels that he has not expressed something in the most suitable way. Something said in **words of one syllable** is supposed to be simple to understand, though any student of language knows that it is not necessarily the length of words which causes difficulties.

Of the proverbs which mention a 'word' or 'words', those most frequently heard are probably **actions speak louder than words** and **many a true word is spoken in jest**. The former sums up the thought that is inherent in many variant sayings, such as **words are but wind, good words without deeds are rushes and reeds**. The latter is so well known that speakers rarely bother to say more than 'many a true word'.

That last remark is true unless the speaker happens to be someone like Don Edwards. In 1986 The Reader's Digest Association in conjunction with The Multiple Sclerosis Society published for charitable purposes an affectionate collection of Mr Edwards' accidental sayings. The title of the booklet set the tone: *My Pear Tree Has Gone Bananas*. Mr Edwards' version of the 'many a true word' proverb mentioned above, as recorded by his office colleagues, was 'never a true word spoken in jest'. They also quote another of his 'word' sayings: 'You're putting words into my house.'

To complete the survey of 'word' expressions, there is the useful exclamation **famous last words**, said when someone has just made a rash statement. 'I've put all my money on that horse, it can't lose,' says a friend. 'Famous last words,' we murmur, indicating our belief that the action will end in disaster. The phrase is said to have been much used by British and American airmen during World War Two if anyone was unwise enough to suggest that a sortie would be trouble-free. The expression implies that a remark will be recalled later and its irony dwelt upon.

■ INCHING ALONG

'I am every inch a president.'

Nigel Dennis *Cards of Identity*

In spite of a general change to the

metric system, 'inches' still feature in English phrases. Both 'inch' and 'ounce' derive from Latin *uncia* 'twelfth part', an ounce still being a twelfth of a pound in Troy weight.

Every inch means 'completely' in the Nigel Dennis quotation above. In the same novel someone says 'You can't trust him an inch', meaning 'you can't trust him by the smallest amount'. Another common expression talks of **coming within an inch** of something 'coming very close to it' or 'very close to doing it'.

If someone takes undue advantage of a slight concession we say: **Give him an inch and he'll take a mile**. In the 16th century he would have taken 'an ell'. 'Ells' are no longer used, but at one time an ell was an English measure of 45 in (114 cm). The Flemish ell was 27 in (69 cm), relating the word more closely to its original meaning of 'an arm's length'. It has been suggested that the English measure was originally a 'double-ell'. The 'bend' or 'bow' of an 'ell' gave us the word 'elbow'.

■ JACK ROBINSON

'If I tell him you're our man, you'll get a letter from him before you can say Jack Robinson.'

C.P. Snow *The Affair*

Before you can say Jack Robinson, meaning 'very quickly', is now seldom heard in everyday conversation. The phrase first appeared in print in Fanny Burney's *Evelina* (1778), in slightly different form. Captain Mirvan announces that he is willing to 'lay ten pounds to a shilling' that he could throw the foppish Mr Lovel head first into a public bath. Another man present says: 'Done! I take your odds!' The captain then says: 'Why,

then, 'fore George, I'd do it as soon as say Jack Robinson.'

Mr Lovel manages to escape his ducking, and soon afterwards makes sneering remarks about the unintelligibility of the captain's 'sea-phrases'. There is no evidence that 'before you can say Jack Robinson' is a sea-phrase, and indeed nothing is known about its origin. An early suggestion that it referred to a man who was in the habit of making brief visits to the houses of his friends, departing even before his name could be announced, is clearly nonsensical. Even had such a madman existed, his name would not have been announced in that form.

Another writer in the 19th century claimed that the phrase was to be found in 'an old play' in the form 'saye Jacke! robys on'. This is totally meaningless, and the 'old play' has never been traced. No notable person called John or Jack Robinson seems to have lived in the 18th century, and in the absence of any other evidence one can only suppose that the name was chosen at random. At the end of the 19th century Kipling and other writers record the variant **before you can say knife**. The last word may be a pun on 'jack-knife'.

■ JAZZING IT UP

'If she wants to get plastered what do we do? It's a free country and all that jazz'.

Peter Draper *A Season in Love*

'Jazz' is a word of uncertain origin according to most dictionaries, though *Webster's New Collegiate Dictionary* confidently says that it is English slang and means 'to copulate with'. In fact, the word has only ever had that sense in black American slang. Of the various theories about the origin of the word, the most favoured is that it derives from the Creole patois of New Orleans and referred originally to erotic music and dancing. Clarence Major, in *Black Slang* says that it is 'a French word meaning sexy or sensuous'.

We can be more definite about the phrase **all that jazz**, in use since at least the 1950s, at first with the meaning 'all that nonsense'. It now means 'all that sort of thing'. 'You mean Strontium 90 and all that jazz' is in Penelope Mortimer's *The Pumpkin Eater*. The phrase usually occurs at the end of a sentence, but J.I.M. Stewart, in *The Last Tresilians*, has: 'The stuff he puts into a nice girl's head! All that jazz inspires artists only in rotten novels.'

■ KEEPING COOL

She was as cool as a cucumber when the boys got there. Opened the door and pointed to the body so calmly you'd have thought it was an everyday thing for her to find her boss murdered.

Vera Caspary *Laura*

Coolness and cucumbers were first associated with one another by Sir Thomas Elyot in *The Castle of Health* (1531). Elyot reported that eating them produced a 'cold and thick humour'. This in turn was said to 'abate lust'. A modern writer discussing cucumbers would be more likely to say that they produce flatulence, but perhaps that in turn has a dampening effect on sexual ardour.

The coolness alluded to in **cool as a cucumber** certainly had sexual overtones in former times. The phrase was often **cold as a cucumber**.

Beaumont and Fletcher, in their *Cupid's Revenge*, have a young man refer with regret to young maids 'cold as cucumbers'. Coldness has mostly given way to coolness, and the phrase is now synonymous with **cool, calm and collected**.

'So, just as calm as a cucumber I arose.'

Truman Capote *My Side of the Matter*

The linking of 'cool' and 'calm' in the latter phrase may have been responsible for the **calm as a cucumber** which now also occurs. Susan Barrett, in *Moses*, has: 'There's my friend Jo, calm as a cucumber, just went for her two weeks' holiday and came back with a baby.' The usual modern form, however, remains 'cool as a cucumber'. 'The way you caught on about that slop was something worth seeing. Bif! Right off. Cool as a cucumber.' So writes H.G. Wells in *Kipps*. Mary McCarthy, in *The Groves of Academe*, refers to: 'Hen sitting opposite, cool as a cucumber.' Margaret Laurence, in *The Diviners*, has a child describe a religious picture, referring to 'Jesus not looking worried at all, not by a long shot. He is standing there cool as a cucumber.' Mordecai Richler, in *Joshua Then and Now*, has a character say: 'Hey, you're some cool cucumber.'

Speakers in the 18th and 19th centuries who used the phrase may have associated it with the placidity of cows, since 'cucumber' was at that time always pronounced 'cow-cumber'. The vegetable in fact has no connection with cows: the process, known as folk-etymology, that led from cucumber to cow-cumber was the same one which made 'sparrow-grass' out of 'asparagus'.

■ KEEPING COUNT

'Maybe if the Committee could throw a little business our way . . .' 'I wouldn't want to do that, Charlie.' 'It was just a thought. Lookin' out for Number One, you know.'

Edward A. Rogers *Face to Face*

Cardinal numbers occur in many popular expressions. The philosophy expressed in **look after** or **look out for number one**, for instance, summed up the 1980s for many commentators. The phrase is obviously based on 'oneself', but influenced also by the fact that 'I' is both the first person personal pronoun and the Roman numeral 'one'. That was not always the case: the English pronoun was 'ic' or 'ich' until at least 1400.

'Number one', in the sense of oneself or one's own interests, seems to have appealed to Dickens. Eric Partridge quotes his remark that 'if a man doesn't take care of No.1, he will soon have 0 to take care of'. In *The Pickwick Papers* Lowten is made to say: 'No man should have more than two attachments – the first, to number one, and the second to the ladies.' There is a more modern reference in Richard Gordon's *The Face-Maker*, where a man is described as 'a bit lackadaisical and over-concerned with number one'. John Updike, in *Rabbit Redux*, has: 'You got to reason outwards from Number One. To you, you're Number One, not the kid.'

Superintendent Thomas's call of that morning had come as yet another blow to hopes of an early capture of the elusive killer. Once again the phrase 'back to square one' had been used.

Frederick Forsyth *The Day of the Jackal*

If research work leads to a dead end we may borrow an expression from the board game Snakes and Ladders and talk about **going back to square one**. Use of the phrase implies a reluctant acceptance of the fact that setbacks can occur at any time as we progress towards a specific point. It is something that must be borne in mind from the outset of any new project – **from day one**, as the modern phrase has it. This probably derives from military jargon.

From the world of busking comes the phrase **one-man band**, used to describe the street-entertainer who has various musical instruments attached to his body and plays on each of them in turn. Metaphorically the phrase refers to a self-employed businessman who does everything himself. There would be a tendency these days to talk about a **one-woman band** if appropriate, though the original form is more concerned with the idea of one person doing everything than with one 'man' doing it.

It *is* almost invariably a man, though, who is said to have a **one-track mind**. Theoretically this could be said about someone who is obsessed with any kind of idea, whose thoughts about it are like a train running on a single-track railway and are unable to change direction. In practice the obsession normally referred to is sex, a subject hilariously assumed to be of far more interest to men than women. **Scatter-brained**, as it happens, is an equally sexist phrase, normally applied to a woman and implying that, far from having a one-track mind, she is unable to think consistently about any single subject.

'It's a perfectly good idea, a most practical idea. Don't you see it'll kill two birds with one stone?'

Malcolm Lowry *Under the Volcano*

A character created by Monica Dickens, in *Kate and Emma*, is certainly not scatter-brained. The author says: 'It was typical of Molly that even in a crisis she could plan to kill two birds with one stone.' This graphic expression has been used in English since at least the 17th century and is still frequently heard. Eric Partridge remarks in passing (in his *Dictionary of Clichés*) that it comes from a Latin original, but does not elaborate. The fact that there is a French version of the saying, *faire d'une pierre deux coups* 'make two hits with one stone', makes his statement more likely. In German, incidentally, the equivalent expression refers to hitting two flies with one swat (*zwei Fliegen mit einer Klappe schlagen*).

The English phrase provides a good example of how metaphorical application can completely obscure literal meaning. No one who talks about killing two birds with one stone thinks for a moment about birds, killing or stones. All the speaker has in mind is that doing one particular thing will bring about two useful results simultaneously. 'Two', at least, is the usual number. In *Under the Volcano* Malcolm Lowry has: 'I'd discovered I might kill several birds with one stone by coming to Mexico.' Similarly, Margaret Drabble in *The Middle Ground* has: 'She had decided to kill several birds with one stone.' Josephine Tey, in *The Franchise Affair*, begins a chapter with the words: 'Robert had decided to kill a great many birds with one stone by spending the night in London.'

'I didn't care two hoots about her.'

Vera Caspary *Laura*

Not to care two hoots about someone or something is **not to care a jot** or **not to care an iota**. The 'not' may be separated from the rest of the phrase,

as when when Berta Ruck writes, in *Ancestral Voices*: 'Extraordinary, to compare that attitude with *now* . . . It wouldn't occur to people to care two hoots about the "peculiar situation". They'd just take it in their stride.'

A 'hoot' is simply a cry of derision which, in former times, was frequently extended to 'hoot-toot'. That may explain the 'two' hoots, but why 'hoot' in the first place? Edward Radford, in *Crowther's Encyclopaedia of Phrases and Origins*, believes that it is a corrupt form of 'jot', itself a form of 'iota', name of the ninth and smallest letter of the Greek alphabet. The latter fact led to the meaning 'the smallest amount', as in a sentence like: 'There's not one iota of truth in that rumour.'

It is easier to account for 'jot' as a form of 'iota' than it is to cast 'hoot' (or 'hooter' as Edward Radford suggests) in that role. For centuries the letters *i* and *j* were interchangeable. There was an earlier phrase **jot or tittle**, where 'jot' referred specifically to the stroke of the letter, 'tittle' to the mark above it. That mark is now a dot but was presumably once a wavy line like the Spanish tilde, seen over the *n* in a word like *piña*. Modern translations of the Sermon on the Mount (Matthew 5.7) say 'not an iota, not a dot, will pass from the law until all is accomplished', where earlier versions had 'not a jot or tittle'.

As soon as I had put two and two together, I realized that I had one duty in regard to this tragedy.

Vera Caspary *Laura*

People who metaphorically **put two and two together** are meant to arrive at an obvious answer, one that need not be stated. They nevertheless sometimes **jump to the wrong**

conclusion. Once we hear the word 'jump' in connection with a 'conclusion', we know that someone has put two and two together and managed to make five, or possibly twenty-two. The simple piece of mathematical activity to which this phrase refers seems to be fraught with danger.

Danger of a different kind is represented by two stools. *The Oxford English Dictionary* records a 16th-century proverb: 'Between two stools, the arse goeth to the ground.' The figurative meaning then, as now, was that the inability to choose between two different possibilities was likely to lead to complete failure. Modern application of **fall between two stools** frequently concerns a choice between two people. Trollope was already using the phrase in that sense in *The Last Chronicle of Barset* (1867): 'She was like to fall to the ground between two stools, – having two lovers, neither of whom could serve her turn.'

A drunk who can only stagger rather than walk might still be described as **three sheets in the wind**. The metaphor accurately conjures up an image of a sailing vessel which is being blown about in gale-force winds, even though 'sheet' in this case refers to the rope or chain attached to a sail, not the sail itself. In high winds the sheet would be loosened and described as 'in the wind'. The desperate lurching of a drunkard clearly reminded early 19th-century seamen of a ship's erratic progress in a storm.

Another 19th-century expression was **three times three**, probably a reference to 'Hip hip hurrah' said three times. We now refer more simply to **three cheers**, or more tellingly – if only half-hearted applause is merited – to **two cheers**.

'Eliot ought to realize all this is within these four walls. Not a word must leak outside.'

C.P. Snow *The Masters*

'You seem free enough – in your talk anyway,' says a character in *Pray for the Wanderer*, by Kate O'Brien. 'Within these four walls,' is the reply. The number of walls is usually specified in this roundabout allusion to privacy, though it is hardly necessary. 'Nothing that has been said in this room or that remains to be said shall go beyond its walls' occurs in *The French Lieutenant's Woman*, by John Fowles.

'People from the four corners of the earth will come to see our work, as pilgrims.'

Richard Gordon *The Face-Maker*

References to the four walls of a room seem more logical than those to the **four corners of the earth**. The phrase reflects the ancient belief that the earth was flat. Isaiah 12.12 has: 'He will raise an ensign for the nations, and will assemble the outcasts of Israel, and gather the dispersed of Judah from the four corners of the earth.'

Another phrase refers to **four-letter words**. The specific allusion, of course, is to a few words which happen to have four letters, known to everybody but considered by many to be highly offensive. Tony Thorne reports, in his *Bloomsbury Dictionary of Contemporary Slang*, that **four-letter man** is also used, referring to 'a contemptible or unpleasant male'. This is not necessarily a man who uses four-letter words, merely one who deserves to be described by one. The user of the phrase leaves it to his audience to decide which particular word is suitable.

'Five' is not a popular number in phrases. **Five-star** is meant to suggest 'excellent' by those advertisers who use it, but the expression would not be used in normal speech. Far more likely to be heard is the comment **six of one and half a dozen of the other**, meaning that there is nothing to choose between two alternatives. This phrase clearly meets a need and has been well used since the 1830s.

'The whole house is at sixes and sevens,' he said crossly. 'We don't want any more mess.'

E.M. Forster *Howards End*

One of the oldest 'number' phrases is **at sixes and sevens**, used of a place or people in a state of confusion and disorganization. William Trevor writes, in *The Old Boys*: 'The men were at sixes and sevens, groping their way to their feet to herald her entry, seating themselves to receive her bounty.' Some writers and speakers would prefer the version **all at sixes and sevens**, perhaps a leftover from a time when the expression had a different meaning. As early as the 14th century, Geoffrey Chaucer referred to **set on six and seven**. He was using a metaphor from dicing which is taken to refer to gambling everything on those numbers.

The difficulty with that explanation, of course, is that dice do not have a number seven. *The Oxford English Dictionary* long ago suggested that 'six and seven' was a corrupt form of *cinque* and *sice* 'five and six'. This is not very satisfactory and many other theories have been advanced. A dispute between the Merchant Taylors and the Skinners about which was to take sixth and seventh place in official processions is sometimes cited, but this stubbornly ignores clear linguistic evidence that dicing gave rise to the expression. A simpler possibility is that the phrase was originally **sixes even**, and that everything was being hazarded on a throw of double six.

The type of person who would take such a risk would presumably have been someone who lived life in a careless way, heedless of the chaos his actions might cause. What certainly seems to have happened is that in the course of several centuries the meaning of the phrase changed from a person who lived heedlessly to a haphazard state of affairs.

'Seven' also occurs in **seven-year itch**, where once again the meaning has changed. The phrase originally referred to an itch, as from poison ivy, that lasted or recurred for seven years. More generally it was used of an unpleasant situation or person that was only got rid of with difficulty. The *Chicago Daily News* (23.6.1949) had the comment: 'He stuck around like seven-year itch.' George Axelrod gave the phrase a new meaning in a play *The Seven Year Itch* (1952) which became a Marilyn Monroe film in 1955. Since that time most people would take the phrase to mean a sexual restlessness which develops in a man who has been married for seven years. Eric Partridge mentions in his *Dictionary of Historical Slang* that 'itch' in the sense of a sexual urge has been in colloquial use since the 17th century.

But here was Dolly, dressed up to the nines, standing at the door to greet them.

E.M. Forster *Howards End*

One over the eight, meaning drunk, is a curious phrase only in its tacit assumption that one may drink up to eight pints of beer or whatever and remain sober. More interesting from every point of view is **dressed (up) to the nines**, wearing clothes that are obviously one's very best. Robert Burns had earlier used 'to the nines' in a general way to mean 'to perfection'.

Some writers ingeniously see in this phrase a corruption of **then eyne**, where 'then' is an oblique form of 'the' which remained in use until at least 1400, and 'eyne' is an alternative plural of 'eye'. This theory would have more to commend it if earlier examples of the phrase could be found. As things stand, there is no evidence that it was used as early as 1400. It would in any case still be necessary to explain why 'to the eyes' meant 'to perfection'.

Professor Weekley mentions that there was once a phrase **to the ninth (degree)** which also suggested perfection. Nine itself can be said to contain this idea. It was a mystical, magical number in ancient times, a trinity of trinities and therefore a perfect plural. Traces of early beliefs surface in the nine Muses of the Greeks, the Novena, the nine orders of angels, the proverbial nine lives of a cat. 'To the ninth degree' or 'to the nines' (the second phrase perhaps a corruption of the former) could easily have suggested the attainment of perfect harmony.

The modern phrase **on cloud nine**, used of someone who is feeling euphoric, can be explained in more prosaic terms. To the US Weather Bureau, 'cloud nine' is the highest band of cloud. The person who is on cloud nine is simply saying that he feels 'high', he's **over the moon**, **walking on air**. He is metaphorically intoxicated, though 'high' in that sense is from rhyming slang: 'high as a kite' – 'tight'.

Celia: *But didst thou hear without wondering how thy name should be hang'd and carved upon these trees?* Rosalind: *I was seven of the nine days out of the wonder before you came.*

William Shakespeare *As You Like It*

A **nine-days' wonder** is someone or something that is of interest for a short time but is then forgotten. The proverb 'a wonder lasts but nine days' dates from the 14th century. 'Wonder' had much the same meaning then as it has now, though it could also refer to evil deeds and destruction. The proverb is therefore capable of many interpretations. It probably meant no more than 'novelty soon wears off' but could be stretched to 'a period of evil soon passes'. Some link it with medieval religious celebrations, said to last nine days, but these were scarcely 'wonders'. Others refer to dogs and cats who are blind until they are about nine days old. The complicated thought is that the public is blinded by a sensation for a few days, then its eyes are opened.

It had been a nine days' wonder, a society elopement, a grand news story.

Winifred Holtby *South Riding*

'Nine-days' wonder' seems to have been a popular phrase in the 17th century. Shakespeare plays with it in *Henry VI*, Part Three. When King Edward speaks of his impending marriage to Lady Grey, there follows the exchange: '"That would be ten days' wonder at the least." "That's a day longer than a wonder lasts." "By so much is the wonder in extremes."' Edward seems to find much to amuse him in that last remark, baffling though it is to a modern audience.

■ LAYING IT ON

'It's so hard to get published if you aren't in the swim, and can't butter up the right people.'

Malcolm Bradbury *Eating People is Wrong*

To **butter someone** 'flatter someone in order to influence him' has been used since the beginning of the 18th century. We would now talk of **buttering someone up**, or would use the alternative expression, to **soft-soap someone**. In both cases the oiliness of the product is being compared to the unctuous words that are used. The speaker is using **sweet-talk**, is **laying it on thick, with a trowel**.

The latter expression refers to the excessive use of paint or varnish. It sounds like modern slang, but the idea was familiar at the beginning of the 17th century. In Shakespeare's *As You Like It*, Celia remarks: 'Well said, that was laid on with a trowel.' She is commenting on the over-the-top phrases used by Rosalind and Touchstone. *The Oxford English Dictionary* has a quotation from the *Law Times* (1893) which combines the 'laying it on' metaphor with 'butter': 'It is nauseous to hear the adulation of Mr Neville, who laid butter on with a spade.'

In former times a possible reply to a flatterer, using a similar 'butter' image, would have been **fair** (or **fine, soft) words butter no parsnips**. The meaning was that flattery or the use of fine language was all very well, but it made no material difference. It might 'butter up' the person to whom the words were addressed but it could not actually provide the money for food, as symbolized by buttered parsnips.

The worldly-wise William Thackeray would have smiled at the thought that fair words and flattery were ineffectual. In *Vanity Fair* he asks: 'Who said that "fine words butter no parsnips"? Half the parsnips of society are served and rendered palatable with no other sauce.'

'Butter' is mentioned in other expressions. **Bread and butter** is used symbolically, for instance, of work that provides an individual or organization with a basic income. When a freelance speaks of 'bread and butter work' he usually means work that it is not very exciting.

'They're all the same, these old soldiers. On the scrounge. They know very well which side their bread's buttered.'

Angus Wilson *Anglo-Saxon Attitudes*

To **know on which side one's bread is buttered** is to 'know where one's interests lie, know whose goodwill is necessary for one's own advancement'. John Braine curiously mixes the idiom with its meaning in *Life at the Top*: 'She'd continue to remind me of my origins and of where my bread was buttered.'

She smiles and languishes, you'd think that butter would not melt in her mouth.

William Thackeray *Pendennis*

It is often a woman who is said to look as though **butter would not melt in her mouth**. (For the origin of this saying, see Introduction, page 12.) The speaker implies that she looks demure and innocent, as if incapable of harming anyone or anything, but it is only an act. She is actually cool and calculating and is probably plotting something diabolical at that very moment. The phrase is used by two different characters to describe Betty Kane, in Josephine Tey's *The Franchise Affair*.

■ LEAD-FREE

'You get the lead out of your ass and turn in some work I can use.'

Mordecai Richler *The Incomparable Atuk*

Get the lead out, in the sense of 'stop wasting time by loafing about', was much used in American military circles in the 1940s and 50s. It is still occasionally heard, sometimes in one of its longer forms. How the speaker completes the phrase depends on how rude he wishes to be. There is an ascending scale which includes **Get the lead out of your feet/pants/ass**. All forms remain purely North American.

The idea of being loaded down with lead, and acting therefore lethargically or sluggishly, can be alluded to in other ways. In *The Wayward Bus*, by John Steinbeck, there is a discussion at one point about cakes and pastries. 'You need something rich in food energy,' says Pimples. 'Rich in lead in the pants,' is the reply.

■ LEAVE-TAKING

'I don't think I'll have anything,' she replied thoughtfully. 'Why this departure?' he said. Kay had suddenly decided to turn over a new leaf, but she felt that this was not quite the right moment to announce it.

Mary McCarthy *The Group*

People have been promising themselves and others to **turn over a new leaf** since the 16th century. The 'leaf' in this case is the sheet of paper in a book which forms two pages.

The expression suggests that one is turning to a blank page in a diary or journal on which one's conduct as from now will be recorded. What has gone before is to be forgotten and a new beginning made.

In *You Can Call It a Day* Peter Cheyney writes: 'I've turned over a new leaf as the English say. I practically never touch the stuff.' This implies quite wrongly that Americans do not use this expression, but James Purdy, for instance, in *Eustace Chisholm and the Works*, has: 'She promised me she'd turn over a new leaf.' Other American examples are easily found.

The new way of life referred to frequently involves drinking less alcohol, as in the above examples. In Anthony Trollope's *Doctor Thorne* a doctor says to his patient: 'We must turn over a new leaf, Sir Roger; indeed we must.' The 'we' is a polite substitution for 'you'. When drinking is not the subject of the leaf-turning it is often womanizing that is to be abandoned.

'You want to take a leaf out of your cousin Walter's book. He has a system in a morning: so many minutes for this and so many for that. You never see him bolting his food or having to run for a bus.'

Stan Barstow *A Kind of Loving*

It would be possible both to 'turn over a new leaf' and **take a leaf out of someone else's book**. The implication is that the pages of the other person's diary record a blameless life. One should therefore imitate that person's actions and life-style, boring though the latter may be. The problem is that most of us would prefer to take a leaf out of a more exciting journal, perhaps that of Gwendolen Fairfax in Oscar Wilde's *The Importance of*

Being Earnest. She travels everywhere with her diary because 'one should always have something sensational to read in the train'.

■ LEG WORK

'You certainly pulled old Morrison's leg last night with that yarn of yours about the secret document,' he said, chuckling amusedly. 'He believed every word of it. Can you beat it? Never suspected for a moment that you were just kidding him.'

P.G. Wodehouse *Cocktail Time*

To **pull somebody's leg** is to make fun of someone, especially by trying to make him believe a story that isn't true. The intentions of the speaker are important - he has basically friendly feelings towards his victim and a harmless joke is intended. Someone who relates a 'cock and bull story', by contrast, may have other reasons for concealing the truth, as when an employee tells a cock and bull story about what made him late. (For the origin of 'cock and bull story' see page 35.)

Nor is pulling someone's leg the same as **leading someone up the garden path**, since once again the motives for deception may be more serious. The latter phrase originally referred to seductive talk in secluded bowers, and still tends to be used of dishonourable conduct in romantic relationships. The light-heartedness of 'pulling someone's leg', on the other hand, is acknowledged by perpetrator and intended victim. The latter, if he sees that an attempt is being made to fool him, is likely to say immediately: **pull the other one (it's got bells on)**.

Pulling someone's leg seems to be related to the idea of metaphorically 'tripping someone up'. Some writers have linked the expression to 19th-century muggers, who tripped people in the streets and then robbed them. It is difficult to see how tripping for such unpleasant reasons could have led to a phrase with a relatively innocent meaning.

While no one ever physically pulls someone else's leg to make fun of him, we sometimes imagine this happening when we use this phrase. In Graham Greene's *The Heart of the Matter*, for instance, a character says: 'John used to pull his leg about it, quite gently you know.' The speaker implies that a leg could be pulled with varying degrees of strength.

The phrase is often found in shortened form as a single verb or noun. Kate O'Brien, in *Pray for the Wanderer*, writes: 'It's impossible not to suspect you of leg-pulling.' 'I don't leg-pull. I'm not at all humorous.' None of this leg-pulling, needless to say, is connected with **stretching one's legs** 'going for a walk to get some exercise'.

The earl's boot, in a glass case, still stood in the hall to prove the truth of the story and give scandal a leg to stand on; for the boot had been found in the queen's room.

Eric Linklater *Poet's Pub*

Eric Linklater uses a phrase in the above quotation which is normally found as **not have a leg to stand on** 'have nothing to support one's opinion or actions'. The allusion is a straightforward one, whereas other expressions imply that we have different sets of legs during our lifetime. 'His wife assured him that he would soon get his sea-legs' is in Upton Sinclair's *World's End*. The phrase suggests that we need to be issued with a special pair of legs before being able to walk about on the deck of a ship without feeling sea-sick.

'He's the youngest of all of us.'
'When people say that,' the old man
told her, I know I must really be on
my last legs.'

Shirley Hazzard *The Evening of the*
Holiday

More commonly, we speak of
someone who is **on his last legs** 'in a
weak condition, with not long to live'.
Once again the implication is that
other pairs of legs have been used
previously. In *The Dynamiter*, Robert
Louis Stevenson uses the phrase to
mean 'nearly destitute': 'I am, dear
boy, on my last legs. Besides the
clothes in which you see me, I have
scarcely a decent trouser in my
wardrobe.'

Other 'leg' phrases which are used
metaphorically make their meaning
clear. To **give someone a leg up** can be
to assist him in a general way, not
just help him mount a horse.
Someone who **has his tail between his
legs** looks as dejected and humiliated
as a dog in that state.

Break a leg! is the curious way in
which superstitious actors wish one
another 'good luck!' before a
performance. Saying something more
positive would presumably tempt the
fates to be vindictive, as when the
sports commentator remarks that a
boxer is looking invincible. This often
proves to be the **kiss of death**,
somehow ensuring that the boxer's
opponent immediately knocks him
out. Leo Rosten, in *The Joys of
Yiddish*, reports that if someone
praises her child, a Jewish mother
traditionally mutters *kayn aynhoreh*
'may no Evil Eye harm him!' in fear
of the envious forces of darkness.
Theatrical slang is said to reflect in
many ways a Yiddish influence.

■ LETTING IT OUT

---

*Instead of broaching the subject he had
come to discuss, he said lamely, 'You
must come over and meet Ethel.'*

James A. Michener *Chesapeake*

To **broach a subject** is on the verge of
becoming a set phrase. The only
'broaching' that most of us do is of a
subject or topic for discussion. 'I
could broach the subject with him, if
you like,' says a character in
Mordecai Richler's *The Incomparable
Atuk*.

'Broach' here means 'open a
discussion about', but the idea that
lies behind it is that something is
being pierced and allowed to flow
out. The original meaning of the
noun 'broach' was a 'spike, pointed
instrument'. The verb meant to
'pierce, stab'. A horse could be
broached with spurs; meat could be
broached with a spit, prior to
roasting; a cask of liquor was
broached when it was tapped.

There is a passage in *All My Sons*, by
Arthur Miller, where the
pronunciation of the word is
discussed:

Keller: *When he comes I like you to
brooch something to him.*

Chris: *Broach.*

Keller: *What's the matter with
brooch?*

Chris: (smiling) *It's not English.*

Keller: *When I went to night school it
was brooch.*

Ann: (laughing) *Well, in day school
it's broach.*

'Brooch' there is used to indicate a
pronunciation that rhymes with
'pooch'. The word 'brooch', meaning
an ornamental fastening used mostly

by women, is pronounced in the same way as 'broach' and is another form of that word. The safety-pin on a brooch is what does the broaching. Another familiar word that eventually derives from the same word has come to us through Italian. 'Broccoli' means 'little shoots' in Italian, but the *broc-* part of the word was once another form of 'broach'.

■ LETTING SOMEONE STEW

'Let dear Margaret stew in her own juice.'

Kingsley Amis *Lucky Jim*

A 17th-century writer talked of 'letting hypocrites, like oysters, stew in their own water'. The modern phrase would be to **let someone stew in his own juice**. The meaning is 'allow someone to suffer the natural, unpleasant consequences of his own folly, be tormented by his own passions'. 'I'd like you to go and see her' says someone in Margaret Forster's *Georgy Girl*. The reply is: 'Well of course, if you want me to, I will. But she'd be best left to stew in her own juice.'

This phrase appears to be a simple metaphor from cooking, borrowed from the French *cuir dans son jus* 'cook in his own juice'. If that were so, the question would be – why the emphasis on suffering and torment? To cook something in its own juice seems to be the right thing to do. An earlier version of the saying gives the clue to the darker implications of the expression. To **fry in one's own grease** was also used metaphorically of suffering torments: the ghastly image that lay behind the phrase was of someone being burned alive.

■ LIP-READING

'She never uttered a word of complaint. She accepted the circumstances she'd chosen and kept her word. So did her husband.'
'Stiff upper lip, in fact.'

Berta Ruck *Ancestral Voices*

Ngaio Marsh, in *Surfeit of Lampreys*, links two similar expressions when she writes: 'We stiffened our upper lips and bit on the bullets.' To **keep a stiff upper lip** is to put up with whatever has to be endured without showing one's emotions. To **bite the bullet** also means to accept pain without showing emotion. The former expression alludes to not allowing the upper lip to quiver, as it does when someone is about to cry. The latter expression refers to the practice in former times of giving a wounded soldier a bullet to bite on. By clenching his teeth on the bullet it would distract him from the pain he was feeling elsewhere.

The 'stiff upper lip' is associated by many with the education of English schoolboys at boarding schools, but the phrase is well used in America. James Purdy, in *Eustace Chisholm and the Works*, has a character abbreviate the phrase: 'You can keep a stiff upper today, if I can.' In the American classic *Uncle Tom's Cabin*, by Harriet Beecher Stowe, George tells Uncle Tom to 'keep a stiff upper lip'.

'I know all about the lip-service they paid. She – Rowena Pringle – paid lip-service and I know how much lip-service is worth.'

William Golding *Free Fall*

When 'lip-service' was first referred to in the 17th century there was a specific reference to those at a church service who mumbled the prayers and voiced the correct responses, but were not really thinking about what they were saying. To **pay lip-service to something** is now used of those who profess belief in something, but do not demonstrate that belief in a practical way. *The Oxford Advanced Learner's Dictionary* offers as a sample sentence: 'He pays lip-service to feminism but his wife still does all the housework.' *The Bloomsbury Dictionary of Contemporary Slang* remarks that 'lip-service' is now 'a humorous euphemism' for fellatio.

Nothing would make him betray his late master's guilty secrets; his lips were sealed.

John Fowles *The French Lieutenant's Woman*

'Be like Mr Baldwin and say your lips are sealed' says a character in E.F. Benson's *Trouble for Lucia*. The Penguin *Dictionary of Modern Quotations* quotes Mr Baldwin rather differently: 'My lips are not yet unsealed.' The meaning is not affected; if one's **lips are sealed** one is clearly saying nothing. In the slang phrase one is **buttoning one's lip**, or **zipping one's lip**. One is not **flipping one's lip** 'talking in an idle way' as another American expression puts it.

One of the proverbs that is well enough known to be left uncompleted is **there's many a slip (twixt cup and lip)**. It serves as a useful warning to those who think that success is certain. Plenty of things can still go wrong at the very last moment.

■ LONG AND THE SHORT OF IT, THE

To make a long story short, the company broke up, and returned to the more important concerns of the election.

Washington Irving *Rip Van Winkle*

When someone says: '**The long and the short of it is . . .**', he is usually about to sum up what he has just been saying. He means that the gist of it, what really needs to be said, is what he is about to say. A similar expression is **to make a long story short**. This is likely to be said when a person realizes that he is becoming tedious, being too **long-winded**, as we also say.

'Our own doctor is long in the tooth, behind the times, against modern methods, you know the kind of thing.'

William Trevor *The Old Boys*

Amongst many other 'long' or 'short' expressions, one of the most used is **long in the tooth** 'rather old'. This was originally applied exclusively to horses, whose teeth appear to get longer as the gums recede with age. Horses are also sometimes said to be **past the mark** when they get past the age of seven, since judging their age by the marks or depressions in their teeth is no longer possible.

'Long in the tooth' is often applied jokingly to humans. Evelyn Waugh writes in *Unconditional Surrender*: 'If you're lucky you get fixed up with a nurse. Cape's got one – a bit long in the tooth but very friendly.' Elizabeth Jane Howard, in *Getting it Right*, has: 'If it *is* a girl you're after, you're not going to meet her in that salon of yours, are you? They all sound a bit long in the tooth there, apart from anything else.'

Edward Blishen rather confuses the issue in *A Cack-handed War* by writing about an older woman who really does happen to have long teeth. One of his characters says: 'Well over forty, she was. Pots of money. Bit long in the tooth, o'course. But Gawd . . . she fancied me. Thought she'd eat me, Ted. Those big teeth. Biting, an' all that.'

'You might be going to Washington to work in the government.'
'That's a long shot, I think.'

Joseph Heller *Good as Gold*

There is a different kind of link with horses in a **long shot**, which is something that has only a slight chance of success. The phrase comes from racing slang, where 'long shot' has been used since the 19th century to mean a bet placed at **long odds**, at fifty to one, say. 'Shot' here means 'attempt', as when a person has 'a shot at doing something', but the original allusion must have been to a target that was a long way off and difficult to shoot at. 'What about this House of Diamonds lead?' asks James Bond, in Ian Fleming's *Diamonds are Forever*. 'Seems a long shot.'

Not by a long shot is used to mean 'emphatically not'. 'We ain't noboddies, not by a long shot,' says someone in Truman Capote's *A Tree of Night*.

'I told you our Sam was a wonder, didn't I? And he hasn't finished yet; no, not by a long chalk.'

Harold Hobson *People Like Benstead*

By a long chalk is a similar British expression meaning 'by a large amount, by far'. In former times it

was likely to be used in the plural form **by long chalks**. Modern writers always make it singular, and often use it negatively. A character in Francis King's *The Needle* says: 'Matty hasn't got the same kind of relationship with that hag of a mother of hers, not by a long chalk.' John Le Carré, *The Honourable Schoolboy*, has: 'Karla's no scholar, he's a soldier. But not blind, either, not by a long chalk.'

'By a long chalk' is explained by *The Oxford English Dictionary* as being related to the use of chalk for scoring points in various games. It would make far more sense if the phrase were connected instead with 'chalk' in its well-attested sense of 'the amount owed by a customer at an ale-house'. 'A long chalk' could easily refer to a long row of marks, indicating the number of drinks consumed. The amount owed would be greater as the line increased in length.

This explanation would also offer an origin for 'not by a long shot' unconnected with 'a long shot' in the betting sense. One meaning of 'shot', recognized by *Webster's Dictionary*, is 'a charge to be paid'.

Mark Twain uses another variant of 'not by a long chalk/shot'. *Huckleberry Finn* has: 'I asked her if she reckoned Tom Sawyer would go there, and she said not **by a considerable sight**'. 'Sight' here means 'amount'. The change in meaning came about through phrases like 'a sight of stars', where 'sight' meant a 'show or display' but could be understood as meaning 'a great number'. There is a reference in the *Paston Letters* (1449) to 'a sight of ships,' where both meanings are still possible. Jane Austen in one of her letters (1800) refers to a 'sight of thanks', enclosing the phrase in inverted commas to show that it was rather colloquial.

*'This business is as broad as it's long,'
contributed the doctor. 'You need us,
Mrs Wilcox, and we need you.'*

E.M. Forster *Howards End*

A situation which is **as broad as it is
long** is evenly balanced to the point
where it makes little difference which
alternative is chosen. It may be that
in the long run 'eventually', it makes
little difference. There is a hint of the
tortoise-and-hare fable in the latter
expression, implying that a sustained
slow progress can eventually achieve
as much as a short sprint. We can
refer to achievement by using another
'long' phrase, saying that someone
has **come a long way** or is likely to **go
a long way** or **go far**.

---

*From birth to death they've been short-
changed.*

James A. Michener *Chesapeake*

To **be short-changed** is to be given less
than the correct amount in change, or
to be 'cheated' in more general terms.
This is not the same as **selling
someone** or **something short** 'not
recognizing the true value of someone
or something'. 'You can't sell Canada
short' says a character in Mordecai
Richler's *The Incomparable Atuk*,
meaning that what the country has to
offer must not be under-estimated.

---

*I encountered some obstacles
deliberately put in my path by upstart
Jacks in office, but I gave them short
shrift.*

Dane Chandos *Abbie*

The brutality and inhumanity of the
past lies behind the phrase to **give
someone short shrift**, which now
merely means 'to treat someone
curtly.' 'Shrift' is connected with the
verb 'shrive', which is to hear
someone's confession and impose a
penance. Another reference to this
verb is found in **Shrove Tuesday**. It
was on this day that people were
'shriven' in preparation for Lent,
which began next day on **Ash
Wednesday**. They also ate heartily
before the Lenten fasting began,
pancakes being the traditional dish
and leading to **Pancake Day** as the
alternative name for 'Shrove
Tuesday'.

A 'short shrift' was once the brief
amount of time allowed to a criminal
to make his final confession, just
before his execution. 'Come, come,
dispatch' says Ratcliff to Lord
Hastings, in Shakespeare's *King
Richard the Third*; 'the Duke would
be at dinner. Make a short shrift; he
longs to see your head'. This is meant
literally: the future king has just
announced that he will not eat his
dinner that night until the head of
Hastings has been brought to him.

■ LUMPING IT

'If they don't like it, they can lump it.'

Alan Sillitoe *Saturday Night and
Sunday Morning*

Many English words which relate to
disagreeable things have the sound
-*ump* in them. Examples are 'dump',
'frump', 'hump', 'grump', 'mump',
'rump'. 'Glump' was a dialect word
still current in the 19th century, used
both as a noun meaning 'a sulky
person' and a verb 'to sulk'. 'Lump'
something, in the sense of 'reluctantly
accept it', is thought to be connected
with such words, perhaps especially
'glump'. Those who are forced to
'lump' something may well be rather
sulky about it.

'Lump' is always used in antithesis to
'like'. The speaker is saying that there

is no choice about this matter, it must be accepted regardless of what the other person feels about it. The phrase that is always implicit in the situation, if not openly stated, is **like it or lump it**. Typical usage occurs in W. Somerset Maugham's short story *Sanatorium*: 'Campbell replied that he had a perfect right to play and if Mr McLeod didn't like it he could lump it.' Mary McCarthy, in *The Group*, has: 'Like it or lump it, some of our best authors are Communists this year.'

■ LURCHING ABOUT

'If a woman's in trouble, I don't leave her in the lurch. That's not my street.'

E.M. Forster *Howards End*

There was a game played in the 17th century called 'lurch.' Little is known about it, but it is thought to have been similar to backgammon. The word 'lurch' was later taken into other games in the sense of what we would now call a 'whitewash', where the loser scores no points at all. From this meaning came phrases like **give someone the lurch** 'get the better of someone' and **have someone on the lurch** 'have someone at a disadvantage'. Both of these are now obsolete, but **leave someone in the lurch** 'leave someone in a very bad situation without assistance' is still very much with us. 'I can't leave her in the lurch after just moving her out here, away from everything she knew and liked in the East,' says the hero of *Face to Face*, by Edward A. Rogers.

The word 'lurch' meaning to 'roll to one side' was originally nautical and not connected in any way with the game of lurch. Yet another 'lurch' was a variant of 'lurk' and meant to

'prowl'. It was this word which led to the name of the dog called a 'lurcher', traditionally used by poachers to catch hares and rabbits.

■ MAKING ONE'S MARK

They desired to keep Chalkeley up to the mark.

E.M. Forster *Howards End*

Keeping someone **up to the mark** 'up to the desired standard' is a nautical metaphor, based on the idea of taking soundings to ensure that there is a sufficient depth of water. The phrase is thus linked with Samuel Langhorne Clemens, or 'Mark Twain', who derived his pseudonym from the call used by Mississippi River boatmen to indicate a water-depth of two fathoms. 'I always find the servants have not been kept up to the mark' is a typical remark of the formidable aunt in *Abbie*, by Dane Chandos.

'She minds me as well as she can. Doesn't come up to scratch half the time, but she tries.'

Harper Lee *To Kill a Mockingbird*

The meaning of **come up to scratch** 'reach a specified standard' has obviously been influenced by 'up to the mark'. A scratch on the ground was originally used in various sports to indicate a starting line, cricket crease or the place where two pugilists or birds in a cock-fight were to face each other. Those who literally 'came up to the scratch', when the phrase was first used, were ready for the fray. Perhaps it could be argued that by so doing they were proving themselves worthy and of a good standard. It seems more likely that because of a 'scratch' being a kind of 'mark', 'up to the mark' and 'up to scratch' were perceived as synonyms.

The 'scratch' version of the phrase is popular, and tends to retain the idea of 'coming' to it. 'I think he'll come up to scratch,' said by someone in C.P. Snow's *The Masters*, means 'I think he'll behave properly and vote for our candidate.' In *Lucky Jim*, by Kingsley Amis, there is the remark: 'Perhaps Christine wasn't coming up to scratch, or not quickly enough, possibly.' Here the reference is to a woman who is not behaving properly in that she is not providing sexual favours.

'Start from scratch to build up a team that will know how to play together.'

Bernard Malamud *The Natural*

The notion of bringing someone to a starting line is more evident in a comment like: 'I'm just in the mood for a good film. The thing will be to get Will up to scratch.' This occurs in Kate O'Brien's *Pray for the Wanderer*. To **start from scratch** 'start from the very beginning' is based on the same idea. The phrase is in common colloquial use.

The Standard, *never a newspaper to be caught off the mark, printed two sets of their late morning edition.*

Mordecai Richler *The Incomparable Atuk*

The Richler quotation above presumably means that the *Standard* is quicker 'off the mark' than any other newspaper. **Quick off the mark** applies literally to an athlete who gets quickly away from the starting line. It is interesting that 'quick off the scratch' does not occur, in spite of the overlapping meanings discussed above. Metaphorically 'quick off the

mark', or the corresponding **slow off the mark**, is applied to someone who responds quickly or slowly to a new situation.

Rose feared that in a desire to give a foreigner pleasure he had overshot the mark. But then, what he had said was more or less the truth.

J.I.M. Stewart *The Last Tresilians*

'Mark' can have a totally different meaning as a 'target'. A misjudgement of distance, wind conditions and the like may cause one to **overshoot the mark**. The phrase is also used metaphorically to mean 'make a mistake as a result of misjudgement of a person or situation'.

There was always something in his feeling that seemed wide of the mark or of too literal or too personal an application.

Mary McCarthy *The Groves of Academe*

Other phrases where 'mark' has the same meaning of 'target' lend themselves to metaphorical use. Someone or something can fall **short of the mark** 'not do enough to achieve the desired object'. To be **wide of the mark** is to be wrong in what one has said or done, as in 'Mrs Renfrew's sensitive conjectures were wide of the mark', a comment in Mary McCarthy's *The Group*.

'He's really overstepping the mark this time.'

Mordecai Richler *The Incomparable Atuk*

Overstep the mark 'say or do more than is wise or acceptable' is rather different. Here the image is of a person stepping across an imaginary boundary line into an area not sanctioned by polite society. To 'overstep the mark' is to **go too far**, as it is also expressed, to break society's unwritten rules.

To **make one's mark** is to make an impression, figuratively speaking, on people in general, to become known to a large number of people for positive reasons. Metaphorically the person who 'makes his mark' becomes as visible as a mark on a sheet of paper. The phrase replaced in the 19th century the expression **of mark** 'important, noteworthy', which had been in use since Shakespeare's day. There is a reference in *King Henry the Fourth*, Part One, for instance, to 'a fellow of no mark'.

'I think the whole system of black marks is grossly unfair. I'm going to bring it up at the next T.U. meeting.'

Monica Dickens *The Fancy*

When we compliment someone by saying that we give him **full marks** for what he has done, we are using an image from the educational world. Such 'marks' are now either numbers or letters but were originally vertical marks placed against a student's name if he answered a question correctly or otherwise distinguished himself. A **black mark**, usually in the form of a cross, could also be made, giving us another phrase which survives as a linguistic token of disapproval. In the Monica Dickens quotation above 'black mark' has a literal meaning, referring to errors made in a factory during wartime.

'A big day in your life, mark my words.'

Barry Oakley *A Salute to the Great McCarthy*

The verb 'mark' also occurs in popular phrases. **Mark my words** literally means 'pay attention to what I say'. The phrase now seems to be used by rather pompous speakers who think that what they say carries a great deal of weight. 'It will appreciate, mark my words,' says a character in R.F. Delderfield's *Theirs Was the Kingdom*, confident that he knows what will become more valuable in the future. Those who use the expression are likely to use it irritatingly often. The narrator of Alistair Maclean's *The Dark Crusader* comments at one point: 'Mark my words,' I said nastily. 'You forgot to say, "Mark my words".'

The phrase has been in use for centuries. Miles Coverdale made use of it in his translation of the Bible (1535), Isaiah 28.23: 'Take hede and hear my voyce, pondre and merck my wordes wel.' A more recent translation has: 'Give ear, and hear my voice; hearken, and hear my speech.' Shakespeare's characters frequently preface remarks with 'Mark me (well)' or 'Mark what I say'; Polixenes also tells his son in *The Winter's Tale*: 'Mark thou my words.'

Mark you is a similar linguistic fossil. Like the similar **mind you** it means something like 'but take note of this', qualifying a previous statement. 'He speaks English very well. Mark you (Mind you), he's been learning the language for ten years.'

■ MAYBE

'Be that as it may,' he said, a phrase Polly disliked . . .

Mary McCarthy *The Group*

Be that as it may was listed by Eric Partridge in the 1940s as a particularly hackneyed and objectionable cliché. He was perhaps rather harsh. *The Oxford Advanced Learner's Dictionary*, 1989 edition, prefers to list it without comment as a standard idiom, because it does actually mean something. It is another form of **that is as may be** 'that may or may not be so', and is a polite way of saying 'I don't necessarily agree with the conclusion you have reached, but for the sake of argument let us assume that it is correct. Nevertheless . . .' Unfortunately, the phrase manages to sound extremely pompous, suggesting an unemotional, humourless speaker who believes himself to be superior.

Mordecai Richler, in *The Incomparable Atuk*, links it with **correct me if I'm wrong**, another phrase which many heartily dislike. It is used hypocritically by those who are convinced that they are right: 'Be that as it may,' says the Richler character, 'well, you correct me if I'm wrong – but I take it you believe that Jews *are* different from other people.'

■ MILLING ABOUT

'*You've been through the mill, as they say, haven't you?*'

Malcolm Bradbury *Eating People is Wrong*

Someone who is forced to undergo a period of hard and perhaps unpleasant training is likely to say afterwards that he has been **put through the mill**. If he is referring generally to hard times that he has experienced he may say that he has **been through the mill**. He is comparing what has happened to him to the grinding of the corn in the mill. 'I've been through the mill as well' is said by a character in Alan Sillitoe's *Saturday Night and Sunday Morning*.

'*He has regarded her as an abominable nuisance – a millstone round his neck – a responsibility.*'

William J. Locke *Jaffery*

A woman in Richard Gordon's *The Face-Maker* says to her potential husband: 'You'd resent me. I'd be just a milestone round your neck.' This looks like a misprint, 'milestone' for 'millstone', but Ngaio Marsh, in a *Surfeit of Lampreys*, has the following conversation: '"We shall have all the rest of it, hung round our necks like milestones." "Millstones, darling," said Henry. "You're wrong," said Charlot. "Hung round our necks like the upper and nether milestones is the full expression. You're thinking of the mills of God."'

The speaker who makes this statement about 'milestones' not 'millstones' is not corrected, implying that the view expressed was that of the author. If so, she was quite wrong. In a traditional mill it is the upper millstone rotating upon the lower or nether stone which does the grinding. The metaphor which uses 'millstone' for 'a heavy burden' is found in the New Testament, at Matthew 18.6: 'Whoever causes one of these little ones who believe in me to sin, it would be better for him to have a great millstone fastened round his neck and to be drowned in the depth of the sea.'

The 'mills of God' referred to by Ngaio Marsh have been mentioned by poets and authors since the 17th century. Best known, perhaps, are Longfellow's grim words in his poem *Retribution*:

Though the mills of God grind slowly, yet they grind exceeding small;
Though with patience He stands waiting, with exactness grinds he all.

The **millstone round the neck** expression occurs regularly in speech and literature. 'I've meant to be a good wife to you, not a millstone' is in Nina Bawden's *George Beneath a Paper Moon*. In Frederic Raphael's *The Limits of Love* the person who says: 'Why do you have to hang a bloody millstone round my neck?' means 'why make me admit that I am Jewish.' The phrase can also be alluded to rather than quoted. In Margaret Laurence's *The Diviners* a daughter says to her mother: 'I won't stay here forever – I'm not the millstone type.'

'The fools bring grist to my mill, so let them live out their day, and the longer it is the better.'

Charles Dickens *Nicholas Nickleby*

Corn which is ready to be milled is known as 'grist'. To say that something is **grist to someone's mill** means that it is something he will be able to make use of profitably. Ralph Nickleby, in the quotation above, is speaking of the Mantalinis. One of Mr Mantalini's better-known utterances, as it happens, is: 'My life is one demd (damned) horrid grind.'

He is certainly no run-of-the-mill postman, he wears a ruffled shirt and a red-spotted bow-tie with his grey uniform.

Sue Townsend *The Growing Pains of Adrian Mole*

Run-of-the-mill means 'ordinary, not special in any way'. The allusion here is either to a mass-produced article from a milling-machine which makes thousands of identical items, or to something which emerges from one of the 'dark satanic mills' of industry. Isaac Asimov, in *Ph for Phony*, says: 'I looked up his name in *Chemical Abstracts* and found the record of a few papers he turned out. Run of the mill.'

■ MIND-BOGGLING

Someone, somewhere, Serge thought, his mind boggling at the idea, loves each one of them . . .

Alexander Fullerton *Other Men's Wives*

The narrator of Joseph Heller's *Good as Gold* is told by a government representative that he has a gift for 'punchy phrases' which would make him useful in Washington. He is pleased about this until he happens to say: 'You're **boggling my mind**.' He is told that this is a 'damned good phrase. I'll bet all of us down here can start getting mileage out of that one right away'.

The sound of 'boggle' seems to appeal to the comic imagination of most people. Few could precisely define the word, though they know that something which 'boggles the mind' is something which is amazing or shocking. For a time, in the 1950s, it became the fashion in literate circles to find new ways of referring to minds and boggling. Alexander Fullerton provides a typical example in *Other Men's Wives*: 'The imagination has its limits, the mind its boggle-point.'

It was originally horses which 'boggled'. The verb means to 'shy, start with fright, be startled'. In the 16th century, horses which boggled were thought to do so because they had seen a 'bogle', some kind of phantom or spectre. The word is therefore connected with the mysterious 'bogey-man'. Scholars think that the ultimate origin of 'boggle' and connected words is to be found in Welsh *bwgwl* 'terror, terrifying'.

'Boggle' is now firmly linked with the mind and things which startle it, especially in the phrases **the mind boggles** and **mind-boggling**. In its earliest metaphorical use, 'boggle' meant to 'raise scruples, hesitate'. Antony tells Cleopatra that she has 'been a boggler ever', meaning that she has always been capricious, but in *All's Well that Ends Well* Shakespeare also uses the verb in its original meaning. The King of France compares a man to a startled horse by saying to Bertram: 'You boggle shrewdly; every feather starts you.'

My father always bellowed: 'You never know what's at the back of his mind!' It had not occurred to me before that I had a back to my mind, but once this area had been brought to my attention as the place where admiration is found, I took a life-lease on the premises.

Nigel Dennis *Cards of Identity*

Other 'mind' phrases are curious if one pauses for a moment to consider their literal meaning. Nigel Dennis makes much in the above quotation of **at the back of one's mind** 'in one's mind but not of central concern for the moment'. He could have amused himself equally with **bend one's mind to something** 'turn one's thoughts toward', and even **change one's mind** 'alter one's opinion', which conjures up an image of mind-transplants.

Everyone would now realize how he had been subtly provoking Harald to finally give him a piece of his mind.

Mary McCarthy *The Group*

To **give someone a piece of one's mind** 'tell someone the blunt, unpleasant truth' is also odd in what it literally says, though as with similar expressions, 'mind' is used to mean the thoughts that are inside the mind. If those thoughts cause one to be undecided, then one can **be in two minds**. Two people, by contrast, can metaphorically **be of one mind** if they agree.

'A great weight being off my mind, I feel in the very heyday of my youth.'

Nathaniel Hawthorne *The House of the Seven Gables*

In the modern idiom we talk about being **under pressure**. The metaphor is often extended as we visualize something heavy pressing down on us; **we have a great deal/a load/a weight on our minds**. 'It's a terrific load off my mind, but the real load is still there,' says a woman in Josephine Tey's *The Franchise Affair*. Ruth Rendell, in *The Tree of Hands*, has: 'Couldn't you find someone else for your mother to stay with? To take a load off your mind?' If the pressure becomes too much and leads to madness we make use of other metaphors and talk of **losing our minds** or **going out of our minds**.

Such phrases we take in our stride, giving no thought to what is literally being said. Only when an unusual word makes an appearance do we notice anything strange. The expressions we use should perhaps boggle our minds more often.

■ MINDING ONE'S MANNERS

This newcomer bore, as to the manner born, the stigmata of poverty and of obedience.

Edward Hyams *Sylvester*

Mary McCarthy, in *The Group*, writes: 'Kay, according to her, should have got married quietly in City Hall instead of making Harald, who was not to the manor born, try to carry off a wedding in J.P. Morgan's church.' **To the manor born** for Miss McCarthy clearly meant born in a manor-house and therefore accustomed since birth to an upper-class life-style. Many people in Britain would agree with that interpretation and use that spelling, influenced perhaps by a long-running television series which used 'To the Manor Born' as a title. The correct form of the phrase, however, is **to the manner born**.

In Shakespeare's *Hamlet*, the prince describes how the king is drinking heavily, with trumpets and drums proclaiming the emptying of each pot. 'Is it a custom?' asks Horatio. Hamlet replies: 'Ay, marry, is't; / But to my mind, though I am native here / And to the manner born, it is a custom / More honour'd in the breach than the observance.' 'To the manner born', for Hamlet, simply meant 'familiar with the custom since birth'. The phrase can therefore be applied to the way of life in any country and at any social level.

■ MINDING ONE'S ONIONS

'But suppose Queen's Rook doesn't win!' I said. 'Let's put something on Little Grange alone.' 'Nonsense,' said Sammy. 'What's the use of caution when you know your onions?'

Iris Murdoch *Under the Net*

To **know one's onions** 'be fully knowledgeable and experienced' is a variant of **know one's stuff**, and in America only, **know one's beans**. Onions have a strong smell and it is just possible that there is an allusion to being able to 'sniff things out'.

Know one's business is another variant of 'know one's onions'. It is presumably a coincidence that 'onions' in the sense of 'business' occurs in colloquial French. *Ce ne sont pas mes oignons* 'these are not my onions' means 'it's no business of mine'. *Occupe-toi de tes oignons* 'look after your own onions' means 'mind your own business'.

'We still got this last one to take,' he said modestly. 'I am not counting my onions till that.'

Bernard Malamud *The Natural*

In the Malamud quotation above, 'onion' appears to mean 'dollar', unless the whole phrase is another form of 'count one's chickens'. 'Onion' is not recorded in any reference works as 'dollar', nor does the phrase occur. The roundness of an onion seems to be the only thing that might link it with a silver dollar. It is certainly the onion's general shape which causes the word to be used for 'head' in the expression **off his onion** 'off his head, crazy'.

■ MONKEY BUSINESS

'Blood is thicker than water, and I do not wish the other boys to make a monkey out of you when you go to school.'

Dane Chandos *Abbie*

To **make a monkey out of someone** is to make him appear foolish. The phrase is linked with **monkey about with something** 'to fool about with it'. **Monkey business** used to mean mischievousness; it now suggests dishonest or unacceptable behaviour. 'Remember; no monkey business; no falling in love' says someone in Mary McCarthy's *The Group*.

In modern slang an 'ape' is a brutal man who uses force rather than reason. To **go ape** is to act like an enraged or highly excited ape. British users of slang might also say that they **couldn't give** (or **care**) **a monkey's**, they 'couldn't care less'. This looks like rhyming slang, which typically does not bother to complete the expression. 'Have a butcher's at that', for instance, means 'have a butcher's hook, a look, at that. It is difficult to know what word is supposed to follow 'monkey's'. I'll **be a monkey's uncle** is a catch-phrase which means 'I'll be damned!', but this cannot be connected. Julian Franklyn's *Dictionary of Rhyming Slang* mentions only 'monkey's tail', used by carpenters for 'nail'.

■ MOUTHPIECE

'My heart was in my mouth when I walked into that room to find you. There are not many men who would have taken the whole thing so calmly.'

Graham Greene *The Quiet American*

Our ancestors, who had a primitive idea of how the body functioned, explained in their own graphic ways the physical sensations induced by intense emotion. They knew that when they were badly frightened their throats became constricted. Their unscientific explanation for the phenomenon was that at such times the heart had moved and was causing the obstruction: a person who was afraid had his **heart in his mouth**.

This assumes that the phrase was meant literally when it was first used. Later it became a situational formula, accepted as a metaphor or simply not questioned too deeply. A modern writer is still able to talk about someone having 'his heart in his mouth' as a way of saying that he is

frightened. In *Theirs Was the Kingdom* R.F. Delderfield writes: 'There she is, getting her things together as offhandedly as a French maid. It's Denzil who has his heart in his mouth.'

'You've been a bit down in the mouth recently.'
'Things haven't been particularly cheerful at Princess Alexandra's.'

Richard Gordon *The Face-Maker*

To **look down in the mouth** has been in use since the 17th century, and reports in a straightforward way on what happens when a person is feeling sad and depressed – the corners of the mouth are drawn downwards. 'Hello, Susie, my love, you're looking a bit down in the mouth – why might that be now?' asks someone in Frederic Raphael's *The Limits of Love*.

'Grandma says Dad's just shooting off his mouth.'

Stephen Vizinczey *In Praise of Older Women*

Several metaphoric phrases, used especially by American speakers, make an analogy between the mouth and a gun. Words are then 'shot' from the mouth. To **shoot off one's mouth** is to speak in a boastful and exaggerated way, like someone who fires a gun into the air simply to make a lot of noise and attract attention to himself. To **shoot a line** is similar; it is to try to impress someone by exaggerating and telling lies. To **shoot the breeze** is rather more pleasant, involving talk that has no particular purpose other than to pass the time in a friendly way. One is metaphorically firing into the wind, at no special target. Expressions with a similar meaning are to **chew the fat** and **chew the rag**, both referring to activities that achieve little.

MY, MY!

'Oh, my eye, how prime! I am so hungry.' Having apostrophised his eye, in a species of rapture, five or six times, the youth took the head of the little table, and Mary seated herself at the bottom.

Charles Dickens *The Pickwick Papers*

Many people still 'apostrophise their eyes', as Dickens describes it in the above quotation. Normally they are expressing disbelief in something that has just been said. Graham Greene, in *The Heart of the Matter*, has: '"There was a rumour in the office", Wilson said, "about some diamonds." "Diamonds, my eye," Father Rank said.' *The Groves of Academe* by Mary McCarthy has: '"I too believe in absolute grading," insisted Domna. Furness laughed. "My eye," he said. "How many Excellents did you give last term?"'

My eye is often exclamatory, as in these examples, but the phrase can be used to mean 'nonsense' in a normal sentence. An example occurs in Evelyn Waugh's *Vile Bodies*: 'She saw no ghosts. "That's all my eye," she said.' In former times the speaker might have said 'That's **all my eye and Betty Martin**,' but the longer version appears to be obsolete. No one ever satisfactorily explained the reason for the additional words, but as usual there was no shortage of fanciful theories. One writer saw in the expression a corruption of Italian *Ah, mihi, beate Martine* 'Ah, bring help to me, blessed Martin.' Another saw in it an appeal to Brito Martis, goddess of Crete.

'Away for a few days,' shouted Percy, 'my foot!'

Muriel Spark *Memento Mori*

Speakers sometimes express disbelief in what has just been said by referring to other parts of their body. 'Beautiful **my hind foot!**' says someone who has just been told that snow is beautiful in Harper Lee's *To Kill a Mockingbird*. Leslie Thomas, in *Tropic of Ruislip*, has the exchange: '"Surely middle-class children like this . . ." "Middle-class **my backside!**"' The more usual version of this occurs in Bernard Malamud's *Pictures of Fidelman*: '"For art," she said, then after a moment, bitterly, "art, **my ass**".'

Speakers in the 18th century were likely to exclaim **my wig!** or **dash my wig(s)!**, presumably as they threw their wigs to the ground in disgust. Milder exclamations which are still perhaps used by some speakers include **my aunt!** and the rather more exasperated **my sainted aunt! my giddy aunt! My word!** is still heard, but not the fuller **upon** (or **'pon) my word!** The 'aunt' and 'word' forms presumably avoid the offensive **my God!**, just as **my land!** (according to Eric Partridge) was formerly used by Canadian and American speakers as a euphemism for **my Lord!** Even more euphemistic is the use of **my!** itself as an exclamation, expanded to **oh my!** or **my, oh my!**

NAIL FILE

'I mean exactly that,' Mr Davison retorted. 'You've hit the nail smack on the head.'

Mary McCarthy *The Group*

As most people who have tried it

know, to hit a nail on the head requires a certain amount of hand and eye coordination. It is remarkably easy to miss the nail and hit one's thumb, and correspondingly satisfying to hit the nail squarely on the head and drive it home. Since it can also be difficult to get to the exact truth of a matter, it is not difficult to see why someone who manages to do so, by deductive reasoning or guesswork, is metaphorically said to have **hit the nail on the head**.

Kate O'Brien, in *Pray for the Wanderer*, has one of her characters comment on the phrase: '"She says my books are 'myth-creating, anti-social, and unnecessary'." "You'll forgive me if I say that Nell usually hits a nail on the head." "It's a waste of energy to hit a nail that's in its place and doing its job."'

'Nail' expressions which are less seldom heard include **nail one's colours to the mast** 'make an open declaration of one's beliefs and allegiances and make it clear that one will not change them'. Another is **a nail in one's coffin** 'anything that hastens one's death or defeat'. As it happens, both phrases are mentioned in *Surfeit of Lampreys*, by Ngaio Marsh, as some young people debate what should be the subject of their charade.

The first was originally an allusion to the flags hoisted by a ship at sea. If they were nailed to the mast, it was impossible for them to be lowered as a token of surrender, or to be changed in some way. The second phrase, often applied to something like a cigarette or alcoholic drink, is meant to suggest that someone is metaphorically constructing his own coffin.

Some speakers might still say 'Let's nail that lie', meaning 'let's prove that it's untrue'. The full form of this old

phrase is **nail a lie to the counter**. The reference is to what shop-keepers and bankers formerly did with counterfeit coins.

■ NECKLINES

'Who's master here? D'ye think as I can't turn ye all out of it neck and crop, if I've a mind?'

Arnold Bennett *Clayhanger*

The phrase **neck and crop** 'completely' appeared in an early 19th-century parody of a Cambridge examination. It was implied that students of the day would be familiar with it, perhaps because they were regularly pitched neck and crop out of public houses. 'Neck and crop' is now little used, other than by old-fashioned speakers such as the hilarious aunt in Dane Chandos's *Abbie*. She says at one point: 'I had intended to throw myself neck and crop into all forms of war activity.'

'That's where I come a cropper with women. Women expect an affair to get better and better, and if it doesn't, they think it's getting worse.'

Mary McCarthy *The Group*

There is dispute about whether the 'crop' in 'neck and crop' refers to a bird's craw or to a cropped head, though the latter is by far the stronger candidate given the existence of **come a cropper**. This slang term from hunting originally meant to be thrown head first from a horse. It now means 'to fall', literally or metaphorically.

'You won't stick your neck out if you don't need to? That's all I'm asking you.'

C.P. Snow *The Affair*

Dane Chandos's Aunt Abbie says to someone who has taken a risk during a game of cards: 'You've stuck your neck out again.' This is a 20th-century expression, and no one has ever specified exactly where one is when one **sticks one's neck out**. By inference the person concerned is on the executioner's block and is about to have his head cut off, to **get it in the neck** as we say of someone who is to be 'severely scolded or punished'. He could equally well be in a train or moving vehicle, risking his life by poking his head out of a window. 'I'm really sticking my neck out for your son,' says a policeman in Mordecai Richler's *Joshua Then and Now*. He means that he is risking his job by concealing certain facts.

'I'm gonna put you in a cab and goodbye, baby. You're getting to be a real pain in the neck.'

Michael Rumaker *Exit 3*

Someone or something that is annoying is a **pain in the neck**. A greater degree of annoyance, perhaps, leads to a **pain in the butt/ass/arse**. The exact location of the metaphorical discomfort is of little importance: the sense of the expression is conveyed by the fact that something or someone is 'a pain', or **gives one a pain**. Peter Benchley, in *The Island*, writes: 'To Maynard, Hiller had fast become a pain in the ass.' 'It's a pain in the neck,' occurs in Tom Wolfe's *The Bonfire of the Vanities*.

'Neck' has been used since the 17th century to mean a narrow strip of land. In the USA, **neck of the woods** took on a special meaning by the end of the 19th century. *The Oxford English Dictionary* quotes M. Schele DeVere, *Americanisms: the English of the New World*: 'He will . . . find his neighbourhood designated as a neck of the woods, that being the name applied to any settlement made in the well-wooded parts of the Southwest especially.' In modern times 'neck of the woods' simply means 'district', as in 'What are you doing in this neck of the woods?'

■ NICE WORK

'Everyone thought I hadn't done a stroke of work – but I had sweated like mad all the time.'

William J. Locke *Jaffery*

It is curious that no one ever says he *has* done a 'stroke of work', the phrase is always used in a negative context. 'I'd never have done a stroke of work again,' says a man in Edward Blishen's *A Cack-handed War*. He is referring to what would have happened had he married a wealthy woman. Sometimes 'stroke' alone is used, as when Barry Hines writes in *The Blinder*: 'He hasn't done a stroke since he came home on Monday.' Originally the phrase alluded to the kind of work done by a blacksmith, striking metal with a hammer. **Not to do a stroke of work** now means to do none of the work that needs to be done, whatever that work happens to be.

George was said to work like a black in the City.

Anthony Powell *Casanova's Chinese Restaurant*

Someone who worked hard, by

contrast, was formerly said to **work like a black**, with obvious reference to plantation slaves. A character in Iris Murdoch's *The Bell* says: 'Let him see a bit of the countryside. He's been working like a black.' Such a phrase would now be avoided by most speakers and writers as being highly offensive in racial terms. **Work like a Trojan** might be used instead. The men of Troy are described by Homer and Virgil as working and fighting courageously. The Trojan allusion is considered to be complimentary, presumably because Trojans worked hard of their own free will.

'It was all in the day's work, no fun and games about it.'

Mary McCarthy *The Group*

A particular task may be easy for some, difficult for others. The former will **make short** (or **light**) **work of it**, considering it to be **all in a day's work**; the latter will **make hard work of it**. Those who are receiving little help from their colleagues may feel like reminding them that **many hands make light work**. The proverb is an ancient one: more recent 'work' phrases include **work to rule** and **out of work**. Also modern is the envious remark **nice work if you can get it**, though this is applied not to having a job, but to any piece of good luck that has come someone's way. Nor is a **nasty piece of work** an unpleasant job that has to be done: the phrase is only used of an untrustworthy, offensive person.

'You see, I've done my homework.'

C.P. Snow *The Affair*

Children who are obliged to do homework may look forward to adult life in the hope that nightly chores will disappear. In many professions, however, they will still be obliged to **do their homework** 'do background research in order to be fully informed about a project'.

'She's done her best to cover you up by gumming the works, creating confusion.'

Dashiell Hammett *The Dain Curse*

To **gum (up) the works** 'cause confusion' is based on the idea of allowing a sticky substance to get into the moving parts of a mechanism and interfere with its normal operation. In Britain the person who does this is said – using a different metaphor – to **throw a spanner into the works**.

'I want you to go for broke today.'

Mordecai Richler *The Incomparable Atuk*

Shoot the works is mainly an American saying. It derives from shooting dice in a game of craps, and refers to gambling every penny one has. In a more general sense the phrase now means not to hold back in any way, to make a maximum effort. A phrase with similar meaning is **go for broke**, based on the idea of staking everything on one last wager. This is now beginning to be heard in Britain.

■ NIGHT LIFE

'Ah, Perce,' he said, 'it'll be all right on the night.' My name isn't Perce, but he called everyone by joke names to save remembering their real ones, and he used vaguely reassuring phrases at the start of a conversation in an attempt to dispel any alarm his appearance might cause.

Ian Jefferies *Thirteen Days*

It'll be all right on the night is a piece of wisdom from the theatre. 'The night' refers to the first night of the production in front of an audience, often better than could be expected after the disasters that have occurred during rehearsals. This is no doubt due to the adrenalin that flows when actors know that they are doing something 'for real'.

In *Talking to Strange Men* Ruth Rendell is referring to a couple's wedding-night when she says: 'It was all right on the night. Strange what an application that common phrase could have. It was just all right. The earth didn't move, nor did he soar to heaven, and he was sure she didn't.'

I need an early night. In fact I am quite tired already.

Anita Brookner *Hotel du Lac*

'Night' occurs in a number of colloquial phrases which are not to be interpreted literally. An **early night** 'a night when one goes to bed earlier than usual' has its corresponding **late night** 'going to bed later than usual'. To have a **good night** 'sleep well' is matched with have a **bad night** 'sleep badly'. We **make a night of it** if we spend much of the night celebrating, perhaps sampling the **night life** of a city by having a **night out**. To **spend the night with someone** euphemistically avoids any reference to 'bed' and 'sexual intercourse', nor does it specify that one is not married to the 'someone', though this is invariably the case.

Luke was probably no more than a ship passing in the night.

J.I.M. Stewart *The Last Tresilians*

Ships that pass in the night are 'people who meet briefly, probably only once'. The metaphor comes from *Tales of a Wayside Inn*, by Henry Wadsworth Longfellow. In Part Three, 'The Theologian's Tale', occurs:

> Ships that pass in the night, and
> speak each other in passing;
> Only a signal shown and a distant
> voice in the darkness;
> So on the ocean of life we pass
> and speak one another,
> Only a look and a voice; then
> darkness again and a silence.

Partridge lists 'ships that pass in the night' in his *Dictionary of Clichés* and says that it is 'particularly hackneyed and objectionable'. The phrase is certainly used frequently, but many would feel that the metaphor retains its freshness.

■ NIPPING OUT

His new-found intimacy with his elder son had been nipped in the bud, but there seemed no reason why he should not see this son he respected.

Angus Wilson *Anglo-Saxon Attitudes*

Instances of the expression to **nip something in the bud** occur in English literature from the early 17th century. The allusion has survived because it makes its point simply and well. Something which is 'nipped in the bud' is deliberately stopped at an early stage. There is the underlying suggestion that what has been stopped was unwanted and potentially embarrassing to whoever did the nipping.

'Nip' in this phrase means to remove by pinching. A slang meaning of 'nipper' in former times was a cut-purse or pick-pocket. Such thieves were often young boys, who had to be able to move through a crowd quickly, or 'nip about'. From all this 'nipper' came to have the general meaning of 'young child' in British slang.

'When this spree's over, it'll be nip and tuck.' Elsa hooked her arm in his. 'I might like you better if you were broke,' she tells him.

John Dos Passos *The Great Days*

Nip and tuck originated in the USA and means 'of uncertain outcome, evenly balanced, questionable'. It appeared in print after 1800 as 'rip and tuck', 'nip and tack' and 'nip and chuck' before settling into its present form. The phrase seems to have first been applied to wrestling matches that were close contests, then extended to other sports. It can now be used of any situation where the outcome is uncertain.

■ NITS AND NUTS

I nudged Wiz. 'He's round the bend,' I said. Wiz didn't answer.
'I said he's flipped, boy,' I shouted.

Colin MacInnes *Absolute Beginners*

Behaviour that others consider to be foolish is likely to attract a wide range of critical words and phrases. The process begins at school, where children roundly tell someone he is **bats**, a **crackpot**, **daffy**, **dopey**, **dotty**, a **nit-wit**, **nuts**, **not all there**, **has a screw loose**. A conversation in William Golding's *Lord of the Flies* runs: '"If we don't get home soon we'll be barmy." "Round the bend." "Bomb happy." "Crackers."'

Twit 'fool' probably developed from 'nit-wit', itself an ingenious insult suggesting that someone's wit or intelligence matches that of a louse's

egg. 'Nit' crops up again in **nit-picking**, now thankfully used mainly in its metaphorical sense of finding fault in a petty manner.

As with all slang, rapid changes occur as fashions change, but expressions such as **round the bend** survive well. Eric Partridge thought that this phrase was nautical in origin, but did not elaborate. It is not listed in *A Dictionary of Sailors' Slang*, by Wilfred Granville. There seems to be no evidence to support the view that 'bend' is used in its technical sense of a knot and that the reference is to a twisted rope, attractive though that theory is. **Round the twist**, of course, is another form of 'round the bend'.

'I sometimes think I shall go off my head. Perhaps I am off it already. That would explain a lot.'

Anthony Powell *Casanova's Chinese Restaurant*

Off one's head 'slightly crazy' is regularly used. 'It drives them all off their heads eventually' says someone in Frederic Raphael's *The Limits of Love*. 'Honestly, I think he's gone off his head' is in Peter Draper's *A Season in Love*. Sometimes 'clean' is added, as in: 'They thought I was clean off my head.' It is also possible to replace 'head' with a slang synonym: 'You thought I was going **off my chump**' occurs in William J. Locke's *Jaffery*. Arnold Bennett, in *Clayhanger*, has: 'I thought she was **off her nut**, but she wasn't.' Isaac Asimov, in *Ph As In Phony*, has: 'I think you're **off your rocker**.' J. Jefferson Farjeon, in his short story *Murder Over Draughts*, has the rather odd: 'It was about a week ago that I first wondered whether he was going **off his dot**.'

The correct reply to an accusation of being crazy, as reported by the Opies in their *Lore and Language of*

Schoolchildren, is quite simple. The accuser is told: 'If you're right in the head, I'll stay as I am.'

■ NOISES OFF

'You give me a royal pain in the ass, if you want to know the truth.'
Boy, *did she hit the ceiling when I said that.*

J.D. Salinger *The Catcher in the Rye*

When we speak about an angry person **hitting the ceiling** we probably have in our minds the image of someone shouting loudly, causing sound waves to bounce back from the ceiling. If his rage causes him to shout even louder we say that he is **hitting the roof**. The person who is angriest of all is said to **go through the roof**. It is of course the noise that goes through the roof, not the person who is making it.

'He's raising Cain in Taipei,' Craw had told him casually.

John Le Carré *The Honourable Schoolboy*

Making lots of noise and generally causing a disturbance is sometimes described as **raising Cain**. 'I can hear the twins raising Cain – you'd best go' says a woman in Margaret Laurence's *The Diviners*. The expression was well enough known in the 19th century for a joke to circulate about Adam and Eve. They were obviously rowdies, it was said, because 'they raised Cain'. The phrase may have alluded to the raising of a notorious, angry trouble-maker from his grave. It could also have been a euphemism for **raising hell** or **raising the devil**, both of which mean much the same as 'raising Cain'. 'Let's back our choices and stir the pot and raise

some hell,' says a character in Robertson Davies's *The Lyre of Orpheus*, where the meaning in this instance is 'let's be unconventional and attract some attention'.

'I wanted to put him in a picture. My partners raised the roof. At that time, no coloureds in movies.'

Garson Kanin *Moviola*

To **raise the roof** normally refers to making a lot of noise in a pleasant way, by cheering or singing loudly. The noise is so loud that it lifts the roof. Garson Kanin, in the quotation given above, obviously links the phrase with 'hitting the roof', since the men referred to were angry at the suggestion that a black American actor should appear on screen.

■ NOSINESS

'It's as plain', returned Solomon, 'as the nose on Parkes's face' – Mr Parkes, who had a large nose, rubbed it, and looked as if he considered this a personal allusion.'

Charles Dickens *Barnaby Rudge*

Something which is **as plain as the nose on one's face** is something that is blatantly obvious. Since 'plain' can also mean 'not attractive', the phrase becomes rather ambiguous when applied to a specific nose. Dickens plays with that idea in the quotation above: Dane Chandos also uses it in *Abbie*. When Aunt Abbie says 'It is as plain as the nose on Grace Bunket's face that Roosevelt is the man for the helm' she is commenting as much on the ugliness of Grace Bunket's nose as Roosevelt's suitability to be president.

In *Anywoman*, Fannie Hurst goes to some lengths to avoid the ambiguity:

'Mark wanted her for a sweetheart. It was plain as the nicely molded nose on Rose's nicely molded face.' Normal use of the phrase, where the speaker merely has obviousness in mind, occurs in *The Pajama Game*, by Richard Bissell: 'It's as plain as the nose on your face we got a showdown on our hands.'

The expression has been in constant use since the 17th century. Shakespeare considered it to be well enough known for him to use it ironically. In *The Two Gentlemen of Verona* Speed says:

> O jest unseen, inscrutable,
>   invisible,
> As a nose on a man's face, or a
>   weathercock on a steeple!

Shakespeare could also have used the phrase **as plain as a pikestaff** to mean 'obvious'. This had begun life in the 16th century in the form **plain as a packstaff** but had quickly been changed. The original reference was to a staff or pole used to carry a pack. It was 'plain' in that, unlike medieval staffs of office, it was unadorned, but the word was soon reinterpreted as 'clearly visible'. 'Plain as a packstaff' has long been obsolete, but the 'pikestaff' variant might still occasionally be used.

'In other words, I have been led by the nose.'
'Yes, I think you have. But it required a generous nose.'

John Fowles *The French Lieutenant's Woman*

Many animals are **led by the nose**: applied to a person, the phrase implies that someone is made to behave exactly as someone else wishes. The expression is an ancient one, and has a biblical model. Isaiah 37.29 has: 'Because you have raged against me and your arrogance has come to my ears, I will put my hook in your nose and my bit in your mouth, and I will turn you back the way by which you came.'

In *The Pickwick Papers* Dickens has: 'We say – we of the profession – that Sergeant Stubbins leads the court by the nose.' A far more significant use of the phrase in literature, however, occurs in *Othello*. Iago comments on the fatal weakness in Othello's character when he says:

> The Moor is of a free and open
>   nature
> That thinks men honest that but
>   seem to be so;
> And will as tenderly be led by th'
>   nose
> As asses are.

'Does she put your nose out of joint?'
Dottie made a brave negative sign.

Mary McCarthy *The Group*

Samuel Pepys noted in his *Diary*, 31 May 1662: 'The King is pleased enough with her: which, I fear, will put Madam Castlemaine's nose out of joint.' Anything 'out of joint' is displaced; the person who **puts someone's nose out of joint** displaces him in some way, or spoils his plans. The sudden appearance of a younger rival is especially likely to 'put someone's nose out of joint'. Sinclair Lewis, in *Martin Arrowsmith*, has: 'He is one of our youngest workers, but you, I believe, are only thirty-three, and you quite put the poor fellow's nose out!'

When Richard Gordon, in *The Face-Maker*, writes: 'So you were Miss Pollock's chaperon? Or was he putting your nose out of joint?' the meaning is: 'Did he spoil your plans? Were you hoping to have a relationship with Miss Pollock yourself?'

'All he could suggest was that I should go on paying through the nose to keep Juliet Rugg's mouth shut.'

Joyce Porter *Dover One*

To **pay through the nose for something** is to pay an excessive price. The phrase is recorded from the 17th century and has never satisfactorily been explained. Some writers talk of a nose-tax 'said to be' imposed on the Irish by the Danes. Why in the 17th century people should suddenly refer to something that may possibly have happened hundreds of years previously is a question such writers prefer not to pose.

Professor Weekley pointed out in the 1920s that extracting money from someone has long been referred to as 'bleeding' them, but it is difficult to see how 'paying through the nose' is, as he suggested, a 'playful variant' of that idea. There may be a connection with another phrase that was used from the 16th century, to **wipe one's nose of** 'to cheat someone out of something'. The metaphorical allusion concealed in that phrase is equally mysterious.

The straightforward use of 'pay through the nose' is seen in George Douglas's *The House with the Green Shutters*: 'They had to pay through the nose for their night's lodging'. Writers have a tendency, however, to link the phrase with other comments on the nose. In *David Copperfield* Dickens has: '"He pays well, I hope." "Pays as he speaks, my dear child – through the nose," replied Miss Mowcher.' This is of a Russian Prince. In *Abbie* Dane Chandos comments: 'She looked down her nose, but she had to pay through it.'

'I hope the other day, I didn't seem to be poking my nose in where it doesn't belong.'

John Updike *Rabbit Redux*

Ruth Rendell writes, in *The Tree of Hands*: 'She wasn't coming back, she wouldn't poke her nose in where she wasn't wanted.' To **poke one's nose in** 'meddle in affairs that should be of no concern' has been used since the 17th century, when **thrust one's nose in** was also common. 'Poke' seems to express the thought more aptly, and is the usual modern form.

'What an old Nosey Parker you are!'

Malcolm Lowry *Under the Volcano*

As a nickname for a person who is constantly 'poking his nose' into other people's affairs, **Nosey Parker** first appeared in the early 20th century. Needless to say, attempts have been made to identify the Parker concerned, on the assumption that the phrase alluded to a specific person. Harold Wheeler, in *How Much Do You Know?*, stated confidently that the reference was to Matthew Parker (1504–75), chaplain to Anne Boleyn and Henry VIII and later Archbishop of Canterbury. Stanley Rogers, in *From Ships and Sailors*, was equally certain that Richard Parker was meant, a man who was hanged in 1797 for leading a mutiny.

That such suggestions can seriously be made is extraordinary, and no doubt other equally unsatisfactory candidates have been proposed. Common sense would appear to dictate that ordinary English people do not start alluding in informal 20th-century conversations to obscure sailors of the past, nor to archbishops who have been dead for centuries. If a real Parker was responsible for the expression, he must have been alive and well-known around 1910. No one named Parker who remotely fits the bill has been discovered.

There may be a connection here with 'poke one's nose in'. The person who does so could be called a 'poker', and indeed the word is recorded in the sense of 'inquisitive person' from the 17th century. 'Nosey' is also recorded as an adjective describing such a person. The phrase 'nosey poker' would very clearly indicate an officiously inquisitive person and a humorous change to 'Nosey Parker' is easily imagined. This must remain pure speculation, since no example of 'nosey poker' has been found, but in the absence of a Parker who was famous for his nosiness, the conversion from word to name status of some such phrase deserves consideration.

'If you went up there and looked, really looked, you'd see it.'
'See what, Will?' Morgan asked.
'Well, a different view of things, that's all. Something more than keeping your nose to the ground.'
'Grindstone's the word,' Morgan said.

Raymond Williams *Border Country*

To **keep someone's nose to the grindstone** has changed its meaning since the 19th century. In *Our Mutual Friend*, Dickens describes how the villainous Wegg proposes to punish Mr Boffin. 'I consider his planting one of his menial tools in the yard, an act of sneaking and sniffing. And his nose shall be put to the grindstone for it . . . I shall not neglect bringing the grindstone to bear, nor yet bringing Dusty Boffin's nose to it. His nose once brought to it, shall be held to it by these hands, Mr Venus, till the sparks flies out in showers.' Wegg's intention is to force Mr Boffin to do hard and monotonous work.

In modern times the phrase still means to work consistently at something which is not pleasant, to keep 'grinding away' as we might also say, but the task is now self-imposed. The allusion is to the sharpening of tools, a job that has to be done slowly and with great care, though the phrase may be applied to work which is purely mental, such as studying for an examination. 'You won't be able to go out in the evenings much longer' says someone in Henry Cecil's *Brothers in Law* to a young man who has to prepare for his bar examinations. 'Nose to the grindstone, my boy.'

Another example of the phrase occurs in Stephen Vincent Benét's *Everybody was Very Nice*: 'Well, we had stuck pretty close to the grindstone for the past few years, with the children and everything.' In Mary McCarthy's *The Group* there is the similar: 'Her tribe of brothers and sisters had kept her Dad's nose to the grindstone; if he had not had so many children, he might have been a famous specialist, instead of a hard-worked G.P.'

'It's been goin' on under your nose for years.'

Ngaio Marsh *Surfeit of Lampreys*

Something that happens **under one's nose** occurs in one's presence without one noticing it. This ability not to see something which ought to be blatantly obvious has been remarked upon since the 16th century. Human nature does not change, and the phrase is still much used. Henry Cecil, in *Brothers in Law*, has: 'It's a fine kettle of fish. Taking machinery from under their very noses.'

To **follow one's nose** 'be guided by instinct' is another 16th-century phrase. Shakespeare has the Fool, in *King Lear*, say: 'All that follow their noses are led by their eyes but [except] blind men; and there's not a nose among twenty but can smell him that's stinking.'

'No thanks, Uncle Charlie, not a drink right now – I just want to powder my nose.'

Stephen Vincent Benét *The Prodigal Children*

Powder one's nose, as a euphemism for going to the lavatory, was originally used exclusively by women but is now sometimes jokingly used by men. The ladies' lavatory in a theatre or other public building is sometimes coyly referred to as the 'powder room'.

'Powder one's nose' came into use at the beginning of the 20th century and attracts comments from writers. In *The Limits of Love*, by Frederic Raphael, there is the exchange: '"I don't know whether you feel like powdering your noses." "We have to be careful of our noses, don't we?" Nat said.' This is said to a woman who is trying to conceal the fact that she is Jewish. Kingsley Amis, in *Lucky Jim*, says of a woman who has been gone for some time: 'I wonder where young Callaghan has got to. Her nose must be fairly thickly encrusted with powder by now.'

Waiting for the Police, by J. Jefferson Farjeon, has a woman being interrogated: '"How long were you out of the room?" "Five minutes, I should say." "A long time to get a handkerchief." "Perhaps. But I not only blew my nose, I powdered it."'

Another relatively modern phrase is **on the nose** 'exactly'. In the days when radio broadcasting was always live, a play would be rehearsed carefully and timed. As it was being broadcast the director would signal to the cast to tell them whether they needed to spin things out or go faster.

A finger on the nose was a welcome sign from the director that they were running exactly to time.

■ NOT IN THE SAME STREET

If two people or things are **not in the same street**, then one of them is probably **streets ahead** of the other. The phrases reflect our tendency to judge people's social status by the street they live in. We then extend the idea to a more general judgement of relative quality. 'Street' is invariable in these expressions: 'not in the same road' or 'avenues ahead' would lead to a certain amount of puzzlement.

'What is it, Swan Lake*?'*
'No, it's modern. It'll be right up your street.'

Barry Hines *The Blinder*

Variation does occur in **up one's street** – within one's range of knowledge and interest. The phrase has been used since the end of the 19th century and gave rise soon afterwards to the mainly American variant **up one's alley**. 'He wouldn't have understood it anyway,' says J.D. Salinger in *The Catcher in the Rye*, 'it wasn't up his alley at all'. This compares with the typically British usage of Joyce Porter, in *Dover One*: 'There's an outbreak of fowl pest or swine fever or something and, naturally, that's far more up his street than one of these vanishing lady larks.' Another British policeman, in Frederick Forsyth's *The Day of the Jackal*, transfers a difficult task to someone else by saying: 'Sorry, Alec, but this really is more up your street.'

No one seems to know who first used the 'alley' form of the phrase, which remains for the time being as much an Americanism as **down one's street** and **down one's alley**, both of which are American synonyms for 'up one's street'. 'Down one's alley', especially, seems to hint that speakers have a bowling-alley in mind rather than a narrow street. As part of a street name 'alley' survives in only a few of the oldest American cities.

■ NOT PANNING OUT

President Truman made it clear that today's blow was no flash in the pan. The showering of high explosive on the power plants was described as a 'new policy of getting tough with the Reds'.

Robert Shaw *The Hiding Place*

The use of **flash in the pan** in the above quotation is especially apt in referring to explosives. 'Pan' was the technical term for that part of the lock in old-fashioned guns and pistols which held the priming. Sometimes that priming 'flashed in the pan' without igniting the charge. From this arose the metaphorical sense of 'flash in the pan', applied to someone or something that begins well but fails to live up to its promise. 'The companies were suspicious he might be a flash in the pan' occurs in Bernard Malamud's *The Natural*, applied to a baseball player.

In a sense, a 'flash in the pan' is someone or something that does not **pan out**. The allusion here is to an entirely different kind of pan, that used in panning for gold. When the gravel and sand in the pan was washed away, leaving gold behind, it had 'panned out', or been successful. The phrase originated in the California gold rush and has been used since the late 19th century.

Another 19th-century phrase that came into slang use along with 'flash in the pan' has not survived. At one time **shut your pan**, where once again

'pan' referred to part of a flintlock, was the equivalent of 'shut your mouth'.

■ NUTS IN MAY

'To put the matter in a nutshell, I fear my dear Susan will get unhinged.'

E.F. Benson *Trouble for Lucia*

Most people who talk of putting something **in a nutshell** 'in a few words' are unaware that the phrase ultimately alludes to the *Historia Naturalis* of Pliny the Elder. In that work, Pliny mentions a copy of Homer's *Iliad* which was small enough to be enclosed in the shell of a nut. This famous *Iliad*, specifically referred to in English from at least the 16th century, established 'nutshell' as a typical example of something small that could enclose a great deal. It led Shakespeare to the well-known exchange in *Hamlet* where the prince tells Rosencrantz and Guildenstern 'Denmark's a prison'. 'Why, then your ambition makes it so; 'tis too narrow for your mind,' says Rosencrantz. Hamlet replies: 'O God, I could be bounded in a nutshell and count myself a king of infinite space, were it not that I have bad dreams.'

The basic idea of a book, or a great many words, being contained in a nutshell soon established itself and has been much used by writers. Thomas Love Peacock, in *Crotchet Castle*, has: 'There, sir, is political economy in a nutshell.' In Henry Cecil's *Brothers in Law* occurs: 'That could be a long story, but I'll make it a short one. In a nutshell, I've got too big for my boots.' Len Deighton, *Funeral in Berlin*, has: 'I say, that's rather good. In an absolute nutshell. I'll write that down. "Expendable hero", that's what Stok is all right.'

Jeremy Brooks, in *Henry's War*, makes the sarcastic comment: 'You've put it in a nutshell the size of the *Queen Mary.*'

The head Hun will find me a tough nut to crack.

Dane Chandos *Abbie*

Other allusions to nuts are self-evident. The hardness of a nutshell leads to someone or something being a **tough** or **hard nut to crack** 'a difficult problem to deal with'. When a job is done or something is bought **for peanuts**, the reference is to a very small sum of money.

'It was a very rum place you landed him in. Half of the people clear nutters.'

Michael Innes *Honeybath's Haven*

One or two phrases derive from 'nut' in its slang meaning of 'head'. **Off one's nut** is a variant of **off one's head** and leads to **nuts** or **nutty** as a synonym for 'crazy'. To **be nuts about someone** is to be 'crazy about, madly in love with' that person. 'Nutty' is sometimes extended to **nutty as a fruit cake**, which in turn leads to a crazy or eccentric person being described in Britain as a **fruit cake**. The same term in America is more likely to be an elaboration of 'fruit' in its slang sense of 'homosexual'. A real **nutter** or **nut-case** 'crazy person' is one who is likely to **do his nut** 'lose control of himself and act in a furious way'.

■ OCCASIONAL DELIGHT

'That's for her birthday. She'll be over the moon when she sees it.'
Margaret Drabble *The Middle Ground*

In Britain, one of the most mocked phrases of the 1980s was **over the moon**, meaning 'extremely happy'. The words were associated especially with footballers or their managers being interviewed immediately after a victory. In response to the clichéd question posed by unimaginative reporters about how they were feeling, they were inevitably 'over the moon'.

Nigel Rees, in his *Dictionary of Popular Phrases*, remarks that by the end of the 1970s the phrase had become notorious. Discussing its origin, he cites an isolated example of the phrase in a diary of 1857, though this was not published until 1927. Other early instances are very rare. Penelope Gilliatt uses it to mean 'delighted' in *A State of Change* (1967) and makes no comment on it, though she does specifically comment on several other idioms in the novel. *Chambers Twentieth Century Dictionary* (1974), makes no mention of the phrase, but includes it in the 1988 edition of *Chambers English Dictionary*.

The words are familiar because of the nursery rhyme: 'Hey diddle diddle, The cat and the fiddle, The cow jumped over the moon.' This is recorded from 1765 and has been 'interpreted' in many different ways. The 'cat and fiddle' is often said to be a corruption of Catherine la Fidèle, a reference to the French wife of Peter the Great of Russia. Bryant Lillywhite in *London Signs* gives examples of 'Cat and Fiddle' tavern signs which date from the beginning of the 16th century. This makes the

'Catherine' allusion impossible. Of more significance, perhaps, is the fact that the small fiddle used by dancing-masters was first referred to as a 'kit' in the early 16th century.

It cannot be said with certainty that 'over the moon' derives from the nursery rhyme, though the cow that jumps over the moon is obviously happy. One would have expected the phrase to have come into use much earlier, were that the case. What is clear is that in spite of, perhaps because of, the notoriety associated with the phrase, it was being used at all social levels in Britain in the 1980s. Prince Andrew and Sarah Ferguson announced their engagement on 19 March 1986, and chose 'over the moon' as the expression that best summed up their feelings.

Shakespeare and his contemporaries were more familiar with **under** or **below the moon**. 'For all beneath the moon' as used by Edgar, in *King Lear*, means 'for everything on earth'. Hamlet also refers to a cataplasm (poultice) made of all the herbs 'under the moon'. The modern equivalent is **under** or **beneath the sun**.

'Does Daniel ever ask about me?'
'Oh, I guess once in a blue moon.'

James Purdy *Eustace Chisholm and the Works*

Once in a blue moon, meaning 'very rarely', has been widely used since the mid-19th century. 'I only come up to London once in a blue moon,' says a character in Christopher Dilke's *Freddie and Son*. The usual explanation given is that the moon does occasionally seem to have a blue tinge.

Professor Weekley thought that 'blue moon' was originally meant to be

'never', since it referred to something nonsensical that never occurred. His view is supported by the 16th century couplet:

Yf they say the mone is blewe,
We must beleve that it is true.

'We are obliged to believe them,' in other words, 'no matter how ridiculous their statements.'

Weekley equated the phrase with **on** or **at the Greek calends**, a literary joke that began in the 17th century. The first day of any Roman month was the 'Calends' or 'Kalends' (hence our 'calendar'), but the Greeks did not use this term. 'On the Greek calends' was a favourite day for settling debts, since it never arrived. It belonged in what the French call *la semaine de quatre jeudis* 'the week of four Thursdays'.

■ OLD HANDS

'Once you make a formal approach I shall wash my hands of you entirely.'

John Le Carré *The Honourable Schoolboy*

Some of the metaphorical expressions which mention 'hands' effectively demonstrate that the simplest images can be the most striking and most enduring. To **wash one's hands of something** is an example, used regularly in speech and writing to disassociate someone from an affair. 'If you're going to regard every suggestion I make as a criticism, then I must wash my hands of the whole matter,' says someone in Angus Wilson's *Anglo-Saxon Attitudes*. John Stroud, in *On the Loose*, has: 'I'm washing my hands of the whole affair; it's no longer my business.' 'I wash my hands of it, it is God's doing,' occurs in Bernard Wolfe's *The Late-Risers*.

Occasionally the phrase is used of one person refusing to have anything to do with another. W. Somerset Maugham, in *The Ant and the Grasshopper*, has the rather clumsy sentence: 'When circumstances forced George to realise that his brother would never settle down and he washed his hands of him, Tom, without a qualm, began to blackmail him.'

None of these modern authors is able to use the phrase with its original intensity, as it occurs in the New Testament, Matthew 27.22. 'Pilate said to them, "Then what shall I do with Jesus who is called Christ?" They all said, "Let him be crucified." And he said, "Why, what evil has he done?" But they shouted all the more, "Let him be crucified." So when Pilate saw that he was gaining nothing, but rather that a riot was beginning, he took water and washed his hands before the crowd, saying, "I am innocent of this man's blood; see to it yourselves."'

'You blunder along hoping everything's going to be all right as long as you don't do any harm. As long as you keep your hands clean.'

Jeremy Brooks *Henry's War*

To **keep one's hands clean** alludes to the same biblical passage. This has the unpleasant alternative form **keep one's nose clean**, where the allusion is obvious. Alexander Fullerton makes sure that the point gets across in *Other Men's Wives*: 'Metromark has to keep its nose clean – because it's a dirty, snotty nose to start with, and they wouldn't want to invite anyone to look at it too closely.' Ian Fleming, in *Diamonds are Forever*, has: 'You made no mistakes so far. You go on that way and keep your nose clean.'

He was through with trying to hold their hands over there. His advice had been disregarded once too often.

J.I.M. Stewart *A Use of Riches*

Another phrase of obvious allusion is **hold someone's hand** 'help someone by offering support and comfort'. Publishing editors traditionally 'hold the hands' of sensitive authors, hence the advice given by a publisher to a new member of staff in Mary McCarthy's *The Group*: 'Encourage them; ride them; tell them what to cut; hold their hand; take them out to lunch.' The expression is also applied at times to people who are newcomers to a situation and are temporarily as helpless as children; they need to **have their hands held**.

'Well, sir, are we to have you with us? Will you lend us a hand?' Winningly he held out his own right hand. Steven-Blair seized it in his own and wrung it with a nervous spasm of emotional loyalty.

Edward Hyams *Sylvester*

To **lend someone a hand** is curious in its literal meaning, but is easily understandable. The work one is able to do, symbolized by the use of one's hands, is temporarily at the service of someone else, lent to him. There is a similar metonymic use of 'hand' in sayings like **many hands make light work** 'a job becomes easier if several people are doing it', **have one's hands full** 'be fully occupied, have plenty of things to do', **turn one's hand to something** 'undertake something', **keep one's hand in** 'put one's skills into practice from time to time in order not to forget them'.

We also talk about leaving a matter **in someone's hands**, if that person is to concern himself with it. The hands may then be assigned the qualities of the person: 'I will leave this in your capable hands.' Raymond Williams, in *Border Country*, has a doctor remark: 'I shall be seeing him regularly.' 'I can see he's in good hands,' is the reply.

'In someone's hands' has its opposite **out of someone's hands**. 'That's **out of my hands**' means: 'I have no control over the matter, it does not fall within my jurisdiction.' A similar pair of phrases related to responsibility are **on one's hands** and **off one's hands**. A parent might say: 'My children are grown up now and have lives of their own. They are off my hands.'

The latter phrase has only a faint connection with an **offhand** manner. This was originally something said or done quickly, without thought, as if one wished to dispose of responsibility for it as soon as possible. That meaning of immediacy is still present when we say: 'Offhand, I can't think of the answer to that.' Something done quickly is also done without ceremony, and it is easy to see how the secondary meaning of 'curtness' became attached to 'offhand'.

Leamas had to hand it to Fiedler; he had guts.

John le Carré *The Spy Who Came In From The Cold*

The thought behind **have to hand it to someone** is that one is obliged to concede something. It is as if the person concerned has proved his right to possession, though the phrase always refers to something abstract, not to a concrete object. The expression carries a strong suggestion of reluctance. 'I have to hand it to you' means: 'I don't much like admitting this, but I must.'

'You want to expose that crook, Slingsby, and then he would eat out of your hand.'

P.G. Wodehouse *Bill the Conqueror*

To **have someone eating out of one's hand** compares the person concerned to an animal that has been tamed. The person was dangerous and difficult to control, but has become submissive and pliant. In *The Honourable Schoolboy* John Le Carré writes: 'Wheel in the Cousins and you'd carry the committee without a shot fired. Foreign Office would eat out of your hand.' The person to whom this is said replies: 'I prefer to stay my hand on that.' To **stay one's hand** 'to take no action' would not be heard in daily speech. In Le Carré's novel phrases of that type help to establish the rather antiquated character of the speaker.

The 'eating out of one's hand' metaphor refers to the voluntary submission of one person to another. Rather harsher control of animals is alluded to when a person is said to **have the whip hand** 'be in a position of control'. Here there is the implication that those submitting are being forced to do so.

And what have they brought up? A failed anorexic who never washes her hair or anything else, snarls at her teachers, and habitually bites the hand that feeds her.

Robertson Davies *The Lyre of Orpheus*

The gentler methods of taming animals or people can lead to problems. Instead of 'eating out of someone's hand' a person may **bite the hand that feeds him**. In this case the person concerned has not been 'tamed' and shows no gratitude for past kindnesses. On the contrary, his response is hurtfully aggressive. In *Jaffery*, William J. Locke makes a character extend the animal metaphor by saying: 'I have been a pet for such a long time – for years, and I've shown myself to be such a bad pet – biting the hand that fed me.'

'However free the hand they give you, it means battles.'

Frederic Raphael *The Limits of Love*

With a **free hand** one can do whatever one wishes, there are no restrictions. 'Surely you saw that I stayed away so that everyone should have a free hand,' says someone in Angus Wilson's *Anglo-Saxon Attitudes*. By contrast, somebody who is forced to work within strict guidelines or consult his superiors every time a decision has to be made, might complain that **one hand is tied behind his back**. 'Free-hand' has a special meaning when applied to drawing: no measuring instruments or other aids are used. 'Free-handed' also has the special sense of 'liberal, generous' when applied to a person.

That's what agents do, work hand in glove with them.

Mary McCarthy *The Group*

If two people are **hand in glove** with one another, they have a close and constant relationship, have mutual interests and cooperate very closely. Muriel Spark, in *Memento Mori*, speaking of the doctors and nurses in an old people's home, prefers the hyphenated form of the phrase: 'They're hand-in-glove.' (For remarks about hyphenation, see Introduction, page 7.) In modern usage the hand in this expression is always *in* the glove. When the phrase was first used in the late 17th century it was written as **hand and glove**.

Lady Arabella felt that the doctor kept the upper hand in those sweet forgivenesses. Whereas, she had intended to keep the upper hand, at least for a while.

Anthony Trollope *Doctor Thorne*

A simple game played in the 17th century led to the phrase **have the upper hand** 'be in a superior position'. Two players put their hands on a stick one after the other, gradually working their way upwards. One ended by having the upper hand. Modern children play their own version of the 'upper hand' game, one laying a hand on a table which another child covers with his own hand. The first child covers this, and has his hand covered in turn. A rapid interchange of hand positions then follows until both become tired of the contest.

He was making money hand over fist.

W. Somerset Maugham *The Verger*

When we speak of someone making money **hand over fist** we are again alluding to a rapid interchange of hand positions. The earlier form of this expression was **hand over hand**, referring to the drawing in of a rope by pulling it with each hand in turn. The rope piles up as does the wealth of the person who is making his money 'hand over fist', but that is by the way. The point is that money comes in as quickly as the rope does.

Arthur prided himself on knowing the wood like the back of his hand.

Alan Sillitoe *Saturday Night and Sunday Morning*

To **know something like the back of one's hand** needs no explanation. The simile is well used, but W. Somerset Maugham preferred to vary it. In *The Unconquered* he says of a man that: 'He knew the city like the palm of his hand.' Maugham often uses his own version of set phrases, and there is no way of knowing whether it was deliberate policy or an occasional slip of memory.

Contrasting life styles are described in two other 'hand' phrases. A luxurious existence has been described since the 14th century as being **waited on hand and foot**. The phrase conjures up an image of servants who place everything within easy reach and bolster one's feet with cushions. **Live from hand to mouth** has been a set phrase since the 16th century, applied to those who are very poor. The expression implies that they are obliged to consume immediately whatever food comes their way because of hunger: as food comes **to hand**, so it is conveyed to the mouth. A **hand-to-mouth existence**, one where no thought can be given to the future because coping with present needs is a constant problem, describes human life at its bleakest.

■ OLYMPIAN MOLEHILLS

'You have done nothing. Talk about a mountain out of a molehill! We shall be afraid to open our mouths.'

Ivy Compton-Burnett *A House and Its Head*

People have been **making mountains out of molehills** 'making trivial matters seem important' since at least the 16th century. 'Molehill' is no doubt contrasted with 'mountain' in this expression purely for the sake of alliteration, a kind of internal rhyme.

Perhaps because of this phrase, 'molehill' was at one time used on its own to symbolize something small. The mountain-molehill contrast could also be used to make a different point. In Shakespeare's *Coriolanus* it describes relative social importance when Coriolanus says: 'My mother bows / As if Olympus to a molehill should / In supplication nod.' Normal modern use is shown by Mary McCarthy in *The Groves of Academe*: 'She had been wondering in secret whether they had not been making a mountain out of a molehill.'

Professor George R. Stewart reports in *American Place Names* that a place called Mole Hill in West Virginia was probably named for a family called Mole. The place name was later changed, and is now Mountain.

■ ONE'S MOTHER TONGUE

For God's sake hold your tongue and let me love.

John Donne *The Canonization*

In **hold one's tongue** 'remain silent, even though one would like to say something', 'hold' is used in its sense of 'restrain', as in **hold your noise**, **hold your fire**. The phrase has been in continuous use since the 9th century, and now conjures up an image of someone grasping his tongue between his fingers to make sure that he says nothing.

The expression constantly occurs in literature, though nowhere more dramatically than in John Donne's famous opening line, quoted above. The heroine of Margaret Laurence's *The Diviners* discusses the 'cruelty' of the poem in an English literature class, on the grounds that the woman might have been as much a poet as Donne himself. 'You would not take it kindly, Miss Gunn,' says the teacher, 'to be asked to hold your tongue?' Miss Gunn agrees that she would not, and is complimented for caring enough about the work of an ancient poet 'to want to go back in time and discuss the matter with him'.

Other literary occurrences include Malcolm's comment in Shakespeare's *Macbeth*: 'Why do we hold our tongues that most may claim this argument for ours?' 'Hold your tongue, for the Lord's sake, and don't mention it any more' is in Dickens's *David Copperfield*. Sheridan's *The School for Scandal* has: 'Sir Peter will hold his tongue for his own credit's sake.' Edward Hyams, in *Sylvester*, mentions a valid reason for remaining silent: ' "There! I never could hold my tongue." The girl was really mortified at her want of professional discretion.'

Never before had he felt so tongue-tied in front of a girl.

Bernard Malamud *The Natural*

Tongue-tied is used metaphorically to mean 'silent because of shyness or embarrassment', but the phrase also had a more literal meaning when it was introduced in the 16th century. It described the condition of someone who was unable to speak because his tongue was attached to the floor of his mouth along most of its length. 'If you're not tongue-tied, would you be so kind as to answer the question' is addressed by a teacher to Morag Gunn in the Margaret Laurence novel mentioned above.

The idea of a tongue being restrained in some way also leads us to talk of **loosening one's tongue**. Alcohol, especially, is thought to have this ability to untie the knots. Once the tongue has been loosened it can start to 'wag', though the mockery and

mild contempt inherent in the notion of **wagging tongues** has long associated the phrase with idle gossips.

'That's poor James giving tongue. He's got a cold.'

Ruth Rendell *The Tree of Hands*

If noise rather than speech is referred to we can speak about someone **giving tongue**. This was originally a term used in hunting, applied to the baying of a hound when it sighted its prey, but it can be humorously applied to humans. In the quotation above, Ruth Rendell is talking of a crying baby.

The cat seemed to have got Norine's tongue, and Putnam Blake was no conversationalist.

Mary McCarthy *The Group*

An insensitive teacher might ask an embarrassed, silent child if **the cat had got its tongue**. The phrase is modern and perhaps comes from a children's story or rhyme. It is a fanciful variant of **have you lost your tongue?**, the sarcastic question addressed to someone who appears to be choosing to say nothing.

'She could say it was a slip of the tongue and she didn't mean green at all.'

Joyce Porter *Dover One*

When **slip of the tongue** came into use in the 18th century, **slip of the pen** was also used. Both phrases refer to an unintentional error of a minor kind, though the listener may think that a **Freudian slip** was made, accidentally revealing someone's true thoughts. In *The Old Boys*, William Trevor has a character called Jarraby who says: 'You will be present on Friday, Boyns?' The conversation continues: '"My name is Swabey-Boyns. I do not address you as Jar." "Dear fellow, a slip of the tongue."' Nigel Dennis also makes much of the phrase in *Cards of Identity*: '"I am sorry. It was a slip of the tongue. I suppose an apology is in order." "Not merely in order. For immediate delivery." "It will take a moment to frame one that will not involve too much loss of face."'

Someone whose 'slip of the tongue' has caused him to say something deeply embarrassing may metaphorically **bite his tongue** 'blame himself for the mistake'. 'Bite one's tongue' can also be used figuratively to mean 'force oneself to remain silent'.

'You can always put your tongue in your cheek.'

Warwick Deeping *Sorrell and Son*

To say something **with one's tongue in one's cheek** is to say it ironically, not meaning it to be taken seriously. Tobias Smollett, in *Roderick Random*, says: 'I signified my contempt of him, by thrusting my tongue in my cheek.' This seems to imply that in the 18th century a tongue thrust in the cheek was the equivalent of poking one's tongue out at somebody. The bulge in the cheek would have conveyed the message to the other person. The later metaphorical use of 'tongue in cheek' would then mean saying something while simultaneously making fun of someone.

This modern meaning of the phrase did not establish itself for at least a hundred years. Richard Harris Barham, in *The Ingoldsby Legends* (1842), has a passage in 'The Black Mousquetaire' which runs:

. . . With that sort of address
Which the British call 'Humbug',
*   and Frenchmen 'Finesse',*
(It's 'Blarney in Irish – I don't
*   know the Scotch,)*
He fell to admiring his friend's
*   English watch.*
He examined the face, And the
*   back of the case,*
And the young Lady's portrait
*   there, done on enamel, he*
'Saw by the likeness was one of
*   the family';*
Cried 'Superbe! – Magnifique!'
(With his tongue in his cheek) . . .

To **humbug someone** at the time meant to 'impose upon, delude someone'. 'Blarney', then as now, meant to 'get one's way by delusive flattery'. Barham perhaps used 'with his tongue in cheek' in the same meaning, but it now no longer implies that someone is trying to persuade or delude another person for an ulterior motive. 'Tongue in cheek' remarks are made purely in fun.

. . . a pal of Miss Stryker's, whose name was on the tip of his tongue.

P.G. Wodehouse *Bill the Conqueror*

Daniel Defoe talks of having arguments **at the tip of one's tongue** in *Moll Flanders* (1722). 'On the tip of one's tongue', as it would now be, serves a useful purpose in allowing a speaker to say that he has forgotten something but feels that he will remember it at any moment. It is temporarily eluding recall. The phrase is also used to refer to something that one can only just prevent oneself from saying. 'It was on the tip of my tongue to tell him what I thought of him.' Truman Capote, in *The Headless Hawk*, has: 'Though the subject was always there on the tip of his tongue, not once had he ever mentioned D.J. to any of his friends.'

It is probably this latter sense which led to the image evoked by the phrase. The suggestion is that words have got as far as the tip of one's tongue, almost out of one's mouth, but have just been held back. In the other sense of the expression it is as if the words have got that far, but refuse to continue past the lips.

'I'm paying through the nose for this, matron. And will not be treated like a schoolboy.'
'I'll thank you to keep a civil tongue in your head.'

Barry Oakley *A Salute to the Great McCarthy*

The 'tongue' is so closely associated with speech that the word itself can mean 'language', as in **mother tongue** 'native language'. From this it is a short step to applying comments about what is said to the tongue that has uttered the words. **Keep a civil tongue in one's head** simply means 'be civil, polite'. We extend the idea in other phrases, imagining that the kind of tongue a person has determines what he says. 'You keep your filthy tongue to yourself' says someone in Frederic Raphael's *The Limits of Love*. A person who can charm others by what he says is said to be **silver-tongued**. We also speak at times about tongues having different sides to them which produce different kinds of words. To **give someone the rough edge of one's tongue** is to berate him, give him a **tongue-lashing**, as we also express it.

The extraordinary versatility accorded to the tongue in popular sayings extends to its supposed ability to assume various shapes. We talk of not being able to **get our tongues round** a difficult word or phrase, or describe the latter as a **tongue-twister**. In such sayings lies buried an age-old folk humour to which most people

have become insensitive. It is probably children, who much enjoy their tongue-twisters, for whom 'tongue-twisting' retains something of the comic quality that it is meant to have.

■ PECKING ORDER

She was pressing against him. Her warm, silky body. A phrase came into his head. It gets the old pecker up. *The manager at the supermarket who was turned on by veiled women.*

Nina Bawden *George Beneath a Paper Moon*

Elizabeth Jane Howard, in *Getting it Right*, has: 'When she thanked him again he gave her a cheery wink – as a kind of telegram to keep her pecker up.' The meaning in this passage of **keep one's pecker up** is 'keep your head up, remain courageous and cheerful in spite of difficulties'. The allusion appears to be to the head of a game-cock, whose head tends to sink when defeat is near.

American writers, if they use this phrase, interpret it differently. Mary McCarthy writes in *The Group*: 'You say your husband can't sleep with you because you're a "good woman". I suggest you enlighten him. Tell him what you do with Harald. That ought to get his pecker up.' 'Pecker' here has its American slang meaning of 'penis', which itself was probably derived from a misunderstanding of the British phrase. The 'penis' meaning of 'pecker' is becoming far more usual in Britain in the early 1990s.

The so-called **pecking order** in a group of people refers to the relative power and influence of the individuals. To be bottom of the pecking order is to be the least important person. The reference is to domestic fowls who establish their dominance by pecking at weaker birds. A far older expression, dating from the 17th century, is **hen-pecked**, said of a husband dominated by his wife.

■ PENNY WISE

First and last, this wedding would cost a pretty penny.

E.M. Forster *Howards End*

The 'penny' has been part of the English currency system since the 8th century as a silver, copper or bronze coin, with differing values. In Canada and some parts of America, 'penny' has long been used to refer to a cent.

The long history of the penny has led to the inclusion of the word in many idiomatic phrases. 'This mourning (i.e. the clothes for it) will cost a pretty penny,' says a character in *Mary Barton*, by Elizabeth Gaskell. Modern writers continue to use **pretty penny** to refer to 'a lot of money'. 'That'll cost me a pretty penny' is said by a character in Bernard Malamud's *The Natural*. Mordecai Richler, in *The Incomparable Atuk*, has: 'It cost me a pretty penny but it was worth it.' Mary McCarthy uses the phrase slightly differently in *The Group*: 'I had the man from Lehmann appraise the contents. It would have brought me a pretty penny.'

'Pretty penny' was probably a reference originally to the so-called gold penny minted by Henry III in 1257. This was a gold coin but not actually a penny – the word was occasionally used in the more general sense of 'coin'.

'Penny for your thoughts, Artie.' He considered. 'I reely don't think I was thinking of anything,' he said at last with a smile. 'I expect I was thinking jest what a Rum Go everything is. I expect it was something like that.'

H.G. Wells *Kipps*

It is still customary to offer a thoughtful-looking person **a penny for your thoughts**. Edna O'Brien has a character use the words in *The Country Girls*, but adds a comment: '"A penny for your thoughts," Baba said to me, but they were worth more. I was thinking of Mr Gentleman.' This kind of reply – that one's thoughts are worth more or less than a penny – has occurred to others. In his *Polite Conversation* Jonathan Swift showed how a young lady could deal with an annoying man in the 18th century: '"Come, a penny for your thoughts." "It is not worth a farthing, for I was thinking of you."'

'A penny for your thoughts' has been in use since the 16th century. The familiarity of the phrase makes possible a shortened form. Monica Dickens writes, in *The Fancy*: '"A penny for 'em," said Edward, finding her staring into space.' The 'penny' in the expression, needless to say, has no special significance; the meaning is 'I would give something to know what you are thinking.'

It's the fullness of the breasts, the spending of pennies in the night, the being sick in the mornings you have to watch out for.

Fay Weldon *Down Among the Women*

In **spend a penny**, by contrast, the penny originally meant what it said. It was formerly necessary in many public lavatories in Britain to insert a penny coin into a slot to gain admission to a cubicle. From this a reference to 'spending a penny' became a euphemism for 'going to the lavatory'. 'Just spend the old penny,' says a man cheerfully, in Peter Draper's *A Season in Love*. *You All Spoken Here*, by Roy Wilder, Jr, says that the equivalent phrase in the southern states of America is **tease the cat**.

'Sorry to interrupt, Sar'nt, the penny's only just dropped.'

John Stroud *On the Loose*

The idea of putting a penny into a slot also gave rise to **the penny's dropped** 'something has now been understood'. A penny coin would sometimes get stuck in a slot machine, preventing its normal working. If some way could be found of making the penny drop into the mechanism, all was well. By analogy, something said to a person sometimes fails to register immediately. If, a little later, light dawns, then 'the penny drops'. Ruth Rendell writes, in *The Tree of Hands*: 'It was at this point, Barry always remembered, that the penny dropped. At this moment, for the first time, he understood that they thought he had murdered Jason.'

In the same Ruth Rendell novel occurs: 'He had no alternative now anyway, he'd gone too far. He had signed the contract and committed himself. In for a penny, in for a pound.' **In for a penny, in for a pound** is proverbial, and implies that once a project has been embarked upon, it must be completed regardless of the cost. The expression is often shortened to 'in for a penny'.

Other proverbs which mention 'penny' include **a bad penny always comes back** – referring literally to a counterfeit coin, metaphorically to a person whose company is not wanted; **a penny saved is a penny gained**; **turn an honest penny** – make an honest living; **penny wise, pound foolish** – said of a person who spends small amounts carefully but large amounts rashly.

'I don't care twopence about Brindlehough.'

Edward Hyams *Sylvester*

Something which is commonplace and of little value might still be described as **two a penny**, though Elizabeth Jane Howard, in *Getting it Right*, comments: 'Two a penny – no, nothing was that any more – two for one-fifty with special offers in the Sunday supplements . . .' In the phrase **not care twopence** 'twopence' is merely a small amount, suitable for indicating how small a value one places on something. 'I couldn't care tuppence how she is, the silly girl,' says someone in Margaret Drabble's *The Middle Ground*.

Many other English phrases, some no longer in current use, mention pennies or money in general. They are fully discussed in *The Guinness Book of Money*, by Leslie Dunkling and Adrian Room.

■ PICTURESQUE EXPRESSIONS

'A little chit you were, when we met last. Pretty as a picture, too.'

Edward Hyams *Sylvester*

To say that someone is **as pretty as a picture** is to compare the person concerned with the ideal representation of an artist. A similar thought lies behind the format phrase whereby we say that someone **looks the picture of** health, happiness, success, or whatever. Of a landscape, or language, we would say instead that it is **picturesque**.

His subsequent interview with the Chief Constable – 'Just to keep me in the picture, old boy' – was not a particularly happy one.

Joyce Porter *Dover One*

Evelyn Waugh, in *Unconditional Surrender*, has the following conversation: '"I put the General and the Commissar in the picture last night. You'll find them very ready to help." "Perhaps you'd put me in the picture." "It's a very pretty picture – an oil painting. Everything is moving our way at last."' Waugh takes the phrase **put someone in the picture** 'inform someone of the facts' to refer to a painting, but it is noticeable that the expression was not recorded in English until 1919, a few years after 'picture' had come to have its new meaning of a 'movie' or 'film'.

To **be in the picture** meant at first 'to be in evidence, to be seen, to be part of what was happening'. This also suggests that the metaphor was drawn from the world of the cinema rather than the art gallery. A natural development of sense allowed 'being in the picture' to mean 'be in possession of all the relevant facts'. A further development has given us **get the picture** 'understand the facts that one is being given'. Barry Oakley gives prominence to the latter phrase in *A Salute to the Great McCarthy*. The last four words of the novel are 'I get the picture.'

■ PIDGIN ENGLISH

'He's put the cat among the pigeons now, the Master has,' Arthur said breathlessly. 'He's got under their skin something terrible this time.'

Tom Sharpe *Porterhouse Blue*

The idea of **putting the cat among the pigeons** seems to appeal to English-speakers. The phrase is frequently used to refer to causing trouble amongst a group. C.P. Snow, in *The Affair*, indicates that the expression is for him a relatively new one: 'He said straight out that Getliffe's note had "put the cat among the pigeons".' Alexander Fullerton, in *Other Men's Wives*, sees no need to use quotation marks: 'You see how you put the cat among the pigeons over there at Metromark?'

'You've got to get me out of here.' Captain Fremantle had more than three years' experience of the army and, as the facts of Guy's predicament were frantically explained, the staff solution came pat: 'Not my pigeon. The Senior M O will have to discharge you.'

Evelyn Waugh *Unconditional Surrender*

'This is my pigeon, not yours,' says a character in Francis King's *The Needle*, meaning 'it's my business'. There is no hidden metaphor in the phrase to **be one's pigeon**. The 'pigeon', more often written 'pidgin', was earlier 'bidgin'. That represented a Chinese speaker's version of the word 'business'. 'Pidgin English' was in use by the middle of the 19th century, enabling Chinese and Europeans to trade at seaports. Later, 'Pidgin' was applied to any kind of simplified language used by those who were otherwise unable to communicate.

The original Chinese-English Pidgin was normally used for bartering, but its applications spread. It was considered to be rather quaint, and books like *Pidgin-English Sing-Song*, by Charles G. Leland, had considerable success. By 1918 this collection of songs, stories and proverbs in Pidgin had already gone through nine editions. Its version of 'Little Jack Horner' runs:

> *Littee Jack Horner*
> *Makee sit inside corner,*
> *Chow-chow he Clismas pie;*
> *He put inside t'um,*
> *Hab catchee one plum,*
> *'Hai yah! what one good chilo*
> *my!'*

It is foolish in modern times to assume that foreigners need to be spoken to in some kind of Pidgin English. There is a well-known story about a lady at an official dinner who sat next to a Chinese gentleman and spoke to him for some time in this way. After dinner, he was called upon to address those present. He stood and spoke for some time in faultless colloquial English, sitting down to generous applause. At that point he turned to his neighbour and asked politely: 'Likee speechee?'

■ PIE CHART

'The Master may dismiss our protests but we have powerful allies,' said the Dean.
'And in the meantime we must eat humble pie and ask the Master to reconsider his resignation.'

Tom Sharpe *Porterhouse Blue*

In **eating humble pie** 'being very apologetic' there is a deliberate pun on eating 'umble' pie. 'Umbles', earlier 'numbles', are certain inner parts of a deer which are suitable for eating. In the 17th century, eating umble pie was no doubt a gastronomic pleasure. It was only in the 19th century that the expression was altered to 'humble pie' and acquired its figurative meaning of being submissive and admitting to being wrong.

John Fowles, in *The French Lieutenant's Woman*, has: 'It is Papa's clause. He wants you to eat humble pie.' This is to do with a man who has broken off his engagement and is being forced to admit that he has behaved badly. In *The Group*, Mary McCarthy writes: 'It was the first time she had seen Harald eat humble pie, and it had given her the most dismal feeling, as if she were a sort of encumbrance.'

'We don't need pie in the sky proposals but practical ideas that will make the areas safer for all women.'

The Observer (8.3.1992)

Pie in the sky is something which sounds good and desirable but is not within practical reach and is unlikely ever to be obtained. The phrase featured in a World War One song which had the line: 'You'll get pie in the sky when you die.' **Easy as pie** 'very easy' is analagous to a 'piece of cake', both being easy to eat. The same thinking leads to the use of **sweetie pie** and **cutie pie** as terms of address. The French endearment *mon petit chou*, often translated as 'my little cabbage', refers in fact to the *chou* which is a light, sweet pastry. The expression is therefore roughly equivalent to 'sweetie pie'.

■ PIN-UPS

'For two pins I'd have you run in.'

Dane Chandos *Abbie*

For two pins means 'for very little'.
Pins have been symbols of slight
value or significance since the 15th
century, when phrases like **not worth
a pin** and **not care a pin** came into
use. *Brewer's Dictionary of Phrase and
Fable* therefore cannot be correct in
saying that **pin-money**, 'money
allowed to a wife by her husband for
her personal expenditure', was so
called because 'pins were once very
expensive'. 'Pin-money' was based on
an archaic French expression *épingles
d'une femme* 'a woman's pins', where
'pins' stood for hair-pins and other
toilet accessories.

'For two pins' was first used in the
19th century and is a fanciful
elaboration of the earlier phrases. It is
still well used. 'A damned funny
business and no mistake. I'd tell you
for two pins' says a character in W.
Somerset Maugham's short story
Flotsam and Jetsam. 'For two pins I'd
come out and tell him a thing or two
about his only child!' is in Edna
O'Brien's *Girl with Green Eyes*.

---

*You could have heard a pin drop, as
the girls agreed later.*

Mary McCarthy *The Group*

In another Edna O'Brien novel, *The
Country Girls*, the author writes:
'Nothing happened. You could **hear a
pin drop**.' The allusion is obvious in
this phrase from the 19th century,
which occurred also at that time as
hear a pin fall. Richard Bissell, in *The
Pajama Game*, uses his own version of
the expression: 'Hasler sat there and
you could hear a paper clip drop.'

■ PITTER-PATTER

*'Perhaps they're afraid the patter of
tiny feet may distract the highly-paid
minds.'*

Alistair Maclean *The Dark Crusader*

'Are we going to hear **the patter of
tiny feet?**' has become a standard
euphemism for 'Are you expecting a
baby?' It is a curious expression. By
the time children are old enough to
run about their footsteps rarely sound
like the light patter of rain on a
window. Berta Ruck makes the point
in *Ancestral Voices*: 'Stamping
overhead. The patter of little feet
(phrase that must I think have been
dreamed up by some corny old
bachelor) could have threatened to
bring a shimmering quivering tinkling
chandelier down with a crash.'

The feet are invariably 'tiny' these
days, but Miss Ruck appears to be
correctly quoting an earlier version.
The Oxford English Dictionary cites:
'**The patter of little feet**, and the
unconscious joyousness of children.'
The line comes from *My
Reminiscences* (1883), by Lord Ronald
Sutherland-Gower. The Dictionary
makes no comment on his marital
status, or whether the phrase he used
was his own invention. He clearly
used it in all seriousness, though it is
now usually a joke. It is also well-
enough known to have been
converted into a format phrase. '**The
patter of tiny criticism**' is attributed to
Christopher Fry.

---

*'What idiot poet invented the phrase
"the innocent laughter of children"?
Watch children at a puppet show,
laughing to see the puppet being hit
over the head. Their innocent laughter
is, more than anything else, nervous*

laughter. Children need a victim because they are small and vulnerable. Once there is a victim, he is the sacrifice that keeps the others safe.'

Rona Jaffe *The Cherry in the Martini*

The sound that is described as a patter is based on 'pat', an onomatopoeic word meant to imitate the actual noise. **Pit-a-pat** and **pitter-patter** are from the same source. The rapid patter of the salesman as he tries to tell you something has a more interesting origin. The Lord's Prayer in its Latin version is known as the paternoster, from its opening words *Pater noster* 'our Father'. 'Patter' derives from *pater* and originally described the rapid repetition of the paternoster. When he launches into his sales pitch the salesman, in a way, is saying his prayers.

■ PLAYING CARDS

'I'll put my cards on the table, Barry. We're not trying to trick you. Honesty is the best policy, don't you think?'

Ruth Rendell *The Tree of Hands*

Card games of one kind and another have been popular in England since the 14th century and have given rise to various metaphorical phrases. To **put** or **lay one's cards on the table**, for instance, is an obvious reference to revealing the truth, being honest. In *My Side of the Matter*, Truman Capote makes the interesting remark: 'Bus people are a close-mouthed buncha dopes. But a train's the place for putting your cards on the table.'

There is a similar allusion in **above-board**. The person in *Tropic of Ruislip*, by Leslie Thomas, who asks: 'Everything proper and above-board?' wants to be sure that no one is gaining an unfair advantage by metaphorically exchanging cards beneath the table.

To **have something up one's sleeve** was originally to **have a card** (or **trick**) **up one's sleeve**, where 'trick' was used in its special card-playing sense. It was clearly another way of cheating, but seems to have lost its pejorative sense. The allusion appears to have been transferred to a conjuror who conceals things in order to 'cheat' his audience harmlessly, merely in order to surprise them. Metaphorically, to 'keep something up your sleeve' now means to have information that one keeps secret until the right moment.

Even someone who is playing a game of cards fairly has the right to **hold his cards close to his chest**. This is merely being cautiously discreet, especially during some kind of business negotiation. One is not **showing** or **revealing one's hand** to an opponent. 'I'll make you show your hand – you see if I don't!' says a character in Arnold Bennett's *Clayhanger*. The speaker in this instance means that he will make a young lady reveal her true feelings.

"E ain't got it to give. But shall I tell yer someone who 'as? If you and me play our cards right?'

John Fowles *The French Lieutenant's Woman*

To **play one's cards right** is to take the necessary actions at the right time and thereby achieve success. This is not so easy if fate or the gods have been unkind to begin with and the **cards are stacked against someone**. Upton Sinclair has a character in *World's End* make the philosophical comment: 'The cards are all stacked against a woman.'

In American slang to **deal someone a poor deck** means to treat someone cruelly or unjustly. In Britain it has been usual to refer to a 'pack' of cards rather than a 'deck' since the late 17th century, but what is dealt is normally a 'hand.' Another American slang expression refers to **dealing (playing/operating) with a full deck**. The negative form is more common, alluding either to someone who is not very intelligent or to someone who is not completely honest.

A car was definitely on the cards.

Frederic Raphael *The Limits of Love*

Something which is said to be **on the cards** in Britain is usually **in the cards** in America. The meaning is the same in both cases: something is likely to occur or be obtained. The form 'in the cards' has caused some to suggest that fortune-telling rather than a card game gave rise to the expression. This remains a distinct possibility. A book about cartomancy was published in Italy by the 16th century; by the 18th century it was as popular in most European countries as astrology is today.

'There are plenty of instances, in the experience of every one, of short courtships and speedy marriages which have turned up trumps – I beg your pardon – which have turned out well.'

William Wilkie Collins *No Name*

To **turn up trumps** is to do better than expected. The powerful 'trump' card was earlier the 'triumph', allowing Shakespeare to pun on both meanings of the word in *Antony and Cleopatra*. Antony tells his attendant that Cleopatra has 'pack'd cards with Caesar, and false-play'd my glory / Unto an enemy's triumph'. We might still say of someone that he **plays his trump card** when he puts forward his most powerful argument during a discussion, especially if it is one that

his opponents are unable to answer. They will be left to **throw in their cards** and admit defeat.

■ POKING ABOUT

What is the veil but a relic of marriage by barter, when the man bought a pig in a poke and never knew his luck till he unveiled his bride?

William J. Locke *Jaffery*

To buy **a pig in a poke** is to buy something without inspecting it first. This particular example of such unwise behaviour has been commented on since the 17th century. Piglets were then sold at markets in 'pokes', or 'bags.' 'Poke' is no longer used in this sense, except perhaps in dialect. The word is connected with 'pouch' and French *poche* 'pocket', originally 'little bag'. 'Pig in a poke', in fact, in an old-fashioned French phrase, becomes *acheter chat en poche* 'buy a cat in a bag'. This makes the point about the foolishness of not inspecting one's goods before buying them. It seems at one time to have been a regular practice of unscrupulous traders to substitute a cat for the piglet.

'You could have told me,' Leopold said angrily.
'Yes, and I was afraid that if I did, my dear cousin, you might let the cat out of the bag. You are so impetuous.'

Christopher Short *The Saint and the Hapsburg Necklace*

It is this same cat which is referred to in **let the cat out of the bag**. That would originally have been the sensible thing to do – reveal what someone was trying to keep secret for unlawful reasons. By contrast, a modern person who 'lets the cat out of the bag' can expect no thanks. The phrase has now come to refer to the revelation of a secret by someone who is unable to be discreet. 'Kay, who had always been a blurter, had let the cat out of the bag' writes Mary McCarthy, in *The Group*.

Joyce Porter, in *Dover One*, reveals a fondness for this phrase. 'She was quite capable of letting the cat out of the bag to Maxine,' says one character. 'I reckon that's let the cat out of the bag, all right!' says another. On the second occasion a cynical policeman comments: 'If it was ever in.'

It's in the bag is not used of cats, but of anything which is as good as certain. 'That meant the majority was in the bag,' says a man who is anticipating the result of an election, in C.P. Snow's *The Affair*. The expression usually refers to something abstract in that way, such as the outcome of a process. More rarely it is used of a person, as when Henry Cecil writes, in *Brothers in Law*: 'He's in the bag, they say.' 'They' are the police, talking about someone against whom they think they have overwhelming evidence. The solicitor who is speaking thinks the man concerned isn't 'in the bag' at all.

The 'bag' in this expression is no doubt the sportsman's game-bag. The hunter theoretically puts into this everything he has 'bagged', even if it is a large animal. Figuratively speaking, 'in the bag' really means 'as good as in the bag', almost a **foregone conclusion**.

'It's a foregone conclusion surely.'

Winifred Holtby *South Riding*

'Foregone conclusion' is interesting because it is an unrecognized Shakespearean quotation that is always wrongly applied. In *Othello*

Iago tells the Moor that he has heard Cassio talking in his sleep about Desdemona. What Iago says appears to be clear evidence that Desdemona has been unfaithful to her husband. Othello interprets it in that way, whereupon Iago pretends to introduce a note of caution: 'Nay, this was but his dream'. 'But this', replies Othello, 'denoted a foregone conclusion.' Cassio, in other words, was talking about something that had already happened.

It seems to have been Charles Lamb, in 'New Year's Eve' (*Essays of Elia*), who first applied 'foregone conclusion' to something that was sure to happen in the future, as if 'foregone' meant 'predestined'. Perhaps, then, we are no longer quoting Shakespeare when we use this phrase to mean 'something sure to happen', we are simply consolidating a rare mistake of Charles Lamb.

■ POLES APART

'I gave him a chance when none of his so-called friends would touch him with a barge-pole.'

Mordecai Richler *Joshua Then and Now*

British and American speakers of English tend to indicate their extreme reluctance to have anything to do with someone or something in slightly different ways. **Wouldn't touch (something/someone) with a bargepole** is usual in Britain. Most Americans would use **wouldn't touch (something/ someone) with a ten-foot pole**. Canadian writers seem to use either or both. Margaret Laurence, for example, in *The Diviners*, has someone say of a snake, 'I wouldn't touch that creature with a ten-foot pole.' A dozen or so pages later another person is made to say of a man, 'I wouldn't touch him with a barge pole.'

The basic idea of keeping one's distance obviously remains the same in either case. Perhaps the sense would be conveyed slightly better, however, if the word 'even' was included: I wouldn't touch it, even with a bargepole/ten-foot pole.

'I haven't seen her since November. She's got this ten-foot pole she'd like to keep me away with.'
Judith Guest *Ordinary People*

Writers sometimes use more idiosyncratic forms of the idiom. Ruth Rendell in *Talking to Strange Men* has: 'He wouldn't touch Martin Hillman now with a two-metre-long pole.' The significance of the very exact 'two metres' is not commented on. John Fowles, in *The French Lieutenant's Woman*, jokes with the phrase. After a servant has referred to a bargepole, his master says: 'Yesterday you were not prepared to touch the young lady with a bargee's tool of trade.'

In *Howards End* E.M. Forster writes: 'I wonder what you'll think of the place. I **wouldn't touch it with tongs** myself.' This was the normal form of the saying from the 14th century onwards. Chaucer makes use of it, for instance, in his 'Parson's Tale'. 'Poles' of one kind or another only began to be mentioned at the end of the 19th century, before tongs had ceased to be familiar household implements. The 'pole' versions of the saying clearly conjure up a stronger image and have replaced the earlier expression.

■ POT BOILERS

'I hear you are in a kettle of fish,' he said, raising his voice somewhat above the din.

'Might call it so,' I said cautiously, sipping my tea. I never overdo my troubles to Dave, for he is so often sarcastic and unsympathetic about them.
Iris Murdoch *Under the Net*

By 'kettle' most people now mean a container with a spout, lid and handle, used to boil water for making tea. In the 18th century the word could also be used of a cauldron, or open pot, while in Scotland it came to have the special meaning of 'picnic'. The reference was to 'giving a kettle of fish', a popular way of providing an outdoor entertainment amongst those who lived near the River Tweed. Freshly caught salmon were thrown into a kettle or pot of boiling water to provide the food for the occasion.

English observers of these occasions were evidently struck by the disorderliness of the scene, with people and utensils scattered about on a river bank. In the 18th century, novelists such as Samuel Richardson and Henry Fielding make ironic references to a 'fine' or 'pretty kettle of fish', meaning a great muddle or mess, a confused state of affairs. This meaning of **kettle of fish** survives, but in modern times the 'confused' element is often forgotten, especially in a **different kettle of fish**. This simply means 'a different person or thing from the one previously mentioned'.

The earlier meaning of 'muddle' is present in Arnold Bennett's *Clayhanger*: 'We shall be having you ill next, and then there'll be a nice kettle of fish.' Henry Cecil, in *Brothers in Law*, makes a character say: 'It's a fine kettle of fish. Taking machinery from under their very noses.' 'Different kettle of fish' is applied to an abstract situation by John Stroud in *On the Loose*: 'This was a different kettle of fish – they knew they couldn't do much about Tod.' Similar usage occurs in Stan Barstow's *A Kind of Loving*: 'Ah,' says Henry, 'but that's a different kettle of fish. That's a different thing altogether.'

The same author, later in the novel, applies the phrase to a person: 'Right behind Hassop there's Mr Althorpe and he's a different kettle of fish altogether.' John Steinbeck, in *East of Eden*, goes a step further, varying the expression to say: 'Liza Hamilton was a very different kettle of Irish.'

'Well, if it isn't the old pots calling the kettle black,' says I.

Truman Capote *My Side of the Matter*

The pot calls the kettle black has been a proverb since the 17th century and still serves a useful purpose. It refers to an accuser having the same fault as the accused. A German proverb uses the same metaphor as the English: *Der Kessel schilt den Ofentopf* 'the kettle scolds the saucepan', though Germans can also say *Ein Esel schimpft den anderen Langohr* 'a donkey reviles the other jackass'.

■ PUNCH LINES

Sergeant Hunter was as pleased as Punch because he got the prize money.

David Walker *Geordie*

The puppet show which later became known as Punch and Judy was first seen in England in the 17th century, having been imported from Italy. Samuel Pepys was a great enthusiast, saying in his diary that it 'pleases me mightily'. **As pleased as Punch**, referring to Punch himself, is recorded from the beginning of the 19th century. 'How does Doria take it?'

asks a character in William J. Locke's *Jaffery*. 'She's as pleased as Punch' is the reply. Later in the same novel occurs: 'You're **as proud as Punch** of your fame and success and all that it means to you.' This comments on the other main characteristic attributed to the puppet.

Punch was earlier Punchinello, or Polichinello in Neapolitan form. Early Italian philologists explained this as a corruption of Puccio d'Aniello, the name of a peasant whose unusual face inspired the puppet-maker. Others claimed it was the name of Paulo Cinella, 'a buffoon at Naples'. Later scholars pointed out that in the Neapolitan dialect *pollecenella* referred to a young turkey-cock, and that the hooked bill of this bird resembled Punch's nose.

'And now comes the punch line.'

Penelope Gilliatt *A State of Change*

Other 'punch' expressions in English refer to the blow with a fist. **Not to pull one's punches,** for instance, is to say what one thinks without bothering to be diplomatic. Something that **packs a punch**, such as an alcoholic drink, has a powerful effect. The **punch-line** of a joke provides its climax, surprising the audience like an unexpected blow.

■ PUNISHING RUNS

When such a gauntlet was thus thrown in his very teeth by Dr Fillgrave, he was not slow to take it up.

Anthony Trollope *Doctor Thorne*

Gauntlets 'gloves covered with steel plates' were part of the armour of a medieval knight. 'Gauntlet' here is a diminutive of French *gant* 'glove'. A knight would issue a challenge by throwing his gauntlet not, as Trollope suggests in the above quotation, in the teeth of his opponent but on the ground in front of him. Sometimes a general challenge was issued by **throwing down the gauntlet**. Whoever **picked it up** was accepting the challenge.

This knightly behaviour has greatly appealed to the popular imagination since medieval times. It is still frequently alluded to metaphorically when any kind of challenge is made.

Others said he deserved to run the gantlope.

Henry Fielding *Tom Jones*

Running the gauntlet was a military punishment of the 17th century, whereby an offender was stripped to the waist and forced to run between two lines of men who struck at him with sticks and knotted ropes. The 'gauntlet' in this instance is an error for 'gantlope', literally a 'gate-run'. 'Gate' here has its sense of 'way, lane' as it still does in many street names in the north of England. 'Gantlope' became corrupted into a more familiar word, but at no time were gauntlets used to strike the man who was being punished. Nor was a 'gantlope' a 'Ghent-run' because the punishment was first used at Ghent, though this was the interpretation of one early writer.

'You'll have to run the gauntlet of publicity.'

Alice Dwyer-Joyce *The Penny Box*

To 'run the gauntlet' is sometimes used in modern times of a physically dangerous activity, as when a character in Mary Stewart's *This Rough Magic* says: 'If one runs the gauntlet of those coasts often enough, it's not surprising if one gets hurt.'

More often the allusion is to being exposed mentally to criticism or anger. 'You had to run a gauntlet of Communists before getting in to see the book editor' says Mary McCarthy, in *The Group*.

■ QUEER FISH

'I should worry about dolls givin' me the air. There's always another one. Who was it said there's as good fish in the sea as those that came out of it?'

Peter Cheyney *You Can Call It a Day*

The consolation that English-speakers normally offer one another when a romantic relationship comes to an end is **There are more fish in the sea** 'there are other people equally pleasant that you have yet to meet'. 'I haven't seen him for ages,' says a woman in *Nurse is a Neighbour*, by Joanna Jones. 'Never mind,' she is told. 'There are lots more fish in the sea.' A similar comment occurs in Peter Draper's *A Season in Love*: 'Never mind, old boy. Plenty more fish in the sea.' Mary McCarthy, in *The Group*, has: 'Forget about Harald. There're other fish in the sea.'

Some speakers would use a different metaphor in these circumstances. 'Never mind. He's **not the only pebble on the beach**' is in James Mitchell's *When the Boat Comes in*. However, the doctor who says to a patient in *Sylvester*, by Edward Hyams: 'I must go. You're not the only pebble on the beach' means only that he has other patients to see.

'You are an odd fish, Stephen. Odd as odd.'

Warwick Deeping *Sorrell and Son*

'Fish' was first applied to a person in

the 18th century. At first the reference was to the kind of person someone tried to 'hook' or 'catch', perhaps in order to swindle him. It was then used as an unflattering term for anyone, especially in conjunction with adjectives like 'odd' and 'queer'. In Edna O'Brien's *The Country Girls* Mr Gentleman is described as an 'odd fish' by the girls. An 'odd fish' is not the same as **Odds fish**!, the curious oath that was occasionally used in former times. 'Odds' was a euphemism for 'God's', while 'fish' perhaps replaced 'flesh'.

'He seems such a queer fish for you to have gone for in that way.'
'Not so queer as all that.'

Kingsley Amis *Lucky Jim*

Queer fish is the same as 'odd fish'. William J. Locke suddenly decides to make much of the phrase in *Jaffery*, saying of his hero: 'Jaffery was always a queer fish where women were concerned. Not a chilly, fishy fish, but a sort of Laodicean fish, now hot, now cold.' In the same novel another fish idiom occurs. The author says: 'My wife and I attended, fishes somewhat out of water amid this brilliant but solid assembly of what it pleased Barbara to call "merchandates".' H.G. Wells in *Kipps*, has his hero use the same expression when he comes into a fortune: 'I'm a regular **fish out of water** with this money.' The allusion to someone who is 'out of his element' is a straightforward one.

Libby usually played up to this, but today she had other fish to fry.

Mary McCarthy *The Group*

To **have other fish to fry** 'have other matters to attend to' is still in modern use, as is the statement that a heavy drinker **drinks like a fish**. The latter phrase is found in the 16th century and was no doubt suggested by the way some fish swim with their mouths open, as if they were constantly drinking. **Neither fish, flesh nor fowl** is a now out-dated phrase meaning 'neither one thing nor the other'. It was also found as **neither fish, flesh nor good red herring**.

Christopher Dilke, in *Freddie and Son*, creates an interesting German-born character of whom he says: 'His English was fluent but inaccurate, being prone to mix idioms such as 'a fish in hot water'.

■ QUESTION TIME

He was going to take her to dinner, and that was where, she expected, if all went well, he was going to pop the question.

Mary McCarthy *The Group*

In theory, any question could be 'popped'. The 'popping' refers to the suddenness with which the question is put, it pops up suddenly and unexpectedly in the middle of a conversation. Conventionally, a young woman was always taken by surprise when a man asked her to marry him, hence the association of popping with that particular, all-important question: 'Will you marry me?'

At one time the familiarity of 'pop the question' allowed a speaker to use 'popping' as a synonym of 'proposing'. An example occurs in Trollope's *Doctor Thorne*, '"Have you spoken to my niece about this, Sir Louis?" "I haven't exactly popped to her yet, but I have been doing the civil."'

A man who assumed that a woman was going to marry him without actually having asked her would be **begging the question**. To 'beg' is to 'ask' in a sense, though in phrases like **I beg your pardon** it is taken for granted that what is asked for will be granted. A similar leap is made in 'beg the question', where assumptions are made unjustifiably. What is assumed may in fact be **out of the question** 'impossible' or merely a **question of time** 'something certain to happen sooner or later'.

Bond decided it was time to put the sixty-four thousand dollar question. 'And where do I come in, Sir?' he asked.

Ian Fleming *Diamonds are Forever*

A **vexed question** is a particularly difficult and troublesome problem that causes much discussion. Answering it will not necessarily bring rewards, as did the original **sixty-four dollar question**. In general terms this is usually the most important, and most difficult, question that has to be answered. The phrase derives from an American television show where a sixty-four dollar question was asked, bringing that amount of prize-money, if answered correctly. 'Now for the sixty-four-dollar question' says someone in Mordecai Richler's *Joshua Then and Now*. In a later series **sixty-four thousand dollars** was the top prize if the contestant answered the final question. The phrase is therefore often found in that form.

An 18th-century proverb says **Ask no questions and you will be told no lies**. It is still sometimes quoted if someone wishes to avoid answering a question. Monica Dickens has a character allude to it in *The Fancy*: '"Ask me no questions, Miss," said Mrs Geek cagily. "I tell no lies."' Ruth Rendell, in *The Tree of Hands*, has: 'If you didn't ask questions, you wouldn't get lies. What's it to you anyway where I

go?' An alternative way of dodging a question by referring to a different proverb is demonstrated in *Joshua Then and Now*, by Mordecai Richler: '"You know what killed the cat?" "Curiosity." "Right."'

■ RABBITING ON

'I could fancy a Welsh rabbit for supper.'
'So could I – with a roast onion.'

Charlotte Brontë *Jane Eyre*

A **Welsh rabbit** is neither Welsh nor a rabbit. The phrase is recorded in the early 18th century, when Englishmen commonly made fun of most other nationalities, including the Welsh. It was not for nothing that the cuckoo was known as the 'Welsh ambassador', though the polite explanation for this was that the bird's appearance each year was followed soon afterwards by Welshmen in search of summer employment.

Indicative of the general attitude to Welshmen were phrases like a **Welsh comb**, meaning the thumb and four fingers; **Welsh diamond**, a name for rock crystal; **Welsh bait**, where 'bait' means food, especially food for animals. 'Welsh bait' given to a horse meant that it was allowed to rest when it reached the top of a hill, but was given no fodder at all. The similar rest without food taken by pedlars was known as a **Scotch bait**.

'Welsh rabbit' was a joke name for what was considered to be a substitute for a real meal, with meat. The word 'rabbit' had no particular significance, it could as well have been lamb, beef or pork. Nor perhaps was 'Welsh' of special significance. At least one 18th-century writer refers to the same dish as **Scotch rabbit**. The simple point being made was that the so-called meat was not meat at all. A similar joke leads to the phrase **shank's pony** or **mare**, a reference to one's two feet rather than an animal.

I am always particularly fond of a tankard of stout and a Welsh rarebit.

H.G. Wells *The Man Who Could Work Miracles*

Already in the 18th century a genteel form of 'Welsh rabbit' had emerged, turning it into **Welsh rarebit**. **Welsh rearbit** was also suggested, on the grounds that the dish was eaten at the end of a meal. Needless to say, there is not a shred of evidence that this was actually the case. As for 'rarebit', no trace of such a word has been found which pre-dates the appearance of 'Welsh rabbit'. Nor does the word occur elsewhere. 'Rarebit' only exists in the context of the spurious 'Welsh rarebit', where 'rabbit' is undoubtedly both the original and correct form.

■ READING SKILLS

'Has he complained?' 'Good heavens, no, of course he hasn't. But I can read between the lines of his letters.'

R.F. Delderfield *Theirs Was the Kingdom*

Many people believe themselves to be discerning enough to **read someone like a book** 'arrive at a clear understanding of a person's character'. They also think that, when necessary, they can **read between the lines** 'discover a meaning that is implicit rather than overtly stated'. 'He paid me a very nice compliment,' says the hero of Joseph Heller's *Good as Gold*. 'Sure, that's what he wrote,' says his father, who is never one to miss a put-down, 'but I could read between the lines.' The expression

came into use at the end of the 19th century and was perhaps suggested by the use of invisible ink, the existence of which had already been known for at least 200 years.

'Reading between the lines' is normally applied, for obvious reasons, to written words. In his novel *Self*, Beverley Nichols shows that it can refer to speech: 'It is perfectly clear from what you have told us – not directly, I admit – but I flatter myself that I have been able to read between the lines.'

'Hope it doesn't take Sam too long to read the riot act.'

Nina Bawden *George Beneath a Paper Moon*

The reading of the Riot Act can have serious consequences in real life. This British Act of 1715 provides that 'if twelve or more persons unlawfully or riotously assemble and refuse to disperse within an hour after the reading of a specified portion of it by a competent authority they shall be considered as felons'.

Modern parents (especially fathers, it would seem) and teachers are obliged figuratively to **read the Riot Act** on numerous occasions, when children's behaviour gets out of hand. That is how they themselves describe reprimanding young wrong-doers. 'My husband's read the Riot Act several times now,' says a woman in Elizabeth Jane Howard's *Getting it Right*. Children themselves would probably define the phrase as 'ranting and raving for a while, issuing threats and ultimatums and making a lot of fuss'.

■ RECONSIDER

All things considered is a fine-sounding phrase, at its most effective when uttered slowly and thoughtfully. It can then give the impression that the speaker really has taken every possibility into account before coming to a decision. Eric Partridge, who mentions that G.K. Chesterton used the phrase as the title of a volume of essays, is less impressed with it, dismissing it as a cliché.

'The best thing,' he agreed. 'All things considered.'
No one has the capacity to consider all things, even if he wished to. From all those things that force themselves on our attention, we select what we can bear to consider.

Shirley Hazzard *The Evening of the Holiday*

The origin of the word 'consider' makes it clear that it was originally the stars which were given close attention. Latin *sidus* could refer to a star, constellation, celestial sign or planet. It gave us our word 'sidereal', as in **sidereal time**, which is measured by the daily movement of the stars. *Considerare* to the Romans meant to examine the stars for omens and portents, or perhaps for purposes of navigation at sea. They also had the word *deconsiderare*, which gave us 'desire'. This seems originally to have meant something like 'notice the absence of', then 'regret the absence of'. That in turn led to the notion of wanting something that was not there, desiring it.

■ REMEDYING MATTERS

She pushed one of the glasses of gin to Mary, who smiled, trying to make a joke of it. 'Good for coughs, is it?' she asked. 'Sovereign remedy,' said Bella.

James Mitchell *When the Boat Comes in*

A **sovereign remedy** uses 'sovereign' in its sense of 'most excellent, supreme'. Such remedies, salves, medicines and herbs have been referred to in literature since the 14th century.

In *The Pickwick Papers* Dickens has Mr Weller Senior announce that he has found a sovereign cure for the gout. Mr Pickwick becomes very excited: 'A sovereign cure for the gout,' said Mr Pickwick, hastily producing his note-book – 'what is it?' 'The gout, sir,' replied Mr Weller, 'the gout is a complaint as arises from too much ease and comfort. If ever you're attacked with the gout, sir, jist you marry a widder as has got a good loud woice, with a decent notion of usin' it, and you'll never have the gout agin.'

■ RIVER TRIPS

'Pacifism. Or to put a true label on it, selling your country down the river.'

Mordecai Richler *The Incomparable Atuk*

In former times a slave in America who was 'sold down the river' was sold to a plantation of the lower Mississippi, where conditions were notoriously harsh. It also meant being separated from one's family, perhaps for ever. To **sell someone down the river**, then, once had a literal meaning that one does not like to contemplate.

The phrase is now used of betrayal, usually for one's own advantage, of a person or organization. 'Who got sold down the river – you or me?' asks someone in Erica Jong's *Fear of Flying*. A baseball player in Bernard Malamud's *The Natural* is asked: 'Ain't you ashamed that you are selling a club down the river?' Bernard Wolfe, in *The Late-Risers*, has: 'Maybe he ought to sell the Lovis information to Blakely? Nah, didn't make sense to sell Lovis down the river for a punk 50.' Typically, these are American writers, but the British writer Alexander Fullerton, in *Other Men's Wives*, refers to 'selling the other chap down the river all he could'.

'How, dear, in your mother's land does one send somebody up the river having sold him down it?'

Dane Chandos *Abbie*

In the above quotation the question is posed by a British aunt to her American nephew. She is referring to the American slang term **send someone up the river** 'send someone to prison'. The river in this case was the Hudson. Prisoners were formerly sent from New York City up the river to Sing Sing Prison at Ossining.

■ ROLL OUT THE BARREL

'You'll end up paying the increase anyway. They've got you over a barrel.'

Richard Bissell *The Pajama Game*

To **have someone over a barrel** is to have him at your mercy, in a position where he cannot prevent you doing what you like. Barry Hines uses the phrase in a sporting context in *The Blinder*: 'Twenty minutes left and we had them over a barrel.' He means 'we were completely dominating the game and could do what we liked'. Bernard Wolfe, in *The Late-Risers*, has: 'He hadn't reported it in his tax returns, and there was a law about that too. Any way you looked at it, he was over the barrel.'

The phrase appears to be relatively modern, and no one is certain of its origin. The 'barrel' is presumably the container for liquid, properly a cask holding 36 gallons (164 l), though the word tends to be used by laymen for a cask of any size. One suggestion is that a person recovered from the sea was laid over a barrel which was then gently rolled back and forth until the water was expelled from the lungs. This supposes that barrels were regularly kept on beaches or by pools where swimmers were likely to get into difficulties. It is also difficult to see why a meaning related to the domination of one person by another would evolve from a situation where someone was engaged in life-saving.

In his *Dictionary of American Slang* Robert L. Chapman suggests that the person 'over the barrel' was about to be flogged. This seems much more logical: against it is the fact that the expression does not appear to have been in use at a time when floggings were relatively common.

'I insisted that the whole thing, lock, stock and barrel, should be by Leonard Benton Curry.'

J.I.M. Stewart *The Last Tresilians*

The phrase **lock, stock and barrel** 'completely' reminds us that a 'barrel' is part of a gun, as (in that phrase) are the 'lock' and 'stock'. 'Over the barrel' does not at any time seem to have been used to mean 'in one's sights' and therefore at one's mercy.

'Well, well. Cash on the barrelhead.'

Steven Bauer *The River*

To pay **cash on the barrel** or **on the barrelhead** is an Americanism for pay **cash on the nail** 'make an immediate cash payment for goods'. Barrels at one time would have been seen in many shops where perishable goods were sold. They were the best containers for items such as butter in days before refrigeration. The barrelhead would have been replaced as soon as a customer was served, whereupon payment was made.

'Cash on the nail' is a much older expression, and is far more difficult to explain. Professor Weekley favoured the idea that it was related to drinking 'on the nail'. This meant draining a glass completely so that only a solitary drop would cover the finger-nail when the glass was inverted. The French phrase *faire rubis sur l'ongle* 'make a ruby on the finger-nail' referred to this custom. Significantly, it led to another French phrase *payer rubis sur l'ongle* 'pay ruby on the finger-nail'. This is still in use and means to 'pay the complete amount'.

■ ROPED IN

'He's got to know all the ropes, you see; he'd be Warden if I didn't crack down on him.'

John Stroud *On the Loose*

The rigging of sailing ships in the early 19th century led to the expression **know the ropes** and the associated **show someone the ropes**. A newcomer in any organization needs to be 'shown the ropes' metaphorically: a young seaman in former times literally had to be shown them and have their functions explained. The seaman who 'knew the ropes' was fully experienced, an old hand. 'I would make a good teacher, perhaps, a man who knew all the ropes and understood why each thing must be done,' says the hero of William Golding's *Free Fall*. In

Ancestral Voices Berta Ruck writes: 'He was able to take with him this lovely wife, Eastern blood in her veins, who, in the bluff English idiom "knew the ropes".'

'I'm at the end of my tether. I shall go mad if this goes on. I'm afraid to go to sleep.'

W. Somerset Maugham *Lord Mountdrago*

To be **at the end of one's tether** is another 'rope' metaphor, this time referring to the rope which secures a grazing animal. Arthur Miller, in *All My Sons*, uses 'rope' itself when Sue says: 'I'm at the end of my rope on it!' The phrase is used of a person's mental state – he or she can 'go no further', nothing that has been tried has succeeded and all patience is exhausted. The person concerned will either erupt into anger or give up in despair.

What could my father do? He was almost at his wits' end . . .

Laurence Sterne *Tristram Shandy*

To be **at one's wits' end** is a phrase of similar meaning, though English people seem to treat the latter as something of a joke. 'Wits' End' is a common English house-name, meant to amuse the passers-by. Washington Irving, in *Rip Van Winkle*, has: 'The man in the cocked hat demanded who he was, and what was his name? "God knows," exclaimed he, at his wits' end.'

The idea of tethering an animal was again originally present in **giving someone rope** 'allowing someone to do what he wants to do'. The strong association of 'the rope' with the hangman's noose, however, caused this expression to be extended to the proverbial **give someone enough rope and he'll hang himself**. The meaning is that freedom of action will make a person over-confident so that he brings about his own downfall.

'Fourteen quid, eh?'
'Money for old rope, son,' he said.

Ian Jefferies *Thirteen Days*

Money for old rope is money earned by doing very easy work. The person who benefits is getting money in exchange for 'nothing', as represented by the 'old rope'. **Money for jam** is now used with a similar meaning, though the original reference was to what would theoretically be bought with the money. It was not **bread and butter** income and could be spent on a luxury item.

In British slang, something that is **ropy** (or **ropey**) is of poor quality. **Ropeable**, in Australia and New Zealand, is used of someone who is going berserk with anger. He should be 'roped up' for his own and others' safety.

She and Iris talked about childminding arrangements for the coming week. Maybe Maureen could be roped in for one day.

Ruth Rendell *The Tree of Hands*

To be **roped in to something** is to be caught with a lasso, as it were, and made to do something one would not necessarily have chosen to do. Volunteers often need to be 'roped in' to projects by persuasive leaders.

The phrase 'being roped in to do something' is so common that it probably fails to conjure up in the minds of those who use it an image of cowboys and lariats. A **frozen rope**, the term used in baseball for a line drive, or straight drive as British

speakers would say, retains its vividness. The ball travels at great speed just above the ground in what appears to be a straight line. It is known by the equally suggestive phrase, a **blue darter**.

■ RUBBING IT IN

They considered themselves the salt of the earth, or of that part of the earth. And I have an idea that they were.

Arnold Bennett *Clayhanger*

The salt of the earth 'people of excellent qualities' is another phrase that was made known by the Sermon on the Mount (see 'hide one's light under a bushel', page 115). Matthew 5.13 records that Jesus told his disciples 'You are the salt of the earth,' though he continued: 'but if salt has lost its taste, how shall its saltness be restored? It is no longer good for anything except to be thrown out and trodden under foot by men.' Modern use of the phrase is shown in Josephine Tey's *The Franchise Affair*: '"When the thought of that girl becomes too much for me, I think of Stanley." "Yes, the salt of the earth."'

The importance of salt in ancient times is shown by the word **salary**, derived from Latin *salarium* 'pertaining to salt' (ultimately from *sal, salis* 'salt') and referring to the sum of money given to a Roman soldier to buy that product. From the same Latin word came 'saler', which survives in corrupt form as salt-*cellar*. Many other words, such as *salami, salad, sauce* and *sausage* contain hidden references to salt if one traces their history back to their roots.

'No English girl worth her salt would consent to be saddled with such a groom.'

Dane Chandos *Abbie*

To **be worth one's salt** is to do one's job efficiently and be worth one's salary. We would expect the phrase to be linked to Roman soldiers and their salaries, but 'worth one's salt' appears only in the 19th century. It may well have been a deliberate introduction by a classicist, though Professor Weekley, in his *Etymological Dictionary of Modern English*, thought that it had a nautical origin. E.M. Forster, in *Howards End*, has: 'If Monet's really Debussy, and Debussy's really Monet, neither gentleman is worth his salt – that's my opinion.'

'You did rub it in a good deal how difficult it was for you to get away.'

E.F. Benson *Trouble for Lucia*

We talk about **rubbing salt into someone's wounds** 'maliciously causing further mental pain to someone who is already suffering'. As it happens, salt might be of use in helping a wound to heal, but its immediate effect would be to increase the pain. This phrase is now rarely heard in full, but **rub it in** is common and unconsciously alludes to it, though the meaning of the shorter form is little more than 'insist on or emphasize something'. 'He's been rubbing it in all evening how I don't mean as much to him as one of Scintilla's whiskers' says someone in James Purdy's *Eustace Chisholm and the Works*. Penelope Gilliatt, in *A State of Change*, has: 'We're all pretty hideous, after all. But don't rub it in. It puts people off.'

'She even sees when I'm offended, without my having to rub her nose in it.'

Sinclair Lewis *Cass Timberlane*

A modern alternative to 'rub it in' is **rub someone's nose in it**. The decidedly unpleasant allusion here is to the training of domestic animals. Many owners rub a dog's nose in its own excrement if it chooses the wrong place as a lavatory. Richard Gordon writes in *The Face-maker*: 'He knew perfectly well he would for years have cut a petty figure at Maria's side, but having his nose rubbed so vigorously in the malodorous fact took away his breath.'

Some things that people say need to be **taken with a pinch** (or **grain**) **of salt**. They need a little flavouring before we can digest them because the remarks are of doubtful quality. There are also some people who will throw a pinch of salt over their shoulder if they happen to spill some accidentally. Why it should be considered especially unlucky to spill salt is not known, unless the idea was put into servants' heads to make them careful. Salt was formerly more valuable than it is now.

In medieval times a large salt-cellar was placed in the middle of the table at a banquet. From this practice arose a saying about dining **above** (or **below) the salt**, according to whether one was among the honoured guests at the upper end of the table or with the riff-raff at the lower end. The phrase is no longer used. A modern speaker might instead refer jokingly to something happening **like a dose of salts** 'very quickly'. This slangy reference to laxative salts would not, needless to say, be an appropriate one to make in polite circles.

■ RUBBING SHOULDERS

'I don't believe you properly appreciate your advantages, Conrad. Being born into a good family. Having a head on your shoulders – '
'Is it fair to count that? Everybody's got one, Grandmother.'

Judith Guest *Ordinary People*

The expression used by the grandmother in the quotation above is seen in its more usual form in Mary McCarthy's *The Group*: 'She has a good head on her shoulders.' Some speakers do leave out the 'good', expecting the listener to supply the word, but Miss Guest rightly points out that intelligent young people are fond of interpreting literally what is said in order to confound their elders. The grandmother is not, as it happens, saying to the boy that he is intelligent in an academic way. To **have a good head on one's shoulders** is to have practical ability and common sense.

The grandmother could also have said that her grandson had **an old head on young shoulders**, meaning that he was more mature than one would expect for someone his age. Had she really wished to flatter she could have told him that he was **head and shoulders above** his contemporaries. This would refer not to physical size but to outstanding mental or physical abilities.

'Always had a big chip on his shoulder, you should have heard him go on about me being above myself, and him only an ignorant working man.'

Margaret Drabble *The Middle Ground*

To **have a chip on one's shoulder** is to have a belligerent attitude, to be bitter, resentful and defiant. A person who is described in this way is convinced that others are prejudiced against him, usually because of his social background or physical appearance. 'Like all martyrs, when you get to know them, he turns out to have quite a chip on his shoulder' says someone in Mary McCarthy's *The Groves of Academe*. Berta Ruck, in *Ancestral Voices*, has: '"One forgives that rather – well, brusque manner." "Yes, as if she had a chip on her shoulder about something."' 'I rather fancy he may have a chip on his shoulder' is in Frederic Raphael's *The Limits of Love*.

This phrase was in use in America by 1830. Contemporary writers explained that when two boys were determined to fight with one another, a chip of wood was placed on the shoulder of one of them. The other was then challenged to knock it off. Typical reasons for wishing to fight could well have led to the metaphoric use of the phrase.

'Let me tell you straight from the shoulder, Rat, you've captivated him.'

James Purdy *Eustace Chisholm and the Works*

A blow which comes **straight from the shoulder** comes directly, with full force. The phrase is used figuratively of things which are said frankly and honestly, with no holding back. Often there is a suggestion that the listener will not like what he is about to hear. 'I'm going to give it to you straight from the shoulder,' is said by a colonel in Mordecai Richler's *The Incomparable Atuk*, but in this case all that follows is: 'Things aren't what they used to be.'

■ SEEING THE LIGHT

'It can be done within the time allowed if I burn the candle at both ends.'

Frederick Forsyth *The Day of the Jackal*

When candles were in daily household use, before electric lighting became available, it was natural that a number of metaphorical expressions should refer to them. The one that has best survived is **to burn the candle at both ends** 'to exhaust oneself by trying to do too many things, especially by going to bed late and getting up early'. One's reserves of energy and strength are consumed at an alarming rate.

The phrase is occasionally confused, as it appears to be in the above quotation from *The Day of the Jackal*, with **burning the midnight oil**. This refers to a temporary spell of working late into the night, especially when preparing for an examination or performing a specific task. Mary McCarthy alludes to the phrase in *The Group*: 'I watched those *magnas* go up for their diplomas and I didn't like the look of them at all; they smelled of the lamp. The midnight oil, dontcha know.' 'Burning the candle at both ends', by contrast, is more often concerned with the pursuit of pleasure than with working excessively hard.

There are some people who live their whole lives in this way. The American poet Edna St Vincent Millay offered this thought on the subject:

> My candle burns at both ends;
> It will not last the night;
> But, ah, my foes, and oh, my
>   friends –
> It gives a lovely light.

The idea of 'burning the candle at both ends' was taken into English from French in the 17th century. In modern French the phrase *brûler la chandelle par les deux bouts* 'burn the candle by the two ends' is still used, referring to a reckless lifestyle that does little good for one's health or bank-balance.

'I say she's the best, the kindest, the gentlest, the sweetest girl in England, and that, bankrupt or no, my sisters are not fit to hold candles to her.'

William Thackeray *Vanity Fair*

We less often hear someone compare two people by saying that one of them **cannot hold a candle to the other**. The original allusion was to a servant, whose duties would have included carrying candles in order to light the way for a master or mistress. The person who 'cannot hold a candle' to the other person is so inferior to him that he is not even fit to be his servant.

Older speakers may still speak of something as being **not worth the candle**. They mean that the effort and expense involved in doing something is not justified by the result. The expression was originally used by gamblers who liked to play for high stakes. A game that was 'not worth the candle' was one in which the sum wagered was not even enough to pay for the candle that provided the lighting.

■ SHEEP AND GOATS

I suppose every family has a black sheep. Tom had been a sore trial to his for twenty years.

W. Somerset Maugham *The Ant and the Grasshopper*

A proverb says that **there are black sheep in every flock**, but most people today would probably follow W. Somerset Maugham and say that there is a black sheep in every family. The 'black sheep' is the one the rest of the family are sorry to have to acknowledge. They feel that he brings disgrace on them by his illegal or immoral behaviour. 'They do not approve of me,' says someone in John Stroud's *On the Loose*. 'I am the black sheep of the family.' In *Doctor Thorne* Trollope philosophizes: 'Fathers are apt to be more lenient to their sons than uncles to their nephews, or cousins to each other. Dr Thorne still hoped to reclaim his black sheep.'

As usual, a writer can play with this phrase if it suits his purpose. In *World's End* Upton Sinclair is discussing a Communist when he writes: 'The black sheep of your family – or perhaps I had better say the red sheep of your family.'

'This has separated the sheep from the goats, all right. Either you're on the side of humanity or you're on the side of your own interests.'

Jeremy Brooks *Henry's War*

Separating the sheep from the goats is a familiar image because of the New Testament. Matthew 25.31 relates what will happen at the Last Judgement: 'When the Son of man comes in his glory, and all the angels with him, then he will sit on his glorious throne. Before him will be gathered all the nations, and he will separate them one from another as a shepherd separates the sheep from the goats, and he will place the sheep at his right hand, but the goats at the left.'

St Matthew goes on to say that the sheep will 'inherit the kingdom prepared for you from the foundation of the world'; the goats will be told 'Depart from me, you cursed, into the eternal fire.' 'Separate the sheep from the goats' in modern usage does not have such a powerful meaning, but refers in general terms to separating good people from bad.

Mary McCarthy remains close to the biblical source when she writes in *The Groves of Academe*: 'The poetry conference figured now in the local mind as an event like Armageddon, to be followed by Judgement and the final separation of the sheep from the goats.'

'They are sharp traders, and that's all right, but what gets your goat is the mask of righteousness they put on.'

Upton Sinclair *World's End*

As for 'goats' themselves, they figure most frequently in English phraseology in **get someone's goat** 'irritate somebody'. No one has satisfactorily explained the 'goat' reference, but there is a French idiom *rendre quelqu'un chèvre*, literally 'make someone into a goat'. The metaphorical meaning is much the same as 'get someone's goat', and the French phrase is obviously easier to explain. The person becomes angry enough to start butting his head against a wall.

'Get someone's goat' is in frequent use. Truman Capote, in *Jug of Silver*, writes: 'Rufus McPherson has finally got his goat.' In *To Kill a Mockingbird,* Harper Lee has: 'He said he was trying to get Miss Maudie's goat, that he had been trying unsuccessfully for forty years.' Later in the novel occurs: 'No matter what anybody says to you, don't you let 'em get your goat.' John Updike writes in *Rabbit Redux*: 'Did you really give Stavros a bang today? Or're you just getting my goat?'

It got up his nose rather the way Charles Mabledene had betrayed Stern.

Ruth Rendell *Talking to Strange Men*

A number of other phrases refer to being irritated by someone or something. Relatively modern is **get up one's nose**, alluding presumably to something that makes one sneeze. A person can **rub someone up the wrong way**, where the allusion is probably to stroking a cat or dog in the wrong direction. To **get on someone's nerves** really means to make him very nervous; to **drive someone up the wall** humorously suggests that he will do anything to escape the person who is irritating him.

There is an obvious allusion in **drive someone crazy** and the American **burn someone up**. To **get on someone's wick** looks like a harmless reference to a candle, but is from **Hampton wick**, rhyming slang for 'prick', penis. A similar indelicate allusion to the body occurs in **get on one's tits**, curiously used by both men and women. This list by no means exhausts the possible ways of stating colloquially that one is annoyed; expressions such as 'get under someone's skin' are dealt with elsewhere in this book.

■ SHIPPING FORECAST

I knew that in her heart she had already won the prize. 'When our ship comes home,' she would say, and at once sternly warn me about 'counting our chickens before they were hatched'.

C.P. Snow *The Affair*

When one's ship comes home refers to some unspecified time in the future when one becomes successful. An alternative form of the expression is seen in D.H. Lawrence's *Sons and Lovers*: 'They're off the little list I'd made to get when my ship came in.'

The phrase may allude to *The Merchant of Venice*. Shakespeare has Antonio express great confidence that he will soon be able to pay Shylock the money he has borrowed on behalf of Bassanio: 'Come on; in this there can be no dismay; My ships come home a month before the day.' Antonio's ships are later reported lost, causing Shylock to demand his 'pound of flesh'. It might seem that Shakespeare was warning of the dangers of placing too much faith in 'one's ship coming home', but at the end of the play we are told that three of Antonio's ships have indeed 'richly come to harbour'.

■ SHUTTING ONE'S CLAM-SHELL

'When he saw me looking blank, he shut up like a clam.'

John Sherwood *The Half Hunter*

A 'clam' is a name applied to various large shellfish with hinged shells, the two sides of which are tightly clamped together. It was this clamping action which gave the bivalve its name, 'clam' having the earlier meaning of a vice-like object. Certain species of clams are especially popular in North America, where 'clam-bakes' may be held on a beach. These have something in common with the Scottish 'kettles of fish' of former times (see page 182).

Blakely remembered another time when the whole town had clammed up on him.

Bernard Wolfe *The Late-Risers*

In American slang, 'clam' or 'clam-shell' was at one time applied to the mouth in a phrase like 'shut your clam-shell'. A person who is a 'clam' is still a secretive person who does not easily open his mouth. To 'clam up' on both sides of the Atlantic is to become silent and refuse to speak. Phrasal references to the clam are based on **shut up like a clam** and have a similar meaning. Examples include: 'He was himself tight-mouthed as a clam' in C.P. Snow's *The Affair*; 'Mooney retained a clam-like silence' in Vera Caspary's *Laura*; 'Everyone shuts up like clams and says nothing' in Maurice Edelman's *The Minister*.

■ SIDE ISSUES

His mother had cancelled the trip 'to be on the safe side'.

Elizabeth Jane Howard *Getting it Right*

To be **on the safe side** is to take no risks. The phrase probably arose when estimating the cost of something. An extra amount was added to allow for items which had possibly been forgotten, and which would convert a profit into a loss. The 'side' would have alluded to the side of the page which listed credits, rather than the debit side of the page.

In many situations where some kind of notional polarity exists, reference may be made to one 'side' or the other. In disputes it is often said that there are two sides to the matter. Debaters might even use a concrete metaphor and refer to the **other side of the coin** 'the opposite aspect of the matter'. When we support someone who favours one argument rather than another we are said to side with that person, or **take sides with him**.

Look on the bright side 'take an optimistic view of a matter' is based on the fact that one could instead take a pessimistic view. To say that someone is **on the wrong side of fifty**, or whatever, 'older than the age mentioned', assumes that to be below any given age is better than being above it.

'I was just going to knock,' she said, 'isn't that funny?'
'I'm splitting my sides,' Jos said.

Margaret Forster *Georgy Girl*

English people have been talking about **splitting their sides** with laughing since at least the 17th century. The phrase is a simple exaggeration. Shakespeare alludes to the idea in *Cymbeline*, when Iachimo says: 'The jolly Briton / Your lord, I mean, laughs from's free lungs, cries "O, / Can my sides hold . . . ?"' Milton's allusion in *L'Allegro* to 'Laughter holding both his sides' is even better known. An especially funny story has been described as **side-splitting** since the 19th century.

Rather more of a mystery is **laugh on the other side of one's face** 'experience a sudden change of mood and become gloomy'. It has been suggested that since the mouth turns upwards when a person is laughing, but takes a downward turn when he is miserable, the phrase may be another way of saying that **one's face drops**. The expression is often used threateningly: 'You'll laugh on the other side of your face in a moment!' and may therefore link with remarks such as 'I'll knock that smile off your face.'

Let the side down uses 'side' in its sense of a team of sportsmen, and is one of the sporting metaphors much loved by male speakers. The person who 'lets the side down' fails to give his colleagues the help they feel they have a right to expect.

■ SINGING BIRDS

Even in your thought, do not curse the king, nor in your bedchamber curse the rich; for a bird of the air will carry your voice, or some winged creature tell the matter.

Old Testament, Ecclesiastes 10.20

Partridge says in his *Dictionary of Historical Slang* that **a little bird told me**, meaning 'I have heard a rumour' or 'Someone I do not want to name told me', dates from the 19th century. He adds that the expression is 'far from literary'. In *The Reader's Handbook*, Dr Brewer provides evidence to the contrary. He gives illustrations from literature to show that a truth-telling bird is mentioned in many folk-tales and is to be found in the *Arabian Nights*, 'The Two Sisters'. The phrase is a good example of what appears to be a childish euphemism which has a long and respectable history. No doubt the idea of birds passing on messages was originally inspired by those birds which can to some extent imitate human speech.

■ SKELETON KEY

'I'm bone idle. I'm delighted to have an excuse for not working.'

Henry Cecil *Brothers in Law*

'Bone' expressions in English include references to both human and animal bones, plus one or two where the 'bone' is not actually a 'bone' at all. The bones of the human body lead to phrases like **bone idle** and **lazy bones**. The latter is now used as a mild, almost affectionate, term of address and is not a serious accusation of laziness. The description 'bone idle' is more contemptuous. Both expressions refer to bodily laziness, 'bones' sometimes standing in for 'body' in a sentence like 'he ran as fast as his bones could carry him'.

A person who is unpleasantly thin may be described as **a bag of bones**. Thinness also gives rise to a comment that is sometimes heard when men and women discuss the relative merits of slim or well-built partners: **the nearer the bone, the sweeter the meat**. This has been accepted as a proverbial truism since the 16th century. By contrast, a remark which is **close** or **near to the bone** is by no means 'sweet', but is one which rather tactlessly reveals the truth.

'I had this intuition you would come here just after the rain broke. I knew in my bones you were coming and that you would make it just too late.'

Carson McCullers *The Heart is a Lonely Hunter*

To **know** or **feel something in one's bones** has been used since the mid-19th century to describe something that is felt intuitively. The knowledge seems to come from within. Jeremy Brooks writes in *Henry's War*: 'He knew in his bones that there were hundreds of millions of human beings in the world whose identities as members of this or that race were worth more to them than their lives.' Bernard Malamud, in *The Natural*, has: 'I feel it in my bones that you will have luck with it.'

Riders of early bicycles had an experience which they literally 'felt in their bones'. Rubber tyres did not yet exist, and their solid predecessors, on primitive road surfaces, made for an uncomfortable ride. The bicycles themselves deserved their nickname **bone-shakers**.

'Bone-shaker' is now merely a historical term. Other 'bone' phrases from the past include the curious exclamation that was used in the 16th century, **bones of me**! This seems to have been the equivalent of **bless my bones**! During the same period **by these ten bones** might be used to swear that something was true. The allusion was to the finger-bones and thus to the hands. In *King Henry the Sixth*, Part Two, one man accuses another of saying that King Henry is a usurper. The accused man denies uttering such words. His accuser holds up his own hands and says: 'By these ten bones, my lords, he did speak them to me in the garret one night.'

Sawbones is another out-dated term. One of the more obscure remarks made by Sam Weller in *The Pickwick Papers* is to a boy who is standing nearby when an old lady faints. 'Now depitty sawbones,' says Sam, 'bring out the wollatilly!' Dickens has previously had Sam explain to Mr Pickwick, who thought that a 'sawbones' might be something to eat, that the reference was to a 'surgeon'. The boy, in his turn, is meant to understand that he is being appointed deputy doctor, and should go in search of some volatile (smelling) salts.

'I've more than a little bone to pick with Bryce,' called Henry.

E.M. Forster *Howards End*

Mary McCarthy writes, in *The Group*: 'It had been a bone of contention between them.' This **bone of contention** 'subject of disagreement' between people has been spoken

about since the 16th century. Then as now a bone thrown onto the ground between two dogs would inevitably lead to a fight, each dog considering the bone to be rightfully his.

The image of a dog gnawing a bone also led to the phrase **a bone to pick**, which at first meant 'a difficulty to solve'. When the difficulty involved someone else it became **have a bone to pick with someone**. The bone that has to be picked is now usually a problem that the other person is thought to have created. The person who has the bone to pick wants to know how and why something has occurred.

Ogden Nash, in his *Lines on Facing Forty*, says:

> *I have a bone to pick with fate,*
> *Come here and tell me, girlie,*
> *Do you think my mind is maturing late,*
> *Or simply rotted early?*

Why your dear mother called it pie I cannot imagine, for, as I made no bones about telling her, I know a tart when I see one.

Dane Chandos *Abbie*

To **make no bones about something** is to say something without hesitation or worry, to be frank about it, even when a tactful or euphemistic approach might have been expected. This phrase always seems to have been used negatively, but is based on the idea of **making bones about something** 'making difficulties or objections, hesitating about'. There was also once a phrase which referred to **finding bones in something** 'finding points of difficulty that perhaps no one else had noticed'.

The original allusion in all these phrases was to finding bones in soup which made it more difficult to eat. To 'make no bones about something' is to do it as easily as one drinks soup which has no bones or other indigestible things in it. Monica Dickens writes in *The Fancy*: 'The doctor, who prepared Mrs Holt for the ordeal of her confinement by making no bones about his doubts that she would come through it, was only partially justified.'

Manley had decided to bone up on Marx before joining the C.P. under a cover-name: today he did that scandalous weekly broadcast to Canada from Moscow.

Mordecai Richler *The Incomparable Atuk*

Students who speak of **boning up on** a subject are perpetuating a long-standing joke. Such students originally made use of translations and other texts published by Henry George Bohn. He was born in London in 1796, though his family came from Germany. He must be unique among publishers in having a verb formed from his name, even though it is in corrupt form. The noun 'bone' or 'boner' is also used in American slang of a diligent student, derived from the same source.

'Boner' has other slang meanings. It can mean a 'stupid mistake', the type of error committed by a **bone-head** 'stupid person'. It can also be connected with **having a bone on**, where the reference is to the erect penis. 'Have a bone on' is described by Robert L. Chapman, in his *Dictionary of American Slang*, as a 'hubristic anatomical mis-statement', a matter of excessive pride, in other words, based on factual error. It was factual error of a different kind which led to *whalebone* being described in that way. The substance concerned is not in fact bone.

'It's desert where you're going. Dry as a bone and hotter'n hell at this time of year.'

Ian Fleming *Diamonds are Forever*

A disguised form of 'bone' is found in **bonfire**, which was once a fire made by burning bones. These could have been dry animal bones (**dry as a bone**, **bone dry** are proverbial) or bones contained in human corpses which were being cremated. Bonfires are now associated with innocent amusement: in the grimmer times of the 16th century they could also be the fires on which heretics were burnt alive.

■ SKIN DEEP

'He's all over you one minute. Then he discovers some reason for getting under one's skin as he did this afternoon.'

C.P. Snow *The Masters*

'I've Got You Under My Skin' is the title of one of Cole Porter's best-known songs. In this instance the meaning is 'you're a part of me, and I can't stop thinking about you'. When Mary McCarthy writes, in *The Groves of Academe*: 'What got under his skin was the *unseasonableness* of this celebration,' the meaning is quite different. Here to **get under someone's skin** has its more usual sense of 'irritate someone'. It makes an unpleasant allusion to an insect which buries itself in someone's skin and causes an itch.

They all very nearly jumped out of their skins; for close at hand a crane had trumpeted once desperately.

Richard Hughes *A High Wind in Jamaica*

The notion of **jumping out of one's skin** is now linked with fright, but all early occurrences of the phrase, from the 16th century onwards, refer to jumping out of one's skin for joy. The phrase makes a straightforward use of exaggeration, in keeping with its purpose of expressing an extreme reaction.

He's only just kept his mother away from this party by the skin of his teeth.

Fay Weldon *Down Among the Women*

By the skin of one's teeth 'with difficulty, barely' is a literal translation of a Hebrew text. The Old Testament, Job 19.20 has: 'My bones cleave to my skin and to my flesh, and I have escaped by the skin of my teeth.' Teeth do not have a skin, but if they did it would obviously be very thin. The image manages to convey the idea of a very narrow escape indeed and has more than proved its worth, being in continual use since the 16th century. Ngaio Marsh in *Surfeit of Lampreys* talks of someone 'hanging on by the skin of his teeth' with reference to his financial problems.

We talk about the metaphorical thickness or thinness of ordinary skin when we refer to someone's sensitivity. A person who can withstand criticism and not be unduly bothered by it is said to have a **thick skin**. Someone with a **thin skin** is all too easily hurt by comments.

'Cheers.'
'Skin off your nose.'

Ian Jefferies *Thirteen Days*

Skin off your nose is one of countless salutations used when drinking with a companion. (Such terms are fully discussed in *The Guinness Drinking Companion*, by Leslie Dunkling.) When not used in those special circumstances, it tends to take the form **no skin off your nose**, meaning 'what has just been mentioned won't do you any harm (and may possibly do you some good)'. The phrase probably originated with the thought: 'There's no need for you to be inquisitive and stick your nose into this affair, which might lead to your nose getting skinned by someone's fist.' Robert L. Chapman's *Dictionary of American Slang* reports that **no skin off one's ass** and **no skin off one's butt** are common variants.

■ SLEEVE NOTES

'You go on hoping to reform them with patience and love, and they go on laughing up their sleeves and doing exactly what they want.'

Jeremy Brooks *Henry's War*

In English phrases the 'sleeve' has to do with secrecy or lack of it. A person who **laughs up his sleeve** is secretly amused, stifling his laughter with his sleeve, as it were, so that others do not hear it. The phrase was formerly to **laugh in one's sleeve**. 'I have laughed in my sleeve to see how she played her game' says someone in Trollope's *Doctor Thorne*. **Smile up one's sleeve** and even **yawn up one's sleeve** were formerly used.

Edward couldn't help feeling gratified by his admiration, because after all, he did know something about rabbits.
'You sly old devil, I'd no idea you'd been keeping something like this up your sleeve.'

Monica Dickens *The Fancy*

Concealment is also the theme of a phrase like have **something up one's** sleeve, especially **have an ace up one's sleeve** 'something effective kept out of sight until it is needed'. American speakers might also describe this as an **ace in the hole**, 'in the hole' referring to a card turned face downwards.

In Shakespeare's *Othello*, Iago explains to Roderigo that he serves the Moor for his own ends. He is one of those, he says, who 'throwing but shows of service on their lords, do well thrive by 'em.' He continues:

> For when my outward action doth
>   demonstrate
> The native act and figure of my
>   heart
> In compliment extern, 'tis not long
>   after
> But I will wear my heart upon my
>   sleeve
> For daws to peck at.

Iago, then, is certainly not one to **wear his heart on his sleeve**, his behaviour does not reveal his true thoughts and feelings. The phrase has remained in use since the 17th century to describe someone who allows his emotions to be seen, especially someone who reveals love for another person. The allusion is to the medieval practice of wearing on one's sleeve a 'favour' provided by one's loved-one in a public display of one's attachment.

■ SNUFFING IT

'He was one too many for you, warn't he? Up to snuff and a pinch or two over – eh?'

Charles Dickens *The Pickwick Papers*

The use of snuff was widespread in the 18th and 19th centuries. Pickwick's male companions are constantly exchanging snuff-boxes and often comment on the relative quality of particular brands. The esteem in which snuff could be held was summed up by Samuel Taylor Coleridge in his *Table Talk*: 'Perhaps it is the final cause of the human nose.'

Up to snuff 'crafty, knowing' was in use as a colloquial phrase, used typically by Sam Weller in the quotation above to refer to Jingle. Trollope comments on it in *Doctor Thorne*: ' "I have been doing the civil; and if she's up to snuff, as I take her to be, she knows very well what I'm after by this time." Up to snuff! Mary Thorne, his Mary, up to snuff! To snuff too of such a very disagreeable description.'

'Snuff' in its other sense, of putting out a candle, also contributed to phrases. In out-dated slang **snuff out** meant 'to die'. The modern version is to **snuff it**. The metaphor occurs again in **snuff movie**, a pornographic film in which one of the participants is allegedly killed.

There is a scene in *Showboat* where Edna Ferber has a midwife baffle a young doctor by talking of **snuffing someone**: ' "Time to snuff her, I'd say." "Well, perhaps it is." He watched her, fearfully, wondering what she might mean; cursing his own lack of knowledge. To his horror, before he could stop her, she had stuffed a great pinch of snuff up either nostril of Magnolia Ravenal's delicate nose. And thus Kim Ravenal was born into the world on the gust of a series of convulsive a-CHOOs!

' "God almighty, woman!" cried the young medico, in a frenzy. "You've killed her." "Run along, do!" retorted the fat midwife, testily, for she was tired by now, and hungry, and wanted her coffee badly. "Never knew it to fail." '

■ SOCIAL CLIMBING

*'Why shouldn't I take a job like
anybody else, and see how it feels to
put in an eight-hour day?'
'Beginning at the bottom of the
ladder?' smiled the father.*

Arnold Bennett *Clayhanger*

Comparing one's advancement in life
to the climbing of a ladder has been
usual for centuries. Shakespeare
philosophises on the subject in *Julius
Caesar*:

> *'Tis a common proof
> That lowliness is young ambition's
> ladder,
> Whereto the climber-upward turns
> his face;
> But when he once obtains the
> upmost round,
> He then unto the ladder turns his
> back,
> Looks in the clouds, scorning the
> base degrees
> By which he did ascend.*

In *King Richard the Second*,
Shakespeare goes a step further and
uses 'ladder' to describe a person who
assists someone in his upward climb.
Richard addresses the Earl of
Northumberland as: 'thou ladder
wherewithal / The mounting
Bolingbroke ascends my throne'. He
goes on to warn Northumberland that
Bolingbroke will hate him once he
has achieved his aim.

*She has struggled so gallantly for
polite reputation that she has won it:
pitilessly kicking down the ladder as
she advanced degree by degree.*

William Thackeray *Book of Snobs*

The view that someone who had been
helped to climb a social or
professional ladder would later
repudiate those who gave him
assistance was formerly expressed in
the phrase **kick down the ladder**. The
phrase is no longer heard, though it is
doubtful that human nature has much
changed. To **see through a ladder** is
another phrase that has disappeared.
'Can't ye see through a ladder?' asks
someone in *Uncle Tom's Cabin*, by
Harriet Beecher Stowe. This was once
a commonplace for: 'Can't you see
what is obvious?'

We do continue to refer to **having a
foot on the ladder** 'being in a position
where one will be able to advance'.
'This will be a godsend to young
Eliot,' says a senile professor in C.P.
Snow's *The Affair*. 'It will put his
foot right on the ladder. There's no
one who deserves to have his foot on
the ladder more than young Eliot.'
This is of a man who is already
extremely successful.

*She had never much cared for a match
based on hard cash and an admitted
hoist up the social ladder.*

R.F. Delderfield *Theirs Was the
Kingdom*

A writer sometimes forgets what he is
literally saying when he uses the
ladder metaphor. Edward A. Rogers,
in *Face to Face*, talks of 'scraping and
digging to make his way up the
ladder', which is a peculiar way of
going about it. The purist might say
that for writing in such a slap-dash
way Mr Rogers deserved to **climb the
ladder**. This colloquial phrase was in
use from the 16th century and had
nothing to do with becoming more
successful. The ladder led to the
gallows, and to 'climb the ladder' was
to be hanged.

■ SONS OF SHE-DOGS

'You're a ham, you son of a bitch, and you know it.'

Stanley Kauffmann *The Philanderer*

Son of a bitch is probably used more frequently in the USA than in Britain. The phrase can form part of phrasal 'you' (see Introduction page 9), be used in third person reference or occur as an exclamation. It is impolite slang and may be softened down as **son of a so-and-so, son of a b.** or **s.o.b.** There is a Sob Lake in Canada which was named for an unpopular early trapper.

'Bitch' has been used as an insulting term for a lewd woman since the 15th century. C.S. Lewis, in his *Studies in Words*, writes: 'Till recently – and still in proper contexts – **bitch** accused a woman of one particular fault and appealed, with some success, to our contempt by calling up an image of the she-dog's comical and indecorous behaviour when she is on heat. But it is now increasingly used of any woman whom the speaker, for whatever reason, is annoyed with – the female driver who is in front of him, or a female magistrate whom he thinks unjust.'

Henry Fielding, humorous as always in *Joseph Andrews*, pretends to find the word so appalling that he cannot mention it. The relevant passage runs: '"Get out of my house, you whore." To which she added another name, which we do not care to stain our paper with. It was a monosyllable beginning with b-, and indeed was the same as if she had pronounced the words "she-dog".' Aldous Huxley resurrects that euphemism in his *Brave New World*: 'Not for you, white-hair! Not for the son of the she-dog.'

'Son of a bitch' was almost certainly known to Shakespeare. He comes very close to using the phrase in *King Lear*, when Oswald asks Kent 'What dost thou know me for?' Kent replies that he knows him, amongst other things, as a 'beggar, coward, pander, and the son and heir of a mongrel bitch'. In *Troilus and Cressida* Ajax calls Thersites 'thou bitch-wolf's son'.

Peter Cheyney, in *You Can Call It a Day*, has an exchange between a man and woman who are having an adulterous relationship. When the man says 'I'm a son of a bitch,' the woman replies 'I suppose that makes me a daughter of a bitch?'

■ SORE THROATS

'We seem to quarrel such a lot. You jump down my throat at everything I say.'
'Well, don't pursue things so much.'

John Harvey *Within and Without*

To **jump down someone's throat** combines the idea of figuratively jumping on someone, 'suddenly attacking him with criticism', and angrily thrusting his words back down his throat. The expression arose in the 19th century and remains in common colloquial use, perhaps because of the startling image it evokes. In modern usage the phrase usually means 'to reply to something that has been said in an angry and critical way', but it can be used of someone who initiates the criticism. In *Clayhanger* Arnold Bennett has: 'You jump down my throat because I spend a bit of money of my own.'

Her voice comes out like a croak. She clears her throat. 'Sorry. Frog in my throat.' Dramatic effect is somewhat marred, second time. Frog in the throat? What a gruesome expression.

Who could ever have thought that one up? Ugh. Those clammy clambering teeny saurian legs in your gullet, for God's sake?

Margaret Laurence *The Diviners*

The throat seems to attract humorous expressions. The rasping sound produced by a temporary hoarseness is attributed to a **frog in the throat**. The phrase was less amusing in former times when it was applied to the thrush, the infectious disease which produces white patches in the mouth and throat.

■ SPEAK OF AN ANGEL

Here lies Nolly Goldsmith, for shortness call'd Noll, Who wrote like an angel, but talk'd like poor Poll.

David Garrick *Impromptu Epitaph on Oliver Goldsmith*

In his *Curiosities of Literature*, Isaac Disraeli has an essay 'The History of Writing-Masters' in which he says: 'There is a strange phrase connected with the art of the calligrapher, which I think may be found in most, if not all modern languages, *to write like an angel*. Ladies have been frequently compared with angels; they are beautiful as angels, and sing and dance like angels; but, however intelligible these are, we do not so easily connect penmanship with the other celestial accomplishments.

'This fanciful phrase, however, has a very human origin. Among those learned Greeks who emigrated to Italy, and afterwards into France, in the reign of Francis I was one Angelo Vergecio, whose beautiful calligraphy excited the admiration of the learned . . . Henry Stephens, who was one of the most elegant writers of Greek, had learnt the practice from our Angelo. His name became synonymous for beautiful writing, and gave birth to the vulgar proverb, or familiar phrase, to write like an angel!'

This was written in the early 19th century, when hand-writing was of much greater importance than it is in this age of word-processors. But if Disraeli's anecdote is correct, then even when 'to write like an angel' was still relatively familiar, it was misunderstood. The epitaph (quoted above) on Oliver Goldsmith, who died in 1874, shows that Garrick applied the phrase – as would any modern reader – to composition rather than penmanship.

'Where the hell's George?'
I gestured towards the door. 'Speak of the devil,' I said.

John Braine *Life at the Top*

Angels play little part in English phraseology. A woman, especially, might ask someone to **be an angel** and do something for her, but we refer to the devil rather more frequently. A typical comment on the sudden appearance of someone we have just mentioned, for instance, is: **Speak (Talk) of the devil!** 'Talk of the devil' in Geraint Goodwin's *The Heyday in the Blood* is said when the local police constable, known as Peepy-Tom, is spotted through the window.

The phrase is a joke, of course, but would not always be appropriate. A character in Kate O'Brien's *Pray for the Wanderer* shows that there is an alternative formula. The friend who appears just as she is being talked about is greeted with: 'Speak of an angel!'

■ SPITTING IMAGES

'Spitten image of his dad, little Alf is.'
Winifred Holtby *South Riding*

In *You All Spoken Here*, Roy Wilder suggests that to be the **spitting image** of someone else was originally to be the 'spirit and image' of that person. The 'r' in 'spirit', he says, could easily have been lost in southern American speech. The same theory could perhaps be applied to being the **dead spit of someone**, except that this is always applied to physical appearance, not to personality and character.

The reluctance to believe that 'spit' and 'spitting' in these expressions really refers to expectoration is understandable, but that is almost certainly the case. In French it has been possible to say, since the 15th century, *il est son père tout craché*, 'he is the very spit of his father'. Jacqueline Picoche suggests, in her *Nouveau Dictionnaire Étymologique du Français*, that the French idiom derives from 'a fairly common symbolism assimilating the act of spitting with the act of generation'.

In Britain the satirical television programme 'Spitting Image' has given this phrase extra prominence. The people portrayed probably feel that they have been roasted on a spit.

■ SPOT CHECK

'Listen here, Atuk, you put me on the spot like last night once more and . . .'
Mordecai Richler *The Incomparable Atuk*

The 'spot' referred to in **put someone on the spot** is metaphorically a 'difficult position', one which requires the person to defend himself verbally. When someone is in a **tight spot** he is literally in a particular place where he is exposed to physical danger. **On the spot** again means in a particular place, but can include the idea of immediacy, of something happening 'there and then'. In a sentence like 'The police were quickly on the spot', 'spot' is used for 'the place where something has occurred'. In **hot spot**, 'spot' means 'place' in a much wider sense. It is an area, perhaps even a whole country, where trouble is likely to occur because of political turmoil or social upheaval.

'People have a soft spot in their hearts for alcoholics,' Hawthorne said.
Graham Greene *Our Man in Havana*

Someone who is 'soft-hearted' is affectionate by nature, easily moved to pity, kind and trusting. A person who is not soft-hearted in general terms may still **have a soft spot in his heart** for someone, 'have a special fondness for that person'. Most speakers do not bother to mention where the 'soft spot' is; X 'has a soft spot for' Y is enough to convey the meaning.

'You were always spiffing in French. You could simply knock spots off me.'
Arnold Bennett *Clayhanger*

'Spot' can also mean a small mark, such as the spots on the back of a leopard. Allusions to the proverb a **leopard does not change his spots** are sometimes found, meaning that people do not change their basic nature. **Knock the spots off** 'be much better than' is thought to have referred originally to American marksmen. They used playing-cards as targets and aimed to drill holes through the 'spots'. The alternative version of this saying, **knock the spots out of,** lends support to this theory of the phrase's origin. **Spot on** 'exactly right, accurate' could also be connected with this idea.

■ STARRY-EYED

'You may thank your lucky stars I am so lovely. After all, looks go a long way on the stage.'

Ngaio Marsh *Surfeit of Lampreys*

If someone thinks that we have been fortunate in some way he is likely to say that we should **thank our lucky stars**. 'Lucky' is sometimes omitted: 'Walter thanked his stars and tiptoed out of the room' is in *Self*, by Beverley Nichols. The expression is probably often used to comment on good fortune by speakers who do not for one moment think of what they are literally saying. They offer ammunition to those intelligent young people who delight in disconcerting their elders by literally interpreting their words. The point is made by Judith Guest in *Ordinary People*: '"You are so protected, you can't imagine what it was like in the old days. I mean, you should just thank your lucky stars every night – " "My what?" he asks. "My lucky what?" She stares him down. "You heard me."'

The saying is based on astrological beliefs that are as common today as they have been for centuries. In *Julius Caesar*, Shakespeare has Cassius say: 'Men at some time are masters of their fates: / The fault, dear Brutus, is not in our stars, / But in ourselves, that we are underlings.' Many other Shakespearean characters, however, comment on stars that are both 'malignant' and 'inauspicious' as well as 'good' and 'happy'. Helena, in *All's Well that Ends Well*, had typical 17th-century beliefs. She tells Parolles

that he was 'born under a charitable star' and believes that 'the luckiest stars in heaven' will enable her to cure the king and win Bertram as her husband. When she achieves her aims it is not difficult to imagine her literally 'thanking her lucky stars'.

■ STEAMING ALONG

'I'm sure you understand that, as her family, we get a bit steamed up about her.'

Elizabeth Jane Howard *Getting it Right*

The discovery that steam could be used to provide power in a steam engine (often called a fire-engine in the 18th century) had the secondary effect of introducing a number of phrases into everyday language. We are still likely to talk of **getting up steam** as we gradually become excited or angry. We can talk instead about **getting steamed up about something** or **someone**. The meaning remains the same – pressure is supposedly building up inside us as it does in a boiler. Our feelings are becoming more intense.

Gus saw no harm in letting Mr. Schneidfer 'blow off steam.'

Mary McCarthy *The Group*

The steam-engine metaphor is continued when we speak of **letting off** or **blowing off steam**, releasing emotional pressure or getting rid of surplus energy. Some people might instead use a **safety-valve** metaphor, but they are still imagining a kind of human steam-engine. This becomes decidedly humorous in the phrase we use about someone who is extremely angry but is trying not to show it. His face goes red and we know that any moment he will explode, since there is **steam coming out of his ears**.

If human energy is harnessed and put to use we can talk about doing things **under our own steam** 'by our own unaided efforts'. At one time we might have said we were ready to go **full steam ahead**, though **full speed ahead** would be used today. Eventually we, or the project we are concerned with, may begin to **run out of steam** 'lose impetus'.

Most people now think of steam as a decidedly antiquated form of energy, as the modern phrase **steam radio** shows. 'Back in the days of steam radio' really means 'at a time when there was no television and everything seemed to be driven by steam, even the primitive radio sets'.

■ STICKY ENDS

'But that isn't the dispute,' Blakely said patiently. 'You fellows always manage to get the wrong end of the stick. There's no dispute about railwaymen's wages.'

Raymond Williams *Border Country*

To **get hold of the wrong end of the stick** now means to misunderstand a situation or something that has been said. E.F. Benson, in *Trouble for Lucia*, has the heroine blithely tell her friend: 'I shouldn't wonder if you'd got hold of the wrong end of the stick somehow. Habit of yours, Elizabeth.'

This expression has been used since the end of the 19th century, but its precise origin was not recorded. In *You All Spoken Here*, Roy Wilder, Jr, says that **get the shitty/dirty end of the stick** derives from log-rolling, where two men would lift a log on a pole held by each of them. 'The shitty end of the stick resulted from horseplay,

from coating one end of the stick or pole in ordure.' Perhaps from this idea of being deceived came the more general meaning of not understanding a situation.

■ STRAW POLL

Mr Baker did not care a straw about it; why should he? He had an heir of his own as well as the squire.

Anthony Trollope *Doctor Thorne*

Straw has been referred to metaphorically as something of insignificant value since the 14th century. **Not care a straw** has been in use since that time. 'Two straws' are of no more value than one, hence the occasional **not care two straws**. E.F. Benson, in *Trouble for Lucia*, writes: 'Lucia did not care two straws what "the common people" were saying.'

'She and a man are in love. All the rest isn't worth a straw.'

E.M. Forster *Howards End*

Not worth a straw 'worth nothing' is an equally ancient expression, while **man of straw** has been used since the 16th century to describe a man of no real power, or a weak opponent. The allusion is to the figures of men made from straw used in various folk-loric festivals.

Towards evening a new solution to his problems occurred to him – he was clutching at straws now: could he find another guardian while he was away?

Robert Shaw *The Hiding Place*

The proverb **a drowning man will clutch at a straw** dates from the 17th century. Someone in a desperate situation will place his hopes in the slightest chance that is offered to him of escape or rescue, however unrealistic that chance may be. **To clutch** or **grasp at straws** usually does service for the whole proverb in modern times. 'You know how it is at times like this,' says someone in John Le Carré's *The Honourable Schoolboy*: 'Clutching at straws, listening to the wind.' This is said at the beginning of a difficult investigation where evidence is hard to find.

The remark about 'listening to the wind' recalls **straw in the wind**, something that gives a slight indication of how things may develop. The allusion is to dropping a straw to assess how hard and in which direction the wind is blowing.

'I was thinking of you when I kissed her.'
Jean sprang up and stamped her foot.
'That's the last straw. That's the finish.'

David Walker *Geordie*

Some reference sources say that **the last straw breaks the camel's back** is a 17th-century proverb, but allusions to the saying in any form before the 19th century are difficult to find. In *Dombey and Son* (1848) Dickens says: 'As the last straw breaks the laden camel's back, this piece of underground information crushed the sinking spirits of Mr Dombey.'

From Dickens onwards, **the last straw** is a popular phrase, used of something insignificant in itself which finally pushes a person beyond the limits of his endurance. Mary McCarthy, in *The Groves of Academe*, has: 'He gave a sudden sharp cry of impatience and irritation, as if such interruptions could positively be brooked no longer. This was the last straw.'

Elaborations of the phrase can occur.

Truman Capote, *My Side of the Matter*, has: '"*This* is the straw that broke the camel's back," says I. "That's not the only back that's going to be broke," says she.' Elizabeth Jane Howard, in *Getting it Right*, has the interesting: '"I have a suspicion that this incident will prove to be the Last Straw." Mr Adrian specialized in last straws, could even be said to be addicted to them.'

The same day Pharaoh commanded the task-masters of the people and their foremen, 'You shall no longer give the people straw to make bricks, as heretofore; let them go and gather straw for themselves. But the number of bricks which they made heretofore you shall lay upon them, you shall by no means lessen it.

Old Testament, Exodus 5.6

The modern saying about **not being able to make bricks without straw** is clearly based on the passage in Exodus, though the meaning has changed considerably. Pharaoh instructed the brick-makers to gather their own straw but did not suggest that bricks should be made without it. 'Bricks without straw' is used of not being given enough money, materials or information to do a specific job. In theory the phrase should have referred metaphorically to being asked to do everything oneself.

Strawberry is an interesting word to etymologists, who have long puzzled over the fruit's lack of connection with straw. Unconvincing explanations of the name include a supposed resemblance between the plant's runners and straws, or between the plant's external seeds and straws. In no other language does the word for 'strawberry' hint at any connection with straw.

A **straw vote** or **straw poll** is an unofficial ballot used as a test of opinion. *Picturesque Expressions*, edited by Laurence Urdang, says that the phrase came into being in the 19th century when straws were handed out to voters. They either broke them to indicate a No vote or left them intact to indicate Yes.

■ STRUNG UP

'I heard the word "string", did I not, Mr Harcourt? What have you to tell us about string? Are you an authority on string?'
'It was strings, not string,' said Mr Harcourt. 'The plural is of even greater interest. The word that goes with it is "pulling", is it not?'
'Not always,' said Mr Jamesworth.

Nigel Dennis *Cards of Identity*

'String' expressions are well used in English. Since the 19th century we have spoken a great deal about **pulling strings**, for instance. The allusion to a puppeteer is obvious, but nonetheless effective. The person who 'pulls strings' is the unseen manipulator of other people, obtaining special favours and privileges from them. To be able to do that one must normally be on good terms with the people concerned or be markedly superior to them socially or professionally. Without such conditions being met, pulling strings becomes difficult. Graham Greene has someone comment on that problem in *The Heart of the Matter*: 'He's cabled that he's pulling strings about the passage. I don't know what strings he can pull from Bury, poor dear. He doesn't know anybody at all.'

Typical circumstances in which it becomes possible to pull strings are mentioned by Leslie Thomas, in *Tropic of Ruislip*: 'He said he used to be mayor and he could pull some strings. And he did.' Beverley

Nichols, however, appears to mean only that a woman can get other people to do what she wants in a general way when he writes, in *Self*: 'Again Nancy had pulled the strings as she had desired.' What is really meant here is that Nancy can 'twist people around her little finger'. (See page 72.)

The noun derived from 'to pull strings' is **string-pulling**, used by Penelope Gilliatt in *A State of Change*: 'We arranged to have his house requisitioned for billets. We did a little string-pulling.'

'It's as well to have a second string to your bow.'

Winifred Holtby *South Riding*

To **have a second string to one's bow** alludes to archery, and to having a spare bow-string that can be used if the first one breaks. Metaphorically the phrase refers to having something in reserve in a more general way. When Mary McCarthy writes in *The Group*: 'Libby decided that she must have another string to her bow,' the meaning is that Libby wants to do something else besides book-reviewing. If there comes a time when book-reviews are no longer offered to her she will be able to turn to her **second string** and still have a source of income.

Alistair Maclean's use of 'two strings' in *The Dark Crusader* is rather different, though the reference is still to having two courses of action. A character says: 'So now you had the two strings to your bow. If you couldn't give your friends every detail of the new fuel, you could give them the fuel itself.' 'Two' strings are normal in this expression, but the number can easily be extended or made indeterminate. Edward A. Rogers, in *Face to Face*, has: 'I wonder if he really left Hollywood because of the chance you gave him, or because he had played out almost every string he had in his bow out there?'

'There's strings attached to everything you do for me,' she said.

Charles Webb *The Marriage of a Young Stockbroker*

When there are 'strings attached' to something there are conditions that have to be satisfied. The expression is a modern development of a common 18th-century idea of having someone **on a string** (on a lead or leash) and thus being able to control him. In modern times it tends to be the absence of strings which is of more concern. A woman might seek an assurance, if a man asks her out to dinner, that there are **no strings attached**, that his offer is not made with specific expectations of what will happen later. Susan Barrett writes, in *Moses*: 'That had been one of Jo's conditions when she accepted the job. "No strings?" she had asked. "No strings," he had agreed.' This is a woman accepting a job from a man who was once her lover.

The 'no strings' are again emphasized in James Mitchell's *When the Boat Comes in*: ' "There would be no strings attached," said Ashton, "not to a loan, I mean." ' Edward A.Rogers, in *Face to Face*, has: 'The party to endorse is the one most anxious to grab the free time with no strings attached.'

'You, of age? Why, thou canst not as yet have left thy mother's apron-string!'

Anthony Trollope *Doctor Thorne*

To be **tied to one's mother's apron-strings** now means being under the influence or domination of one's mother at an age when one ought to be an independent adult. The expression has been used in that sense since the early 19th century and appears to be a simple allusion to maternal possessiveness, or timidity about facing adult responsibilities. Earlier, however, it was the wife's apron-strings that were mentioned, and the phrase had legal significance.

An **apron-string hold** or **tenure** in the 17th century referred to property to which a husband had access only by virtue of his wife. He might inherit it at her death, or it could revert to another descendant of her father. Such arrangements gave the wife considerably more power than was usual. It was actually the property, then, rather than the husband, which was **tied to a wife's apron-string**, but it is easy to see how the phrase took on the meaning of feminine domination. That in turn suggested a mother rather than a wife and led to the usual modern form of the saying.

The idea of being 'tied to one's mother's apron-strings' has been taken into French as *pendu aux jupes de sa mère* 'hanging from one's mother's skirts'. The variation *être toujours dans les jupes de sa mère* 'always in one's mother's skirts' reverses the situation and takes the blame away from the mother. It is now the child who is 'clinging to the mother's apron-strings' rather than being tied to them.

The word **apron** itself is of interest because it is a mistake. The Old French word *naperon* (Modern French *napperon* diminutive of *nappe* 'table-cloth') was taken into English. 'A naperon' was then misinterpreted as 'an apron'. Similar mistakes led to **adder**, earlier 'nadder', from Old English *naedre* 'snake' and **orange** instead of 'norange', from Spanish *naranga*, Arabic *nārang*.

■ STUFFING SHIRTS

We run a conservative business, but we're not all stuffed shirts, in spite of what the radicals say.

Stephen Vincent Benét *Everybody was Very Nice*

A **stuffed shirt** is a pompous and pretentious person, all show and no substance. The metaphor referred originally to a shirt in a shop window, offered for sale. Shirts would now be displayed on mannequins, but the latter were only introduced in the 19th century. Previously a shirt would have been filled with paper, forming the 'stuffed shirt' of this expression.

'Who are you to judge her?'
'Keep your shirt on,' Mark said. 'I didn't make any comments.'

Vera Caspary *Laura*

Keep your shirt on is invariably used as an imperative, and means 'don't lose your temper'. The reference may be to the angry man who strips to the waist in order to fight someone. To **lose one's shirt** in the 19th century meant 'to become angry', but this seems to have been replaced in modern slang by **lose one's rag**. The 'shirt' reference is retained in the phrase **get shirty with someone**, which again means to 'become angry'.

'Listen – put your shirt, undershirt, cuff-links and sleepy-suit on Larksong. She can not *lose.'*

Roger Longrigg *Daughters of Mulberry*

To **lose one's shirt** in modern times means to 'lose all one's money' because one has **put one's shirt** on a horse. The latter phrase means 'bet everything one has, including the shirt off one's back'. John Le Carré, in *The Honourable Schoolboy*, has: 'Number seven in the third, you can't go wrong. Put your shirt on it, okay?' It is sometimes said of a person who is generous to the point of foolishness that he would **give someone the shirt off his back**.

■ SURE THINGS

'I'd bet my bottom dollar that whoever did that job takes his Sunday off like the rest of us.'

Vera Caspary *Laura*

To say that one is willing to **bet one's bottom dollar on something** is to imply that one is absolutely certain about it. The 'bottom' dollar is at the bottom of a stack, and is the only one remaining to the gambler. The phrase is used in Britain as well as America. In *Lucky Jim*, by Kingsley Amis, a discussion about a painting of a nude includes the line: 'She's female all right, you can bet your bottom dollar on that. And "bottom" is the exact word.' Some speakers would say instead 'you can **bet your boots** (or **your life) on that**'.

Other ways of expressing certainty include saying that something will happen **as sure as eggs is eggs**. The syntax of the phrase supports the view that this is a humorous or misunderstood use of a mathematician's statement 'as sure as X is X'. The phrase was familiar to Sam Weller, who sings a song which includes it in Dickens's *The Pickwick Papers*.

It's a cinch 'it's certain' is from cowboy talk. The 'cinch' is a multiple-stranded girth, fastened by latigos (long straps), used to secure a pack or saddle. American speakers sometimes intensify this phrase by saying that something is a **lead-pipe cinch**, thought to be a reference to the ease with which a lead pipe can be bent.

■ SWEAT-BAND

In the sweat of your face you shall eat bread till you return to the ground.

Old Testament, Genesis 3.19

No sweat has become a fashionable alternative in modern times for 'no problem, nothing to worry about'. Someone who nevertheless thinks he does have something to worry about because of the situation in which he finds himself may be told by unhelpful friends that he will just have to **sweat it out**.

These phrases refer to the sweat induced by anxiety. Sweat produced by physical exertion is healthier, and there is a certain pride in being able to say that one's living is earned **by the sweat of one's brow**. An alternative in former times was **by the sweat of one's face**. Both phrases are based on God's words to Adam as he expelled him from Eden after the Fall. In modern terminology Adam might have been told that he must **sweat blood** 'work to the utmost'.

Peter Draper, in *A Season in Love*, suggests a feminine version of 'by the sweat of one's brow'. One of his characters is made to remark: 'She's going to get there by the sweat of her bra.'

■ TABLE TALK

No girl had ever taken a man away from her. If any taking was done, she had done it. Who could it be who was turning the tables on her?

Jetta Carleton *The Moonflower Vine*

When **the tables are turned**, the situation that existed previously, whereby one person was in a superior position to another, has been reversed. The person who was in the stronger position is now in the weaker. Someone who brings about this change by his own efforts is said to **turn the tables** on the other person. Elizabeth Jane Howard, in *Getting it Right*, has: '"Who's asking questions now?" Mr Lamb was enjoying the turned tables.'

The fact that this expression, in use since the 17th century, has always referred to 'tables' in the plural suggests that 'table' is used in its special sense of one half of a folding games board, as in back-gammon. The metaphor is certainly meant to suggest a competitive board-game which has reached a point where one of the players has an advantage. The board is then reversed so that each player continues with what was his opponent's game.

The phrase is sometimes used to refer simply to a changed situation but not to superiority or otherwise. Thomas Hughes writes in *Tom Brown's Schooldays*: 'It was no light act of courage in those days, my dear boys, for a little fellow to say his prayers publicly, even at Rugby. A few years later, when Arnold's manly piety had begun to leaven the school, the tables turned.'

■ TAKING TO THE BOATS

If you didn't get to go with a girl whenyou were sixteen or seventeen, you sort of missed the boat and unless you got engaged and married that was it.

Ruth Rendell *Talking to Strange Men*

The naval expression to **miss the boat** means 'to be late for an appointment ashore' and refers specifically to the boat ferrying liberty men from the ship. We now tend to use the phrase in a more general way to mean 'fail to respond to an opportunity'. The image in our minds is of missing the boat that would take us back to the ship, with the result that it sails without us.

Another naval phrase is **push the boat out**. In the wardroom, this means to be 'in the chair' and buy a round of drinks. A television advertisement (1992) which says 'At Sainsbury's prices, you can afford to push the boat out' certainly does not mean that. 'Pushing the boat out' has come to mean 'celebrate without worrying about the expense', extending the original idea. Wilfred Granville includes the saying in his *Dictionary of Sailors' Slang*, but offers no explanation of the metaphor. The original meaning seems to suggest doing something for others, as when one pushes a boat away from a quay for the benefit of those on board.

'The admission only puts you in the same boat as everyone else.'

John Wain *A Travelling Woman*

There is no evidence that **to be in the same boat** 'be in the same situation, often an unpleasant one' was ever a nautical term. Anthony Trollope, in *Doctor Thorne*, seems to have a lifeboat in mind when he makes a character say: 'We are in the same boat, and you shan't turn me overboard.' That is probably the image that most of us have as we use the expression. 'We are all in the same boat, old and young,' says someone in E.M. Forster's *Howards End*. The phrase has been in general use since the middle of the 19th century.

'My father comes a-lookin' over him, and complicates the whole concern by puttin' his oar in.'

Charles Dickens *The Pickwick Papers*

We no longer speak of a meddling person as having **an oar in another's** (or **every**) **boat**, but we refer to this saying when we ask someone why he feels the need to **put/shove/stick in his oar**. He is interrupting a private conversation or meddling with something that doesn't concern him. There is usually someone in every office who 'has to stick his oar in', as his colleagues will complain. Robertson Davies, in *The Lyre of Orpheus*, describes a meeting where someone says 'I withdraw.' One of his colleagues replies: 'You mean you withdraw till next time you feel like sticking your oar in.'

He felt a lurching desire to rock the boat of their conventions by some untoward and scandalous revelation.

Mary McCarthy *The Groves of Academe*

Someone who **rocks the boat** is one who **makes waves**, as we also say. He disturbs a situation which is satisfying as it is. Bernard Malamud writes, in *Pictures of Fidelman*: 'Intimately eating together excited Fidelman, and he sat very still, not to rock the boat and spill a drop of what was so precious to him.' The phrase became fashionable around 1950, helped along by a lively song in Frank Loesser's musical *Guys and Dolls*. Malcolm Bradbury quotes it in *Eating People is Wrong*: 'What you're trying to say is, "Sit down. You're rocking the boat."'

'To make waves' would seem to be derived from 'rocking the boat'. Robert L. Chapman, in his *Dictionary* of *American Slang*, says instead that it is from 'the joke in which a person just arrived in hell, and hearing beautiful, serene singing, finds that it is being done by inmates standing in chin-high excrement and cautiously chanting "Don't make waves."'

■ TALK OF THE TOWN

Other passengers sent me to Coventry.

Alistair Maclean *The Dark Crusader*

Sending someone to Coventry is usually a punishment inflicted on someone who has broken the unwritten rules of a group of people. In *Abbie*, by Dane Chandos, the formidable heroine says of her husband: 'I put him in Coventry at once and refused to say or listen to anything he said unless it were in Double Dutch.' It is unusual to 'put' someone in Coventry, and only Aunt Abbie would have such a reason for putting someone there.

'Sending someone to Coventry' means suspending all normal social contacts with the person concerned, treating him as if he did not exist. The significance of 'Coventry' in this expression as opposed to any other city has long been debated, and no conclusive explanation can be given. Most often quoted is *The True Historical Narrative of the Rebellion and Civil Wars in England*, by Edward Hyde, Earl of Clarendon. This was first printed 1702–4, nearly 30 years after the earl's death.

Clarendon says that the citizens of Birmingham, being especially wicked, had taken to attacking small parties of the king's men. These they either killed or took prisoner and sent to Coventry. Coventry, at that time, was a Parliamentary stronghold where

such prisoners would have been well guarded. There is also a legend that soldiers generally were not liked by Coventry's citizens, who refused to have normal social relations with them. Royalist soldiers who were there as prisoners would presumably have had an especially bad time of it.

Coventry's other main claim to fame from a linguistic point of view derives from the Lady Godiva story of the 11th century. The tailor who peeked at Godiva as she rode naked through the city, protesting against increased taxes, was the original **peeping Tom**.

■ THREADING ONE'S WAY

'Mantovelli's life is hanging by a thread. He'll be lucky if he lasts a month.

John Welcome *Stop at Nothing*

The person mentioned in the above quotation, whose life is **hanging by a thread**, does not long survive. On the next page we are told that he is dead: 'The thread has snapped at last.' This is not the point of the original story, as told by Cicero. Damocles, who lived in the 4th century BC, was a courtier of Dionysius. When Damocles told his master how fortunate he was to enjoy such wealth and power, Dionysius invited him to a banquet so that he could see for himself what that luxury meant.

At the feast Damocles looked up and saw a sword hanging over his head, suspended by a single horse-hair. Needless to say, he was unable to relax and enjoy the occasion and began to understand the precarious nature of such happiness. From the story also comes the phrase **sword of Damocles**, which refers – as does 'hanging by a thread' – to imminent danger.

'That's what I started to say,' Kay went on, remembering. 'I lost the thread for a minute.'

Mary McCarthy *The Group*

It is tempting to connect the phrase **lose the thread** with another ancient story. According to the Greek myths, Theseus found his way to the centre of the labyrinth in Crete by means of a magic ball of thread. After killing the Minotaur, he found his way out again by winding up the thread. From this, one could imagine 'thread' being used metaphorically for something that runs through a complex argument and has to be followed to take one from the beginning to the end. It is certainly something like that which is in our minds when we talk of 'losing the thread' of what we are saying. In *Rabbit Redux*, by John Updike, the hero is watching a skit on television when his son interrupts him. We are told: 'Rabbit loses the thread of the skit a little, there has been a joke he didn't hear.'

■ TIN POTS AND PANS

'I've been brought up to think you a little tin god.'

Margaret Forster *Georgy Girl*

'Tin' is thought of as a cheap and flashy substitute for more valuable metals. **Little tin gods** are people we are perhaps obliged to respect though they do not merit it in themselves. Rudyard Kipling used the phrase in his poem *Public Waste* to refer to British government officials in India. Such people might also be described contemptuously as **tinpot** officials, again alluding to their inferiority and pettiness. In American slang, **tinhorns** could be used with roughly the same

meaning. The reference in this case was originally to petty but flashy gamblers who used a horn-shaped container made of tin to shake the dice.

'Fancy? Is that your real name?'
'Sure. My father had an unorthodox and poetic soul . . .'
'Your father had a tin ear.'
Robert Krepps *Fancy*

Another American slang term refers to having a **tin ear** 'having a poor judgement of musical quality'. The phrase suggests that such a person would not be able to distinguish between a finely-tuned instrument and the tinny sound of a poorly-tuned piano. Such sounds gave rise at the end of the 19th century to the nickname **Tin Pan Alley** for the area on Seventh Avenue, just off Broadway, where composers and publishers of popular music were gathered. The name was later transferred from New York and used of the Denmark Street area of London for similar reasons.

'Why did you do that? To show off? Oh, that puts the tin lid on it!'
Nina Bawden *George Beneath a Paper Moon*

When we come to **put the tin lid on something** (or **put the lid on something**) we see that deciding on the precise meaning of colloquial phrases can cause severe problems at times for the people who compile English dictionaries. According to *The Concise Oxford Dictionary* (1990) these are two forms of the same phrase, which means either 'be the culmination of' or 'put a stop to'. *The Oxford Advanced Learner's Dictionary* (1989) says that the reference in either phrase is to 'the final event that provokes an outburst', which sounds very like 'the last straw'.

Collins Cobuild English Language Dictionary (1987) explains: 'If you say that someone has put the lid on an activity or a piece of information, you mean that they are preventing or restricting the activity or are not allowing the information to become known by other people.' No comment is made about the 'tin lid' version. *Chambers English Dictionary* (1988) has 'put the lid on it – to end the matter: to be a culminating injustice, misfortune, etc.' Elsewhere, it has 'put the tin hat, lid, on – to finish off, bring to an end, suppress'. The Longman *Dictionary of the English Language* (1984) says that 'put the (tin) lid on' is 'to ruin, put paid to'.

'To put the lid on' can certainly mean 'to conceal or suppress'. In this sense it contrasts with **take (blow) the lid off something** 'reveal something that was meant to be secret'. But used during an argument, the phrase 'That puts the lid on it' means something like 'After that last remark or action there is nothing more to be said.' It would normally be in this sense only that it would be possible to say 'That puts the tin lid on it' or 'That puts the tin hat on it.'

It is almost impossible to know in which order the various forms of the phrase came into being, on which metaphors they were based and when the different meanings arose. With some expressions which have not been long in use, individual speakers and writers form their own idea as to their meanings and use them accordingly. It is necessary to refer each time to the context in which a phrase is used to see what is meant.

'Put the lid on something' in the sense of concealing it, was probably an allusion originally to putting the lid on a jar in order to seal it. But 'lid' has long had the slang meaning of 'hat', and in military slang 'tin hat' was the usual term for a steel helmet.

It is easy to see how 'put the tin hat on something' emerged as a military version of 'put the lid on it'. 'Put the tin lid on something' could then be seen as a blend of the two. The interpretation of 'lid' as 'hat' could also have led to the change in meaning, wherby 'put the lid on' came to mean something like 'that caps it all'.

■ TO HELL WITH IT!

'Here have I been going hell-for-leather up and down the country.'

Mary Webb *Gone to Earth*

Hell for leather means 'as quickly as possible' and is applied in the above quotation to riding on horseback, as are all early instances of the expression. Ernest Weekley, not one to put forward frivolous suggestions, wondered whether the phrase was a corruption of 'all of a lather'. A present-day speaker would probably say that he rode **like hell** 'very quickly', though this can mean 'very much, extremely' in a sentence like 'It hurts like hell.'

Libby was going to make her way, come hell or high water.

Mary McCarthy *The Group*

Come hell or high water 'no matter what the difficulties' has been claimed as an American cowboy expression, referring to the 'hell' of driving herds of cattle across open country and the 'high water' that had to be forded at each river. 'High water' does seem to suggest a hazard, though **high-water mark**, literally the mark left by a high tide, is used figuratively of 'excellence'.

'There's going to be hell to pay at home.'

Upton Sinclair *World's End*

The dictionaries gloss **all hell to pay** as 'severe punishment to be faced'. There is a hint that **all hell will break loose**, that there will be 'great noise and confusion'. The latter phrase has been in use since the 17th century. In *Paradise Lost* Milton asks:

> But wherefore thou alone?
> Wherefore with thee
> Came not all hell broke loose?

A lifetime of happiness: no man alive could bear it: it would be hell on earth.

George Bernard Shaw *Man and Superman*

A number of miscellaneous phrases mention 'hell'. **Hell on earth** seems to have been Shaw's invention at the turn of the century. It is applied to very unpleasant situations. We say that someone **hasn't a hope in hell** of achieving something, if we think he has no hope at all. This is sometimes expanded to **hasn't a cat in hell's chance**. The 'cat' reference is bizarre, unless there is a connection with the more logical American expression **hasn't a snowball's chance in hell** (Snowball being fairly common as a name for a cat). The shortened form of 'snowball's chance in hell' occurs in *The River* by Steven Bauer: 'We're in for it bad, I think. We don't have a snowball's chance.'

'If you expect things to be fair, you'll be waiting until hell freezes over.'

Margaret Laurence *The Diviners*

Until/Till hell freezes over replaces the dull 'forever'. In statements like **go to**

hell, 'hell' is synonymous with 'the devil'. The exclamatory **Hell's bells!** intensifies 'Hell!' by means of the rhyme, but the 'bells' have no other significance. Perhaps the most curious 'hell' expression, given all the gloom and doom that attaches itself to the word, is to do something **for the hell of it** 'do it purely for fun'.

■ TO THE LETTER

'The corvette is carrying their President, so you'll have to mind your p's and q's. We're expected to be diplomats on occasion, you know, eh?'

Edward Hyams *Sylvester*

A number of English phrases refer to individual letters. To **mind one's p's and q's** 'to be careful not to speak or act impolitely, not be socially inept' is a typical example. It often occurs as an imperative piece of advice, but can be used in other ways. 'Minding Hen's p's and q's is not my idea of a picnic' is said by a character in Mary McCarthy's *The Groves of Academe*. J.I.M. Stewart, in *The Last Tresilians*, has: 'Burntisland realized that he had spoken words angrily and aloud. It was something he had once or twice noticed himself doing of late. I'll gain a reputation, he thought, for eccentricity if I don't mind my Ps and Qs.'

An earlier saying was **learn one's p's and q's**. It referred to the difficulty young children sometimes have when learning to write. They are likely to confuse the letters p and q, just as they do b and d. There is little doubt that the idea of 'minding one's p's and q's', in the sense of being very careful about what one was doing, was transferred from learning to write to general social behaviour.

Amateur etymologists are always

reluctant to accept a simple explanation, and ingenious alternatives have been proposed. One fanciful explanation involves the keeping of a tally in an ale-house. A landlord who was told to mind his p's and q's was being told, or so runs the tale, not to chalk up q for 'quart' instead of p for 'pint'. The story is nonsensical, but many will swear to its truth. An even more far-fetched story concerns French dancing-masters, who supposedly told pupils at one time to mind their *pieds* 'feet' and *queues* 'pigtails'.

'Remember our little talk here has been strictly on the Q.T.'

James Purdy *Eustace Chisholm and the Works*

Bernard Wolfe, in *The Late-Risers*, has: 'Aly Khan, supposed to be potchkying around in Paris broken-hearted on account of the Princess Margherita walking out on him, was really in this country on the q.t.' **On the q.t.** means 'on the quiet, in secrecy'. The q.t. obviously derives from the word 'quiet', but it is impossible to say why this curious abbreviation came into general use at the end of the 19th century. 'Strictly' is often associated with the phrase, which Arnold Bennett uses in a slightly different way in *Clayhanger*: 'This is strictly q.t.! Nobody knows a word about it, nobody! But of course I thought I'd better tell you. You'll say nothing.'

'The doctor tells us they don't know but what the side effects may be worse. You know: the big C. My figuring is, take the chance, they're just about ready to lick cancer anyway.'

John Updike *Rabbit Redux*

Many other phrases contain letters that are simply the initial letters of the words concerned. In Britain an **L driver** is a 'learner' who is obliged to display 'L plates' on his vehicle. To **get the big E** is to 'get the elbow, be dismissed from one's job'. In the USA **the big H** is 'heroin', while **the big C** is a euphemism for 'cancer'. Another American euphemism refers to a **T and A show**, characterized by a generous display of women's bosoms and backsides. The words being avoided are 'tits' and 'asses'. In British slang there was a similar avoidance of the second word when the **DA haircut** became fashionable after World War Two. The hair was cut to resemble a duck's tail (arse).

Sweet FA is sometimes used by British speakers to mean 'nothing at all'. Some would expand it to **sweet Fanny Adams**, but they would still avoid using the expression in polite society. The 'FA' or 'Fanny Adams' is considered to be a euphemism for 'fuck all'.

That may be so, but Fanny Adams was earlier Royal Navy slang for stew or hash. The name is said, on the authority of *The Oxford English Dictionary*, to be that of a young lady who was murdered in the 19th century. Wilfred Granville, in a *Dictionary of Sailors' Slang*, says her body was cut to pieces and disposed of in a copper, hence the use of her name for a stew containing pieces of meat. The Merchant Navy is said to use 'Harriet Lane', the name of a girl who was murdered and disposed of in similar style, instead of 'Fanny Adams'.

'All these old-fashioned goings on would suit you to a T.'

Harriet Beecher Stowe *Dred*

'That's him to a "T",' she cried – 'like a navvy!' says a character in *Sons and Lovers*, by D.H. Lawrence. **To a t** 'to a nicety, exactly' was earlier **to a tittle**, and is therefore another simple abbreviation. (For 'tittle' see page 133.) *Brewer's Dictionary of Phrase and Fable* wrongly relates the saying to the use of a T-square.

U and **non-U** were much heard in the late 1950s, after an article by Professor A.S.C. Ross on 'Linguistic class-indicators in present-day English' had been taken up by Nancy Mitford. 'U' stood for 'upper-class', especially in relation to speech-habits. Professor Ross pointed out that only non-U speakers used certain words, such as 'cutlery' for 'knives and forks', 'toilet' for 'lavatory' or 'loo'. Countless ordinary people temporarily became worried about the words they were using.

The three Rs, meaning 'reading, writing and arithmetic' or more generally 'a fundamental education', is clearly not a simple use of initial letters. The phrase was a joke used by Sir W. Curtis (1752–1829) which quickly caught on. It manages to suggest how those who have not had the benefits of an education might mispronounce and misspell the words concerned.

Letter-phrases that do not include abbreviations include to **dot the i's and cross the t's** 'complete the final details of a contract, the main points having been agreed'. The allusion is an obvious one. The word-order is not important and the phrase is sometimes seen or heard as 'cross the t's and dot the i's'.

'I would enjoy it in a case-history, you understand? But I flatly refuse to become personally involved. Once agree to be Mr X today and tomorrow you become X marks the spot.

Nigel Dennis *Cards of Identity*

To get **from A to B** is to 'get from one place to another', the letters having no particular significance other than their sequential order. In some phrases there is a reference to the conventional use of a letter. An **X-rated film**, for instance, is one which formerly in Britain and still in the USA would be classified with an 'X' to indicate that it was considered unsuitable for viewers under 18 years of age. Amongst its other uses, X designates an unknown person or thing, indicates a mistake or a position (**X marks the spot**), and symbolizes a kiss or a vote.

An X film, in colloquial American English, might be said to rate only a **gentleman's C**, to be 'no more than satisfactory'. The reference is to the grade traditionally given by colleges to well-bred but lethargic students.

■ TOOTH WISDOM

Coffee was served and Lena took three lumps of sugar in hers.
'You have a very sweet tooth,' said Arrow.

W. Somerset Maugham *Three Fat Women of Antibes*

References to a **sweet tooth** 'a liking for sweet and sugary things' occur in the early 17th century, when 'tooth' was still often used for 'eating', and more specifically for the sense of taste. Such usage had been common for centuries: when Chaucer talked of keeping something 'for your own tooth', he meant keeping it to eat yourself. To 'love the tooth' once meant to be fond of eating good food.

'Sweet tooth' was presumably known to Shakespeare, but the nearest he comes to using the expression is in *The Two Gentlemen of Verona*. When

Launce is discussing his sweetheart he lists amongst her vices the fact that she has a **sweet mouth**. The change of wording may have been deliberate, since we are told soon afterwards that the girl concerned has no teeth. 'Sweet tooth' remains in common use.

They shall no longer say: 'The fathers have eaten sour grapes, and the children's teeth are set on edge.' But every one shall die for his own sin; each man who eats sour grapes, his teeth shall be set on edge.

Old Testament, Jeremiah 31.29

The relationship between taste and teeth is seen again in **set one's teeth on edge**, said of something that causes an unpleasant sensation. The phrase is a literal translation from the Hebrew in the passage from Jeremiah quoted above. Originally it was applied only to a bad taste, but by Shakespeare's time it could be used, as it often is in modern times, of a rasping noise. In *King Henry the Fourth*, Part One Glendower mentions two such sounds (the first a brass candlestick being turned on a table):

> *I had rather hear a brazen*
> *   canstick turn'd,*
> *Or a dry wheel grate on the axle-*
> *   tree;*
> *And that would set my teeth*
> *   nothing on edge,*
> *Nothing so much as mincing*
> *   poetry.*

Until that time his greatest battle, fought tooth and nail and lost without glory, was against baldness.

Gabriel Garcia Marquez *Love in the Time of Cholera*

The earlier form of **fight tooth and nail** was 'fight with tooth and nail',

but even in the 16th century the phrase was mostly used figuratively. The phrase is often used with reference to defensive action and the allusion is obvious: someone who is prepared to continue fighting even to the point where he is reduced to biting and scratching is someone who fights 'with all his might, doing everything he possibly can to avoid defeat'.

'Maybe we finally got our teeth in something.'

Bernard Wolfe *The Late-Risers*

Getting one's teeth into something is becoming fully involved in it and giving it all one's concentration, as one normally does with whatever one is eating. A similar metaphor gives rise to the idea of **biting off more than one can chew** 'attempting to do something that is beyond one's capabilities'.

'It may be that he has settled down this year and gotten the bit between his teeth.'

Mary McCarthy *The Groves of Academe*

The 'bit' that is part of a horse's bridle is also connected with 'biting'. It is a mouthpiece that a horse bites on as well as something that bites into a horse's mouth. The phrase **take the bit between one's teeth** originally meant to become unmanageable, since a horse which did this prevented the bit from hurting its mouth and was able to ignore it. It could go wherever it felt like going, at its own unchecked speed. The modern meaning of the phrase interprets the idea of this free running as enthusiasm for what one is doing. A person who 'has the bit between his teeth' is doing something with great energy and determination.

There is still a suggestion of lack of control, since it would be difficult for others to stop him.

Scarlet gritted her teeth . . .

Fay Weldon *Down Among the Women*

To **grit one's teeth** is to keep one's jaws tight together so that the teeth are literally grating against one another. It is something one tends to do quite naturally when in a determined mood. Since the 19th century the phrase in this form has been used figuratively to refer to summoning up one's courage and facing one's difficulties. Typical modern usage would be: 'The recession will be with us for quite a while yet. We'll just have to grit our teeth and see it through.'

The earlier form of this expression was to **set one's teeth**. An example occurs in the famous 'Once more unto the breach, dear friends' speech in *King Henry the Fifth*. Henry says:

> Now set the teeth and stretch the
>   nostril wide;
> Hold hard the breath, and bend up
>   every spirit
> To his full height.

'From his last remark, lying in his teeth to the end, I gather he's biding no more.'

Alistair Maclean *The Dark Crusader*

Someone who tells outrageous lies is said to **lie in** (or **through**) **his teeth**. The 'teeth' have no special significance here, other than being connected with speech. Other phrases which use **in the teeth of** generally refer to the idea of facing opponents at close range. To do something 'in the teeth of' fierce criticism is to do it in spite of the opposition. To be 'in the teeth of' a strong wind is to be advancing directly into it.

'It's the first year the club has been open,' went on Mr Tuckerson. 'And we're having a lot of teething troubles.'

B.S. Johnson *Travelling People*

The problems experienced by young babies as their teeth begin to grow are alluded to in **teething troubles**. Metaphorically, these are problems that arise in the early stages of an enterprise. The phrase also conveys the idea that such problems are to be expected, and that they will soon be sorted out.

■ TREE TOPS

In those days we thought an Indian judgeship about equal to a county-court judgeship at home. His Honour – a pretty title, but still, not the top of the tree.

Virginia Woolf *Night and Day*

To be **at the top of one's tree** is a very different thing from being **up a tree**. The former expression simply means to be at the top of one's profession. 'But you *are* one of the survivors, Delver. Right up at the top of your tree,' says a character in J.I.M. Stewart's *The Last Tresilians*. To be 'up a tree' is mainly an American term which means to be 'cornered, at someone else's mercy', like a raccoon which has taken refuge in a tree when being chased by dogs.

Opossums in similar circumstances are likely to climb a gum tree. To be **up a gum tree** therefore had a similar meaning at first to 'up a tree'. The reference to 'gum', however, seems to have suggested stickiness and changed the meaning to being 'stuck, unable to continue because ideas are lacking'.

'We need chaps like you. All-rounders. There are too many specialists. Can't see the wood for the trees.'

Derek Jewell *Come In No.1 Your Time Is Up*

Not to see the wood for the trees has been proverbial since at least the 16th century. The expression is ambiguous, but 'wood' has its meaning of 'a collection of trees, a small forest', not the 'substance which composes a tree'. The phrase remains in use because it can still usefully be applied to those who become so involved with details that they lose their view of the totality. *Other Men's Wives*, by Alexander Fullerton, has: 'A bit of flattery about her acumen, and if you let her spot the trees she won't see the woods closing in around her.'

There was another 'wood' expression in the 17th century: people spoke of being **in a wood** if they were in a difficulty. The idiom would now only be used negatively. 'We are not yet **out of the wood(s)**' implies that we are still 'in the wood' and means that 'we still have problems'.

The phrase **money doesn't grow on trees**, in use since the 19th century, is also meant to have implications. Children are meant to understand by it that parental resources are not infinite, that money has to be earned, that demands for pocket-money have been excessive recently. They probably understand quite quickly that they are going to have to listen to a lecture before they get a hand-out.

It can be said that other things, or even people, 'do not grow on trees'. In *Come In No.1 Your Time Is Up*, by Derek Jewell, the reference is to businessmen when someone says: 'Good men don't grow on trees.'

Ian Fleming, in *Diamonds are Forever*, has Tiffany Case say to James Bond: 'Can't you tell me something nice about my dress or something instead of grumbling the whole time about how expensive I am? You know what they say. "If you don't like my peaches, why do you shake my tree?"' Bond replies: 'I haven't started to shake it yet. You won't let me get my arms round the trunk.' The saying referred to, of obvious meaning, is not in general use.

■ TUNING UP

'What a daft thing to do, to get a girl into trouble. He'll just have to face the music, like our Dave did.'

Alan Sillitoe *Saturday Night and Sunday Morning*

Metaphorical allusions to music are not as frequent in English as one might expect, but some expressions are well used. **Face the music** is one, most of the meaning being contained in the verb 'face'. Someone who 'faces the music' **faces up to** the consequences of his actions, accepts responsibility for them and stands ready to take his punishment. 'I am willing to face the music. It was my fault,' says a character in *Sylvester*, by Edward Hyams. R.F. Delderfield, *Theirs Was the Kingdom*, has: 'Stay put man, and face the music. You're in this as deep as me.'

It has been suggested that the phrase alludes to a performer going on stage to face the pit orchestra and the audience. This theory has little to commend it; nor has the notion that it refers to a soldier responding to a bugle call, facing up to whatever it involves. Soldiers obeying such a call have not committed an offence for which they must now accept punishment.

The probability is that 'music' in this expression is used ironically, or means the kind of 'uproar' that is produced by 'rough music'. The latter was traditionally made by banging pots and pans and generally making a din in order to annoy somebody. The person whose offence has been discovered is probably going to be subjected to loud and angry condemnation, someone is going to make a **song and dance** 'a lot of fuss' about it and that is the kind of 'music' that must be faced.

'Face the music' has been in regular use since the mid-19th century. A more recent expression, used when someone hears something that greatly pleases him, is 'that's **music to my ears**'.

'Even some of my dear brother directors have changed their tune, and the union bosses are quite enthusiastic now.'

Angus Wilson *Anglo-Saxon Attitudes*

To **change one's tune** 'change one's opinion or attitude to a noticeable extent' dates from the 16th century. The phrase alludes to a **change of mind** or a **change of heart** which is quickly apparent to others. **To the tune of** 'to the amount of' is another old phrase, found in the 18th century (in Daniel Defoe's *Colonel Jack*) as **at the tune of**. The reference here may be to the sound of chinking coins.

'I suppose the man who pays the piper calls the tune.'

Alistair Maclean's *The Dark Crusader.*

The proverb **he who pays the piper may call the tune** is found in the 17th century. Its familiarity is such that many speakers would not bother to complete it, contenting themselves

with 'who pays the piper'. It serves as a reminder that whoever is providing the money for a project, has the right to decide how it is spent.

'You buy the paintings at a song, practically,' Connie said.

Bernard Wolfe *The Late-Risers*

Something bought or sold **for a song** is disposed of at a very low price. (**At a song**, in the above quotation, is unusual.) Shakespeare's *All's Well that Ends Well* has the Clown say of Bertram: 'Why, he will look upon his boot and sing; mend the ruff and sing; ask questions and sing; pick his teeth and sing. I know a man that had this trick of melancholy sold a goodly manor for a song.' In George Douglas's *The House with the Green Shutters*, a builder says to his client: 'There's not a thing in your house that a man in your position can afford to be without, and ye needn't expect the best house in Barbie for an old song!'

At Angmering, Sussex, there is a house called 'Arches' which was 'bought for a song', as its owner Bud Flanagan liked to say. He and his partner Chesney Allen made a small fortune from their song 'Underneath the Arches'.

■ UNBEARABLE BEHAVIOUR

'Who said I was angry?'
'Come off it. You've been like a bear with a sore head all day.'

Jeremy Brooks *Henry's War*

The phrase **like a bear with a sore head** 'irritable, peevish' has been used since at least the beginning of the 19th century. 'Lisa says I go around like a bear with a sore head' is a typical occurrence, in Stephen Vincent Benét's *Everybody was Very Nice*. It is not known who first used the simile, nor do we know whether it was originally used humorously as it is today.

'It's a mad, crazy world we live in,' he observed to him. Jenkins nodded sagely. 'It's a bear-garden,' he said.

Malcolm Bradbury *Eating People is Wrong*

Bears with sore heads would certainly have been found in bear gardens, where bear-baiting took place between the 14th and 17th centuries. In this so-called sport, a bear was chained to a stake and dogs set on it. The kind of spectator who enjoyed such entertainment can be imagined, and bear gardens became notorious for the riotous behaviour that occurred there. Figuratively, to turn a place into a **bear garden** was to act as people did in such places.

Thomas Hardy, in *Fellow-Townsmen*, writes: 'Her mouth and brow showed only too clearly that the turbulency of character which had made a bear garden of his house had been no temporary phase of her existence.' In *The Masters*, a novel set in a Cambridge college, C.P. Snow has: '"Winslow gave a lamentable exhibition last night. He makes the place a perfect bear garden." It seemed to me a curious description of the combination room.' A better known quotation is Lord Macaulay's remark, in his *History of England*, that: 'The Puritan hated bear-baiting, not because it gave pain to the bear, but because it gave pleasure to the spectators.'

■ UNIFORMITY

'Are you a man of the cloth?'
'Which cloth?'
'The table cloth?' chuckled Mex.
'The loincloth,' muttered Hook.

Michael Rumaker *The Desert*

A man or woman **of the cloth** is a Christian minister or priest, the phrase normally being restricted to formal or literary use. Mordecai Richler, in *The Incomparable Atuk*, has a priest say: 'I'm a man of the cloth myself, hardly a thespian,' which may reflect the manner in which some priests refer to themselves in conversation.

The phrase came into use in the 16th century, when 'to wear someone's cloth' meant to wear a uniform which indicated that one was in the service of that person. It seems to have been Bishop Hall, at the beginning of the 17th century, who pointed out that the distinctive clothing worn by clergymen showed that they were God's servants. 'Of the cloth' then, in its modern sense, really means 'of God's cloth'.

'Of the cloth', however, was by no means restricted to clergymen in former times. It could be applied to any profession which was marked by the wearing of special clothes. Even in the 19th century it was still possible for a writer to refer to a naval officer as 'a man of our cloth', meaning 'a man who wears the same uniform as we do ourselves'. Such usage has died away other than for clergymen.

'We must use our cunning and cut our capers according to our cloth.'

Ngaio Marsh *Surfeit of Lampreys*

In the above quotation Ngaio Marsh

adapts the proverbial **cut one's coat according to one's cloth**. The words might still be applied as a warning to those who appear to be living beyond their means, especially if they are trying to maintain former standards in spite of a drastically reduced income. The message is that one must adapt oneself to circumstances, doing only what one can afford to do.

■ UNIMPORTANT PLEASURES

'Men in his position have to make a hundred decisions a day. I expect he looks on this as very small beer – and just puts it off until he's got important things finished.'

C.P. Snow *The Masters*

Small beer refers to weak beer, and figuratively to something or someone of little importance. 'Small', with this specialized meaning 'of low alcoholic strength', was formerly applied to wines and spirits as well as beer. It was also occasionally used to describe what we would now call 'soft' non-alcoholic drinks. Application of 'small beer' to a person occurs in Nina Bawden's *George Beneath a Paper Moon*: 'Any diplomat is fair game, but I'm very small beer. Not a valuable hostage!' Bernard Wolfe, *The Late-Risers*, has a reference to 'small-beer anecdotes'.

Beer and skittles are referred to metaphorically in British English to mean 'pleasure', in what is usually a negative reminder that 'life is not all beer and skittles'. Skittles, a form of ninepins, was once frequently played outside public houses. Charles Dickens probably suggested the phrase, though Sam Weller in *The Pickwick Papers* refers specifically to 'porter and skittles', porter being the 'stout' beer favoured by market

porters. When Mr Pickwick decides to go to the Fleet prison rather than pay damages to Mrs Bardell for breach of promise, he notices that some of the prisoners appear to be enjoying themselves. Sam says: *'They don't mind it; it's a reg'lar holiday to them – all porter and skittles. It's the t'other vuns as gets done over vith this sort o' thing; them down-hearted fellers as can't svig away at the beer, nor play at skittles neither; them as would pay if they could, and gets low by being boxed up. I'll tell you wot it is, sir; them as is always a-idlin' in the public-houses it don't damage at all, and them as is alvays a-workin' wen they can, it damages too much.'*

In *Abbie*, by Dane Chandos, 'beer and skittles' is applied unusually to a person. Aunt Abbie says that her personal maid 'is by no means all beer and skittles', not always easy to deal with or wholly pleasant.

■ VERBAL SKETCHES

Everything's all right, everything's fine, keep it that way. On an even keel, as his grandfather would say.

Judith Guest *Ordinary People*

The keel of a ship runs lengthwise along its base, with the framework radiating from it. When a ship is **on an even keel** it is without sideways movement. Applied to a person, the phrase means to proceed through life in a steady, undisturbed way.

The phrase is made considerably more interesting in Judith Guest's *Ordinary People*, by being associated with the personal speech pattern of one man, the grandfather of the central character. The author comments early in the novel that it is easy to spot the clichés, as she calls them, that are used by other people.

There is little doubt that Miss Guest practises such phrase-spotting in real life.

The grandfather is established as having a number of favourite expressions. At one point he says: '**Let's get this show on the road**, folks!' The young central character is immediately reminded of a game he and his brother used to play – Grandfather Trivia. 'What does he say after a horseshoe ringer?' 'That's **one for the good guys**!' 'What time does he get up in the morning?' '**At the crack o' dawn!**' 'When will he eat liver?' '**When hell freezes over!**'

One might describe this as an idiolectal caricature, or verbal sketch. In this man's private language 'let's get started' is always 'let's get this show on the road'; 'early morning' is always 'at the crack of dawn', 'never' becomes the more emphatic 'when hell freezes over'. We all have such private languages, tending to make heavy use of certain favourite words and phrases which are probably as familiar to our friends as our faces.

■ WALKIE TALKIE

'And what would you judge to be his walk of life?'
'A scholar,' Alabaster pronounced.

J.I.M. Stewart *The Last Tresilians*

Walk of life has been used since the 18th century to describe both a person's social standing and his profession. 'Walk' is used for 'movement, activity', but in the occupational sense of the phrase there may at one time have been a specific allusion to a roundsman. The expression is used in formal speech and writing, as in Virginia Woolf's *Night and Day*: ' "A legal family?" Mrs Milvain inquired. Mr. Hilbery shook his head. "I should be inclined

to doubt whether they were altogether in that walk of life," he observed.'

French walk (or **Spanish walk**) is rather less formal. Both terms are American and describe what happens when someone is given the **bum's rush**. A person is grasped by the back of his collar and the seat of his trousers and propelled (rushed) towards the door. The 'bum' in 'bum's rush', incidentally, refers to a tramp, not to the buttocks. Nor is a 'French walk' what is called in Britain a **frog march**, even though **Frog** is a common nickname for a Frenchman (based on the assumption that Frenchmen are constantly eating frogs' legs). A 'frog march' originally meant that someone, such as an unruly prisoner, was carried face downwards, held by the arms and legs. The phrase is now often applied to other methods of forcing someone to walk in a particular direction, such as twisting his arm behind his back and urging him forwards.

■ WEATHER REPORT

Arthur told me that Abbie was 'a bit under the weather' . . . When she is 'under the weather' it means she has been thwarted.

Dane Chandos *Abbie*

There are probably many people for whom a phrase has a personal interpretation, as in the quotation above. **Under the weather** is a good example, since there so many different things can cause someone to feel rather ill and be depressed. The phrase is based on the belief that atmospheric conditions affect the way a person feels.

'We needn't make heavy weather of it. If the boy hates being there, or Nick is unpleasant to him, we'll move him back to the house.'

Iris Murdoch *The Bell*

There are not many other phrases which mention 'weather', which is surprising when one considers how the English love to discuss that subject. To **make heavy weather of something** is to make something more difficult than it really is. The phrase is probably of nautical origin, conjuring up an image of a ship ploughing through heavy seas. To **keep a weather eye open** 'be watchful and alert' is also a sea phrase. 'I naturally kept my weather eye agog for a suitable piece of wood,' says the heroine of Dane Chandos's *Abbie*.

We describe things which have long been exposed to the elements as **weather-beaten**. The Scandinavian languages all have a word which means **weather-bitten**, also found in 17th-century English. In *The Winter's Tale* Shakespeare describes 'the old shepherd, which stands by like a weather-bitten conduit of many kings' reigns'. The Shakespearean word has merged with 'weather-beaten', though it deserved to survive in its own right.

■ **WEIGHT WATCHING**

'The fact that you are my husband will carry immense weight.'

E.F. Benson *Trouble for Lucia*

The wife who makes the remark quoted above is the local mayoress, and it is probably the importance of that office that she thinks will **carry weight**. Not that E.F. Benson's Lucia is a modest person; she would think that she conferred great importance on her husband at any time, mayoress or not.

'Weight' has for centuries been used to mean 'importance', as in 'a person of some weight'. In primitive societies the only people who become physically bulky are rich enough both to eat well and pay others to labour on their behalf.

Someone over-impressed by his own importance may at times **throw his weight around** 'behave aggressively and arrogantly to those who are lower down in the same hierarchy'. The 'weight' in this case again refers metaphorically to the importance of the position a person holds, not to his physical weight. The latter is rarely mentioned in phrases, though an informal suggestion that someone should sit down might be expressed as 'Why don't you **take the weight off your feet**?'

She was worth her weight in gold, which Gavin had once considered must make her very valuable indeed.

Elizabeth Jane Howard *Getting it Right*

To be **worth one's weight in gold** is simple hyperbole in western societies. The phrase obviously refers to the traditional ceremony in some eastern countries in which a potentate is literally weighed against a weight of gold or precious stones. This is a public demonstration both of his personal wealth and his symbolic value to his people.

They paid for their board; they shared the work of the house with her – in fact, they did more than their share. So why complain? They're pulling their weight.

Margaret Laurence *The Diviners*

To **pull one's weight** 'do one's fair share of the work' is a relatively modern expression, based on a rowing metaphor. Each member of a rowing team is required to 'pull his weight'. The origin of the phrase appears to have been in Eric Linklater's mind when he made a character in *Poet's Pub* say: 'A man with a good athletic record, any man with a Rowing Blue, can do well in this house if he cares to pull his weight.'

■ WHAT A DISH!

'He's awfully hard to talk to,' she remarked. 'And not your cup of tea at all.'

Mary McCarthy *The Group*

The Englishman's fondness for a **cup of tea**, or **cuppa** as it sometimes becomes jokingly, is well attested. Metaphorical use of the phrase to mean in more general terms 'something one is partial to' began in the 1920s. It is still often used in that sense. 'Rosie Whittaker wasn't his cup of tea' occurs in Ruth Rendell's *Talking to Strange Men*. Frederick Forsyth, in *The Day of the Jackal*, has: 'A political killer is an extremely rare bird. It's not quite the English cup of tea, is it?'

Americans probably consider the phrase to be the archetypal Briticism. They also seem to imagine that **dish of tea** is still used in England, as it was in the 18th century when Addison was writing his *Spectator* essays. He and his contemporaries often drank a dish of tea, coffee or chocolate, but 'dish of tea' would only be used in modern Britain by a literary *poseur*. American writers sometimes use the phrase as a synonym of 'cup of tea', as when Bernard Wolfe, in *The Late-Risers*,

writes: 'It wouldn't be exactly my dish of tea – pretty lightweight.'

Sir Roger was most efficacious when in his cups.

Anthony Trollope *Doctor Thorne*

Addison and his friends would also have spoken about someone being **in his cups** if he was intoxicated. 'Cups' at the time were similar to those now presented as sporting trophies and were the normal drinking vessels for wine.

■ WHISTLES WET AND DRY

'The wine shall be kept to wet your whistle when you are story-telling.'

Charles Dickens *David Copperfield*

'May you never be without a drop to wet your whistle' is a cheerful remark in Trollope's *Doctor Thorne*. 'Here, sport, wet your whistle' is said by someone handing over a glass of wine in *The Honourable Schoolboy*, by John Le Carré. Englishmen have been referring to 'having a drink' as **wetting one's whistle** since the Middle Ages. The phrase is used by Chaucer in *The Canterbury Tales*. 'Whistle' is used for the throat, or perhaps more exactly for the windpipe. Some writers have turned the phrase into **whet one's whistle**, on the basis that some kinds of whistle have to be sharpened, but 'wet' is the correct form.

As it happens, a wooden whistle if wet would be of little use. It has to be dry and clear before it will produce a 'clean' sound. We refer to the latter in the phrase **as clean as a whistle**, which can mean either 'very clean' or 'very skilfully'. In former times the comparisons **as dry as a whistle** and as **clear as a whistle** were also used.

Today we talk about **blowing the whistle on something** 'bringing something to an end' or **blowing the whistle on someone** 'informing on someone responsible for illegal activity'. The latter phrase was originally based on the idea of summoning the police, the former to the whistle which brings an end to various open-air games.

There is no connection in either case with **whistle-stop**. The allusion in this case is to a small American town where trains only stop to pick up passengers if specially signalled to do so. Alternatively they blow their whistles to indicate that they are stopping to let off passengers. It has become the custom for politicians to pay brief visits to such places, delivering short speeches from a train's rear platform as part of a 'whistle-stop election campaign'.

Sometimes he did not write for weeks, while poor Kay went whistling in the dark.

Mary McCarthy *The Group*

To **whistle in the dark** means to 'try to overcome one's fear'. The phrase is normally used metaphorically, though many people really do whistle if they are walking down a dark road at night and are worried about what is lurking in the shadows. It is possible that doing so helps them to relax, since a whistling sound could not be produced if the throat muscles were tense.

There are still some speakers who reply to an unwelcome request for money or something similar by saying: 'You can **whistle for it**.' The meaning is 'you have a very slight chance of obtaining it'. The saying ultimately refers to a sailors'

superstition in the days of sailing-ships. When a ship was becalmed, it was believed that whistling for the wind would cause it to blow. It is easy to see from this how 'whistling for it' came to mean 'asking in vain for something'.

In an article in *The Times* (16.5.1992) Philip Howard used the expression **worth a whistle**. This phrase is not in daily use, and few would recognize the allusion to Shakespeare's *King Lear*. It is Goneril, the king's eldest daughter, who tells her husband 'I have been worth the whistle.' She means 'worthy of some notice'. Her husband replies: 'O Goneril! / You are not worth the dust which the rude wind / Blows in your face.'

■ WHY THE DICKENS?

'Now what the dickens is this about Beauty going to Spain?'

Upton Sinclair *World's End*

In *The Merry Wives of Windsor* Ford asks Mistress Page about the young man who is with her. She replies: 'I cannot tell what the dickens his name is my husband had him of.' **What the dickens**, then, was in use long before Charles Dickens made the surname famous and has nothing to do with him. The phrase is an example of the common practice in former times of substituting a harmless word or name for one which might give offence. 'Dickens', ultimately a diminutive form of Richard, replaces 'devil' or 'Old Nick'. The ingenious suggestion was made as early as 1656 by Thomas Blount that 'Dickens' was a form of 'devilkins'. Unfortunately, no evidence has come to light which supports this attractive theory.

'What the dickens' has been a well-used phrase, along with its variants

where the dickens, why the dickens, etc. Examples include: 'What the dickens are you talking about?' in E.M. Forster's *Howards End*, where even the euphemism causes offence. The conversation continues: 'Now, Charles, you promised not to say those naughty words.' *Jaffery*, by William J. Locke, has: 'That's just it – what the dickens does it matter to you?' Later in the same novel occurs: 'Why the dickens did I order a big breakfast?' 'Where the dickens is she?' is in Charlotte Brontë's *Jane Eyre*.

'The dickens' also occurs in other contexts as a substitute for 'the devil'. *Babbitt*, by Sinclair Lewis, has: 'When a fellow's worked like the dickens all day, he doesn't want to go and hustle his head off.'

■ WILDLIFE

He had sown his wild oats – one had to somewhen – and now he was happily married.

H.G. Wells *Kipps*

In the New Testament, at Matthew 13.4, is the parable about the sower and the seeds. Some were devoured by birds, some fell on stony ground or on thorns, some fell on good soil and led to a good harvest. Galatians 6.7 also has: 'Do not be deceived; God is not mocked, for whatever a man sows, that he will also reap.' The proverbial **sow one's wild oats** uses a similar metaphor, this time comparing the actions of a young man who behaves in an irresponsible way to a sower who uses wild oats instead of good grain. 'Wild oats' is a specific name for a tall grass that commonly grows as a weed in cornfields. Sowing wild oats instead of grain would be a very foolish thing to do, as time would later reveal.

The association of 'sowing one's wild oats' and young men behaving wildly has occurred since the 16th century. The expression is used as a euphemism for dissolute behaviour of all kinds, but especially of a sexual nature. That has been made explicit in the modern slang phrase **get one's oats**, which refers to male sexual gratification. Often the reference to 'wild oats' is indulgent, as it is in the H.G. Wells quotation above. Other writers philosophize at some length about the implications of the phrase. Trollope, for example, has this to say in *Doctor Thorne*: ' "Let a young fellow sow his wild oats while he is young, and he'll be steady enough when he grows old." "But what if he never lives to get through the sowing?" thought the doctor to himself. "What if the wild-oats operation is carried on in so violent a manner as to leave no strength in the soil for the produce of a more valuable crop?" '

The difference between Robbie Budd and most others was that they didn't consider it necessary to tell their future brides about the wild oats they had sown.

Upton Sinclair *World's End*

In *Howards End*, E.M. Forster makes a different point: 'He confused the episode of Jacky with another episode that had taken place in the days of his bachelorhood. The two made one crop of wild oats, for which he was heartily sorry, and he could not see that those oats are of a darker stock which are rooted in another's dishonour. Unchastity and infidelity were as confused to him as to the Middle Ages.'

Respectable young women, needless to say, were not and perhaps still are not expected to sow their own wild oats. They are left to decide what their attitude will be towards the wild oats sown by a husband-to-be. Ivy Compton-Burnett, in *A House and Its Head*, offers an interesting view: 'Do you think you could marry me? You know about my wild oats, and that is said to be so important, though I should have thought it would be a mistake. There is nothing for you to find out.'

■ WIND BREAKS

The Marchesa uttered this gently, so that it rather took the wind out of his sails.

J.I.M. Stewart *A Use of Riches*

Phrases of nautical origin are well-used in English. Those connected with sailing ships seem to have appealed especially to the popular imagination. One such phrase is **take the wind out of someone's sails**, which even land-lubbers know puts a vessel under sail at a disadvantage and prevents its forward motion. Applied to a person, the phrase normally means 'take the wind out of' someone, dent his confidence and make him uneasy. 'Telegram took the wind right out of my sails' says someone who has been very surprised, in John Le Carré's *The Honourable Schoolboy*.

The phrase is also sometimes applied to a situation. When Mary Stewart writes, in *This Rough Magic*: 'Godfrey was taking the wind out of this sail, too, before it had ever been hoisted,' she means that someone is raising a subject with the police that sooner or later they would have mentioned.

'We never do anything illegal.'
'You sail near the wind sometimes. And things go wrong, even things that start innocently.'

Ruth Rendell *Talking to Strange Men*

Someone who sails **near/close to the wind** is doing something that is dangerous and almost illegal, or something which very nearly offends good taste. The literal meaning of the phrase at sea is to sail almost in the direction from which the wind is blowing, a risky procedure.

'Sometime in the next year or two you are going to have to give your wonderful talents a decisive bent.'
'I shall see which way the wind blows. I can feel it blowing pretty hard already.'

Nigel Dennis *Cards of Identity*

To **see which way the wind blows**, in its figurative sense, is to wait and see what is likely to happen. It is the very opposite of **throwing caution to the winds**, which is what a naturally cautious person does when he suddenly decides to take a chance.

'Even Archie's people know there's something in the wind.' What a silly phrase that was.

Clifford Hanley *The Taste of Too Much*

Something in the wind derives from hunting rather than sailing. The allusion is to the scent of an animal, detected by the hounds. If 'something is in the wind' it means that there is game nearby, which in turn means that something is about to happen. The phrase tends to be used when people suspect or sense that something significant will soon occur, though they have no concrete reason for thinking so. 'Well, Roger, what's in the wind?' is used as a greeting in Anthony Trollope's *Doctor Thorne*, an alternative to 'what's happening?'

To **get wind of something** is another hunting metaphor alluding to a scent. We use it very aptly when we hear a rumour about something that was meant to remain a secret.

'He's already got the wind up; he called up the store just now, spying out the land.'

Mary McCarthy *The Groves of Academe*

To **get the wind up** 'become alarmed or frightened' and **put the wind up someone** 'frighten someone' are 20th-century British slang terms, though both are already out-dated. 'Windy' in the sense of 'frightened' perhaps survives with older speakers. Professor Weekley thought that these terms derived from the world of aviation, but there is little doubt that the wind referred to is intestinal, as it is in **breaking wind**.

■ WONDERLAND

'You don't mean to tell me that you came over here on your own money when you could have charged it to the firm. Well . . . well . . . wonders will never cease.'

Peter Cheyney *You Can Call It a Day*

Wonders will never cease is an exclamation of surprise that someone has acted in a certain way. First recorded use of the phrase is in a letter to the actor David Garrick, written 13 September 1776 by Sir Henry Dudley. The phrase is not complimentary to the person concerned, it being implied that he or she was not thought capable of such positive behaviour. When Dickens makes Sam Weller say 'Wonders 'ull never cease' in *The Pickwick Papers*, it is because Sam has just seen Jingle weeping with remorse and gratitude. Geraint Goodwin, in *The Heyday in*

the Blood, has the saying in the form 'Wonders never cease'. Derek Jewell, *Come In No.1 Your Time Is Up*, has the exchange: ' "The plane was early." "Miracles never cease." '

In the name of wonder might still be used by an exasperated speaker who is about to ask why somebody has acted in a certain way. The formula makes it clear that the questioner is very surprised. Similar opening remarks include **It's no wonder that** 'It's not surprising that', and **I shouldn't wonder** 'I wouldn't be surprised'. A person who **does wonders with** or **works wonders with** someone or something 'achieves surprising results'.

Wonder Woman has been achieving such results since she first appeared in *All-Star Comics* in 1941. This Amazon first went to America from Paradise Island to help that country win World War Two. Her possession of a magical lasso and feminium bracelets which repel bullets, as well as various other super-powers, made her task that much the easier. Her exploits would have surprised Sir Arthur Conan Doyle, who first used the phrase 'wonder woman' in *The Case Book of Sherlock Holmes* (1927). (The reference was not, as one might have expected, to Irene Adler but to Violet de Merville.)

■ WOOL-GATHERING

'Vulkan is a thorough-going, dyed-in-the-wool, black-hearted, London-shrunk, copper-bottomed bastard.'

Len Deighton *Funeral in Berlin*

Dyed-in-the-wool usually refers to someone's opinions and means that they are 'long-standing and unlikely to change'. The original allusion was to ideas imparted to children which would stay with them for the rest of their lives. Their thinking was 'coloured' at an early stage. They were like wool which was dyed in its raw state, before being made into yarn. When Mary McCarthy, in *The Group*, says 'Priss herself was a dyed-in-the-wool liberal' we know that Priss has been liberally-minded since her youth and that it would be surprising if she changed.

'I like your wool,' said Gold. 'He told me he likes my wool,' he heard her relating to his brothers-in-law Irv and Max. 'But I think he's trying to pull it over my eyes.'

Joseph Heller *Good as Gold*

People have talked about **pulling the wool over someone's eyes** 'deceiving or deluding someone', since the end of the 19th century. By that time **jerseys**, as they were called before they became **sweaters** and **pull-overs**, were widely worn. Needless to say, as these garments are put on or taken off, the wearer is momentarily unable to see what is happening. There can be few parents who have not tickled a child at this moment while helping him to dress or undress. The metaphorical meaning of the expression seems to have arisen from this idea of taking advantage of someone while his view was obscured, though the phrase is now sometimes used of something more serious than tickling.

Frederic Raphael, *The Limits of Love*, has: '"I know what's going on. You don't have to pull the wool over my eyes." "Nobody's pulling anything over your eyes."' In *The Groves of Academe* Mary McCarthy writes: 'Mulcahy was not much impressed. "You let him pull the wool over your eyes," was the verdict he returned.'

An altogether more idiosyncratic

version of the phrase occurs in Truman Capote's *My Side of the Matter*: '"Don't think you can pull the sheep over our eyes," says Olivia-Ann. "We weren't born just around the corner, you know," says Eunice.' The latter comment is also unusual: **weren't born yesterday** would have been the normal way of saying that they were not foolishly immature.

I drifted into the kind of wool-gathering that music induced in me.

C.P. Snow *The Affair*

Someone who is **wool-gathering** is acting in an absent-minded way, day-dreaming, letting his fancy wander in all directions. The phrase came into metaphorical use in the 16th century. At that time those who were unfitted mentally for more serious work were assigned the task of gathering the tufts of wool torn from sheep by bushes and brambles. Robertson Davies, *The Lyre of Orpheus*, has: 'Darcourt was eating and wool-gathering at the same time, a frequent trick of his.'

■ WORLD LANGUAGE

Jack Ford was going up in the world.

James Mitchell *When the Boat Comes in*

World has many different meanings, reflected in expressions which include the word. Someone who is **going up in the world** is improving his position in society, with 'world' describing the social environment in which he lives. Others may be **coming down in the world**. The person who travels to a far-away place, then meets a stranger who was at school with his father, will remark that **it's a small world**, thinking of 'world' as the planetary body on which we live, with its various countries.

'She'll have you like a shot, old Beth. Thinks the world of you.'

John Le Carré *The Honourable Schoolboy*

The sense-development of 'world' is especially complex, the original meaning being 'a period of human existence', contrasted in early religious writings with eternity, the **world without end**. We now mainly associate the word with the earth itself and the people who live on it, but it can mean 'a great deal' in **think the world of** someone.

'You think when you've done that, the world'll be at your feet. It won't be, Will.'

Raymond Williams *Border Country*

Consider also the various shades of meaning in the following: **live in a world of one's own** 'have thoughts, dreams and attitudes which are peculiar to oneself'; **man** or **woman of the world** 'with wide-ranging experience, not easily surprised or shocked'; **out of this world** 'wonderful'; **the outside world** 'life as it is lived by those not members of a particular community or professional group', **on top of the world** 'very happy'; **have the world at one's feet** 'have the opportunity to do anything one wants'; **think the world owes one a living** 'believe that because one did not choose to be born, others are obliged to provide whatever is necessary to sustain one's existence'.

Not long for this world implies that someone is 'likely to die soon'. Margaret Laurence, in *The Diviners*, has the exchange: '"Christie – how is she?" "Not long for this world, Morag," Christie says abruptly, and the euphemism sounds odd, coming from him.'

'Stephen will be getting the best of both worlds.'

Mary McCarthy *The Group*

The plural form 'worlds' is used in phrases like **worlds apart**, an exaggerated way of referring to a great difference. Two people are said to be 'worlds apart' in their views on a subject, for instance, if they hold opposing views. To **get the best of both worlds** is 'to benefit from two sets of circumstances or ideas that would normally be incompatible. In the Mary McCarthy quotation above, Stephen is a baby who will be part breast-fed, part bottle-fed. His mother is convinced that he will thus be getting 'the best of both worlds'.

WORD AND PHRASE INDEX